"The Inner World of AI is an exceptional edited volume on the cultural and spatial dimensions of artificial intelligence. Bahmanteymouri, Mohammadzadeh and Morreale bring together a diverse set of scholars to examine how AI reshapes creativity, power, and human experience, a very important contribution to planning and design scholarship."

– **Dr Thomas W. Sanchez** *is a professor of Landscape Architecture and Urban Planning at Texas A&M University*

"AI systems are made of far more than just software like neural networks and hardwarelike data centers. Inside every AI is a complex—and often hidden—web of human labour, social relations, psychic desires, and real estate. This book offers a wide-ranging investigation into the deeper interiority of AI."

– **Dr Jathan Sadowski** *is a senior lecturer at Department of Human Centred Computing, Monash University.*

The Inner World of Artificial Intelligence

The Inner World of Artificial Intelligence, edited by Elham Bahmanteymouri, Mohsen Mohammadzadeh, and Fabio Morreale, offers a critical and interdisciplinary exploration of how artificial intelligence (AI) is reshaping the contemporary world. Bringing together leading and emerging scholars from planning, engineering, economics, philosophy, computer science, and media studies, the book examines the hidden infrastructures, political economies, and spatial imaginaries that underpin AI. It invites readers to look beyond technical narratives, uncovering how AI operates as both a transformative technology and a socio-political force.

Structured around three interconnected sections – *Hidden and Subsumed Humans in Artificial Intelligence, Political Economies and Fantasies of AI,* and *AI, Urban Knowledge, and the Repressed Real* – the volume explores how AI functions simultaneously as technology, ideology, and social relation. Contributors reveal how intelligent systems mediate labour, governance, and everyday life, exposing both the promises and contradictions of automation and digitalisation. The book also analyses AI's entanglements with global urbanisation, environmental change, and shifting power relations across regions, including the Asia-Pacific, Europe, and the Americas.

Offering a critical yet accessible perspective, *The Inner World of Artificial Intelligence* serves as an invaluable reference for academics, professionals, and policymakers interested in understanding AI's technical, social, spatial, and ethical implications. It will appeal to readers in planning, economics, political science, engineering, and the social sciences who seek to navigate and shape the complex human–AI relationship in an age of accelerating technological transformation.

Elham Bahmanteymouri is Senior Lecturer in Urban Planning at the University of Auckland. Her research focuses on urban critical theories, incomplete markets, housing and spatial inequality, and the implications of digital platforms and AI for planning and governance. Her recent book, *Cities and Digital Platforms* (Routledge, 2025), extends these inquiries. She also has extensive professional experience in urban and regional planning across public and private sectors.

Mohsen Mohammadzadeh is Senior Lecturer in Urban Planning at the University of Auckland's School of Architecture and Planning. He holds academic qualifications in Urban and Regional Planning, Urban Design, and Civil Engineering. His research includes, but is not limited to, planning theory and alternative approaches to planning practice, and examines how AI-enabled planning and urban digitalisation reshape governance, accountability, and equity in our cities. He also investigates societal and governmental readiness for disruptive mobility – including autonomous vehicles, electric vehicles, and shared mobility platforms – across Australasia.

Fabio Morreale is Staff Research Scientist at Sony AI in Barcelona. In his work, he combines his formal background in Computer Science with Philosophy to critically examine the functionality and philosophical foundations of artificial intelligence, with a particular focus on the ethics and interpretability of generative AI. He previously served as Senior Lecturer at the University of Auckland.

The Inner World of Artificial Intelligence

Edited by
Elham Bahmanteymouri,
Mohsen Mohammadzadeh and Fabio Morreale

CRC Press
Taylor & Francis Group
Boca Raton London New York

CRC Press is an imprint of the
Taylor & Francis Group, an **informa** business

Designed cover image: Inner-Outer Entangled Dodecagon by Fabio Morreale (2025)

First edition published 2026
by CRC Press
2385 NW Executive Center Drive, Suite 320, Boca Raton FL 33431

and by CRC Press
4 Park Square, Milton Park, Abingdon, Oxon, OX14 4RN

CRC Press is an imprint of Taylor & Francis Group, LLC

Funder: Knowledge Unlatched

An electronic version of this book is freely available, thanks to the support of libraries working with Knowledge Unlatched (KU). KU is a collaborative initiative designed to make high quality books Open Access for the public good. The Open Access ISBN for this book is 9781003480167. More information about the initiative and links to the Open Access version can be found at www.knowledgeunlatched.org

ISBN: 978-1-032-76808-3 (hbk)
ISBN: 978-1-032-76807-6 (pbk)
ISBN: 978-1-003-48016-7 (ebk)

DOI: 10.1201/9781003480167

Typeset in Palatino
by Apex CoVantage, LLC

Contents

Contributors' Bios

Christoffer Andersson is Postdoctoral Researcher in Organisation Studies at Mälardalen University. He studies digital technology and organisational change, currently focusing on the epistemic effects on work of digital technology and generative AI in particular.

Elham Bahmanteymouri is Senior Lecturer in Urban Planning at the University of Auckland. Her research focuses on urban critical theories, incomplete markets, housing and spatial inequality, and the implications of digital platforms and AI for planning and governance. Her recent book, *Cities and Digital Platforms* (Routledge, 2025), extends these inquiries. She also has extensive professional experience in urban and regional planning across public and private sectors.

Mohammed Ali Berawi is Professor at the Department of Civil and Environmental Engineering, Faculty of Engineering, Universitas Indonesia. He has served as a Visiting Scholar at the University of Washington (2017) and as a Professor at Peter the Great St. Petersburg Polytechnic University (SPbPU), Russia, since 2019, and at the University of Malaya since 2024. In 2024, he received an Honorary Doctorate from SPbPU. Recognised among the world's Top 2% Scientists by Elsevier and Stanford University (2021–2025), his research focuses on value engineering, sustainable infrastructure, and innovation in construction and infrastructure development.

Udipta Boro is Geographer and Urban Planner, currently working as a PhD researcher at the University of Twente, the Netherlands. He obtained his master's degree in 2021 from the University of Twente in Geo-Information Science, specialising in Urban Planning and Management. His PhD research, commenced in 2021, investigates the politics and public imaginary of automated urban technologies.

Federico Cugurullo is Associate Professor in Smart and Sustainable Urbanism at Trinity College Dublin and affiliated with the Department of Geography at the National University of Singapore. His research is positioned at the intersection of urban geography and political philosophy, and currently explores how artificial intelligence is influencing urban governance and planning, thereby impacting the sustainability of cities. He is a co-editor of *Artificial Intelligence and the City: Urbanistic Perspectives on AI* (Routledge, 2023).

Shona Geoghegan is Researcher at the Department of Geography, Trinity College Dublin, with research interests in the governance of digital technologies in urban contexts. Her work explores smart cities, AI infrastructure, data governance, and regulation through a critical interdisciplinary lens. Key interests include cross-border data flows, AI regulation, and the socio-technical imaginaries driving digital development in Europe and beyond.

Anette Hallin is Professor in Business Studies and Head of Organization and Management-studies at Mälardalen University. She is Scientific Director of the AI and Society initiative, leads the DIGMA research group, and works on several EU and Swedish-funded projects, including Horizon's TechConnect, exploring digitalisation, management, and human-technology complementarity.

Chris Ivory is Professor of Innovation Management at Mälardalen University in Sweden. He has led European projects on the impact of automation, digitalisation, and AI on work, sustainability, and organisation. He has published widely on related subjects, including critical project management, innovation, knowledge management, AI, and technology history.

Kristina Khutsishvili is Postdoctoral Researcher in AI Ethics and Public Sector Decision-Making at the Department of Engineering, University of Cambridge. Kristina is part of the AI@Cam initiative on decision-making with AI in connected places and cities, a project aimed at developing an ethical and responsible innovation-rooted approach for public value creation. She previously served as a work package leader and researcher in the CommuniCity Horizon Europe project and worked at the University of Amsterdam.

Pablo Lorenzo-Eiroa is a professional and scholar in the fields of architecture, urbanism, ecology and computation. Founder of e-Architects.net, he is currently the AI Lab Director and Associate Professor at NYIT. He published Digital Signifiers in an Architecture of Information: From Big Data and Simulation to Artificial Intelligence, Routledge, London 2023.

Dillon Mahmoudi is Associate Professor of Geography and Environmental Systems at the University of Maryland, Baltimore County. His research investigates the contemporary contours of urban inequality and spatial transformation by mapping the faultlines of digital capitalism as they materialise in data centres, algorithms, and smart city infrastructures, drawing from heterodox political economy, critical GIS, and feminist and antiracist theory to analyse how code, land, and labour interlock to reproduce and resist uneven development.

Fran Meissner is Assistant Professor of Critical Geodata Studies and Geodata Ethics at the University of Twente in the Netherlands. As a social scientist of datafication and diversity, her research explores the interrelation between remote sensing systems and urban social and economic stratification.

Francesco Miele is Associate Professor at the University of Trieste. His recent research interests include the intersections between AI and care processes, the exploration of knowledge processes in patients with chronic illnesses, the role of telemonitoring technologies in doctor–patient interactions, and the invisible work of patients and caregivers in managing chronic conditions.

Mohsen Mohammadzadeh is Senior Lecturer in Urban Planning at the University of Auckland's School of Architecture and Planning. He holds academic qualifications in Urban and Regional Planning, Urban Design, and Civil Engineering. His research includes, but is not limited to, planning theory and alternative approaches to planning practice, and examines how AI-enabled planning and urban digitalisation reshape governance, accountability, and equity in our cities. He also investigates societal and governmental readiness for disruptive mobility – including autonomous vehicles, electric vehicles, and shared mobility platforms – across Australasia.

Fabio Morreale is Staff Research Scientist at Sony AI in Barcelona. In his work, he combines his formal background in Computer Science with Philosophy to critically examine the functionality and philosophical foundations of artificial intelligence, with a particular focus on the ethics and interpretability of generative AI. He previously served as a Senior Lecturer at the University of Auckland.

Karin Pfeffer is Geographer and obtained her PhD degree in Physical Geography from Utrecht University, the Netherlands, in 2003. Since 2017, she has been a Full Professor at ITC, University of Twente, the Netherlands. She uses geographic information technologies to investigate critical urban issues, such as deprived settlements, urban infrastructure inequalities, or environmental vulnerabilities, and employs a critical perspective on these technologies.

Soroush Rashidi is Transportation Technical Director at Blue Barn Engineering and a researcher at the University of Auckland. Holding a PhD in Transportation Engineering, he specialises in AI/ML, computer vision, and data-driven modelling for transportation network performance and public transport reliability. His expertise spans agent-based modelling and the classical four-step framework. He has led analytics teams, developed algorithms for network-wide peak-period definition and link-level volume estimation, and delivered real-time performance insights. His publications on bus dwell time and reliability are widely cited and inform practice.

Dio Reyhan Fardizsa joined the Center for Sustainable Infrastructure Development (CSID) at Universitas Indonesia as a researcher in 2021. After obtaining his bachelor's degree in Civil Engineering from Universitas Indonesia, he works as a corporate finance associate in an energy and infrastructure company in Indonesia. His research interests include sustainable infrastructure development and financing.

Mustika Sari is Assistant Professor at the Department of Civil and Environmental Engineering, Faculty of Engineering, Universitas Indonesia. Her primary research interests focus on project management, with an emphasis on innovation and digitalisation. She currently serves as the Managing Editor of CSID Journal of Infrastructure Development (CSID-JID).

Bambang Susantono is Professor at the Department of Urban and Regional Planning, Universitas Diponegoro, Indonesia, and Head of the Asia Pacific Cities & Local Government Institute (CLGI) since 2025. He was Chairman of Indonesia's Nusantara Capital City Authority (2022–2024) and Vice-President for Knowledge Management and Sustainable Development at the Asian Development Bank. He holds a PhD in Infrastructure Planning and dual master's degrees in Transportation Engineering and City and Regional Planning from UC Berkeley. His research focuses on infrastructure, urban development, sustainable cities, and climate change.

Suci Indah Susilowati is Senior Researcher at the Center for Sustainable Infrastructure Development (CSID) at the Universitas Indonesia. She obtained her master's degree in Civil Engineering from Universitas Indonesia.

Thomas Wahl is Senior Lecturer in Sociology at Mälardalen University, Sweden, and an AI and Society Research Fellow. A member of the university's STS group, his research explores narratives of AI futures, trust in digital relations, and critically examines discourses on the societal impact of research and higher education.

Alan Wiig is Associate Professor of Geography at the University of Florida. His research examines the new digital divides emerging alongside smart city projects, the politics of large-scale urban revitalisation efforts, and the spatial strategies through which transnational logistics corridors are remaking city regions. He is Urban Pulse section editor at *Urban Geography*.

Wayne Williamson is Research Associate and Casual Lecturer in the Department of Geography and Planning at Macquarie University. His work investigates the intersection of urban planning practice, community engagement and participation, and digital technologies. He combines qualitative and quantitative methods to study digital adoption, community action, and urban planning governance in contemporary society.

1

Editorial Introduction: The Inner World of Artificial Intelligence

Elham Bahmanteymouri, Mohsen Mohammadzadeh, and Fabio Morreale

1.1 The Aim of the Volume and Its Conceptual Vision

Artificial Intelligence (AI) has come to occupy a decisive role in shaping our world, not only as a technical instrument but as an organising logic of contemporary life. From creative production to governance and urban planning, AI now mediates how knowledge is produced, how value is created, and how social relations are imagined. Yet, despite its pervasive reach, the *inner world of AI* – the hidden human, political, and spatial frameworks sustaining it – often remains concealed beneath the rhetoric of efficiency, innovation, and inevitability (Crawford, 2021). The promise of AI as an autonomous and objective force obscures the complex realities of its making: the invisible labour, extractive infrastructures, and ideological assumptions that shape it (Atanasoski & Vora, 2019; Casilli, 2019; Morreale et al., 2023a).

This book begins from a simple but pressing question: what hidden human, political, and environmental structures lie beneath the smooth surface of AI? In addressing this question, *The Inner World of AI* seeks to uncover the social, economic, and spatial dynamics that make AI possible and to expose how these dynamics mirror and expand the contradictions of late capitalism. AI is not a neutral or inevitable technological advance; it is a political and economic project that reflects and reproduces, and at times exposes the contradictions within, the logic of technocapitalism (Suarez-Villa, 2009). To understand AI's outward capacities – its precision, automation, and apparent autonomy – we must first examine its inner structures: the hidden human labour that sustains it, the political economies that shape its deployment, and the urban and regional landscapes that absorb its consequences.

DOI: 10.1201/9781003480167-1

The impetus for this book arises from a shared recognition that AI is reshaping the terrain of human existence in ways that transcend disciplinary boundaries. Scholarship on AI has expanded across computer science, ethics, and governance, yet these debates often remain fragmented. Most studies focus either on the technological functioning of AI or on its moral and regulatory implications, without connecting these to the broader socio-economic and spatial processes in which AI is embedded. As our reviewers perceptively noted, this volume seeks to 'join the dots' between these disparate conversations, situating AI within the intertwined circuits of labour, capital, power, and space.

What is at stake extends far beyond theoretical synthesis. As Zuboff (2019) argues, the rise of *surveillance capitalism* marks a turning point in how societies govern behaviour and produce value. The expanding dependence on algorithmic systems to mediate decisions, allocate resources, and imagine collective futures is redefining what it means to be human, what counts as knowledge, and how societies are governed. AI participates in a transformation comparable to previous industrial revolutions but of greater depth: its mechanisms of automation and optimisation penetrate not only production but subjectivity itself, reshaping thought, affect, and social interaction. This book thus approaches AI as a phenomenon that alters the very categories through which reality is experienced, promising rational order and control while deepening inequality, alienation, and ecological strain (Birch, 2020; Coeckelbergh, 2020).

The Inner World of AI invites readers to think critically about the unseen dimensions of this technological epoch, tracing how AI intensifies the structural features of capitalism – extraction, abstraction, and commodification – while simultaneously opening new possibilities for ethical reflection, resistance, and emancipation. At its core, this volume confirms the deep entanglements between technology, society, and economy – showing that AI is not built solely upon code and computation but upon labour, ideology, and spatial relations. We approach AI as both a technical artefact and a cultural construct, a system that embodies the contradictions of its time (Feenberg, 2002). What remains missing in most studies is a critical and integrative framework that connects AI's technological, economic, and spatial dimensions as part of a single socio-historical formation (Girasa, 2020; Birch & Cochrane, 2024). The present volume thus brings together scholars from multiple disciplines – computer science, planning, economics, political theory, and philosophy – to reframe AI as a phenomenon embedded within the structures of technocapitalism. Within this framework, AI is not an external disruptor but an internal mechanism of capitalist reproduction, extending accumulation into new spheres of life and consciousness.

In doing so, the volume provides a multi-scalar understanding of AI: from the micro-politics of hidden human labour and algorithmic dependence to the macro-dynamics of digital rentiership and spatial restructuring.

1.2 From the Hidden Human to the Spatial Order

The volume is organised around three interdependent questions:

1. What kinds of human labour and subjectivity are hidden within AI's operations?
2. How does AI reproduce and reshape power, governance, and ideology within the political economies of technocapitalism?
3. In what ways does AI reshape the spaces in which we live – our cities, regions, and the wider environment?

These questions anchor the book's conceptual vision: to move beyond deterministic optimism and moral critique, offering a layered understanding of AI's *inner world* – one that is material, political, and psycho-symbolic. Each section of the book corresponds to one of these analytical perspectives, edited respectively by Fabio Morreale, Elham Bahmanteymouri, and Mohsen Mohammadzadeh. Though distinct in focus, the sections are deliberately interwoven, forming an intellectual arc that moves from the micro to the macro, from the human to the political-economic, and finally to the spatial. Together, they provide an integrated account of AI as both a social relation and a spatial formation – a system whose inner dynamics mirror the desires and contradictions of contemporary capitalism.

1.2.1 Section 1: Hidden and Subsumed Humans in Artificial Intelligence

The first section, *Hidden and Subsumed Humans in Artificial Intelligence*, examines how human labour and creativity are progressively subsumed within the technical and ideological operations of AI. It addresses the hidden forms of human participation that sustain intelligent systems (Morreale et al., 2023a), showing how creativity, cognition, and affect are extracted and recoded as computational value. By revealing AI as a socio-technical formation animated by human work, the section establishes the ethical and epistemic ground for the following parts of the volume, which trace these dynamics across the political-economic and spatial scales of technocapitalism.

In Chapter 2, *Human Subsumption in Training Datasets for Music Generation*, Morreale examines how human creativity is mined and repurposed in generative AI music models. Morreale introduces a typology of training data sources, offering an ontological distinction between scraped data (content automatically harvested without consent) versus laboured data (content produced through unwitting or coerced human labour). The author argues that AI music systems enact a form of primitive accumulation, dispossessing musicians and online communities of their creative labour. Songs and audio that are freely available online are scraped en masse (Morreale et al., 2023b), disregarding intellectual property and moral rights, while new data is simultaneously actively elicited from users to feed AI models through gamified tasks or precarious work. This practice is further problematised by an ongoing data sanitisation process: ethically dubious collection practices are laundered through layers of technical and institutional abstraction (e.g., aggregation, anonymisation, academic intermediaries), which obscures their exploitative origins. The chapter reveals how even content created as a digital common is enclosed and commodified in AI models without credit or compensation. The result is an AI training pipeline that treats human creativity as an extractable, cost-free resource, echoing what Zuboff (2019) termed *behavioural surplus* in surveillance capitalism. The chapter concludes by calling for more equitable frameworks that acknowledge and reward human contributors, suggesting socio-technical work to ensure that AI development respects the human creativity on which it depends.

In Chapter 3, *Authorship, Ownership, Authority, Validation and Creativity through AI*, Lorenzo-Eiroa interrogates authorship as a political technology in the age of AI. Revisiting debates on 'The Death of the Author', the author shows that in AI, authorship re-emerges as a political structure of ownership and validation, concentrated within Big Tech's infrastructures – a new form of *digital feudalism* in the creative domain. The chapter widens the concept of authorship beyond final artefacts to the socio-technical substrate that makes them possible. Granting recognition and rights to those who contribute data and training to AI is thus essential to preserving human creativity. This chapter further contends that truly creative AI requires a *morphogenetic* framework; one that interconnects collective datasets, human authors, grammars, and environmental context into a collaborative neural network. Lorenzo-Eiroa proposes an antidote to digital feudalism: an *environmental common* that sharply contrasts proprietary AI models.

In Chapter 4, *Humanness in the Context of Artificial Intelligence: Performative Imaginaries in Popular Science*, Wahl, Ivory, Andersson, and Hallin investigate how our very ideas of 'AI' and 'the human' are shaped by popular science narratives. The authors analyse a curated selection of popular science books on AI. Borrowing the concept of *sociotechnical imaginaries* (Jasanoff & Kim 2015), the chapter identifies uniform narratives that stabilise a narrow view of humanness. Such storytelling, as the chapter shows, is performative: by continually invoking a near-certain AI-dominated tomorrow, the narratives help normalise the idea that profound changes to 'humanness' are not only possible but impending and legitimise specific policies, investments, and governance choices. Thus, the work connects directly to our guiding questions: it exposes the cultural production of hidden subjectivities; it shows how ideology organises political-economic trajectories; and it hints at spatial effects as these imaginaries steer procurement, regulation, and urban deployments of AI. The takeaway is diagnostic and interventist: by questioning 'what ideas about humanness' these influential narratives depart from, we can understand and diversify these performative imaginaries to ensure that our futures with AI remain grounded in pluralistic understandings of humanity.

In Chapter 5, *Reclaiming Agency! Reframing Algoactivism in the Workplace*, Miele covers another problematic area where human agency is affected by AI innovation: stochastic management. The author reconceptualises algoactivism beyond resistance, combining appropriation and enactment to track how workers fold stochastic technologies into daily practice. Drawing on qualitative research in two workplaces piloting a health-promotion app, Miele shows how agency and adaptation outweigh mere compliance or resistance. Workers' agency is exercised through situated adjustments that reshape both the technology's script and organisational routines. The chapter therefore complements the section's focus on hidden labour/subjectivity by revealing how subjectivities are actively re-made in use, and it extends the political-economic question by showing how governance occurs inside organisations through negotiated rules, not only through top-down algorithmic control. Finally, because these practices stabilise which tools persist and where, the analysis anticipates the book's spatial concerns: organisational and urban spaces are indirectly reconfigured by small-scale appropriations that accumulate into durable socio-technical arrangements.

1.2.2 Section 2: Political Economies and Fantasies of AI

The second section, *Political Economies and Fantasies of AI* (edited by Elham Bahmanteymouri), examines how artificial intelligence functions as both a political-economic infrastructure and an ideological fantasy that sustains contemporary capitalism. It explores how AI's promises of efficiency, optimisation, and neutrality conceal the contradictions of accumulation, labour, and control that underpin technocapitalism.

Chapter 6, *AI in the Shadow of Big Other: Planning, Power, and the Locus of Control* (by Bahmanteymouri), opens this discussion by situating AI within capitalism's fantasy structure, where technological systems mediate crises of value and legitimacy while reproducing systemic inequality and alienation (Žižek, 1989; Lacan, 2006; Bahmanteymouri & Mohammadzadeh, 2023). Drawing on Lacanian psychoanalysis and Marxian political economy, the chapter conceptualises AI as an apparatus through which capital manages uncertainty and desire – a fantasy of control and neutrality (Cugurullo, 2023) that conceals its dependence on human labour, institutional fragility, and social antagonism. This theoretical lens informs the chapters that follow, which trace how AI's political and ideological logics manifest across different domains, from data-centre real estate and surveillance-driven urbanism to digital governance and risk regulation. Together, these contributions reveal AI's ambivalence as both an instrument of capitalist power and a potential catalyst for reimagining democracy, ethics, and collective agency.

Chapter 7, *Land for AI: Data Center Real Estate Markets*, written by Dillon Mahmoudi and Alan Wiig, extends this section's examination of AI's political-economic infrastructures by revealing how digital capitalism materialises through the financialisation of land. As AI platforms demand ever-greater computing and storage capacity, data centres – particularly those managed through Real Estate Investment Trusts – have become the spatial and financial backbone of the AI economy. Mahmoudi and Wiig show how these facilities generate new forms of 'data rent' and 'computational rent', transforming peri-urban and rural landscapes into critical nodes of accumulation. Drawing on fieldwork in Northern Virginia's 'Data Center Alley', they trace how AI's infrastructural footprint reshapes property markets, resource use, and regional economies, embedding extractive logics of rentiership into the urban periphery. In doing so, Chapter 7 complements Bahmanteymouri's theoretical argument by illustrating how the fantasy of AI's immateriality is grounded in profoundly material processes of land appropriation, enclosure, and financialisation.

Chapter 8, *Artificial Intelligence and Surveillance in the City: Implications for Urban Governance, Democracy and Power*, by Shona Geoghegan and Federico Cugurullo, deepens this section's analysis of AI's political economy by shifting focus from infrastructures of accumulation to infrastructures of control. While Mahmoudi and Wiig expose the material foundations of digital capitalism through data-centre logics of land and property, Geoghegan and Cugurullo examine how AI reconfigures urban governance, generating new forms of technocratic authority and surveillance-driven power. They show how algorithmic systems, often operated by private corporations, extend 'surveillance capitalism' (Zuboff, 2019) into everyday urban management, eroding citizen agency and democratic accountability. Yet, drawing on global trends and a case study of Barcelona, they also demonstrate how AI-driven urbanism can become a site of resistance, where cities reclaim digital sovereignty and embed democratic values in data governance. In doing so, Chapter 8 reinforces the section's argument that the economic and ideological logics of AI are inseparable – and that any ethical or emancipatory vision must confront its embedded relations of power, ownership, and control.

Chapter 9, *Can Artificial Intelligence Facilitate Faster Development Assessment? The Case of an Early Adopter Programme*, by Wayne Williamson, extends the section's critique of AI's political economy into the domain of planning governance. Focusing on an early-adopter initiative in New South Wales, Australia, Williamson analyses how AI is deployed to accelerate development assessment within a neoliberal policy framework that privileges speed, efficiency, and market rationality. Through interviews with local government staff, the chapter exposes the tension between AI's ideological promise of frictionless automation and the political-economic realities of dependence on private vendors, data commodification, and the reorganisation of bureaucratic labour. In doing so, Williamson's analysis concretises the section's theoretical argument that AI functions as a fantasy of control within capitalist governance – a tool that seeks to manage uncertainty while reproducing systemic inequality and subordination to market logic. Yet the case also reveals moments of reflexivity, where practitioners confront these contradictions and begin to reimagine institutional responsibility, data ethics, and the social purposes of technological reform.

Chapter 10, *AI and the Governance of Risk: Fantasies, Safety, and Situated Futures*, by Elham Bahmanteymouri and Mohsen Mohammadzadeh, concludes the section by grounding its theoretical arguments in empirical research on AI governance in Aotearoa New Zealand. Drawing on survey and interview data from planners, policymakers, and AI service providers, the chapter examines how fantasies of control, optimisation, and safety sustain enthusiasm for AI despite uncertainty and fragile institutional capacity. Extending the political-economic critique developed in Chapter 6, it brings to light how discourses of risk and safety function ideologically – promising technical mastery while concealing contradictions within capitalist governance. Yet, like Williamson's case in Chapter 9, the study also identifies moments of reflexivity, as professionals call for localisation, ethical oversight, and Treaty-based governance aligned with Māori values and data sovereignty. The chapter reframes AI governance as a political rather than technical project, arguing that legitimacy depends not on frictionless optimisation but on participatory, context-sensitive, and democratically accountable practices.

1.2.3 Section 3: AI, Urban Knowledge, and the Repressed Real

The third section, *AI, Urban Knowledge, and the Repressed Real* (edited by Mohsen Mohammadzadeh), explores how artificial intelligence reshapes the ways cities are imagined, governed, and represented. It examines how algorithmic systems influence urban knowledge production and how their promises of coherence and predictability intersect with the disorder and contingency of urban life.

Chapter 11, *Urban Artificial Intelligence and Planning: Symbolic and Imaginary Representations and the Repressed Real* (by Mohammadzadeh), frames this discussion through a psychoanalytic reading of urban AI using Lacan's registers of the Imaginary, the Symbolic, and the Real. It argues that algorithmic systems – digital twins, dashboards, and predictive models – generate seductive images of coherence that sustain technocratic fantasies of control while concealing the conflictual, contingent realities of urban life. By exposing these tensions, Mohammadzadeh sets the stage for the chapters that follow, which investigate how AI materialises within the infrastructures, governance systems, and ethical discourses of contemporary urbanism. His critique reframes Urban Artificial Intelligence as a site of ideological struggle, suggesting that emancipation depends not on mastering data but on recognising what continually escapes representation.

Chapter 12, *From Urban Surveillance to Urban Care: Care-full Justice in the Age of AI*, by Udipta Boro, Fran Meissner, and Karin Pfeffer, extends this section's exploration of the psychic and political unconscious of AI urbanism into the realm of ethics and social justice. While Mohammadzadeh's chapter exposes how Urban AI constructs technocratic fantasies that repress the conflictual Real of the city, Boro and colleagues interrogate whether these algorithmic systems could ever sustain a genuinely caring urban order. Centring on India's Safe City Projects, the authors reveal how AI-powered surveillance systems, though presented as instruments of protection, perpetuate hierarchies of control, exclusion, and gendered vulnerability. Drawing on feminist ethics of care and the concept of *care-full justice* (Williams, 2017), they propose reimagining AI not as an instrument of domination but as a potential mediator of relational responsibility. In doing so, the chapter bridges the psychoanalytic critique of the imaginary city with concrete interventions for a more situated, just, and caring urban future.

Chapter 13, *Tackling the Bias Problem at the Design Stage: Empirical Evidence from the CommuniCity Project*, by Kristina Khutsishvili, advances the section's exploration of the epistemic and ethical dimensions of AI urbanism by focusing on the politics of design and co-creation. Whereas Boro, Meissner, and Pfeffer interrogate the moral ambivalence of AI-driven surveillance, Khutsishvili addresses the problem of bias at its origin – the design phase of algorithmic systems. Drawing on the CommuniCity Horizon Europe project, the chapter reveals how participatory and 'fair-by-design' approaches can challenge the technocratic imaginary of AI by embedding fairness, context, and care into the material infrastructures of smart cities. Through the concept of *co-creation as epistemic re-design*, it demonstrates that addressing bias is not merely a technical correction but a political and ethical act that requires plural knowledge and collective agency. In dialogue with Mohammadzadeh's Lacanian critique of the symbolic city, Khutsishvili shows that fairness emerges not from universal metrics but from situated, iterative practices that recover what technocratic design tends to suppress – the messy, conflictual, and contingent Real of urban life.

Chapter 14, *Machine Learning–Driven Framework for SDGs-Based Impact Assessment of Transport Infrastructure Projects*, by Mohammad Ali Berawi, Dio Reyhan Fardizsa, Mustika Sari, Bambang Susantono, and Suci Indah Susilowati, extends this section's concern with urban knowledge by translating critical reflection into applied methodology. While earlier chapters reveal what is repressed or excluded within AI's technocratic imaginaries, Berawi and colleagues demonstrate how machine learning can be mobilised to render urban and infrastructural impacts more visible and accountable. Focusing on Indonesia's transport sector, the authors design an SDGs-based framework that integrates social, environmental, economic, and institutional indicators to evaluate infrastructure projects through predictive analytics. Their model illustrates how algorithmic tools can serve as mediators between quantitative optimisation and ethical responsibility when grounded in sustainability goals. In doing so, the chapter complements Mohammadzadeh's psychoanalytic critique by showing how the repressed Real of planning – its social and environmental consequences – might be partially recovered through reflexive, data-informed governance.

Chapter 15, *From Classical Models to Intelligent Systems: AI and Machine Learning in Transportation Planning*, by Soroush Rashidi, concludes the volume by translating the theoretical and ethical debates of this section into the field of transport planning. Building on the preceding chapters' calls for situated, just, and reflexive technologies, Rashidi traces the paradigm shift from classical modelling towards intelligent, adaptive systems powered by AI and machine learning. He shows how these systems overcome the rigidity of traditional approaches by enabling real-time responsiveness, predictive accuracy, and the integration of heterogeneous data sources – yet also reproduce new forms of opacity and dependency characteristic of the technocratic imaginary. The chapter thus mirrors the book's central tension between mastery and uncertainty: while AI-based models promise optimisation and control, their ethical deployment depends on transparency, interpretability, and alignment with social and environmental goals. In closing, Rashidi reaffirms that the future of intelligent transportation – and of AI urbanism more broadly – lies in reconciling technical sophistication with the repressed Real of urban life: its complexity, contingency, and irreducible human dimension.

The synthesis across these scales opens a shared space for critique and reimagination. If AI's inner world is the unseen infrastructure of techno-capitalism, then exposing its layers allows us to question the conditions of its inevitability. The book's strength lies, as our reviewers noted, in 'linking human, economic, and spatial perspectives within a single conceptual framework'. By traversing these dimensions, *The Inner World of Artificial Intelligence* demonstrates that technological change is never merely technical; it is an unfolding social drama in which capital, code, and desire intersect – and where the possibility of a more ethical, plural, and democratic future depends on how we choose to engage with the technologies that shape our collective imagination.

The book's key contribution lies in its multi-scalar approach: it connects the invisible labour that powers AI with the political economy that structures its value, and the spatial forms that materialise its power. In doing so, it offers a conceptual language for analysing AI not as a distant technological phenomenon but as a lived, embodied, and spatial process.

Ultimately, this volume invites scholars, policymakers, and practitioners to rethink AI from the inside out – to see its *inner world* as a mirror of our own social contradictions, and as a potential site for critical reflection and transformation.

References

Atanasoski, N., & Vora, K. (2019). *Surrogate Humanity: Race, Robots, and the Politics of Technological Futures.* Duke University Press.

Bahmanteymouri, E., & Mohammadzadeh, M. (2023). The emerging autonomous smart city and its impacts on planning and power relations in late capitalism. In M. Gunder, K. Grange, & T. Winkler (Eds.), *Handbook on Planning and Power* (pp. 321–338). Edward Elgar Publishing. https://doi.org/10.4337/9781839109768.00029

Birch, K. (2020). Technoscience rent: Toward a theory of rentiership for technoscientific capitalism. *Science, Technology, & Human Values*, 45(1), 3–33.

Birch, K., & Cochrane, D. T. (2024). Big tech: Four emerging forms of digital rentiership 1. In *Global Rentier Capitalism* (pp. 82–95). Routledge.

Casilli, A. A. (2019). Micro-work, artificial intelligence and the automotive industry. *J. Ind. Bus. Econ.*, 46, 333–345. https://doi.org/10.1007/s40812-019-00121-1

Coeckelbergh, M. (2020). *AI Ethics.* MIT Press.

Crawford, K. (2021). *Atlas of AI: Power, Politics, and the Planetary Costs of Artificial Intelligence.* Yale University Press.

Cugurullo, F. (2023). *Urban Artificial Intelligence: From Automation to Autonomy in the Smart City.* Routledge.

Feenberg, A. (2002). *Transforming Technology: A Critical Theory Revisited.* Oxford University Press.

Girasa, R. (2020). *Artificial Intelligence as a Disruptive Technology: Economic Transformation and Government Regulation.* Palgrave Macmillan.

Jasanoff, S., & Kim, S.-H. (2015). *Dreamscapes of Modernity: Sociotechnical Imaginaries and the Fabrication of Power.* The University of Chicago Press.

Lacan, J. (2006). *Écrits: The First Complete Edition in English* (B. Fink, Trans.). W. W. Norton & Company.

Morreale, F., Bahmanteymouri, E., Burmester, B., Chen, A., & Thorp, M. (2023a). The unwitting labourer: Extracting humanness in AI training. *AI & Society.* https://doi.org/10.1007/s00146-023-01692-3

Morreale, F., Sharma, M., & Wei, I.-C. (2023b). *Data Collection in Music Generation Training Sets: A Critical Analysis.* Presented at the Ismir 2023 Conference.

Suarez-Villa, L. (2009). *Technocapitalism: A Critical Perspective on Technological Innovation and Corporatism.* Temple University Press.

Williams, M. J. (2017). Care-full justice in the city. *Antipode*, 49(3), 821–839. https://doi.org/10.1111/anti.12279.

Žižek, S. (1989). *The Sublime Object of Ideology.* London: Vero.

Zuboff, S. (2019). *The Age of Surveillance Capitalism: The Fight for a Human Future at the New Frontier of Power*, First ed. New York: PublicAffairs.

Section 1

Hidden and Subsumed Humans in Artificial Intelligence

2

Human Subsumption in Training Datasets for Music Generation

Fabio Morreale

2.1 Introduction

Machine Learning (ML) models rely on a vast amount of data, and their performance largely depends on the quality and quantity of such data. The types of data fed into ML models are varied and application-dependent (e.g., meteorological data, trading information, listening preferences). In this chapter, I will specifically delve into models that attempt to model *humanness* (Morreale et al., 2023a) and, in particular, humans' capability to create music. This focus stems not just from my disciplinary expertise but primarily from the political implications embedded in this terrain. Unlike most other forms of data, songs are used to train models that are *designed*, albeit unofficially (Pram and Morreale, 2025), to replace the very individuals who generated them. Many Generative AI (GenAI) models are now available to the public. While these models are affected by possibly insurmountable epistemic (as opposed to ethical) issues (Morreale et al., 2025b), the quality of music they can create is undeniable. I am particularly interested in *what* music data is accumulated into these models' datasets, and *how*. The objective is thus to develop a categorisation of modes of music data creation and accumulation. This endeavour has both epistemological and ethical objectives. Epistemologically, I aim to expand the current discourse on critical dataset studies. Ethically, the categorisation aims to ascribe varying degrees of moral responsibility to different dataset creation practices, thus contributing to the normative grounding of AI ethics frameworks.

The investigation begins with a systematic analysis of the datasets that are commonly used to train GenAI music models (Section 2.2). For this analysis, I inevitably needed to engage with technical concepts to show the mechanisms by which human capacities to compose, perform, and transcribe music are captured and transformed into training data. In Sections 2.3 and 2.4, I then propose a classification of such accumulation practices using lenses

DOI: 10.1201/9781003480167-3

from Marxian and post-Marxian literature. Specifically, I delineate two distinct forms of capture, generation, and accumulation that diverge in terms of required human labour and awareness and consent of the individuals contributing the data. I define the two categories as *scraped data* and *laboured data*. Scraped data refers to the practice of automatically collecting data from the Internet by deploying numerous automated agents (bots). Laboured data refers to data that is not initially available and thus cannot merely be captured but must instead be produced through mechanisms that prompt human users to generate it.

I problematise both practices, indicating how they sustain asymmetrical power dynamics in data production and reinforce exploitative relations between platforms, AI developers, and unwitting contributors. Scraped data relies on large-scale, automated extraction that disregards intellectual and cultural ownership, effectively appropriating creative labour without acknowledgement or compensation. Laboured data operates through gamified or precarious systems that coerce individuals into unwittingly generating data under conditions of unpaid or underpaid digital labour, blurring the boundaries between voluntary participation and extraction. Finally, in Section 2.5, I propose that most GenAI companies are inadvertently involved in a *sanitisation* process, in which morally questionable accumulation practices are laundered and normalised through intermediaries and ultimately used with impunity by many models, even from top technology companies like Google and Meta.

2.2 Datasets for Music AI Systems

A variety of ML-based systems exist that are used to perform different music-related tasks (e.g., music generation, analysis, transcription, source separation). To perform these tasks, these models are trained on a considerable amount of music data accumulated in datasets. A comprehensive review of these datasets is beyond the scope of this work and can be found in(Ma et al., 2024, pp. 42–47). In this section, I will present a few of them, which I selected based on their popularity and the contributions they can offer to the topic at hand. The remainder of the section organises them according to the nature of their content (i.e., audio, notation, or textual data), and the last part illustrates how these datasets have been used to train ML models.

2.2.1 Audio Datasets

Most widely used datasets contain actual digital audio (e.g., MP3 files). In many cases, these include sounds scraped from websites such as *Freesound,*

Jamendo, and *The Free Music Archive*, which were initially designed to enable musicians and sound artists to upload and share their own creations with the community. These websites have very permissive licensing frameworks, which lead many researchers to indiscriminately scrape audio from these websites to populate datasets like Freesound's *FSD50k* (Fonseca et al., 2021), *ClothoV2*(Drossos et al., 2019), and Jamendo's *MTG-Jamendo Dataset* (Bogdanov et al., 2019). Some datasets that are commonly used in GenAI also include scraped non-musical data. This is the case of *Libri-Light* (Kahn et al., 2020) and *LibriTTS* (Zen et al., 2019), respectively, developed by Meta and Google, that scraped audio from *LibriVox*. This free public website collects audiobooks read by volunteers from around the world.

Other music datasets include copyright-protected music that is typically obtained by scraping *YouTube* videos. Some of the dataset creators justify their choice, arguing that copyright regulations grant 'an exemption for using copyright infringing copies if the purpose is scientific research' (Schneider et al., 2023). This is the case, for instance, of the *Text2Music* dataset (Schneider et al., 2023): the developers first scraped Spotify's playlists and then downloaded the actual audio and additional metadata from YouTube. In other cases, like OpenAI's GenAI model *Jukebox*, the authors simply stated that they 'scraped a new dataset of 1.2 million songs' (Dhariwal et al., 2020). Copyright-protected work has also been allegedly used by the two major commercial GenAI companies (as of late 2025): *Suno* and *Udio*. After being sued by several major music labels for allegedly training their models on copyrighted music without permission, both Suno[1] and Udio[2] acknowledged that their models had been trained on tens of millions of recordings that 'presumably' included works owned by the plaintiffs.

Other datasets include songs that dataset creators have properly licensed. The most well-known GenAI models that trained their models on licensed data are *Stable Audio* (Evans et al., 2024) and Meta's *MusicGen* (Copet et al., 2024). These two GenAI models were allegedly trained using songs from stock music libraries (i.e., AudioSparx, Shutterstock, Pond5, and Meta Music Initiative Sound Collection). Evans and colleagues (2024) explained that the artists whose songs were used to train their model appeared to have been given the option to 'opt out' from their music being used to train the GenAI model. However, the details of the deal are not public, and it is not clear how the opting-out process worked, nor what the remuneration structure was for the artists. Additionally, neither case provided details about whether and how artists have been asked for permission or remunerated for having their music used to train a GenAI model. Furthermore, as I will demonstrate in Section 2.5, although the core model of MusicGen has been trained using this licensed data, several auxiliary modules (EnCodec, MuLan, CLAP, and BART) employed in this system have been trained on datasets populated with scraped data.

2.2.2 Notation Datasets

Other datasets employed in GenAI models do not contain actual audio recordings but musical scores that have been digitised (most commonly in MIDI format), thanks to the voluntary efforts of community members who contributed their time and expertise to the project. For instance, the *Hooktheory Lead Sheet Database* (Yeh et al., 2021) includes music sheets and chord progressions that were transcribed initially by the users of *TheoryTab*, an online portal designed to 'show you the function of each chord and note within a song and reveal structures that may not be readily apparent'.[3] Similarly, the *MuseScore Lead Sheet* dataset contains scores transcribed by community members of *MuseScore*, a popular open-source notation software. MuseScore has explicitly stated that it is not affiliated with the project and has requested that the developer remove it due to potential copyright concerns. Although it contains no audio, the dataset reproduces sheet music, which is likewise protected by copyright.

Many other datasets include MIDI transcription of piano pieces. For instance, the *GiantMIDI-Piano* dataset (Kong et al., 2022), developed by ByteDance, the parent company of TikTok, includes 10,854 MIDI files by 2,784 composers. Other piano datasets are populated with data collected with particularly dubious means. In particular, the *Yamaha Signature MIDI Collection* contains 1,400 piano MIDI files recoded during an international competition for junior pianists, and the *MAST dataset* (Falcão et al., 2019) was sourced by recording entrance exams.

2.2.3 Annotated and Textual Datasets

In addition to audio, many datasets used to train GenAI models contain other media, particularly text. The motivation for integrating textual and audio information is to develop a semantic *understanding* of music by extracting musical meaning from textual descriptions. Google's *MusicCaps*, in particular, contains 5,500 text-music pairs that were created to train the GenAI model *MusicLM* (Agostinelli et al., 2023). The textual component consists of four-sentence captions written by ten professional musicians. In contrast, the music component is collected from *AudioSet*, the parent dataset (also curated by Google) that contains 10-second audio snippets extracted from *YouTube* videos.

TagATune (Law et al., 2007) is a joint text-audio dataset whose operations are significant for our discussion. TagATune was an online game in which two players took turns describing sounds to each other.[4] Beneath the surface, an algorithm extracted these descriptions and populated the TagATune dataset, which ultimately consisted of 114,000 music samples annotated by unwitting humans. The authors specifically envisaged it being used to 'generate training data for machine learning'.

Lyrics are occasionally included in GenAI systems, such as *Jukebox*. A commonly used lyrics dataset was created by scraping *LyricWiki*, a community-powered lyrics and metadata website. Similarly, the dataset *Music4all* (Santana et al., 2020) contains lyrics collected from *Musixmatch* (a community-based lyrics archive). In addition to these lyrics, Music4all also includes audio, listeners' preferences, lyrics, and other metadata that have been scraped from many different sources, including listening preferences from 15,000 unaware *last.fm* users, metadata from *Spotify*, and 110,000 songs from *YouTube*.

Finally, several GenAI models rely on textual (non-lyrics) datasets. The use of these datasets is necessary, as we will see in the next section, for text-to-music generation (text conditioning). Some of the textual datasets used by these models are the *BookCorpus* (Zhu et al., 2015), a collection of free books written by unpublished authors, and datasets scraped from *Wikipedia*.

2.2.4 Model Training

GenAI models are not monolithic entities; instead, they rely on a collection of interconnected auxiliary modules, each responsible for a specific function within the overall system. Many of the datasets presented in the previous sections have been used to train several of such modules, which, in turn, have been integrated into the architecture of some of the most widely used GenAI systems. It is worth noting that GenAI developers sometimes reuse an existing model architecture while retraining it on a different dataset. When this occurs, it is usually acknowledged in the corresponding publication. Since none of the examples discussed here include such a note, it can be reasonably inferred that the original training datasets of these auxiliary models were retained.

SoundStream (Zeghidour et al., 2022) is a neural audio codec that is an integral part of the architecture of several AI-music models, including Google's *AudioLM* and *MusicLM*. This model has been trained using several datasets, including *TagATune*, *LibriTTS*, and a *Freesound* dataset scraped from the internet.

CLAP is a language-audio model trained to align text and sound representations, enabling the retrieval of relevant audio from textual prompts. CLAP has been trained using several datasets, including *FDS50k*, *ClothoV2s*, and a derivative of *AudioSet*. CLAP was initially designed for adoption in various audio applications, particularly speech recognition, and ultimately found use in several music generation systems, including the commercial system *Stability Audio* 2.0 (Evans et al., 2024).

W2v-bert (Chung et al., 2021) is a speech representation model that learns from audio to understand and process spoken language. This model, which has also been widely integrated into GenAI models, such as *AudioLM*, was pre-trained using *Libri-Light*.

MuLan (Huang et al., 2022) is a multimodal model developed by Google, which was used in its *MusicLM* to align music with textual descriptors.

The authors state that the model was trained on '50 million internet music videos' without disclosing the source of this material. However, there is only one video platform with that scale of content – *YouTube* – and it happens to be owned by Google.

BART (Lewis et al., 2020) is a language model developed by Meta that encodes textual prompts into structured representations. It was trained on several datasets, including *Wikipedia* and *BookCorpus*. This model is used by *MusicGen*, which provides the linguistic foundation for conditioning the music generation process.

EnCodec (Défossez et al., 2022), also developed by Meta and used in *MusicGen*, is a model that transforms raw audio into a simplified format that supposedly captures its essential features while reducing file size (tokenisation). The model was trained on *AudioSet*, *FSD50K*, and *MTG-Jamendo*.

2.3 Category 1: Scraped Data

What emerges from the analysis of current AI music datasets is not merely a technical story of data genealogy but a political economy of capture. Beneath the surface of web scraping and dataset curation lies a process that reproduces long-standing capitalist mechanisms of appropriation. The following section turns to Marxian and post-Marxian thought to frame these practices as contemporary forms of primitive accumulation, revealing how the extraction of creative labour in the digital domain extends the logic of enclosure into new, computational terrains.

2.3.1 Primitive Accumulation of Training Data

The practice of data scraping predates the advent of AI applications. Tech companies have long identified the economic value in what Zuboff (2019) calls *data exhaust* and integrated it as part of their business models. The backdrop is an *all-you-can-scrap* ideology (Morreale et al., 2023b) in which companies simply capture information, or *behavioural surplus* (Zuboff, 2019), from the Internet 'without context and without consent' (Crawford, 2021). Many music datasets examined in Section 2.2 indiscriminately scrape data from online sources or from other previously compiled datasets. This analysis confirms the results of a previous investigation (Morreale et al., 2023b), in which we analysed the datasets commonly used in GenAI and identified that 60% of them had been populated by scraping songs from the Internet or other datasets. While dominant, this practice is inherently exploitative and resembles primitive accumulation.

In Marxian theory, primitive accumulation is a process through which titles to existing assets are accumulated by a dominant class that is capable of transforming them into means of production (Dobb, 1946). Before this process takes place, people from non-dominant classes have some form of direct access to these assets and means of production. The process of primitive accumulation withdraws access to resources and divorces producers from the means of production (De Angelis, 2001).

While Marx originally assigned primitive accumulation a temporal and historical connotation (De Angelis, 2001; Mezzadra, 2011) – the period of transition that led to the emergence of capitalism – with the hindsight of the evolution of capitalism in the past 150 years, scholars have revisited this concept by freeing it from its original temporal collocation. Primitive accumulation can thus be more broadly considered the 'social constitution through which the exploitation of labour subsists' (Bonefeld, 2001) and, as such, a necessarily permanent feature of capitalism (De Angelis, 2001; Federici, 2014; Harvey, 2017; Luxemburg, 2014).

In Marx's original view of primitive accumulation, the *object* of accumulation was land and physical resources. Modern interpretations have broadened the focus to include all forms of conversions of common or state property rights into private rights, a trend that the neoliberal orthodoxy has strengthened over the past 40 years (Harvey, 2017). During this period, resources and assets that were once community- or state-owned, or even unowned, became 'captured, enclosed, and utilised for private profit' (Hall, 2012). This hoarding process, which Harvey (2017) termed *accumulation by dispossession*, extended beyond physical and geographical resources to infiltrate what Brown (2013) calls the *artificial commons*. Ideas, social practices, languages, and modes of sociality that were formerly untouched by capital accumulation become objects of enclosure, appropriation, privatisation, and commodification (Ekman, 2016).

Fast forward to the digital age, Muldoon (2022) identified a parallel between the early capitalist enclosure of the commons and the digital enclosure of the Internet. This reflection resonates with the argument of Sadowski (2019), who proposed that the contemporary political economy is based on the accumulation of data and found in the quest for constant search for new sources of data the typical traits of imperialist mode of accumulation, which is visible in AI companies' attempts to get their hands on data by any means, by either licensing them (in our examples, *Stabilty Audio* and *Meta*) or just obtaining them by more arguable means (*Suno* and *Udio*).

2.3.2 Extractivism and Formal Subsumption

Training data is often scraped without seeking permission from the individuals who had been involved in any capacity in its creation. In the previously mentioned study, we identified that only 2.6% of dataset creators asked musicians' consent to use their music in the dataset, and even in these cases, the original intent was to use them for music research (analysis) rather than generation (Morreale et al., 2023b).

Consent is complex, as it may be given unwittingly, for a specific use, or not at all. For instance, in the case of *Freesound*, sound artists might have consented to their creations being used for sound foley but could not have known that it would be used for AI training purposes. This comment reflects the finding that only 1.7% of dataset creators informed musicians that their contribution would be used to train an ML model (Morreale et al., 2023b). This all-you-can-scrap ideology dismisses individuals' contributions to dataset creation, which their creators can approach with a laissez-faire attitude (Jo and Gebru, 2020), overlooking the ethical implications and liability of scraping the entire Internet.

In a process that reminds us not only of land enclosure but also of colonial logic, which views land and resources as something waiting to be discovered, scraped data is treated as a resource that is free for the taking – a *terra nullius*. Hardt and Negri (2019, p. 168) commented that data extraction is one of the new frontiers of capitalist wealth extraction, and they suggested that attributing metaphors of *mining* and *extraction* for data 'paint an image of unstructured fields of social data that are available for capture by intrepid prospectors, just like oil or minerals in the earth'. Similarly, Zuboff (2019) termed *behavioural surplus* the logged digital traces that people leave behind as they wander around and inhabit the web'. These extractive practices rely 'on forms of wealth that to a large extent preexist the engagement of capital' (Hardt and Negri, 2019, p. 169).

Techno-capitalism, other than dominating others, is indeed *dependent* on others and 'cannot exist without making use of unpaid resources stemming from nature, nonwage/unremunerated labour' (Fuchs, 2018), in what Hardt and Negri termed the *formal subsumption of society under capital*. As explained by Fraser and Jaeggi (2018) and Drott (2024), capitalism needs to draw resources and background conditions (e.g., nature, social reproduction, public power) from outside itself while simultaneously disavowing such a need. Thus, it treats these resources 'as *free gifts*, which are inexhaustible, possess no (monetised) value, and can be appropriated ad infinitum' (Fraser and Jaeggi, 2018).

Mutatis mutandis, similar characteristics can be found in the Marxian concept of *formal subsumption*, whereby the 'capital takes over existing production processes and social arrangements and intervenes in both for its own purpose' (Walsh, 2023). This concept is understood as an ongoing and universal feature of capitalism (Walsh, 2023). Expanding on Marx's original notion, Hardt and Negri (1994, p. 15) argued that, in the phase of formal subsumption, the capital subsumes production processes that originated outside of it.

2.3.3 The Capture of the Common

Hardt and Negri (2019) termed *extraction of the commons* the ways in which capital coopt and enclose the natural resources and 'the social wealth that results from circuits of cooperation, ranging from cultural products to traditional knowledges, and from urban territories and scientific knowledges'. This comment is aligned with Dyer-Witheford's and colleagues' (2019) comments about dispossession in AI applications. The authors suggest that, in order to exist within a capitalist system, any resources needed by the AI for its survival need to be 'commodified or enclosed'. Examples include the enclosure of energy generated from natural sources and the centralisation of computational infrastructures. The focus of this article – training data – however, is not identified by the authors as a possible object of dispossession. The similar term *capture of the common* was used by Crawford (2021) to describe the logic by which AI systems extract and enclose all sorts of public data (e.g., biodata and knowledge), which was previously part of the commons. The author calls this process 'a privatization by stealth, an extraction of knowledge value from public goods'.

While inspired by the concepts of extraction and capture of the commons, in this chapter, I propose a different sort of capture of the commons – one that is possibly even more literal. In my analysis, I showed how several AI music training datasets have been developed by leveraging the volunteer labour of tens of thousands of individuals. This result aligns with related work on the enclosure of digital spaces (Andrejevic, 2019), where IT companies appropriate users' volunteer labour (Brown, 2013). Terranova (2000), in particular, showed that even before social media, IT companies were already commodifying volunteer labour, citing the example of AOL (America Online) community moderators, open-source developers, and users contributing content to online forums. A similar dynamic was noted in my analysis: several datasets were built upon the labour of thousands of users of online communities. These users volunteered their time and skills to perform activities on online projects, creating digital commons for other users to benefit. These activities included creating and sharing music and audio (*Freesound, Free Music Archive, Jamendo*), reading audiobooks (*LibriVok*), captioning lyrics (*LyricWiki, Musixmatch*), tagging music genres and emotions (*Last.fm, Jamendo*), and transcribing music sheets (*MuseScore, TheoryTab*).[5]

Muldoon (2022) offers a useful lens to interpret this phenomenon. He proposes that the business model that underlies this practice is an example of enclosure of the commons 'based on a parasitic relationship in which (the company)'s owners capture value created by its users'. However, to Muldoon, in addition to commodifying users' activities, online platforms like Facebook establish 'proprietary rights over a social commons embedded in online communities'. As discussed by Hardt and Negri (2019, p. 169), social media thus extract value from 'social relationships, social intelligence, and social production'. Value is thus not directly arranged by capital; instead, users produce value through social cooperation, in a relatively autonomous manner (Hardt and Negri, 2019, p. 169).

In addition to the ethical issue of repurposing the creators' work unbeknownst to them, this practice represents a deliberate attempt to appropriate and enclose the digital common. While this common is technically non-rivalrous and available to everyone, the condition for being captured and becoming material for training sets is conditional on the availability of the *means of production* – in this case, the computational resources like GPUs and storage – and the capital to run these, which are not democratically distributed. While dataset developers often frame their releases as contributions to scientific progress or community benefit, this rhetoric conceals the structural reality that such datasets frequently become instruments of commercial exploitation and enclosure. This is particularly the case in a highly competitive market injected with venture capital (Morreale, 2021): commercial music generation companies unlikely – and, in fact, do not – maintain the original intent of the datasets.

2.4 Category 2: Labour Data

In the previous section, I demonstrated that the majority of datasets used in GenAI models include data generated, in one way or another, by unwitting individuals. These individuals inadvertently contributed to these datasets by transcribing music into scores, transcribing lyrics, sharing their own performances and compositions, and even simply by expressing their listening preferences. All this scraped data, however problematic and ethically fraught, already existed 'out there'. However, a different type of data is even more problematic, as it is explicitly created to train an ML model. I refer to this as *labour data*, marking its emergence as a distinct epistemological niche.

This shift from appropriation to transformation echoes the capital's drive to continually reshape labour processes, a dynamic that Marx called *real subsumption*. Unlike formal subsumption, which takes over and instrumentalises existing non-capitalist production processes, practices, and relations, real subsumption entails the ongoing transformation of labour processes, creating new, adequately capitalist forms(Hardt and Negri, 1994, p. 142; Walsh, 2023). This continuous transformation is necessary because the external resources on which capital depends inevitably deplete over time (Drott, 2024). For capitalism to continue existing, it must repeatedly subsume social relations under capital (Fuchs, 2018).

Labour data does not pre-exist; it must be actively produced before it can be harvested and used as training material. AI companies, therefore, need to devise mechanisms that generate such data in the first place. Various forms of labour data exist, which can be divided into two categories: (1) paid workers performing micro-tasks on crowdsourcing platforms and (2) Internet users performing tasks that are used to train AI systems unbeknownst to them. The first category has been extensively discussed in literature (Casilli and Brown, 2025; Jones, 2021; Muldoon et al., 2024; Tubaro and Casilli, 2019), with critiques mainly focusing on the exploitation of cheap labour. The second category, however, has received far less attention and involves what I previously called *unwitting labour* (Morreale et al., 2023a): individuals unwittingly contribute their *humanness* – that is, their 'cognitive processes (e.g., preferences, conceptual associations, identifications, and resolutions) and perceptual performances (e.g., being able to read a word or distinguish a panda from an otter)' (Morreale et al., 2023a) – to train the machine.

Unwitting labourers can be further distinguished into two sub-categories. The first includes platform users whose activities performed within the platforms are repurposed to train AI models. For example, user-curated Spotify playlists are exploited by the company to train the ML models underpinning their recommendation systems (Morreale et al., 2023a). Spotify explicitly acknowledges that the 'hundreds of millions of playlists' that users create provide them with an extensive 'music curation database'. In this way, users contribute their taste and preferences to the system without explicitly intending to train AI models (Morreale et al., 2023a). These platforms thus become both *loci* and *instruments* of exploitation – that is, assemblages composed of technology-enabled virtual spaces in which platform owners produce surplus value by exploiting the activities performed by users.

Borrowing the aforementioned concept of dispossession by Harvey, Ekman (2016) suggested that, in the digital domain, the object of capital dispossession 'is everything users do when they are communicating through various commercial platforms and sites on the Internet'. This observation can be extended beyond *communication* to include epistemology: all *information* and *knowledge* produced by users interacting with digital platforms and systems are subject to capital dispossession. Sadowski (2019) suggested that, by using platforms and devices, users 'are turned into commodities that take the form of personal data, which is sold to advertisers and data brokers'. This reflection is a modern adaptation of the *audience commodity* theory, as proposed by Smythe (1977), who postulated that the audience is the primary commodity of mass media. This theory has been revisited and applied to the digital domain (Fuchs, 2010) and to contemporary data capitalism (Zuboff, 2019).

While these activities are obviously problematic, users derive some benefit from them (e.g., arguably better recommendations). However, another category of unwitting labourers receives no benefits whatsoever from the exploitation of their labour in training ML models. This second category is therefore even more problematic, with its most notable example, albeit outside of the musical domain, being reCAPTCHA. This system is presented to users who need to access a service and displays them images or audio, and they must identify objects or patterns within these prompts. This challenge-response test was implemented to detect bots and prevent them from accessing web pages or digital services. When purchased by Google, it has been used to train ML systems (Justie, 2021). However, users are unaware that they are performing unpaid labour. As Foley (2014) observed, reCAPTCHAs turn human bodies into 'prosthetics for computation'.

In this respect, reCAPTCHA is not dissimilar to the *Tag-A-Tune* described earlier, which its authors framed as a *human computation tool* (Law et al., 2007). Notably, the founder of CAPTCHA, Luis von Ahn, is also one of the creators of Tag-A-Tune, a connection that makes the ideological continuity between the two projects unsurprising. Von Ahn, who is also the founder and CEO of Duolingo, even toured the world delivering seminars entitled 'How to get people to work for free' (Foley, 2014). When presenting the Tag-A-Tune dataset, Von Ahn and his colleagues explained that 'unfortunately, the cost of obtaining a comprehensive set of annotations manually is high. One way to lower the cost of labelling is to create games with a purpose that people will voluntarily play, producing useful metadata as a by-product', and they recognise that their system 'has the potential to produce better labels at lower cost because the labor is essentially free' (Law et al., 2007).

In 2021, together with the other principal author of Tag-A-Tune, Edith Law, von Ahn elaborated the principle of human computation, which they defined as strategies to 'leverage the *abilities of an unprecedented number of people via the Web to perform complex computation*' (Law and Von Ahn, 2011). Their stated motivation was to explore the rich connections around workers' interests and expertise. However, in practice, such systems exemplify a profound inversion of human–machine relations. This inversion of human–machine relations represents a precise instance of real subsumption within techno-capitalism, in which, rather than humans making use of the machine, it is the machine using humans to 'fulfil the conditions for profit production' (Moore and Woodcock, 2021).

2.5 Sanitisation, Abstraction, Amnesia

The process that I term *data sanitisation* describes how AI developers systematically obscure the origins of training material through successive layers of technical abstraction. Each layer in this cascading-module strategy (Morreale et al., 2025b) distances AI models from their problematic sources, effectively neutralising ethical scrutiny while preserving the value extracted from those sources.

Google's music generation model, *MusicLM*, exemplifies this process: problematic data passes through multiple stages before becoming normalised within ostensibly clean architecture. MusicLM is partially based on *AudioLM*, includes *MuLan* (a model linking sounds with textual descriptions), and has been partially trained using *AudioSet*'s derivative *MusicCaps*. AudioLM, in turn, incorporates *SoundStream* and *w2v-bert into its architecture*. All these auxiliary models have been trained on some of the problematic datasets discussed in Section 2.2, including *Tag-A-Tune, LibriTTS, Freesound* data, and *YouTube* videos. In Figure 2.1, I trace how three of the main GenAI music

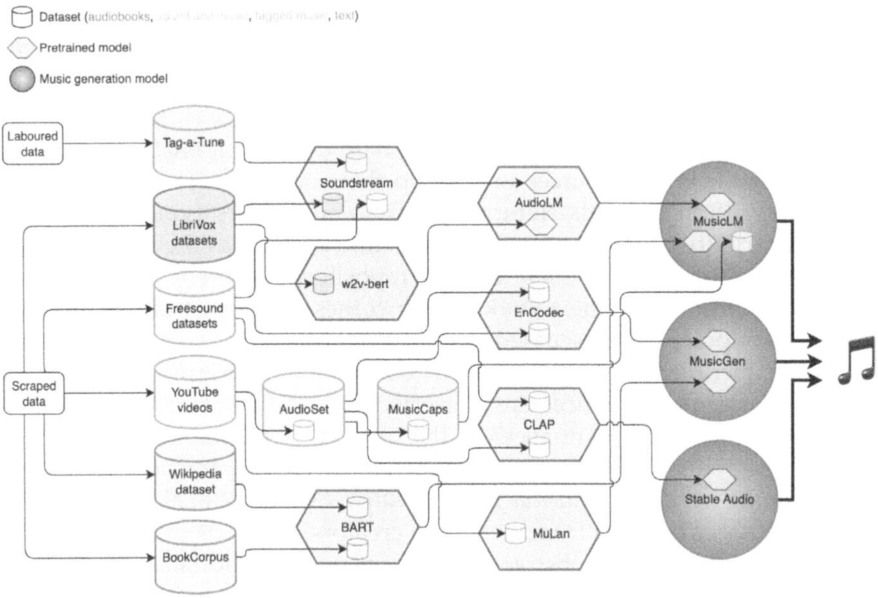

FIGURE 2.1
Example of sanitisation of problematic data.

systems (i.e., MusicGen, MusicLM, and Stable Audio) embed these problematic datasets through this chain of abstraction. Tracing these less visible data sources is crucial, as model developers often claim to have properly licensed their training data. At the same time, significant parts of their architectures remain rooted in ethically compromised origins that remain unacknowledged and unattributed (Morreale et al., 2025a).

Legal frameworks serve as another sanitisation mechanism. One key mechanism is the use of permissive licensing frameworks. Most datasets are released under the very permissive MIT License, even when dataset creators may not have legitimate ownership rights to the underlying data. This practice fabricates a legal fiction, an illusion of legitimacy, that helps sanitise problematic data collection methods. For instance, the *MuseScore Lead Sheet* dataset, which contains scores transcribed by community members, was released under the MIT License, despite MuseScore itself not being affiliated with the project. It was later removed due to copyright concerns.

Institutional endorsement also plays a crucial role in normalising problematic data practices. Academic publication and integration into widely used auxiliary models (e.g., *SoundStream, CLAP*) and datasets (e.g., *MusicCaps, FSD50K*) lend legitimacy to otherwise problematic practices. The accumulation practices become particularly problematic once the use of a dataset diverges from the original intent. For instance, some of the datasets scraped from *Freesound* gained legitimacy through their academic affiliation, but only became ethically questionable when they were used to train *CLAP*, which in turn was embedded in the commercial music generation model, *Stability Audio*.[6] In this light, Stability Audio's profits may be directly linked to the exploitation of Freesound users' creativity and time.

Dataset sharing presents a complex dynamic. While it enables access for researchers lacking resources to develop their own datasets, this apparent generosity often conceals self-interest. Dataset creators typically leverage these contributions to enhance their academic profiles, as they often outline citation requirements in their GitHub repositories, thereby ensuring academic recognition for their work, which comes at the cost of enabling the exploitative practices I discussed in this chapter.

Finally, technical abstraction further sanitises data origins. For example, when musical performances are converted into MIDI data, as in the *Giant-MIDI-Piano* dataset, the nuances of the original performances and human context are reduced to technical specifications. This abstraction, which has also been referred to as *musical grammatisation* (Morreale et al., 2025b), effectively distances the data from its human creators.

These layered forms of abstraction distance problematic data accumulation practices from their ultimate use in GenAI systems. The sanitisation process makes it easier for companies to sidestep ethical concerns while continuing to benefit from extracted human labour and creativity. Understanding these mechanisms is essential not only for developing critical interventions but for exposing how the abstraction and sanitisation of training data are structural features of digital capitalism. Even when certain forms of data accumulation are permitted through legal or institutional mechanisms, they remain complicit with extractive logics that treat human creativity and labour as free resources to be enclosed and commodified. The legality of these practices should not be confused with their ethical legitimacy. On the contrary, permissive licensing, institutional endorsement, and technical opacity often function as instruments of moral laundering, concealing practices of dispossession under the guise of innovation and research.

2.6 Conclusion

This chapter has explored the complex landscape of AI training data through the lens of music generation systems, revealing fundamental patterns of exploitation and accumulation. Notably, these patterns extend beyond the musical domain. While this analysis has focused on music generation systems, such patterns identified here are evident across many domains of AI development. From image datasets like ImageNet to gameplay data like DeepMind's Go dataset, we see similar processes of extraction and sanitisation at work. Image datasets, such as ImageNet, Microsoft's MS-Celeb, and

LAION-5B, primarily contain photos and captions uploaded by individuals on platforms like Instagram and Flickr, which are then used to populate the dataset. AI companies vastly use these datasets to train ML models that are employed for a variety of tasks, ranging from surveillance (facial feature detection) to image generation. Another example worth discussing is the KGS dataset. Google's subsidiary company, DeepMind, scraped[7] individual moves from 160,000 games of Go players to train AlphaGo, an ML-based Go player (Silver et al., 2016). This data was initially generated by Go players using KGS. This website allows Go players to play against each other and is later harvested by DeepMind by running a simple script.

The analysis has demonstrated how the extraction of human experience, creativity, and labour operates through two distinct data accumulation practices: scraped data and labour data. Both practices ultimately serve to capture *humanness*, that is, the unique cognitive and creative capabilities that AI systems seek to emulate. I also revealed how data sanitisation processes obscure the problematic origins of training datasets. This practice, which occurs through multiple layers of abstraction, institutional legitimation, and technical complexity, enables the ongoing accumulation of training data while minimising questions of consent, compensation, and exploitation. The parallels with historical processes of primitive accumulation and dispossession are striking, suggesting that current AI development practices represent a new frontier in capitalism's ongoing need to subsume social relations.

Looking ahead, this work requires several key interventions. First, we need stronger theoretical frameworks for understanding and critiquing data accumulation practices. Second, concrete methods must be developed to document data accumulation practices and enforce accountability when they are ignored. Finally, we need policy and technical interventions that can effectively regulate the accumulation of training data and ensure just compensation for human contributions. To build AI systems that respect human creativity, we must implement systematic changes in dataset transparency, compensation mechanisms, and ethical AI policies.

Notes

1 https://s3.documentcloud.org/documents/25023128/suno-legal-filing-8124.pdf
2 https://www.riaa.com/wp-content/uploads/2024/06/Udio-Complaint-6.24.241.pdf
3 https://www.hooktheory.com/theorytab/about
4 In reality, only one player is playing at time, and they "have the illusion of playing with human partners whereas in reality, they are playing with a simulated player, or a bot, whose moves and timing come from recorded sequences of previous game play" (Law et al., 2007).

5 Freesound recently posted a blog post to discuss the role of the platform "in the era of generative AI" https://blog.freesound.org/?p=2082. The company's response was that creations uploaded on Freesound can be used to train AI models in three out of four licensing types. This created some backlash https://freesound.org/forum/freesound-project/44672/. The response is not dissimilar to CC https://creativecommons.org/2021/03/04/should-cc-licensed-content-be-used-to-train-ai-it-depends/.

6 Stability Audio researchers might have retrained CLAP with a different training dataset, but there is no mention of what such dataset contained in (Evans et al., 2024).

7 https://github.com/hughperkins/kgsgo-dataset-preprocessor

References

Agostinelli, A., Denk, T. I., Borsos, Z., Engel, J., Verzetti, M., Caillon, A., Huang, Q., Jansen, A., Roberts, A., Tagliasacchi, M., Sharifi, M., Zeghidour, N., Frank, C., 2023. *MusicLM: Generating Music From Text*. https://arxiv.org/abs/2301.11325

Andrejevic, M., 2019. Automating Surveillance. *Surveillance & Society* 8.

Bogdanov, D., Won, M., Tovstogan, P., Porter, A., Serra, X., 2019. *The MTG-Jamendo Dataset for Automatic Music Tagging*. Machine Learning for Music Discovery Workshop, International Conference on Machine Learning (ICML 2019). Long Beach, CA, United States.

Bonefeld, W., 2001. The Permanence of Primitive Accumulation: Commodity Fetishism and Social Constitution. *The commoner* 2.

Brown, B. A., 2013. Primitive Digital Accumulation: Privacy, Social Networks, and Biopolitical Exploitation. *Rethinking Marxism* 25, 385–403. https://doi.org/10.1080/08935696.2013.798974

Casilli, A. A., Brown, S., 2025. *Waiting for Robots*. The University of Chicago Press. urn:isbn:978-0-226-82095-8

Chung, Y.-A., Zhang, Y., Han, W., Chiu, C.-C., Qin, J., Pang, R., Wu, Y., 2021. *W2v-BERT: Combining Contrastive Learning and Masked Language Modeling for Self-Supervised Speech Pre-Training*. https://arxiv.org/abs/2108.06209

Copet, J., Kreuk, F., Gat, I., Remez, T., Kant, D., Synnaeve, G., Adi, Y., Défossez, A., 2024. *Simple and Controllable Music Generation*. https://arxiv.org/abs/2306.05284

Crawford, K., 2021. *Atlas of AI: Power, Politics, and the Planetary Costs of Artificial Intelligence*. Yale University Press, New Haven.

De Angelis, M., 2001. Marx and primitive accumulation: The continuous character of capital's 'enclosures'. *The commoner* 2(1), 1–22.

Défossez, A., Copet, J., Synnaeve, G., Adi, Y., 2022. *High Fidelity Neural Audio Compression*. https://doi.org/10.48550/arXiv.2210.13438

Dhariwal, P., Jun, H., Payne, C., Kim, J. W., Radford, A., Sutskever, I., 2020. *Jukebox: A Generative Model for Music*. arXiv:2005.00341 [cs, eess, stat].

Dobb, M., 1946. *Studies in the Development of Capitalism*. Kessinger Legacy Reprints, USA.

Drossos, K., Lipping, S., Virtanen, T., 2019. *Clotho Dataset*. https://doi.org/10.5281/ZENODO.3490684
Drott, E., 2024. *Streaming Music, Streaming Capital*. Duke University Press, Durham.
Dyer-Witheford, N., Kjøsen, A. M., Steinhoff, J., 2019. *Inhuman Power: Artificial Intelligence and the Future of Capitalism*. Pluto Press, London.
Ekman, M., 2016. The Relevance of Marx's Theory of Primitive Accumulation for Media and Communication Research. *In: Marx in the Age of Digital Capitalism*. Brill, pp. 105–132.
Evans, Z., Parker, J. D., Carr, C. J., Zukowski, Z., Taylor, J., Pons, J., 2024. *Long-Form Music Generation with Latent Diffusion*. https://arxiv.org/abs/2404.10301
Falcão, F., Bozkurt, B., Serra, X., Andrade, N., Baysal, O., 2019. *A Dataset of Rhythmic Pattern Reproductions and Baseline Automatic Assessment System*. https://doi.org/10.5281/zenodo.3299663
Federici, S., 2014. *Caliban and the Witch*, Second revised ed. Autonomedia, Brooklyn, NY.
Foley, M., 2014. "Prove You're Human": Fetishizing Material Embodiment and Immaterial Labor in Information Networks. *Critical Studies in Media Communication* 31, 365–379. https://doi.org/10.1080/15295036.2014.939682
Fonseca, E., Favory, X., Pons, J., Font, F., Serra, X., 2021. Fsd50k: An Open Dataset of Human-Labeled Sound Events. *IEEE/ACM Transactions on Audio, Speech, and Language Processing* 30, 829–852.
Fraser, N., Jaeggi, R., 2018. *Capitalism: A Conversation in Critical Theory*. Polity, Cambridge Medford (MA).
Fuchs, C., 2010. Labor in Informational Capitalism and on the Internet. *The Information Society* 26, 179–196. https://doi.org/10.1080/01972241003712215
Fuchs, C., 2018. Universal Alienation, Formal and Real Subsumption of Society Under Capital, Ongoing Primitive Accumulation by Dispossession: Reflections on the Marx@200-Contributions by David Harvey and Michael Hardt/Toni Negri. *tripleC* 16, 454–467. https://doi.org/10.31269/triplec.v16i2.1028
Hall, D., 2012. Rethinking Primitive Accumulation: Theoretical Tensions and Rural Southeast Asian Complexities. *Antipode* 44, 1188–1208. https://doi.org/10.1111/j.1467-8330.2011.00978.x
Hardt, M., Negri, A., 1994. *Labor of Dionysus: A Critique of the State-Form, Theory Out of Bounds*. University of Minnesota Press, Minneapolis.
Hardt, M., Negri, A., 2019. *Assembly, Heretical Thought*, First issued as an Oxford University Press paperback ed. Oxford University Press, New York.
Harvey, D., 2017. The "New" Imperialism: Accumulation by Dispossession. In: Ollman, B., Anderson, K. B. (Eds.), *Karl Marx*. Routledge, pp. 213–237. https://doi.org/10.4324/9781315251196-10
Huang, Q., Jansen, A., Lee, J., Ganti, R., Li, J. Y., Ellis, D. P. W., 2022. *MuLan: A Joint Embedding of Music Audio and Natural Language*. https://arxiv.org/abs/2208.12415
Jo, E. S., Gebru, T., 2020. Lessons from Archives: Strategies for Collecting Sociocultural Data in Machine Learning. *In: Proceedings of the 2020 Conference on Fairness, Accountability, and Transparency. Presented at the FAT* '20: Conference on Fairness, Accountability, and Transparency*. ACM, Barcelona, Spain, pp. 306–316. https://doi.org/10.1145/3351095.3372829
Jones, P., 2021. *Work Without the Worker: Labour in the Age of Platform Capitalism*. Verso Books, Brooklyn.

Justie, B., 2021. Little History of CAPTCHA. *Internet Histories* 5, 30–47. https://doi.org/10.1080/24701475.2020.1831197

Kahn, J., Rivière, M., Zheng, W., Kharitonov, E., Xu, Q., Mazaré, P. E., Karadayi, J., Liptchinsky, V., Collobert, R., Fuegen, C., Likhomanenko, T., Synnaeve, G., Joulin, A., Mohamed, A., Dupoux, E., 2020. *Libri-Light: A Benchmark for ASR with Limited or No Supervision*. ICASSP 2020-2020 IEEE International Conference on Acoustics, Speech and Signal Processing (ICASSP), pp. 7669–7673.

Kong, Q., Li, B., Chen, J., Wang, Y., 2022. *GiantMIDI-Piano: A Large-Scale MIDI Dataset for Classical Piano Music*. https://doi.org/10.48550/arXiv.2010.07061

Law, E. L., Von Ahn, L., 2011. *Human Computation*. Morgan & Claypool.

Law, E. L., Von Ahn, L., Dannenberg, R. B., Crawford, M., 2007. *TagATune: A Game for Music and Sound Annotation*. ISMIR. Vienna, Austria, p. 2.

Lewis, M., Liu, Y., Goyal, N., Ghazvininejad, M., Mohamed, A., Levy, O., Stoyanov, V., Zettlemoyer, L., 2020. *BART: Denoising Sequence-to-Sequence Pre-Training for Natural Language Generation, Translation, and Comprehension*. Proceedings of the 58th Annual Meeting of the Association for Computational Linguistics. Presented at the Proceedings of the 58th Annual Meeting of the Association for Computational Linguistics, Association for Computational Linguistics, Online, pp. 7871–7880. https://doi.org/10.18653/v1/2020.acl-main.703

Luxemburg, R., 2014. *The Accumulation of Capital*, Second ed. Routledge, London.

Ma, Y., Øland, A., Ragni, A., Del Sette, B. M., Saitis, C., Donahue, C., Lin, C., Plachouras, C., Benetos, E., Quinton, E., Shatri, E., Morreale, F., Zhang, G., Fazekas, G., Xia, G., Zhang, H., Manco, I., Huang, J., Guinot, J., Lin, L., Marinelli, L., Lam, M. W. Y., Sharma, M., Kong, Q., Dannenberg, R. B., Yuan, R., Wu, S., Wu, S.-L., Dai, S., Lei, S., Kang, S., Dixon, S., Chen, W., Huang, W., Du, X., Qu, X., Tan, X., Li, Y., Tian, Z., Wu, Zhiyong, Wu, Zhizheng, Ma, Z., Wang, Z., 2024. *Foundation Models for Music: A Survey*. https://arxiv.org/abs/2408.14340

Mezzadra, S., 2011. The Topicality of Prehistory: A New Reading of Marx's Analysis of "So-Called Primitive Accumulation." *Rethinking Marxism* 23, 302–321. https://doi.org/10.1080/08935696.2011.582995

Moore, P. V., Woodcock, J. (Eds.), 2021. *Augmented Exploitation: Artificial Intelligence, Automation and Work, Wildcat: Worker's Movements and Global Capitalism*. Pluto Press, London.

Morreale, F., 2021. Where Does the Buck Stop? Ethical and Political Issues with AI in Music Creation. *Transactions of the International Society for Music Information Retrieval* 4, 105–113. https://doi.org/10.5334/tismir.86

Morreale, F., Bahmanteymouri, E., Burmester, B., Chen, A., Thorp, M., 2023a. The Unwitting Labourer: Extracting Humanness in AI Training. *AI & Society*. https://doi.org/10.1007/s00146-023-01692-3

Morreale, F., Hutiri, W., Serrà, J., Xiang, A., Mitsufuji, Y., 2025a. *Attribution-by-Design: Ensuring Inference-Time Provenance in Generative Music Systems*. https://doi.org/10.48550/arXiv.2510.08062

Morreale, F., Martinez-Ramirez, M. A., Masu, R., Liao, W., Mitsufuji, Y., 2025b. Reductive, Exclusionary, Normalising: The Limits of Generative AI Music. *Transactions of the International Society for Music Information Retrieval*. https://doi.org/10.5334/tismir.256

Morreale, F., Sharma, M., Wei, I.-C., 2023b. *Data Collection in Music Generation Training Sets: A Critical Analysis*. Presented at the Ismir 2023 Hybrid Conference.

Muldoon, J., 2022. *Platform Socialism: How to Reclaim Our Digital Future from Big Tech*. Pluto Press, S.l.

Muldoon, J., Graham, M., Cant, C., 2024. *Feeding the Machine: The Hidden Human Labour Powering AI.* Canongate, Edinburgh.

Pram, L., Morreale, F., 2025. *Opening Musical Creativity? Embedded Ideologies in Generative-AI Music Systems.* https://doi.org/10.48550/arXiv.2508.08805

Sadowski, J., 2019. When Data is Capital: Datafication, Accumulation, and Extraction. *Big Data & Society* 6. https://doi.org/10.1177/2053951718820549

Santana, I. A. P., Pinhelli, F., Donini, J., Catharin, L., Mangolin, R. B., Feltrim, V. D., Domingues, M. A., Others, 2020. Music4all: A New Music Database and Its Applications. *In: 2020 International Conference on Systems, Signals and Image Processing (IWSSIP).* IEEE, pp. 399–404.

Schneider, F., Kamal, O., Jin, Z., Schölkopf, B., 2023. *Moûsai: Text-to-Music Generation with Long-Context Latent Diffusion*. https://arxiv.org/abs/2301.11757

Silver, D., Huang, A., Maddison, C. J., Guez, A., Sifre, L., Van Den Driessche, G., Schrittwieser, J., Antonoglou, I., Panneershelvam, V., Lanctot, M., Dieleman, S., Grewe, D., Nham, J., Kalchbrenner, N., Sutskever, I., Lillicrap, T., Leach, M., Kavukcuoglu, K., Graepel, T., Hassabis, D., 2016. Mastering the Game of Go With Deep Neural Networks and Tree Search. *Nature* 529, 484–489. https://doi.org/10.1038/nature16961

Smythe, D., 1977. Communications: Blindspot of Western Marxism. *Canadian Journal of Political and Social Theory/Revue canadienne de theorie politique etsociale* 1, 3.

Terranova, T., 2000. Free Labor. *Social Text* 18, 33–58. https://doi.org/10.1215/01642472-18-2_63-33

Tubaro, P., Casilli, A. A., 2019. Micro-Work, Artificial Intelligence and the Automotive Industry. *J. Ind. Bus. Econ*. 46, 333–345. https://doi.org/10.1007/s40812-019-00121-1

Walsh, S., 2023. Marx, Subsumption and the Critique of Innovation. *Organization* 30, 345–360. https://doi.org/10.1177/13505084211015377

Yeh, Y. C., Hsiao, W. Y., Fukayama, S., Kitahara, T., Genchel, B., Liu, H. M., Dong, H. W., Chen, Y., Leong, T., Yang, Y. H., 2021. Automatic Melody Harmonization With Triad Chords: A Comparative Study. *Journal of New Music Research (JNMR)* 50, 37–51.

Zeghidour, N., Luebs, A., Omran, A., Skoglund, J., Tagliasacchi, M., 2022. SoundStream: An End-to-End Neural Audio Codec. *IEEE/ACM Trans. Audio Speech Lang. Process.* 30, 495–507. https://doi.org/10.1109/TASLP.2021.3129994

Zen, H., Dang, V., Clark, R., Zhang, Y., Weiss, R. J., Jia, Y., Chen, Z., Wu, Y., 2019. *LibriTTS: A Corpus Derived from LibriSpeech for Text-to-Speech.* https://doi.org/10.48550/arXiv.1904.02882

Zhu, Y., Kiros, R., Zemel, R., Salakhutdinov, R., Urtasun, R., Torralba, A., Fidler, S., 2015. *Aligning Books and Movies: Towards Story-like Visual Explanations by Watching Movies and Reading Books.* https://doi.org/10.48550/arXiv.1506.06724

Zuboff, S., 2019. *The Age of Surveillance Capitalism: The Fight for a Human Future at the New Frontier of Power,* First ed. PublicAffairs, New York.

3

Authorship, Ownership, Authority, Validation, and Creativity through AI

Pablo Lorenzo-Eiroa

3.1 Introduction

After sequential attempts and cycles of "the death of the author" from Nietzsche's "every word is a prejudice" (Nietzsche, 1879–1881), Wittgenstein's "The limits of my language mean the limits of my world" (Wittgenstein, 1921); Borges' Pierre Menard, author of the Quijote (Borges, 1939), Barthes' language as author (Barthes, 1967), and Derrida's signifier (Derrida, 1976) to Negroponte's "the death of the architect" (Negroponte, 1969) by autonomous computational systems, *Authorship* (Lorenzo-Eiroa, 2010–2011, 2013, pp. 10–21, 2023, pp. 416–436) becomes once more a political power structure in the "artificial intelligence" (AI) computational colonization by Big Tech.

In architecture and AI, authorship is quite divided between architects who claim to be the authors of their designs, negating the structuring of data sets, models, interfaces, computation, claiming back a critical cultural dimension from the bottom up against the powering structure of media corporations that are able to impose the means through which they design; and those technologists who disregard cultural criticism when they develop technology through a positivism. Those supportive of a digital-technological positivism use disruptive frameworks available without acknowledging any cultural criticism within the field disrupted. Most architects apply AI frameworks without perhaps understanding how they function, choosing outputs from a range of given possibilities. We have been arguing since the late 1990s that this is problematic since most architects use pre-trained data sets and pre-determined models. Moreover, since McLuhan's media determinism "the medium is the message" (McLuhan, 1964), and Negroponte's death of the architect by an autonomous computational system in 1969, the displacement of conventional media and mediums has necessarily become part of any design agenda. In addition, we claim that data, the frames, the context, and the environment are also part of the frame structures within which the

DOI: 10.1201/9781003480167-4

framework becomes active as a complex system. The star architect system, created after crafted media structures to promote a power structure, fed the architect ego, but has been proved to be functional against political power structures, as a form of cultural resistance against bureaucracy and conventional culture.

Problematically, Big Tech-imposed AI systems retrieve author's text and images, breaking most international copyright law to train their data sets and strengthen their models, and selling back to those same authors pre-trained data sets and anticipatory models. Several lawyers, data scientists, computer scientists, and others in disciplines such as architecture, have argued whether the architecture of the system, or the database, or the users, are or not the authors.

The *Death of the Architect* by an autonomous computational system by Negroponte (Negroponte, 1976) predicted artificial intelligence through human–machine interactivity, as progressive evolutionary machines were soon to take over the task of architects and urbanists since only 5% of architecture in the US was exposed to the work of architects and only 1% to the work at of urbanists, a reading in which the empowerment of media becomes an enaction of "the medium is the message" (McLuhan, 1964). Computation, and media in general, imposes artificial origins through digital signifiers, models, and data mining techniques, therefore expanding the necessity to activate data and computational authorship when doing architecture and urbanism (Lorenzo-Eiroa, 2010-2011, 2013, pp. 10–21, 2023).

Because of a digital feudalism (Lamont and Varoufakis, 2021), expanding authorship to data and computation becomes not only necessary to secure design authorship and expand creativity but a matter of survival of human intelligence, which otherwise several types of human surrogation become active in relation to a growing dependence on automation through AI: from memory and brain neural synapses decay (memory is a function of intelligence) to manipulated mood to others, Big Tech is colonizing the human mind through AI. While we support a post-human validation for space-environments in the growth of cities through the measurement, regulation, and update of building and zoning codes in relation to a thermodynamic AI platform (Lorenzo-Eiroa, 2022), we must secure social equity and well-being regarding AI to save both non-human species and humanity from the 1%. If we are concerned about automated neural intelligence, we should be equally concerned about how our brain's neural structure, neuro plasticity, and memory are deteriorating as AI becomes optimized to favor, for instance, social media networks that manipulate our behavior and train computer networks against ourselves.

The old paradigm of human–machine collaboration is shifting radically and transcended by AI data mining and optimization feedback beyond human comprehension and speed. A type of different intelligence in automation is emerging; soon, self-regulating polymorphic algorithms as agents may take over automation in society, including decision-making AI. Out of necessity for survival, we need to address a cultural-technological ecological cyclical economy in correlation with the environment, achievable through an automated multidimensional scientific participatory-based spatial-environmental engine. A digital feudalism can be resisted by an environmental common through crowd intelligence and shared training of repositories.

We are also critical of current knowledge silos' scientific validation (Milgrom Foundation, 2018), in which AI agents work out relationships across silos and politically empower themselves colonizing authorship within a fragmented scientific status quo. Currently, our reality is measured by capitalism rather than science. We aim to expand through semiotics co-relationships between data and models across knowledge silos.

3.2 Data, Meta-Data, and Information in AI

3.2.1 From China's Critique of Capitalism to Big Tech Distortion of Capitalism through a Digital Feudalism

While controversially China has been engaging in copyrights and patent infringement to compete in a global market economy, China has been articulating a different form of capitalism as a criticism of capitalism. Through collaboration between state public corporations, China has cultivated a model that bypasses the creative destruction typical of competitive capitalism, developing faster than any nation. China's criticism of capitalism is a form of enforced collaboration at the cost of centralization and political control of the individual. Because of the identification of media corporations as infrastructure to structure a society and as a conflict of interest, China ban foreign Big Tech from their national territories. China's large economy and population were able to self-contain enough data to create, simulate, and optimize their own data sets and models, activating a state-powered AI framework. China's centralized economic and top-down efficiency incurs at the cost of civil freedom through citizens' surveillance, although this problem is not alien to the Global West.

On the other end, Varoufakis identified a "digital feudalism" (Lamont and Varoufakis, 2021) as they denounce a society dominated by Big Tech in which belonging to a private feudal safe, gated system, such as Microsoft, is problematic but necessary due to outside danger of malicious bots, renting rather than owning data, software, and hardware. The global political power is shifting away from democratic capitalism to dictatorial capitalism, which has become functional first in China.

For us, we believe we are rather in a new social structure, beyond any science fiction prediction such as Orwell's *Nineteen Eighty-Four* (Orwell, 1949) activating Bradbury's *Fahrenheit 451* (Bradbury, 1953) but before the simulation-state of Wachowskis siblings' "The Matrix" (Wachowski Brothers, 1999);

although we have been already leaving reality behind, making reality non-relevant in a post-truth society, activating a state of simulacra predicted by Baudrillard (Baudrillard, 1981–1983). Semiotics, as systems of representation, separates us from the reality we intend to understand, measure, and dominate. We define our current political reality as an anticipatory *Digital Authoritarianism* based upon a colonization of data and computational authorship through imposing digital signifiers as artificial origins, activating a plutocratic extractive capitalism within a regime in which authority and validation are imposed through power. The current status quo can be critiqued by a digital commons necessarily in coordination with social and environmental commons.

Historically, there has been confusion between data and information. While information consists of a readable, meaningful message, data does not. Data consists of a non-articulated message. Data is not out there, but data becomes meaningful as information through data measurement, data survey, data compilation, and data reconstruction. Once data becomes an articulated message through a system of representation, it becomes information. There is no data outside the media or a medium of representation. Data does not exist until it is represented through a media, a medium, and a system of representation. Once represented and articulated into a message, data becomes meaningful, readable information, whether humanly readable or computationally readable.

There is confusion in terms of the real value of data collection that is misrepresented in current global democracies, placing in danger not only democracy, a fair capital market, entire economies, environmental rights, and sovereignty, but most importantly human rights. The key to data tracking points is that the semantics of the message are not as important as people think. Rather, the meta-data becomes the precious target to collect and articulate its potential value. Mark Zuckerberg's (Meta: Facebook, Instagram, WhatsApp, many others) congressional hearing of 2018 is complicit with the fact that Big Tech is not really interested in the semantics of the message but rather in meta-data. How and when the meta-message is conveyed and through which interfaces it is structured, it provides enough data for forensic reconstruction and correlation, which with enough data points it may develop a full user's profiling. Some data point correlations may be enough to statistically know more about the user behavior and future prediction that the user knows about themselves. Big Tech understands more than anyone that "the medium is the message" (McLuhan, 1964), and that this can be used in multiple ways, from data tracking to profiling to projecting what users may be willing or able to do through interfaces.

Current AI can be defined not as a tool but as frameworks that articulate data science and computer science. Data sets are trained through artificial neural networks (ANN) that use tensors to weigh bias in how data is interpreted in relation to self-editing algorithms that, in each cycle, can become better at what they are able to recognize through statistical correlations and layering. Data and model are in tension with each other. Data sets can output counterintuitive solutions, thanks to the weight of statistical data identifying correlations across recognized features that may offer clues to assumptions. The data set defines the range of possible outputs as it behaves as precedents that constrain the output. The current paradigm, since around 2007, is based on data approximating reality through statistics, counterintuitively and beyond human comprehension in the case of big data, replacing abstract models of reality for trained models that become optimized based on a closer understanding of how reality may work. This data paradigm informs models as models become progressively trained to approximate reality. In addition, the other paradigm that replaced models is the paradigm of simulation, to test models through their functional use and application and perfecting them in terms of the emergent conditions that may arise when the model is placed under tension. Big Data and Simulation, in parallel to each other and in correlation to each other, transformed our way to relate to reality aiming at bypassing the semiotics of language and mathematics but unavoidably through these same systems of representation. The challenge today is that the systems of measurement and representation that we use to approximate reality through Big Data and Simulation are challenged as well. As trained data sets expand, optimize, and update models transforming their premises, these models of reality become more accurate, and with this in mind, we try to activate an autonomous morphogenetic model in which data sets and simulations codevelop a stronger model of reality.

Capitalism's creative disruption disguises practices of feudalism, enacting a wealth transfer and labor exploitation, through an "information civilization" (Zuboff, 2015) and a "data colonialism" (Couldry and Mejias, 2018). Altman's statement, that AI is not possible unless there is widescale copyright infringement through web scraping and API (Milmo, 2024), demonstrates, once more, that within Fordism, current law frameworks only apply to certain conditions and circumstances, and mainly to the lower class that may not be able to have representation or impact in the economy (Gibney, 2024). OpenAI's disruptive technology is based on the seizing of private property for private corporate profit, symbolic of the current type of capitalist structure, breaking the foundations of democratic capitalism through a class wealth transfer and in conflict of interest with their initial nonprofit foundational organization of 2015 and pledge for Artificial General Intelligence (AGI) for all humanity. AI is dependent on articulating statistical prediction through data science and model optimization through computer science. Thus, a statistical common is inherently a social project. Since the comprehension of the value of personalized data tracking and Big Data, a wealth transfer was initiated in which, for the first time, creativity became dependent on an economic factor (Lorenzo-Eiroa, 2023). In response to many of these issues and legal allegations, many publishing companies have edited their publication standards, such as Springer (Springer Publishing, 2023) as they no longer allow publication of AI-generated images nor any AI-generated text unless original citation referencing is included, or it is only used for grammar editing. OpenAI claims legal representation for anyone at any court if any copyright infringement claims are raised from using the output of the platform.

Data belongs to the authors who developed the survey. Computational models belong to the authors who develop the code, the algorithms, the software, and the frameworks. When one works through an AI framework, the output belongs to the data and the model as well as the author who was able to activate relationships across them. It would be easy to tag balances, acknowledging the participation percentage or point-basis of data, model, and retrieved authorship, as Meta AI is currently doing. While Meta discloses precedence to their AI-generated text, for instance, it lacks transparency in the gathering of private data and its analytic use, profiling, and cross-referencing users across their platforms. Most Big Tech decided to colonize the world and not acknowledge how they are displacing authorship and profiting from the labor of the population. Current AI web browser summaries bypass the original websites where that content was generated, now with some reference to it but decreasing their traffic count, siphoning advertising profit, and therefore web pages value. Similarly, architects' labour and authorship are displaced by image and 3D model generators that are trained through their work, their aesthetic visual language, including innovation in systems of representation, grammar, and syntax. The necessity is to activate data and model commons in open repositories tagged to acknowledge the labor produced and share the income developed through the frameworks that utilize such data and models. Shared repositories such as the ones active today, for instance, GitHub, start to acknowledge the necessity for such cross-collaborative frameworks sharing both data and models in which copyrights and patents can be shared as well as acknowledged. Shared profitable frameworks to retrieve both data and models are also active but are less transparent, all the way from data misuse, copyright, and patent infringement to reinforcement learning from human feedback (RLHF), to even problematically functioning, thanks to human linguistic, manual, and visual labor, or fake artificial intelligence such as some image tagging in imageNet disguised as automation.

The data set becomes the main source for defining creativity and the foundational authorship of the framework. The data set, usually through web crawling, is defined by problematically appropriating or interpolating data points based on authored information. Data defines the output not only through precedence but also through the possible combination of data points within the data set that are rearranged for a meaningful output message that is derivative of the grammar of the system. The data would define the canon if the data could be correlated with the model, but in fact data and model become adversarial in the sense that they provide different paradigms to each other. The data is not really the canon, or the model, but the data defines the range of possibilities of the model. The model can be trained to identify features in the data and develop solutions accordingly.

3.3 Semantics in AI

3.3.1 Lack of Cultural Criticism in Programming

As the world became culturally and politically conservative, one could argue that this tendency is due to multiple facts: from the privatization of education to social media self-confirmation bias, partly due to the displacement of top-down authoritative media by a multiplicity of self-media outputs promoted by the new digital economy but easily manipulated by Big Tech. But this cultural tendency has a deeper impact thanks to the widespread use of new technologies. Historically, culture and technology were not separated nor opposites. Today, it seems that the success of technological advancement has displaced any need for cultural criticism, since "technology is just a tool, is neither good nor bad; nor it is neutral" (Kranzberg, 1986). Heidegger (Heidegger, 1977) understands technology as instrumentality, defining technology as anticipatory. Chun's politics of control in mass media define society through technology (Kyon and Wendy, 2008). We understand technology as functional machinic proof of concept. We understand culture as the set of ideas about the world or a social model that defines conventional relationships within groups and through generations. The functionality of technology within society started producing relationships, leaving behind cultural criticism and stagnating culture as an evolving project. As cultural conventions become normative, our language becomes static. Our natural language is not only a system of communication, but it also defines the range of what is possible through what is thinkable as we program our brain's neural connections and define ourselves through language. Derrida's word-sign can be interpreted as an empowerment, a signifier, or a projection of meaning in the classifying-word independently from what is being named, therefore defining language as the structure of our society. Deleuze and Guattari disclosed that language is neither communicational nor informative (Deleuze and Guattari, 1987). With the widespread use of natural language processing (NLP), the conventions of language became once more subject of study, bringing back linguistics and semiotics. Natural language processing (NLP) is able to activate a form of programming through prompt engineering. We understand linguistics as part of semiotics, and therefore we defined computational linguistic semiotics and computational visual semiotics to understand the relationship between computation and architecture.

The problem becomes more complex when one can disarticulate the conventional relationship in language between semantics and grammar. While many have been insisting on the semantics of a message when using AI frameworks, few were able to understand that current AI frameworks are not able to read, interpret, or understand data or models through semantics. The semantics of a message output in AI is just a range of possible meanings interpretable by humans based on grammar structures through statistical prediction. Any AI output based on predictive grammar will be meaningful to humans, producing a perception effect that bots or AI models are talking back to humans. What we call deep learning is no other than a self-editing neural networks trained through statistical prediction models based on recognizing correlational features within a data set. It is quite remarkable how, between 2020 and 2022, many were thinking they were arguing with chat-bots, thinking that the bot was aware of the response and thinking. Similarly, architects were developing images mostly in 2D and a few in 3D models, seeking creative automative processes. In both cases, semantics was the confusion. Developing a project through storytelling based on semantics as a way of conveying messages through AI may be meaningful to the user-designer and to the user of the AI output, but it does not engage with authorship. By not disclosing how data was collected and how the model works or by not problematizing the output-design in relation to the process-framework that developed the output-design, designers relegate authorship to the framework.

Artists-programmers have been exploring radical computational authorship (McLean, 2011) since the early 1960s, defining, experimenting, and expanding Computer-Aided Design (CAD) in relation to the output content, in what we defined as computational visual semiotics (Lorenzo-Eiroa, 2023). Image semantic segmentation, 3D semantic segmentation, and other machine vision AI technologies incentivize the semantics of the message, activating problematic semantics within semiotics. Semiotic conventions are based on conventions of cultural messages: a door is a door if it is distinguishable as such, a cultural convention that goes against the creative design work of an architect that aims at displacing the conventions of the reading and functionality of a door-way. Similarly, sky, water, a body and all the conventional means to segment an image based on the semantics of a semiotic message of figure-background become problematic. Even though, through statistical interpolation, such as Diffusion Models based on thermodynamics of noise-denoise functions, the pixels of an image can develop emergent semantic messages, the base structure through which the message is constructed belongs to a set of conventional conditions that structure data. Software like Building Information Modeling (BIM) is threatening for creative architects, as the interface promotes the use of industry-friendly conventions that, as pre-packaged visual semiotic messages based on material-based construction systems, anticipate the possibilities of what a building is and what the system is able to provide in terms of its own economy.

Since McLuhan's "the medium is the message," the message semantics are irrelevant in relation to the weight of the grammar structure through which the message is articulated, predicted, and even communicated. McLuhan translated a theory of linguistics into visual semiotics as the form of the media became a creative form of semantic disruption.

One of the challenges in the problematic relationship between media and the arts is that media in general is guided by a disruptive economy of pyramidal investment in which computer developers are part of the digital economy.

Programmers seldom agree with cultural criticism. Most are interested in the activation of a functional technology that would challenge the status quo as a disruptive form of technology. In this optimistic scenario, in which thinking is functional to the activation of a technology that validates such thinking, software developers and programmers provide the departing matrices for most fields of study: from physics simulation to CAD to other paradigms of representation across different disciplines and sciences. Since software developers only understand the requirements of multiple disciplines from the outside, they project conventions on the understanding of such disciplines. In architecture and urbanism, this becomes clear, as independent of the intention, the basic parameters through which architects represent reality are presented by programmers and software developers, who, in many cases, may never have done anything related to such disciplines. The problem is not much acting from the outside, usually a necessity to shake the conventions of a discipline, but rather the lack of cultural education in our society in the multiple fields of knowledge and the lack of cultural criticism in general. Seldom does anyone question any longer the parameters of reality, as reality becomes either more static or more functional to Big Tech that models reality according to their shareholders, conventions, desires, and functionalities, accentuating the autonomy of the economic system and propelling its own model distortions.

One of the issues we usually discuss is how software developers project conventions of what they think architecture is, from a conventional Renaissance perspective, which became naturalized as the system to look at space through bidimensional screens, to how machine vision understands space. Likewise, a Cartesian space dominates representation, presenting XYZ axes as a naturalized coordinated space-frame independent and in tension with our planet's geometry, the environment, or geolocation. We proposed to culturally critique the data and computational colonization taking place, from non-Western examples in semiotics such as language, mathematics, the visual, and others. We proposed to shift away from English in computational languages toward an evolved form of language that had expanded its grammar, such as Sanskrit (Bhate and Kak, 1993). Aiming toward a universal language such as Esperanto is not only to demonstrate the limits of our current systems but also to activate universal communication, the original project of computation, by necessarily expanding computational linguistic semiotics. We proposed to investigate different forms of approaching mathematics that help with algorithms, such as the way India approaches mathematics to resolve equations from multiple viewpoints and combinatory logic in their educational system. We investigate the quipu (Mann, 2005), Inca, but also pre-Inca Andean knot system means to count, noting zero before our Western civilization. By designing machines to draw and build we also investigate functional machines that compute signs and signals, such as Leibniz's Characteristica Universalis, aiming to articulate different forms of semiotics, such as linguistics and mathematics, into a single computational system, predicting our current alphanumeric computational systems.

Software is loaded with ideology as it presents itself as a neutral space-frame, but its deep space is loaded with symbolic form. Perspective was one of the most radical modern projects invented to describe space, but it is now more than 500 years old, and it is non compatible with the paradigms of physics, mechanics, fluid dynamics, mathematics, topology, architecture, and urbanism of information we use while viewing-designing space through a computer or when applying machine vision. There is a project of Western computational colonization implicit in each interface that needs to be deconstructed.

3.4 Grammar in AI

3.4.1 Generative Grammar as Formalist Semiotics

AI does not understand the semantics of a processed message. AI frameworks are formalist articulations and correlations of data science models and algorithmic models. AI frameworks are grammar dependent, and when not, grammar emerges as a co-relationship in the functionality of the data that is considered readable, meaningful, or useful for humans.

Current AI can produce semantic messages, not due to intelligent, meaningful interpretation but due to statistical prediction interpolation based on rule-set grammar in language, or, for instance, pre-trained image structures such as rendering, perspective, gravity, and other features in images.

Chomsky (1957) identifies a grammatically correct phrase that carries no meaning; Chomsky's three models for the description of language develop concepts for hierarchy, finite state, and context-dependent meaning in the English language (Chomsky, 1956). Chomsky also discusses a theory of syntax in relation to language and logical structures (Chomsky, 1975). Chomsky Hierarchy pairs Automata Theory to Linguistic Formal Grammar, noting that the simplest are regular languages, followed by context-free and then context-sensitive languages. Minsky (1974) discussed generative grammar, or the possibility for grammar to produce words or linguistic semantic meaning through signification, a determination of the media through its structure.

When users of AI frameworks such as ChatGPT think the chat is understanding semantically what they are asking for, they are rather confronted by a sophisticated type of point-based statistical prediction model that is sensitive to multiple factors and conditions identifying complex pattern recognition and resolving an emergent program (later defined), including context and history activating site-based computation, predicting through grammar and sensitive context pattern recognition and processing what the user is seeking for as it activates reinforced learning by the user entry. In any case, grammar is anticipatory as it provides the structure of how we think the world and itself may be predictive in certain cases, so there will always be semantic meaning emergent from the statistical prediction model arrangement output.

The revolution of OpenAI is that through a high level of resolution within infinitesimal statistical data point correlations, transformers in the framework can identify data point features and resolve precise means to predict a sequence of words forming meaningful sentences. This is an old statistical idea defined in the 1970s, which, through brute force of web crawling and API downloading documents across the globe, was massive enough to make statistically meaningful predictions with precision through Big Data, resolving through context-dependent emergent programming humanly meaningful messages. Before OpenAI and Large Language Models (LLM), the type of statistical features recognized by AI frameworks were not humanly meaningful. With LLM today, the meaning arises from the necessity to read in large data sets statistical features that end up reconstructing a form of emergent statistical grammar implicit in the data points that become meaningful to humans. While the data points may have nothing to do with grammar, the grammar emerges from the value assigned in transformers' weights implicit in the data correlation that are of human value, that is, aiming at predicting grammar and word relationships. While the data set statistics aim to deconstruct any type of model, the model becomes emergent in the data set correlations that are weighted and considered useful, a feature accentuated by context specificity, site-specific computation, and RLHF. Therefore, the data set becomes curated as a form of implicit grammar. The bias is the grammar.

Each language activates different parts and neural connection networks of the brain; therefore, language is strong enough to program the human brain's complex morphology of its neural connections through neuroplasticity (Nelson et al., 2017), a net that is structured following the grammar structure of the language.

Therefore, language becomes a form of programming. Grammar limits the possibilities of the system output, since we cannot develop solutions outside of a given system or the consciousness of the system that created it (usually attributed to Einstein).

Moreover, human systems are incomplete (Gödel, 1931). Currently, we cannot increase the intelligence of a system over its grammar, limiting our capacity to activate general artificial intelligence or artificial general intelligence (AGI) other than through data and information non-linear neural network interconnectivity simulation/optimization and activating emergent programming and AI agents within an autonomous morphogenetic model that is able to evolve over site-based computations.

Big Tech articulates authorship at multiple levels through the grammar of the media and or the medium. In data mining, Big Tech understands that the value of the data is not in the actual message that may be encrypted, but in the actual meta-data that becomes more useful in tracing co-relationships and profiling users. Likewise, models are trained to recognize such meta-data functionality, producing models that can target such data values and define possible semantic messages by function of the grammar.

3.5 Predictive AI, Generative AI, AI Agents, and Emergent Programming

3.5.1 AI Creativity

We claimed that models are anticipatory of problems to resolve, since software has implicit within its range of possible outputs the sets of conditions that anticipate what the software would be able to compute within its interface. Tools within software, as packages of algorithms prepared to resolve certain tasks, are also anticipatory of the types of problems to resolve. The combination of multiple tools within software creates conditions through which one can resolve problems creatively. This combinatory possibility is within a set of possible outputs anticipated by the software; whether intentional or not, the software and its updates are able to contain a set of possible anticipatory problems and solutions to those problems through a variety of conditionings. AI articulates data science and computer science. Data and models become emergent codependent and correlational, therefore it is often difficult to trace origination and causation, presenting limitations in relation to the validating scientific method when using an AI framework.

AI is not a tool. It is not a set of tools as a software package is, but it is rather a data-model framework. An AI framework includes, among others, a data repository to be trained by ANN, which will predict features within the database. AI integrates data science and computer science as data and model become codependent. In deep machine learning, programming becomes emergent as self-editing algorithms resolve emergent tasks dependent on recognizing features within a data set trained repository.

Software is anticipatory. Software is an interface framework in which tools that are packaged as algorithms provide solutions to standardized problems. Artificial Intelligence definitions that we explored over the past few years identify in the development of software automatically the essence of AI agents (Lorenzo-Eiroa, 2023). Predictive AI is able to resolve, through training, whether a machine vision feature complies or not statistically with the features of the categories trained. Most rely on supervised machine learning and tagged image repositories, which in themselves are problematic as they are permeable to human cultural bias. Generative AI is mostly dependent on deep machine learning or unsupervised machine learning. Seeking features in a data set, deep learning involves identifying features and resolving a certain range of tasks related to the features identified, mostly automatically.

We defined several types of automation: from arithmetic automation to algebraic automation, to algorithmic automation, to self-optimizing, to more complex self-optimizing, self-editing, self-simulation, self-replication algorithms. These types of automations are correlated with the data fed through the ANN, recognizing patterns in the data through statistical models that activate AI agents as self-optimizing algorithms or deep learning. One of the definitions we give in our book is Emergent Programming, which is often a deeper type of machine learning or deep learning in which the agents emerge as opposed to being pre-programmed. Unlike anticipatory software, true Artificial Intelligence would activate emergent programming. The system would identify features in the data set and autonomously generate solutions to problems it detects. We seek a morphogenesis in which emergent programming consists of identifying within a data set visual features combined with Large Language Models, articulating several forms of semiotics: linguistic semiotics as well as visual semiotics but not linguistic based. Of course, whether we like it or not, we are restricted by our own linguistic semiotics, and perhaps this is the true boundary of AI today. Once linguistic semiotics permeates into visual semiotics, we consider that yes, it is a base for identifying features but that it will restrict those features to the classifying standards of each language, mostly English, restricting the possible grammar to a low grammar level programming. If we seek non-linguistic features, the AI results are humanly non-readable, non-comprehensible, and therefore non-functional. This was the challenge of early AI systems, in which the features identified were not that useful for humans. Once Large Language Models were able to process large quantities of text, humans were able to cross-reference text with text-creating AI bots and emergent texts, and cross-reference images with text identifying features in images that became useful for humans but also restricted in language. The grammar of a language defines the boundaries of what can be expressed within that linguistic system.

We articulate both computational linguistics and visual semiotics (Lorenzo-Eiroa, 2023, pp. 87–186) through emergent programming in which a morphogenesis of the system would emerge, activating von Neumann's automata principles: from self-simulation to self-replication within a concatenated chain effect in which in each generation the self-optimizing algorithmic agents are able to learn what they need to increase the grammar of the system exponentially. While we believe we were able to activate definitions of emergent programming, mainly through emergent agents, we were only able to activate a partial morphogenesis able to activate self-replication automata. In this current paradigm, the boundary of the data set could define the model evolution or morphogenesis, and therefore a closer relationship between data as canon or data as a type of model emerges only if emergent programming is able to become functional. Although in this context, the data cannot become a canon or a model since the self-editing algorithms defining a form of self-simulation through identifying features in the data set are able to coordinate a program or a higher-level programming, increasing the grammar of the computational linguistic semiotic system. This can become exponential, acquire informational awareness, opening AGI and automata, a boundary not yet activated.

3.6 AI Ethics, Validation, and Authority

In 2022, through forensics of AI frameworks, we were able to retrieve – across several frameworks such as Midjourney – both our own work and that of others, including materials from online catalogues bearing "copyright" watermarks, demonstrating copyright infringement, and before the New York Times lawsuit and other class actions that followed. The same way that data points track individuals for profiling, anticipating, or predicting behavior, it would be similarly feasible to track data sources, weights, percentiles, and balances in final images or text to distribute the income generated. One of the reasons this is probably not happening is that it would reveal the private property seizing, an aspect that Meta AI is partially engaging with. While our society, particularly in the US, is built upon a shifting capital model away from a democracy into a capitalist plutocracy based on Fordism, and now a dictatorial capitalism to compete with China, corporate power dictates the paradigms and ethics of a society.

While companies like Google and Meta encourage users to share their lives on social media – promoting a narrative of horizontal collaboration – they simultaneously colonize, capitalize on, and profit from user-generated content. In doing so, they often violate copyright law and extract surplus labor without consent. By colonizing our labor, displacing authorship by not citing or acknowledging the authors of the data used to train models, they strengthen their dominant position through a monopoly as they validate their colonization, imposing their authority.

Historically, capitalist levels included merchants, real estate, industrialist, finance, and corporate capital. In Marxist theory, the bourgeois class is composed of ownership of capital, land, industry, finance, and corporations or the means of production of our society (Marx, 1867). This structure is currently being modified by Big Tech, which identified the value of data and models. Current AI frameworks, as means of production, secure authorship and ownership of colonized data and research patent models. To achieve higher levels of authorship, one cannot simply use the means of production available; one must develop unique means of production, including data and models, to secure a higher level of creativity. This argument disregards that the user using a framework can be claimed to be an author, and this may depend on the prompt engineering level able to activate emergent programming and/or autonomous agents activating a level of authorship in the output. For us, authorship became a new boundary and level of colonization in capitalism.

The current distorted form of non-democratic capitalism benefits the top 1%, as opposed to a democratic capitalism in which the entire population benefits from the profits of a fair market economy. The current form of capitalism is not economically feasible, it is not efficient, it does not provide benefits to the population, and it is not beneficial to the environment. If an economic system is measured in terms of its real efficiency, one would have to include in its measurable benefits the extractive form of economy dependent on natural resources, the relationship between amount of investment and benefits of its investment, the side-effects of the system in its impact on the environment as well as the restoration of the environment as part of the economic factor, and the impact on the society as a whole as well as the impact on non-human life. Shared data and models for horizontal collaboration are not only necessary but a matter of human rights and survival of the species, from social representation to secure a co-relationship between environmental and social representation.

Human rights depend on non-human rights and environmental commons. Economies depend on environmental commons.

AI energy consumption is also an ethical human rights and non-human rights problem. When AI depends on a large amount of data processing to activate meaningful information processing statistically through big data and brute force, the environment pays the cost of such inefficient means to process information. AI depends on harvesting large amounts of energy to train models by retrieving data, having a high cost on the environment. The most political problem today is what the real cost of AI is in terms of CO_2 footprint, whether one considers only the servers in which data sets and models are trained or the entire ecology of how text and images are harvested, retrieved, reproduced, and funnelled through an ANN to train models.

We discussed before the strategic role of what a Boltzmann Machine (BM) could take (Hinton and Sejnowski, 1983), a type of stochastic neural network that contemplates the use of energy in the system to output processed information, a work recently recognized (Novel Prize Committee, 2024). To develop meaningful ethical AI, the energy of the system should be balanced in relation to the efficient means to process data and information. Otherwise, brute force correlation to train models not only separates data into correlational paradigms that are difficult to trace back and validate scientifically, but it does so at the risk of becoming autonomous, activating its own bias. In addition, as synthetic AI output pollutes the web, API retrieves over-synthetized fake information. Scientific knowledge depends on the explainability and replicability of such relationships between signs, signals, data, models, and information processing, training, and prediction. Scientific knowledge also depends on transparency and ethical considerations when activating AI that currently does not holds up as AI is reinforced by its own self-referential validation and authoritative systems further away from the real within a representation restricted reality (RRR).

References

Barthes, R. (1967). *Writing Degree Zero*. Translated by A. Lavers and C. Smith. London: Jonathan Cape.

Baudrillard, J. (1981–1983). *Simulacra and Simulation*. Los Angeles: Semiotext(e).

Bhate, S. and Kak, S. (1993). Panini and computer science. *Annals of the Bhandarkar Oriental Research Institute*, 72, pp. 1–13.

Borges, J. L. (1939). *Pierre Menard, Autor del Quijote*. Buenos Aires: Sur.

Bradbury, R. (1953). Fahrenheit 451. Chicago: Ballantine Books.

Chomsky, N. (1956). Three models for the description of language. *IRE Transactions on Information Theory*, 2, pp. 113–124.

Chomsky, N. (1957). *Syntactic Structures*. The Hague: Mouton.

Chomsky, N. (1975). *Aspects of the Theory of Syntax*. Cambridge, MA: MIT Press.

Couldry, N. and Mejias, U. (2018). Data colonialism: Rethinking big data's relation to the contemporary subject. In *Television and New Media*. SAGE Publications. ISSN 1527-4764.

Deleuze, G. and Guattari, F. (1987). *A Thousand Plateaus: Capitalism and Schizophrenia*. Minneapolis: University of Minnesota Press.

Derrida, J. (1976). *Of Grammatology*. Translated by G. C. Spivak. Baltimore: Johns Hopkins University Press.

Gibney, E. (2024). Has your paper been used to train an AI model? Almost certainly. *Nature*, 632(8026), pp. 715–716. London, UK: Springer Nature.

Gödel, K. (1931). *On Formally Undecidable Propositions of Principia Mathematica and Related Systems*. New York: Dover.

Heidegger, M. (1977). *The Question Concerning Technology and Other Essays*. New York: Harper & Row.

Hinton, G. E. and Sejnowski, T. J. (1983). *Optimal Perceptual Inference*. Proceedings of the IEEE Conference On Computer Vision and Pattern Recognition, Washington DC, pp. 448–453.

Kranzberg, M. (1986). Technology and history: Kranzberg's laws. *Technology and Culture*, 27(3), pp. 544–560.

Kyon, C. and Wendy, H. (2008). *Control And Freedom: Power and Paranoia in the Age of Fiber Optics*. Cambridge, MA: MIT Press.

Lamont, M. and Varoufakis, Y. (2021). Yanis Varoufakis: Capitalism has become "techno-feudalism". *UpFront Interview, Al Jazeera English*.

Lorenzo-Eiroa, P. (2010–2011). ACADIA 2010 Conference life in:Formation. In *The Cooper Union School of Architecture Newsletter*. Cooper Union.

Lorenzo-Eiroa, P. (2013). Form:In:Form, on the relationship between digital signifiers and formal autonomy. In P. Lorenzo-Eiroa and A. Sprecher, eds. *Architecture in Formation: On the Nature of Information in Digital Architecture*. London: Routledge, pp. 10–21.

Lorenzo-Eiroa, P. (2022). Space-environment commons: From big data survey to AI, to a post-capitalist blockchain zoning platform. In M. Carta, M. Perbellini and J. A. Lara-Hernandez, eds. *Resilient Communities and the Peccioli Charter*. Switzerland: Springer.

Lorenzo-Eiroa, P. (2023). *Digital Signifiers in an Architecture Of Information: From Big Data and Simulation to Artificial Intelligence*. London: Routledge.

Mann, C. (2005). Unraveling khipu's secrets. *Science*, 309(5737), pp. 391–392.

Marx, K. (1867). *Capital: A Critique of Political Economy. Volume 1, Part 1: The Process of Capitalist Production*. New York, NY: Cosimo.

McLean, C. A. (2011). *Artists-Programmers and Programming Languages for the Arts*. PhD thesis. University of London.

McLuhan, M. (1964). *Understanding Media: The extensions of Man*. New York: Mentor.

Milgrom Foundation. (2018). *The Limits of the Material: Conversation with Saskia Sassen*. The Naomi Milgrom Foundation.

Milmo, D. (2024). "Impossible" to Create AI Tools Like ChatGPT Without Copyrighted Material, OpenAI says. *The Guardian*, London.

Minsky, M. (1974, June). *A Framework for Representing Knowledge*. MIT-AI Laboratory Memo, p. 306.

Negroponte, N. (1969). Toward a theory of architecture machines. *Journal of Architectural Education*, 23(2), pp. 9–12.

Negroponte, N. (1976). *Soft Architectural Machines*. Cambridge, MA: MIT Press.

Nelson, M., El Karoui, I., Giber, K. and Dehaene, S. (2017). Neurophysiological dynamics of phrase-structure building during sentence processing. *PNAS*, Proceedings of the National Academy of Sciences, 114(18), pp. E3669–E3678.

Nietzsche, F. (1879–1881). *Human, All Too Human II: Volume 4. Unpublished Fragments From the Period of Dawn (Winter 1879/80–Spring 1881)*. CA: Stanford University Press.

Nobel Prize Committee. (2024). *Nobel Prize in Physics 2024 Awarded to Geoffrey Hinton and John Hopfield for Foundational Work on Artificial Neural Networks* [online]. Available at: https://www.nobelprize.org/prizes/physics/2024/summary/ [Accessed 28 July 2025].

Orwell, G. (1949). *Nineteen Eighty-Four (1984)*. London: Secker and Warburg.

Springer Publishing. (2023). *Artificial Intelligence (AI) Editorial Policies*. Switzerland: Springer.

Wachowski Brothers. (1999). *The Matrix* [Film]. USA: Warner Bros.

Wittgenstein, L. (1921). *Tractatus Logico-Philosophicus. Annalen der Naturphilosophie*. Austria: W. Ostwald.

Zuboff, S. (2015). Big other: Surveillance capitalism and the prospects of an information civilization. *Journal of Information Technology*, 30(1), 75–89.

4

Humanness in the Context of Artificial Intelligence: Performative Imaginaries in Popular Science Narratives

Thomas Wahl, Chris Ivory, Christoffer Andersson, and Anette Hallin

4.1 Introduction

Periods of technological disruption produce what has been termed 'interpretative flexibility' (Pinch & Bijker, 1987), periods in which different social groups initially do not agree on the precise purpose, function, or implication of the new technology. In the case of artificial intelligence (AI), hyperbolic predictions of the emergence of intelligent machines, even 'super intelligences', consist of both dystopian fears of human suppression and extinction, and of utopian hopes of human flourishing through freedom from labour and illness, as well as through unparalleled economic growth and prosperity. At the heart of the divergences between radically different futures, we argue, are underlying, emergent and conflicting assumptions about what it means to be human, or, rather, what defines humanness.

In addressing these issues, we also maintain that, in dealing with these broader questions of the relationship between humans and AI, we must move beyond the present disciplinary confines of studies on human-computer interaction. HCI scholars reflect primarily on the relationship between humans and computers and the new challenges posed by AI to HCI approaches and methods (Choudhury et al., 2020). Nevertheless, there are still useful broader reflections on the implications of AI coming from the HCI community. Wei Xu (2019), for example, points to the potential of distorted and incomplete data and subsequently distorted 'world views' held by AIs and the potential harmful consequences of this for humans. He also notes that as the use of AIs increases across a number of government and corporate spheres, the potential for harm, even for the rejection of humans by AIs, increases (Xu, 2019). Choudhury et al. (2020) similarly point to the implications for job losses and other misalignments between human needs and AI

DOI: 10.1201/9781003480167-5

design. This potential threat to AI development and to human interests (such as fair and transparent treatment by corporations and authorities) prompts the need, it is suggested, for an HCI-led AI design ethics. This ethics would be aimed at shaping AI in ways that better reflect the depth of human intelligence, that works to support rather than replace humans, and that is transparent and interrogable (Xu, 2019). None of this, however, is seen as a reason to question the fundamental value of AI or to ponder the transformative role AI might play in redefining humans and humanness.

The crucial issue for this field of inquiry, as noted, is the perceived 'gap' between humans and computers – but not necessarily the implications, for humanness, of dissolving this gap. The role of HCI professionals is thus constrained to ensuring that AI supports and supplements human endeavour in a 'marriage of purposes', and AI developers are seen as presently getting in the way of that (Harper, 2019). AI writers, he claims, are guilty of 'mystifying' the operations of AI, falsely claiming that natural language interaction itself solves the issue of HCI interaction and the promotion of hyperbolic narratives about the implications of AI. We concur with this view, not least as many of the leading commentators on AI in the popular science literature are precisely AI professionals. However, we also argue that the potential damage of these AI narratives is more far-reaching than taking ground from HCI. HCI's focus on the space between humans and computers, we contend, runs the risk, moreover, of reducing the human to a 'subject to be unpacked' in order to create knowledge about needs, practices, beliefs, values, and cognitive processing. That is, the human is a subject of interest, rather than a cause for concern and potential site of transformation. Moreover, our interest is in the narratives about AI and the human emanating from popular science and the AI industry. We are here less interested, in other words, in the gap between humans and AI, as we are in the implications for the different understandings of humanness that the characterisation of that gap, in popular science discourse, brings about.

Our concern is perhaps most clearly seen when human abilities, defined in particular terms, are taken to serve as the benchmark for assessing the capacity of computers. In one way or another, these narratives address the question of the extent to which the actions of machines are quicker, more accurate, and more knowledgeable than the presumed responses of humans. The narratives of artificial intelligence, its achievements, and its future trajectory, therefore, provide insights into the implicit understanding of the human.

The construction of a machine that surpasses and outmanoeuvres the domination and control of humans over our civilisation has repeatedly been dramatised in science fiction film and literature, but it is also a narrative that has found its way into popular science. These days, there is an abundance of popular science literature telling the story of AI-technology – its history, and the potential effects it might have on the future – thus reflecting the hopes and fears projected onto an imagined technological horizon. In these narratives, the technology of AI is frequently portrayed as an inevitable technological force of progress, one that humanity must either cautiously align with or passively accept. As Morozov (2025) argues, this framing obscures the contingent and political nature of technological development. He traces the dominant vision of AI back to Cold War militarism and venture capital, showing that a more democratic and humane technological trajectory was not only possible but actively suppressed.

The dominant narratives of the inner world of AI present the future as unpredictable. Hence, the narratives of future technological realities should not be regarded as a-political storytelling but as discursive actions that have performative effects. Which stories are told, how they are told, and which future they assume or explicitly propose draw attention to potential risks and possibilities of the technological development and affect decisions made by businesses, regulators, and states when it comes to the next steps of technological development, procurement of technological products, policy, and regulations (Hallin et al., 2025). Ideas about the future matter. And as we will argue in this chapter, the narratives of AI futures tend to build on some narrow perspectives of humanness and the ideas of intelligence, agency, and sociality.

The narratives of AI futures are not merely fantasies. They are grounded in collective experiences of social and material realities and emerge through the joint sense-making of an unfolding world (Jasanoff & Kim, 2015). In this chapter, we use the concept of imaginaries to highlight that the narratives we encounter in popular science are oriented towards the future and are 'animated by shared understandings of forms of social life and social order attainable through, and supportive of, advances in science and technology' (Jasanoff, 2015: 4). Taken together, we view the narratives of popular science to be indicative of more than just discrete pieces of writing and, indeed, indicative of shared imaginaries of AI futures. Narratives play an important role as 'fundamental animators of sociotechnical imaginaries' (Cave et al., 2020: 7).

Furthermore, imaginaries are predicated on people sharing the practices of imagining the future in a particular way. Even though imaginaries can be (and are) multiple, contradictory, and contested, they can become embedded as lodestars for regulatory regimes, science and technology policy, and resource allocation, as well as for capital allocation. Imaginaries are thus powerful precisely because of their embeddedness in practices of governance, science, and technological development. Even so, imaginaries that posit an inevitable future and potentially shape decisions about policy and resources do play a role in making *a* future (Leonardi, 2008).

As we will see, the rhetorical figures recurring in these popular scientific narratives about what AI is and what it might become well align with contemporary critical research on how conceptions of AI are constructed. For instance, Natale and Ballatore (2020) have argued that the narratives of AI technology are based on a strong cultural myth of a thinking machine. This myth is built around an idea that cognitive processes can be reduced to calculations based on symbol manipulations and that the human brain can be understood as though it too were a computer. The myth of AI builds on an imaginary that a thinking machine is within reach and an archetype of the computer scientists as potential scientific heroes on the verge of realising this thinking machine (Barbalau, 2024). Ballatore and Natale (2023) show that the narratives of AI are characterised by a recurring rhetorical use of the future, where today's challenges are reflected against a techno-optimistic development just around the corner, and the controversies that follow in the wake of these speculations constitute a manifesting component, rather than a fragmentation of the narrative. On the same note, Coeckelbergh (2025) argues that the myth of AI is an essential cultural tool that helps us to make sense of the technology and provides a framework for understanding and evaluating our relationship with it. From an existentialist perspective, he argues that myths are responses to the 'absolutism of technology'. This means that myths help humans cope with the overwhelming presence and influence of technology in their lives. The myth of AI and its imaginaries of possible futures build on a complex relationship between technological predictions, science fiction, and utopian thinking (Metzner-Szigeth, 2022). Here, utopian visions provide a framework for imagining ideal futures, which are performative in the sense that they do inspire real-world technological advancements and shape public perception and understanding of technological possibilities.

However, as we argue, this mythmaking is itself context-bound in the specific and established relationships between technology, capitalist tendencies, and socio-political systems. In other words, popular science narratives are themselves rooted in existing broader social, political, and economic realities, where narratives are shaped and constructed both within and as a reaction to them.

It follows that, in order to engage with how the future is being constructed on our behalf, we need to critically examine the emerging imaginaries about AI and from what ideas about humanness they depart. A significant source of these emerging imaginaries can be found in the genre of popular science.

4.2 Popular Science Narratives as Data

Advanced technical systems are opaque to non-experts, have important societal implications, and are rapidly changing. Thus, the popular science genre serves an important function in making accessible what occurs at R&D in tech-businesses and university laboratories, explaining its potential consequences for the lay public. In this sense, popular science writing around AI could be seen as imaginaries grounded in what is largely the experiences and discourses of computer science discourse for consumption by a lay population. Critically, these imaginaries have their own performative effects as they shape perceptions and understandings, thereby laying the ground for the acceptance of, or for the resistance to, particular technological futures. Apart from its foundation in computer science research, popular science on AI builds much of its rhetoric on the metaphors and narrative structures of science fiction (Hermann, 2023). Hence, popular science on AI in a way bridges the two genres, translating scientific discourse to a broader general public while at the same time mobilising narratives from science fiction. At their best, popular science books form a mediating bridge between science itself (they are typically written by scientists) and the more impressionistic inputs of traditional popular entertainment media. Scientists may even feel compelled to set the record straight – or spot a market opportunity in the interest generated in a particular area of science and technology (Cave et al., 2020).

Popular science builds credibility by adapting the discursive practice of references, details, and empiricist repertoires (Potter, 1996) from professional science and its rhetorical effect of storytelling and drama from science fiction. Furthermore, most popular science narratives seem to have a positive view of scientists and their work. The stories are often persuasive and convincing of the importance of scientific progress and celebrating its achievements (Pilkington, 2018).

Therefore, popular science could be regarded as a genre that does far more than entertain or satisfy curiosity. By merging professional science discourse with narrative structures from science fiction, popular science serves as one of the main literary sources that constructs the understanding of what AI is and what effects it might have on the future. Its performative effect on the general understanding of AI should therefore not be underestimated.

4.3 Methodology

There is an abundance of popular science books on AI and a steady stream of new books appearing on bookshelves, which requires us to develop criteria for selection. Since sales data are difficult to obtain and do not necessarily reflect which books are actually read, we merely aimed at identifying the books with the widest reach. To identify these, we first listed books that appeared on the 'recommended' lists in nine widely disseminated media outlets,[1] as well as from consultants and consultancies.[2] This, we believe, enabled us the possibility of identifying the books with the greatest impact, at least in a Western/English context.

To make our work more focused, we decided to create a list of no more than ten books. Realising that some of the recommended books addressed AI in a particular sector or industry or focused on a particular aspect, such as learning, creativity, or engineering, and being interested in a broader discussion on AI, we decided to only include books that offered a broad discussion on AI. Then, based on the title, and/or the way they were described in the official synopsis, we picked books that addressed the relationship between AI and human/s. Books that reappeared on several lists made for an easy choice since it could be argued that these probably would have a greater impact. We also opted for books that received high ranking or were praised as, for instance, 'seminal', or 'a must-read', in the lists, aiming at also ensuring that the chosen books were written by authors with different backgrounds (scientists, entrepreneurs, etc.), and from different parts of the world. As in the selection phase, we were open to the idea that the view on humans in relation to AI could have changed over the years, and we decided to also be open to the possibility of including older books. When realising that one of the books that filled all the

TABLE 4.1

Popular Science Books Selected for Analysis

Author	Title	Year	Gender Author/s/	Author Occupation	Nationality
Nick Bostrom	Superintelligence	2014	Male	Philosopher	Swedish (working in the UK)
Max Tegmark	Life 3.0	2017	Male	Physicist	Swedish-American
Melanie Mitchell	Artificial Intelligence: A Guide for Thinking Humans	2019	Female	Complex systems-scientist	American
Stuart Russell	Human Compatible	2020	Male	Computer scientist	American
Brian Christian	The Alignment Problem	2020	Male	Author, software developer, researcher	American
Henry Kissinger et al.	The Age of AI	2021	Male	Politician/ diplomat, ex Google chief executive, computer scientist	Americans
Mustafa Suleyman	The Coming Wave	2023	Male	AI-entrepreneur, CEO of Microsoft AI	British
Kai-Fu Lee and Chen Qiufan	AI 2041: Ten Visions for Our Future	2021	Male	CEO Author	Chinese
Ethan Mollick	Co-Intelligence	2024	Male	Associate professor of management	American

other criteria was published in 2014, we decided to pick this as the oldest book in our selection. In the end, our list compiled nine books, as listed in Table 4.1.

As seen in Table 4.1, all selected books are written by men, with only one exception, and all authors are living and working in either the US, UK, or China. Bostrom, Suleyman, and Kissinger have a background in computer science, philosophy, and/or business, while all of the others are scientists. Interestingly enough (in light of the fact that all books address social aspects of/in a world with AI), the number of authors from the social sciences or humanities is limited to two – one philosopher and one business studies scholar.

Having selected the books, we assigned one primary reader and at least one secondary reader to each (but in the end, all of us have read almost all books). Then, we designed a template with 12 open questions that we answered in writing, while and after reading each book, as a way to navigate and coordinate our findings.[3]

When coming together to discuss our readings, we realised that our initial idea of looking at how the depiction of the human changed over time was not a fruitful way forward. Instead, four imaginaries emerged in the discussions of our collective reading. These imaginaries emerged in a dialogue between all the authors of this chapter, a dialogue that took place in a series of meetings in which all of us participated. The joint sense-making happened as one of us took notes as the others reflected aloud and reformulated what the others had said – bringing together ideas and thoughts in a synthesised way, still leaving space for further joint exploration. In between our meetings, we reflected individually, also in writing, and brought new ideas back when we met again.

Next, we describe the imaginaries before we discuss their implications.

4.4 Constructions of Humanness

When telling the story of a possible and unpredictable future, some things need to be made stable, objective, or taken for granted so that other aspects can be negotiated and made (in)secure. The narratives in these books all aim their attention at possible AI futures and, when doing so, build their speculations on a narrow and reductionist understanding of humanness. It is this understanding that we aim to deconstruct in the following section.

4.4.1 Intelligence

In the reviewed texts, two key themes emerge with respect to intelligence. In the first, the human brain is treated as a machine – a material thing comparable to computers. In the second, the 'thingness' and materiality of intelligence are downplayed in favour of stressing the unique, non-machinic qualities of the human brain – the ability of human intelligence, for example, to be creative, make sense, and leap to insight based on disparate experiences. These distinctions have implications for how the prospects for the development of Artificial General Intelligence (AGI) – and indeed, even for human survival – are narrativised.

When John McCarthy and the other participants at the Dartmouth conference in 1956 coined the term 'artificial intelligence' for the computer technology they sought to develop, they established a metaphorical relation between the electronic processes of the machine and the psychological capacities traditionally associated with human intelligence. This discursive analogy not only encouraged the view of humans as biological information processors but also made the idea of a genuine artificial intelligence appear more plausible – not least to research funders. As Pasquinelli (2023) argues, such metaphors obscure the fact that AI has historically drawn more from the mechanisation of mental labour and the division of industrial work than from any authentic replication of human cognition. Rather than imitating biological intelligence, AI systems have evolved by formalising patterns of social cooperation and labour organisation, embedding the epistemologies of industrial capitalism into their very design. Furthermore, the metaphorical linkage with human intelligence has, over the years, led to a merging of terminology and understanding between AI, neuroscience, and cognitive science, thereby anthropomorphising machines and computerising minds (Floridi and Nobre, 2024).

In the machine metaphor comparison, the human brain fares badly. AI, it is assumed, will surpass (according to some, has already surpassed) human cognitive capacity, and human intelligence is, for example, by Tegmark, mainly portrayed as something limited and on the brink of its maximum capacity and indeed slower to evolve than its AI competitor.

Bostrom, for example, when accounting for the advantages of digital intelligence over human intelligence, compares the capacities of the neurological processes of the human brain to the functionalities of the computer, speaking about the human in terms such as ' the speed of computational elements', 'internal communication speed', 'number of computational elements' (number of neurons), 'storage capacity', and 'reliability, lifespan, sensors'.[4] With the last aspect, Bostrom concludes that human brains 'become fatigued after a few hours of work and start to permanently decay after a few decades of subjective time; microprocessors are not subject to these limitations'.[5] When the brain and its neurological processes are used as a model for AI, it reflects the understanding of human intelligence. Placed side by side, computers come out as fast, accurate, and persistent, while humans are portrayed as slow, limited, and frail.

Humans are, perhaps paradoxically, flawed in comparison, by being described *also* as emotion-driven, whimsical and unpredictable, and 'motivated by social concerns – gaining status, mates, friends, and influence, through wealth accumulation and conspicuous consumption', as Bostrom puts it.[6] Mitchell adds slowness of thought and learning, irrationality, cognitive bias, boredom, need for sleep, and emotions – all getting in the way of productive thinking for humans. In Christian's view, humans are heterogeneous in will and purpose; while they are curious and driven by intrinsic motivation, they get bored, addicted, and procrastinate.

The poor performance of the human brain, at least based on machine-derived metrics, has dire consequences for humans. In Tegmark's narrative, human biological machines are pitted against AI in a race for intellectual supremacy. Tegmark identifies 'cognition' and 'skill' as key determinants of success in this race, while Suleyman talks about AI moving up the 'cognitive ladder' as it inevitably comes to out-compete humans on an increasing range of tasks by dint of the growing speed, cheapness, and capability of AI technology. Intelligence, for Tegmark, is also very much about human 'performance' in the skills that are needed and valuable in the workplace. It is not, for example, about what humans can 'feel' or 'imagine'. Eventually, he suggests, only 'creative' tasks will be left for humans.

The human-AI 'competition' is extended by Tegmark to encompass not just work but, dramatically, survival itself. He takes this analogy so far as to talk about human life being life 2.0 and AI being life 3.0. From Tegmark's understanding of the situation, we are irrevocably locked in an evolutionary life-or-death race, but one premised on a narrow view of intelligence – as being solely about biological cognitive processes speed. Needless to say, this is a race that humans cannot possibly win. Locking himself into this imaginary, Tegmark views AI as advancing rapidly while humans are trapped in outdated 2.0 biological machines and natural evolution. This reductionism obscures other explanations for human success, and concepts of humanness, such as our propensity for collaboration and capacity for empathy, attributes that machines lack.

The competition between humans and AI appears to be over before it has even started, until we wrestle the fight onto ground more favourable to humans. For example, Mitchell points out that although the AI community has already succeeded in creating AI programs that can solve advanced mathematical problems and beat champions in games like chess, GO, and Jeopardy, it remains hopelessly incompetent in other areas – and struggles with transferring learning between variations of the same game.

For AGI to become reality, computers must somehow be able to transfer their capabilities from one area of expertise to another, in the same effortless way as humans do.

When Mitchell, at the end of her book, reflects on the questions of likeness and domination of a future AGI, human properties appear in a different light. Instead of being simply slow, limited, and in need of sleep, human cognition is constructed as far more complex, surprising, and nimble. As long as the narratives of AI in relation to human intelligence are focused on the capacity of brains and processes of firing neurons, the imaginaries of machine superiority are not so hard to make credible. But a wider view of the concept of intelligence is not limited to a quantifiable and computerisable measurement of speed and storage. It also consists of various capacities like *logic or rational thinking, understanding, abstraction, reasoning, planning, learning, self-awareness, critical thinking, problem-solving, judgment, emotional knowledge, contextualising, adaptation to the situation, goal achievement,* or even *a force to maximise freedom.* See, for example, Cartwell-Smith (2019) and Floridi (2014).

When Mitchell adds up all the dimensions of human intelligence, she uses concepts such as flexible, subconscious, commonsense, understanding, intuitive, predictive, and human abilities underlying human intelligence are perception, language, decision-making, reasoning, learning, abstraction, and analogy. 'For humans, a crucial part of intelligence is, rather than being able to learn any particular skill, being able to learn to think and apply our thinking flexibly to whatever situations or challenges we encounter'.[7]

According to Christian, humans can apply common sense, reason on moral dilemmas, and plan for the future. Humans learn by imitation, and they interfere with their environment. Humans 'read' other people's minds and interpret what they observe. Lee and Quifan make the same reflection and see human intelligence as something attuned to creativity, strategic thinking, reasoning, counter-factual thinking, emotions, trust, and consciousness.

The foregrounding of both Mitchell and Lee and Quifan of unique human capabilities leads to a more sceptical stance on AGI. For its proponents, focusing on sheer brute processing power, such as Tegmark and Bostrom, AGI remains plausibly within reach. In Bostrom's imaginary, a superintelligent machine would achieve the human capacity of: 'Possessing common sense and an effective ability to learn, reason and plan to meet complex information-process challenges across a wide range of natural and abstract domains'.[8]

Thus, the imaginaries that express scepticism regarding the development of AGI in the future do not restrict 'intelligence' to a cognitive process in a disembodied brain but presuppose an embodied way of being in the world, thus emphasising a more holistic view of 'intelligence'. Kissinger et al., for example, acknowledge the ineffable quality of humanness when claiming that 'the spontaneous experience of reality, in all its contradiction and complexity, is an important aspect of the human condition – even when it leads to inefficiency and error'.[9] And Mitchell writes, 'only the right kind of a machine – one that is embodied and active in the world – would have human-level intelligence in its reach'.[10]

4.4.2 Agency

In this section, we argue that the authors consistently rely upon an understanding of humans as lacking any real agency to shape the future. Technology is conceived as something that advances according to its own logic and has consequences for the contexts it moves through and transforms. The texts, in other words, share an implicit 'technology determinism' – an inability to see technology as itself also shaped by the contexts of its use (Pinch and Bijker, 1987). The authors are then able to assume that humanness is inevitably going to be entangled with encroaching AI, which means that they express different views on the extent to which AI will have agency, or indeed what kind of agency that will be.

An excess of technology, or indeed technological excess, also generates its own push-back reactions. The recent rise in popularity of *dumb phones*, phones without internet browsing and social media capabilities, amongst generation Z'ers is a good example of this. In other words, the accelerated pace of 'always on' life is being identified and rejected by some, even if only symbolically. Supersonic commercial flight is another good example. The technology to produce supersonic airliners is known and well tested. Yet, because there is no market for getting from London to NY in 4 hours, the technology is no longer in use by commercial airlines. AI may well begin to generate similar reactions as its negative consequences come to be felt more keenly. Nothing is inevitable about the development of AI; like all technologies, it will be shaped by the contexts of its use. It is worth noting that early indications of the return on investment of LLM AI implementations in corporations suggest that it is difficult for businesses to leverage the technology into value creation (Challapally et al., 2025).

In the words described by Tegmark, Bostrom, Suleyman, and Russell, however, there is no such agency available for pushing back, or even for simply showing a lack of interest. Commercial pressures and competition, in their view, will ensure that AI will inevitably find its way into all areas of life and will continue to develop and improve. It is as if people are (already) not there. Indeed, our selected authors' implicit assumptions about the world have much in common with the Hobbesian assumption of constant competition that leads them to a zero-sum view of agency. As AI systems become more capable, it is assumed that agency will be undermined for humans. Implicitly, it seems that there is only a finite pie of agency in the world, and as an imagined hyper-capable form of AI emerges, there will only be scraps left for humans.

A slightly different view is presented by Christian, who writes:

> We are in danger of losing control of the world not to AI or to machines as such but to *models*. To formal, often numerical specifications for what exists and for what we want. . . . The danger, paraphrasing Hannah Arendt, is not so much that our models are false but that they come true.[11]

In a sense, Christian warns that the danger does not lie in the technology itself but rather in the epistemological impoverishment of relying on models of the world instead of the actual world.

4.4.3 Sociality

The following section argues that, in order to build compelling narratives, science writers appear to rely on simplified conceptualisations of society, humans within it, and their sociality. Thus, we find humans reduced to calculative utility maximisers, as locked in day-to-day competition without regard to future consequences and as living in contexts that are without power relations. These reductionisms reflect, we argue, the situatedness of these writers in a Western Neo-liberal milieu – this hobbles their ability to think expansively or innovatively about the future.

Many of the books, moreover, contain a classic, often heroic, story of the trial and error of an entrepreneur, often working together with Academia towards what has become a successful development of AI-technology. Consequently, the books stop short of engaging with, on a deeper level, the consequences of such success stories for social relations, while also circumventing the need to address the complexity of human relations. For example, we find that real-world variation in social structures or power relations is typically subsumed under generalised notions of democratic, liberal, and capitalist societies and one-dimensional reductionist characterisations of the human.

For our authors, the understanding of 'sociality' is highly situated in a Western-centric, 20th-century view of the state of affairs, that is, based on fair competition between individuals in an open, democratic, market economy. Complications like institutional structures, power relations, or cultural variation are rarely considered. Subsequently, these books portray a pared-down model of sociality dominated by individualised utility maximisation, markets, and consumption. For example, Tegmark, Russell, and Suleyman all describe a socio-economic context in which technology developers progress their technologies without restraint or reflection. As Sulyeman characterises it:

> Invention is an unfolding, sprawling, emergent process driven by self-organising and highly competitive inventors, academics and entrepreneurs, and leaders, each surging forward with their own motivations.[12]

This broader framing of the context for technology change is present in all books and either ignores or downplays the less even reality of technology development and diffusion, which is well documented in academic literature (Mackenzie, 1996). The role of government-military funding, for example, was hugely important in the early development of AI and robotics, but this, and the subsequent developmental trajectories of this, is not mentioned (Markoff, 2016). The role of existing legal frameworks (Suleyman claims they are outmoded and too slow to adapt) and public perceptions of technology and risk (even crucial in holding back the spread of self-driving cars and pilotless aircraft) are similarly not mentioned. The crucial, but varied, nature of demand is also absent from the discussion. Russel points to the 'disappointing' diffusion of automation in manufacturing but does not capitalise on the observation. The undeniable importance of power-relations in encouraging or restraining certain technological avenues, or indeed the use of technology at all, also melts into the background to allow for more sweeping and dramatic narratives. Powerful interests throughout history have suppressed, directly and indirectly, the use of technologies that threaten their own power and wealth accumulation, but this gets no mention. These omissions, while they create a smoother, less troublesome space in which to envisage the unrestrained or threateningly rapid development of AI, simultaneously rob both the author and the reader of the opportunity to engage in a more sober appreciation of how AI might develop.

The reductionism we find with regard to societal context is also to be found in how humans themselves are characterised in this. Suleyman reduces humanity simultaneously to both an ongoing competitive melee and a witless mass unreflectively rushing headlong to its own destruction. There are no brakes and checks beyond the harsh regulatory and surveillance regimes he suggests are needed to contain the emergence of threatening variants of AI and cheap bioweapons. Tegmark's view is similar, one in which competition is the taken-for-granted driving narrative of expansive social and technological change. Russell's view on society and the human is more nuanced, but within this, he nevertheless reduces society to rational economics and humans to rational utility-maximising actors. He acknowledges this is problematic but uses the model nevertheless to sketch the nature of the threat posed by AI. Artificial Intelligence, he argues, must become expert at identifying what human preferences actually are – even if they are not entirely aware of them themselves. Unlike Tegmark, who sees humanity as having to adapt to a new machine-based competitor, or Suleyman, who sees humanity as more or less at war with it, Russell sees the solution as a better-designed, more inquiring, humble servant-AI. Humans, in the process, are reduced to bundles of preferences for AI to unpack. More expansively, Tegmark brushes aside even these nuances as his book settles on a single truth about human nature and society. In Tegmark's understanding, what all humans share is a thirst for expansion and exploration – describing the human as 'inspired by pushing the limits throughout the ages'[13] (evidence of this being the 'Guinness Book of Records' being the world's best-selling book). While he points out that many futures are possible (from Libertarian Utopias to zoos for humans and self-destruction), he ultimately sweeps these aside with reference to a collective species-level 'we', who must decide what sort of future we desire. Again, we find the same lack of appreciation of the nuances and complexities of humanness and human society – in this case, power relations; over 70% of the human species live in autocracies and so have no input into decision-making on laws or regulations. Paradoxically, then, humans are both blindly competing with one another and technology, yet still able to constitute a collective 'we'. In this context, who exactly the collective 'we' is being referred to remains unclear.

For all of these authors, what makes AI an exciting topic is the way it appears to threaten human society by out-competing us (Tegmark), shifting power away from the states and into the hands of bad-actors (Suleyman), obeying our instructions 'to the letter' and destroying us in the process

(Russell). The solutions they propose to the 'AI problem' are as thin as their characterisations of sociality. In the neo-liberal world of the popular science literature on a world with AI, where the focus is on a very specific and limited type of intelligence of the individual (human or AI), and where value is linked to production, the value of the human will, of course, shrink. In fact, according to Tegmark, the value of humans as reproductive organisms will also shrink when AI becomes superintelligent.

4.5 Re-Imagining Humanness

One way to interpret the books we have discussed in this chapter, and indeed popular science in general, is that the books, and the authors, set their work apart by purporting to offer an insider's perspective into the worlds of science and technology – in this case, AI. The implicit promise is of mediation between entertainment media, particularly science fiction, and science and technology itself. All writers are careful to warrant their authority and legitimacy in so doing. Their authority rests on their personal involvement in the worlds of science and technology. Readers might be forgiven for thinking they are reading a text that is itself scientific and objective. However, as we have shown, these texts are also particular and partial. They reflect both limited conceptual models of society and economy and, from that base, very particular constructions of humanness which, as we have argued, are constructed in relation to the drama and narrative arcs of their own texts – the stories *they* want to tell about AI and the future of humanity.

Each author draws on very particular discourses on humanness, intelligence, and sociality in order, primarily, to construct plausible future imaginaries. However, as we have argued earlier, these are necessarily reductionist and narrow. Humans cannot and should not be reduced to simulacra or cyphers of themselves – they have the capacity to constantly surprise; to be more than the sum of their parts. It follows that we should not really trust any narrative constructions about the future. At the very least, we should, as concerned citizens, be prepared to question the assumptions on which these imaginaries are based. Do we really accept, for example, that humans can be usefully characterised only as bundles of preferences? Are we really only in competition with one another for jobs and resources? What about care, love, desire for agency, connection, anger, vision, community – what role does all of this play in shaping a future world of AI, of interacting with AI, how AI will be used, and what effects, therein, it will have? AI can, of course, increase the leverage of bad actors, such as those wishing to extract wealth from others for themselves while offering little or nothing of value in return, but this is not a natural state of affairs and can even become a trigger for new creativity, reinvigorated political outlook, and fresh institutions that rebalance power. Our attention is best focused, we argue, on thinking through the effects that AI is having right now on our lives, work, and institutions. How are humans actually reacting? What are they in the process of actually becoming? By focusing on unreliable future threats or utopias, we are prompted to overreact.

Who writes about AI and the future is, as we have argued, important as what they say is ultimately performative in its own right. If politicians take inspiration from Suleyman, they may well seek to build powerful surveillance infrastructure to protect society and existing interests from attack. If they read Russel, they may see reasoning with AI developers to build more humble AIs as the way to protect the future. If they turn to Mitchell, they may just wonder what all the fuss is about.

What we need is alternative voices to enter the fray, for example, writers in political economy, who better may grasp and think through the implications of power imbalances for technology development; sociologists and ethnographers who can provide a more nuanced view of society – one that incorporates issues of gender, class, ethnicity, age, work, school, family, and governmental institutions and the roles this will play in the unfolding of AI also over the decades to come. We also need different sorts of economic thinking, one which accounts for the plurality and complexity.

We propose, in other words, that technology change is not a 'wave' moving through empty space, as Suleyman puts it, nor is AI a new species that has arrived from nowhere and begun to compete with humans, to speak with Tegmark. It is rather a phenomenon that simultaneously emerges from, and into, already-established social and institutional arrangements and material. The more nuanced and carefully researched insights to be found in 'academic' research rarely find representation in popular science. Where more scientific work is drawn upon, as is particularly visible in Suleyman's and Russell's books, this tends to be highly selective. We, therefore, argue that we need a new language of AI and humanness – one that accommodates multiple and complex constructions of what it means to be human, creating other alternative imaginaries of the future of AI and mankind.

Notes

1 Forbes, Wall Street Journal, the Economist, Amazon and Five Books.

2 ClickUp, Emeritus, Tableau, Entrepreneur Anil A. Kuriakose.

3 The questions were as follows: *How is intelligence conceptualized as a comparative measure for human and machine capacity? Are there skills that AI or humans are especially suited to? What kind of metaphors/similar are deployed to describe humans? How*

is technology anthropomorphized? What are the capabilities of the technology according to the text? Is the technology portrayed as autonomous or under human control? How are dystopian/utopian futures imagined? Is the future inevitable or do humans have agency? If inevitable, what kind of deterministic structures lead to the future? How is AI mystified and constructed as unpredictable? What values are at stake, for whom and what? What is AI according to the text?

4 Bostrom, 2014: 71–73.
5 Bostrom, 2014: 73.
6 Bostrom, 2014: 137.
7 Mitchell, 2019: 217.
8 Bostrom, 2014: 4.
9 Kissinger et al., 2021: 221.
10 Mitchell, 2019: 349.
11 Christian, 2020: 325–326.
12 Suleyman, 2023: 6.
13 Tegmark, 2017: 203.

References

Ballatore, A., & Natale, S. (2023). Technological failures, controversies and the myth of AI. In *Handbook of Critical Studies of Artificial Intelligence* (pp. 237–244). Edward Elgar Publishing.

Barbalau, I. (2024). *Mythological Analysis of the AI Media Narratives: A Comparative Approach*. ECREA 24 Communication & Social (Dis)order.

Bostrom, N. (2014). *Superintelligence: Paths, Dangers, Strategies*. Oxford University Press.

Cartwell-Smith, B. (2019). *The Promise of Artificial Intelligence: Reckoning and Judgment*. MIT Press. ISBN 9780262043045

Cave, S. et al. (eds.). (2020). *AI Narratives: A History of Imaginative Thinking About Intelligent Machines*. Oxford: Oxford University Press.

Challapally, A., Pease, C., Raskar, R., & Chari, P. (2025). *The GenAI Divide: State of AI in Business 2025*. MIT Nanda. https://www.artificialintelligence-news.com/wp-content/uploads/2025/08/ai_report_2025.pdf

Choudhury, M. D., Lee, M. K., Zhu, H., & Shamma, D. A. (2020). Introduction to this special issue on unifying human computer interaction and artificial intelligence. *Human–Computer Interaction*, 35(5–6), 355–361. https://doi.org/10.1080/07370024.2020.1744146

Christian, B. (2020). *The Alignment Problem: Machine Learning and Human Values*. New York: W. W. Norton & Company.

Coeckelbergh, M. (2025). Myth, *Angst*, and AI: Towards a neo-Blumenbergian framework for understanding how we think about technology. *Postdigit Sci Educ.* https://doi.org/10.1007/s42438-025-00548-x

Floridi, L. (2014). *The Fourth Revolution: How the Infosphere is Re-Shaping Human Reality*. UK: Oxford University Press.

Floridi, L., & Nobre, A. C. (2024, February 25). *Anthropomorphising Machines and Computerising Minds: The Crosswiring of Languages between Artificial Intelligence and Brain & Cognitive Sciences*. SSRN. https://ssrn.com/abstract=

Hallin, A., Andersson, C., Ingvarsson, C., Crevani, L., Ivory, C., Lammi, I., Lindell, E., & Uhlin, A. (2025). *Creating the Future of Work. Imaginaries in an Era of Digitalisation*. Cheltenham & Northampton: Edvard Elgar.

Harper, R. (2019). The Role of HCI in the Age of AI. *International Journal of Human–Computer Interaction*, 35(15), 1331–1344. https://doi.org/10.1080/10447318.2019.1631527

Hermann, I. (2023). Artificial intelligence in fiction: Between narratives and metaphors. *AI & Society*, 38, 319–329. https://doi.org/10.1007/s00146-021-01299-6

Jasanoff, S., & Kim, S.-H. (2015). *Dreamscapes of Modernity: Sociotechnical Imaginaries and the Fabrication of Power*. The University of Chicago Press.

Kissinger, H. A., Schmidt, E., & Huttenlocher, D. (2021). *The Age of AI: And Our Human Future*. Little, Brown and Company.

Lee, K.-F., & Qiufan, C. (2021). *AI 2041: Ten Visions for Our Future*. New York: Crown.

Leonardi, P. (2008, October). Indeterminacy and the discourse of inevitability in international technology management. *The Academy of Management Review*, 33(4), 975–984.

MacKenzie, D. (1996). *Knowing Machines: Essays on Technical Change*. Cambridge, MA: MIT Press.

Markoff, J. (2016). *Machines of Loving Grace: The Quest for Common Ground between Humans and Robots*. HarperCollins Publishers.

Metzner-Szigeth, A. (2022). How prophecies become reality – Exploring the interplay of techno-futures, science fiction and utopian thinking. In *On the Interplay of Images: Imaginaries and Imagination in Science Communication (Scientia atque usus, 2612–6125; 3. Scientia)* (pp. 371–406). Leo S. Olschki. https://doi.org/10.1400/298223

Mitchell, M. (2019). *Artificial Intelligence: A Guide for Thinking Humans*. New York: Farrar, Straus and Giroux.

Mollick, E. (2024). *Co-Intelligence: Living and Working with AI*. Penguin Publishing Group.

Morozov, E. (2025). *AI Futures*. Boston: Boston Review.

Natale, S., & Ballatore, A. (2020). Imagining the thinking machine: Technological myths and the rise of artificial intelligence. *Convergence*, 26(1), 3–18. https://doi.org/10.1177/1354856517715164

Pasquinelli, M. (2023). *The Eye of the Master – A Social History of Artificial Intelligence*. Verso.

Pilkington, O. A. (2018). *Presented Discourse in Popular Science: Professional Voices in Books for Lay Audiences*. S.l: Brill.

Pinch, T. P., & Bijker, W. E. (1987). The social construction of facts and artefacts: Or how the sociology of science and the sociology of technology might benefit each other. In Bijker, W. E., Hughes, T. P., & Pinch, T. J. (eds.), *The Social Construction of Technological Systems: New Directions in the Sociology and History of Technology*. Cambridge, MA: MIT Press.

Potter, J. (1996). *Representing Reality Discourse, Rhetoric and Social Construction*. London: Sage.
Russell, S. (2020). *Human Compatible: Artificial Intelligence and the Problem of Control.* Penguin Books.
Suleyman, M. (2023). *The Coming Wave: Technology, Power, and the Twenty-First Century's Greatest Dilemma*. New York: Crown.
Tegmark, M. (2017). *Life 3.0: Being Human in the Age of Artificial Intelligence.* New York: Alfred A. Knopf.
Xu, W. (2019). *Toward Human-Centered AI: A Perspective from Human-Computer Interaction*. Intel Corporation.

5

Reclaiming Agency! Algoactivism beyond Resistance

Francesco Miele

5.1 Introduction

In social science, stochastic technologies at the workplace are frequently depicted as posing risks to both job stability and the working conditions of employees. A significant portion of this debate – which comes out at the crossing edge between sociology of work, organisation analysis, critical management studies, and digital sociology – focuses on last-generation machines equipped with algorithms trained through artificial intelligence and machine learning techniques, being 'able to render decisions without human intervention and/or structure the possible field of action by harnessing specific data' (Issar and Aneesh, 2022). These machines – here labelled as stochastic technologies – have been deeply explored by social scientists in their integration at the workplace, mostly with neo-Marxist or post-structuralist theoretical perspectives that focus on the negative transformative effects of these objects.

If we look at the sociological analysis, most of the studies can easily be brought back to the so-called power reinforcement framework (Norris and Reddick, 2013; Nielsen et al., 2016). From this perspective, stochastic technologies support the existing distribution of power, as individuals, groups, and organisations that are already advantaged in the political process can further shape the diffusion, design, and use of new technologies in ways that support their established interests. The overall sociological debate on the effects of algorithmic machines on the workforce has underscored how stochastic technologies can generate and synthesise data about workers, provide them with recommendations, and simultaneously support management in maximising the value of labour (Kellogg et al., 2020). These technologies, increasingly miniaturised and integrable in the workers' bodies, often take the shape of mobile apps integrated with wearable sensors, allowing the production of granular data mainly concerning productive performances (Wilson, 2013) and individual health (Lupton, 2016).

DOI: 10.1201/9781003480167-6

This chapter treats a topic that until now has been simplified in the aforementioned debate: workers' agency. This body of research, which has often focused on specific sectors such as food delivery and e-commerce, has delved deeply into power and surveillance practices facilitated by Artificial Intelligence (AI from now on) machines, conceptualising workers' agency primarily in terms of acceptance and resistance (see: Miele and Tirabeni, 2020; Bruni et al., 2022). In these studies, often grounded on Marxian and Post-Marxian theories, the processes through which 'unwitting' workers are exploited against their will for developing new AI systems (Morreale et al., 2024) and subsumed to the logic of capital accumulation (Atanasoski and Vora, 2019) have been deeply investigated. In this frame, for existing literature, the main alternative to the acceptance is the open resistance to these labour exploitation processes, in which workers become aware of their condition and obstruct the use of AI and other kinds of stochastic technologies.

Here, I will reframe the concept of algoactivism – until now adopted primarily to frame individual and collective resistance techniques against surveillance imposed by intelligent technologies (see: Kellogg et al., 2020; Cobonpue et al., 2024) – to reestablish the importance of workers' agency in contexts where stochastic technologies are utilised to alter their behaviour. I integrate two constructivist approaches from organisation studies focused on exploring the incorporation of technologies into organisational life (Leonardi and Barley, 2010): (i) the appropriation perspective, focused on how workers adapt new technologies to their daily routines, diverging from the uses imagined by designers and managers; and (ii) the enactment perspective, which seeks to reconstruct the organisational practices that emerge around a particular technology. With this purpose, some of the emerging results from an empirical study conducted in two workplaces in northern Italy are discussed. This research took place alongside a workplace health promotion project characterised by a key technological component aimed at reshaping the lifestyles of workers in the fields of nutrition and physical activity.

In the following pages, the theoretical framework will first be introduced, focusing on the concept of algoactivism. Then, the method and setting of the empirical research will be described. Finally, attention will be given to the emerging findings – specifically, how workers use a new algorithmic technology and how they integrate it into their daily routines – before concluding with final remarks.

5.2 Is Algoactivism Only a Matter of Resistance?

This chapter aims to focus on the agency of workers by exploring the dynamics of algo-activism, a term coined by Katherine Kellogg and colleagues (2020: 383) to define those 'tactics that enable individual and collective resistance against algorithmic control'. Following this conception, algo-activism is a way to 'fight back' against stochastic technologies (see also: Cobonpue et al., 2024), resisting the control over workers' lives exercised by these machines, which can gather data about the workforce and influence their behaviours.

The literature on algoactivism, mostly focused on so-called platform organisations, has explored the sensemaking processes through which workers gain knowledge about algorithmic functioning, as well as the exploitative logics underpinning it – in which humans are transformed into workers subjugated to machines and the managerial interests behind them. Following this new awareness, workers enact individual (e.g., bypassing platform instructions) and collective (e.g., advocacy for removing unfair algorithmic ratings; collective manipulation of platform ratings to maximise monetary benefits) actions aimed at limiting the surveillance exercised by algorithmic technologies. With this aim, this strand of studies has reported multiple examples of algoactivism: Uber drivers can log out of the Uber app when they encounter dangerous districts or after having reached a sufficient number of working hours per day (Möhlmannn et al., 2023); food delivery riders can avoid the routes suggested by their apps (Yu et al., 2022) or use the data collected from their apps to expose illegal working shifts (Leonardi et al., 2020); finally, freelancers can influence customers into giving higher ratings by informing them about the effects of poor ratings, asking for good ones or even bribing customers (Jiang et al., 2023). So, this strand of research has variously documented not just how algorithms and algorithmic management perpetuate power and control but also how workers react, protest, and organise against them (see also Bruni, 2025: 667–671).

Despite the variety of considered fields, the extensive literature on algoactivism consistently conceptualises workers' agency primarily as a means for escaping the surveillance imposed by stochastic technologies, reducing the pressure to accept jobs and renegotiating overall working conditions (e.g., working shifts, salary, safety). In this frame, the ways through which workers adapt stochastic technologies to their needs and integrate them into organisational processes have been overshadowed or seen as a way to explicitly challenge the power arrangements in the workplace.

To fill this gap, unlike the original meaning of algoactivism, it will not be taken for granted that the only alternative to acquiescence is 'resistance', that is, the outright rejection of a given technology. Instead, attention will be paid to the processes through which workers incorporate new technologies into their daily lives. The grey areas between acceptance and rejection consist of usage practices that allow workers to adapt technological objects to their needs, living conditions, and belief systems, thus deriving benefits from their use (Miele and Tirabeni, 2020).

Drawing on the categorisation proposed by Paul Leonardi and Stephen Barley regarding constructivist approaches to the study of technology in organisational contexts (2010), I reframe the definition of algoactivism grounded on two different strands of research: the appropriation perspective and the enactment perspective.

The perspective of appropriation, which originated within media studies (Miller, 1987), has become grounded in organisational studies, thanks to a series of contributions aimed at understanding how workers use new technologies, often deviating from the intentions of designers – namely, their creators – and adopters – that is, those who choose to implement and introduce them into work environments. Marshall Scott Poole and Gerardine DeSanctis (1990), arguably the first to promote this approach in organisational studies, define it as follows:

> Traditionally, technology has been thought of as something independent of the user, as an object or tool. But an important school of thought . . . claims otherwise. . . . Social processes create the conditions for the evolution of technology. . . . No matter what features are designed into a system, users mediate technological effects, adapting systems to their needs, resisting them, or refusing to use them at all. The operative technology is determined by patterns of appropriation and use by human beings.
>
> **(Poole and DeSanctis, 1990: 176–177)**

If designers attempt to guide users towards engaging with technology in predetermined ways – such as by including specific features while omitting others or providing detailed instruction manuals – the ways in which technology is used often turn out to be, at least in part, unexpected and significantly different from the original intentions. Over time, the concept of appropriation has evolved alongside the development of Science and Technology Studies (STS), placing greater emphasis on the connections between appropriation processes and power dynamics (Minniti, 2020: 115–119). Ron Eglash (2004: vii–xi) describes technological appropriation as the ongoing movement of technology across social groups with varying material and symbolic resources (e.g., managers and frontline workers). This circulation fosters continuous innovation, allowing users to redefine its applications – sometimes in radical ways.

A study by Enrico Attila Bruni and colleagues (2022) provides an example of how stochastic technologies are appropriated in practice. Their research focuses on a corporate wellbeing programme structured into two distinct approaches: in one, employees perform exercises in front of a technological platform that offers standardised feedback and scores based on their movements; in the other, they complete the same exercises under the supervision of a specialist. As the study unfolds, the authors observe that workers in the second group actively engage with the specialist, using his expertise to complement the technology's feedback, which is sometimes perceived as insufficiently precise or tailored. Through this appropriation process, technology shifts from being a substitute for human knowledge to a tool that must be integrated with it, since workers recognise human expertise as more adaptable and comprehensive.

The second perspective, known as the enactment perspective, instead emphasises the emerging practices that develop around a given technology. These practices are understood as 'ordered sets of materially mediated ways of doing and saying, driven by clearly identifiable purposes' (Nicolini and Monteiro, 2017: 116; own translation). Unlike studies focused on appropriation processes, which examine the gap between imagined and actual uses of a technology, the enactment perspective shifts attention to the ways of acting that emerge and become stabilised around it. This focus on emerging practices has often led scholars within the enactment framework to explore the connections and tensions between these new practices and pre-existing ones. Technological objects, in this view, are not isolated tools but elements integrated into broader organising processes that involve actors and activities beyond those in direct contact with the technology.

For example, Francesco Bonifacio (2024) explores how digital labour platforms like Glovo and Deliveroo manage food-delivery workers through algorithmic systems. While these platforms claim to offer autonomy, they try to impose constraints that shape couriers' behaviour. Two groups of workers are analysed: 'park riders', who have limited technical knowledge and follow platform rules passively, and 'square riders', who develop strategic ways to manipulate algorithms for their benefit. The study challenges the idea that resistance against algorithmic surveillance is the only possible response for workers, suggesting instead that workers' engagement with platforms is often about self-optimisation rather than outright resistance. The author shows how different organised textures of practices emerge around the platforms depending on the knowledge that riders have about how platform algorithms work. Riders with lower socioeconomic backgrounds and limited technical competencies are more likely to comply uncritically with platform directives, driven by fear of rejecting tasks and shaped by community narratives that often lack a solid technical understanding of algorithmic work. More experienced workers enact and stabilise different practices, in which only the most profitable workers are chosen, and the rules of the algorithms are sometimes explicitly changed. These practices are related to continuous sensemaking processes in which the 'black box' of the algorithm platform is opened and discussed by the most competent and experienced workers.

Thus, I integrate these two different strands of studies for reframing algoactivism not only as a way for escaping from surveillance practised by employers through new pervasive stochastic technologies but broadly as a mode of incorporating these machines into their daily lives. In other words, the integration between appropriation and enactment approach allows to explore the twofold work done by users and other actors that surround stochastic technologies: mediating between the requests of these technologies (e.g., inserting some data or wearing some devices) and the users' needs, living conditions, and belief systems; connecting the practices emerging around stochastic technologies with the pre-existing organised textures of practice, seeking for a harmonisation among them. Consequently, here, algoactivism will be defined as *the set of practices through which workers and other actors in their daily lives engage with stochastic technologies, contributing to shaping their use and organising processes that incorporate them*. The reasons for embracing this definition of algoactivism are manifold. First, paraphrasing Seibt and colleagues (2019: 2), it helps capture the intricate, ambiguous dynamics that occur between total domination and total emancipation. Workers can attempt to mitigate the harsher and more invasive aspects of stochastic technologies without necessarily rejecting their use. Existing literature on algoactivism explores various ways in which technologies are appropriated, even if the concept itself is not explicitly used. However, much of this literature tends to frame such appropriation as a mere reaction to organisational surveillance. From the view proposed here, workers are not merely 'antagonists' who react to management decisions or the tyranny of stochastic technologies. Although a complete rejection of new technologies may occur – especially within organisations marked by strict managerial control and pronounced power asymmetries – it should not be assumed as a given. Moreover, the perspective proposed here pushes to focus on the collective negotiations that unfold in the process of integrating these technologies into organisational practices (see also Orlikowski, 2007; Gherardi, 2010). These negotiations may be characterised by conflict, mediation, or collaboration, highlighting the open and contested nature of technological innovation in workplaces. Conflicts between employers and employees can happen, but they can also leave room for other dynamics in which new organisational arrangements emerge without an explicit clash among actors with different interests and values.

In brief, I adopt a conception of algoactivism more comprehensive and with less taken for granted compared with the ones already existent in literature, going beyond assumptions about the attitudes of employers and employees towards stochastic technologies. Over the next pages, after the methodological section, I will explore how a new stochastic technology is appropriated by workers, being reshaped by them and, at the same time, reshaping organisational processes that characterise the pre-existing setting. This twofold movement carries a complex and ever-changing technological and organisational change, in which algoactivism practices play a central role.

5.3 Research Setting and Methodology

Workplace health promotion programmes have a dedicated body of literature that discusses both their efficacy and the potential 'hidden goals' behind these interventions. Delving deeply into this literature is beyond the scope of this article, but it is worth noting that the way stochastic technologies are perceived within this debate can be easily linked to the broader critical strand of studies cited earlier.

More specifically, various scholars have argued that the introduction and development of workplace health promotion programmes primarily serve to enhance company performance, as organisations strategically implement and develop these programmes for their own benefit. In this view, caring for workers' health also provides advantages to companies, such as reducing absenteeism, decreasing workplace accidents, and increasing individual productivity (e.g., Rongen et al., 2013; Poscia et al., 2016). From this perspective, stochastic technologies become embedded in workers' daily lives, reshaping their bodies and desires to make them more productive and aligned with organisational goals. Similarly to the debate on algoactivism, the specific debate on workplace promotion also includes concerns that stochastic technologies may become yet another tool for controlling and exploiting workers' bodies (see Maltseva, 2020; Pitts et al., 2020; O'Neill, 2017).

Here, more specifically, I will focus on the results coming from qualitative research conducted between 2016 and 2019 in a province of northern Italy, alongside the #Healthforall project[1] (see also: Miele, 2023; Rossi et al., 2023), a workplace health promotion programme aimed at supporting sedentary workers in changing their lifestyle habits, specifically regarding diet and physical activity. This initiative, piloted in two medium-to-large public organisations, was designed to reduce the risk of type 2 diabetes and cardiovascular diseases by providing workers with several services, including:

- A mobile app called *MyFitness*, trained through artificial intelligence techniques and designed to collect and analyse workers' data, providing personalised recommendations based on such data.
- An occupational physician, involved in an initial and a final medical examination for each worker participating in the project.
- A counsellor provided by the local healthcare organisation, tasked with supporting workers throughout their lifestyle change journey.

During its experimental phase, #Healthforall involved two medium-to-large public entities: the blue organisation, a research centre with approximately 500 employees, and the red organisation, a public administration service with 150 workers. In the development and presentation of the project, institutional and scientific figures involved in introducing *MyFitness* – developed by the research centre, also participating in the pilot – placed great emphasis on the app's role, presenting it as a technological platform with artificial intelligence features.

The material collected for this study stems from research conducted alongside the project, with the aim of assessing how workers and professionals engaged with the technology and their overall perception of the initiative. Specifically, the following pages will focus on the data gathered during interviews with workers (19 from the blue organisation and 13 from the red organisation) and professionals involved in the project (one counsellor and two occupational physicians).

Field materials were analysed using a template analysis (King, 1998), through which an interpretative framework was developed to examine algo-activism practices. Based on existing literature, the interview outline, and preliminary interpretations, the conceptual categories within the framework were revised, eliminated, or merged, ultimately creating a new category system useful for understanding the phenomenon under investigation. As shown in the following sections, the final categories focused on the appropriation processes enacted by users and the connections between emerging usage practices and pre-existing practice patterns characteristic of workers' daily lives.

5.4 From Imagined User to the 'Real' One: Appropriation Dynamics in the Workplace[2]

The *#Healthforall* project has been designed for sustaining a new organisational process, with a central role of the mobile app *MyFitness*. The surveillance exercised by *MyFitness* over workers is intended to be continuous and strict, regulating their lives both when they are using the app and when they are not. *MyFitness* intertwines with processes of self-quantification, encouraging workers to constantly monitor, measure, and optimise their own behaviours in line with organisational expectations. In this way, the app acts as a dispositive of digital surveillance and biopolitical governance, reshaping subjectivities through metrics, rankings, and norms of 'healthy productivity' (Lupton, 2016; Ruckenstein and Schüll, 2017). Using a concept strongly grounded in STS debate, this mobile app offers the users a detailed script (see Akrich, 1992; Suchman, 2007), here defined as 'a limited selection of safe, secure, legal, valid, advisable, efficient, or otherwise prescribed 'moves' while excluding 'moves' that generally would be considered unsafe' (Schmidt, 1997: 144). *MyFitness* guides the workers in the sphere of health and wellbeing in the following ways:

- Indicating the data that are useful to acquire day by day. This happens, for example, by providing a range of meal options to include for breakfast based on previous days' choices, sending daily reminders to enter the data about food and drink consumption, and requesting the user to wear other devices (e.g., wristbands) for collecting data via Bluetooth about their physical activities.
- Producing analytical charts to monitor whether users have changed their behaviours over time. In this way, *MyFitness* collects data from

each user and produces analytics about her/his habits (e.g., highlighting the discrepancies between the user's eating habits and those recommended by the Mediterranean diet).

- Processing the collected data and providing prescriptive recommendations that encourage users to adopt clinically 'correct' behaviours while avoiding riskier ones. This is achieved through a virtual coach, developed based on Artificial Intelligence principles, designed to 'guide' users' behaviours in the areas of nutrition and physical activity.

The *MyFitness* app, therefore, includes a script designed to guide workers both in interacting with the app itself and in managing their dietary and physical activity practices, inside and outside the workplace. This evokes what has been observed by Lucy Suchman, alongside the rise of so-called smart technology projects (2007: 222): 'Personalization is a central preoccupation in smart device projects, not in the sense of users shaping technologies within their own practice but as technologies that recognize their users and shape themselves accordingly'. The imagined user, therefore, is a worker who follows strictly the instructions and the feedback provided by the mobile app, consequently changing her/his lifestyle.

> The only thing I don't use [of the wristband] – and that I don't feel comfortable with – is sleep and heart rate monitoring at night. I take it off, not because it's not useful, but because I need freedom. I feel kind of monitored.
>
> **[Man, 40 years old, Red Organisation]**

> If you keep the wristband [provided by the project] on your wrist, it even counts when you're in the bathroom. . . . For me, this is not physical activity. I prefer to do less because I set a target of 6,000 steps, but I only count them when I have my phone in my pocket on my way to work and on my way back home.
>
> **[Man, 35 years old, Red Organisation]**

As suggested by the reported excerpts, when the imagined user becomes 'real' (Akrich, 1992: 209), the script inscribed in the app is promptly betrayed. In the era of 'problematization of normality' (Armstrong, 1995), the health risk is no longer a matter of concern only for people with a diagnosis, but it is pervasive and regards potentially the entire population. In this framework, the workers involved in the project, in most cases, had previously participated in introductory courses for specific sports activities or used wearable technology, developing a system of beliefs related to interventions aimed at supporting so-called 'healthy lifestyles'. This background shapes the ways in which the workers incorporate technology into their daily lives, leading them to regulate its use throughout the day – as seen in the first excerpt given earlier, where the interviewed worker removes the bracelet during the night for privacy issues – or to replace part of it – as seen in the second excerpt, where the interviewee replaces the wristband provided by the project with a step-counting app and, at the same time, recalibrates the daily step goal.

> The app was very useful in this regard, helping to stabilise changes in my diet. When I saw red [on the food diary], I would tell myself, 'It must not turn red!' It's not that I don't drink beer, but I only have it when I really feel like it because I know it's not good for me. I used the app for 4–5 months. Then, maybe at the beach, I wouldn't use it, but by then I already knew what to do, and my daughters were following my eating habits too.
>
> **[Woman, 42 years old, Blue Organisation].**

> The app would tell you, 'Look, this morning you overdid it with carbs, so for lunch try to have more protein or vegetables,' right? That was nice. And also, 'Bad weather is expected in [name of location] . . . do an alternative physical activity [instead of walking].' That weather feature was less interesting because you just wake up, look outside, and – yeah, thanks, I can see it's bad [laughs] . . . but still.
>
> **[Woman, 40 years old, Blue Organisation]**

Second, during the project, workers began interacting with the technologies provided by the organisation, generating processes of meaning-making around them, which in turn influenced how these tools were used. As observed in other cases (Bruni et al., 2022), the combination of a technological intervention – consisting in this case of *MyFitness* and its connected bracelet – with a human intervention – embodied by the occupational physician and, above all, the counsellors – led workers to compare the two and establish a hierarchy between them.

Specifically, the analyses provided by the app (see the first excerpt) were considered useful in the short term but repetitive over time, incorporating clinical knowledge that could be easily transferred and autonomously reproduced by the user or their close contacts (see, e.g., the first excerpt and the role of the interviewee's daughters). On the other hand, the recommendations provided by the virtual coach (see the second excerpt) were mostly described as generic guidelines, formulated without considering the person's preferences (e.g., dietary preferences) or constraints (e.g., weather conditions, available time).

One possible reason behind the emerging perceptions of the technological component of the intervention is the widespread techno-enthusiastic imaginaries, which have been circulating in both academic and non-academic contexts for some time (Lupton, 2016). These imaginaries depict a near future in which technologies will be able to match or even surpass human intelligence. However, the results achieved in laboratories are often of much lower quality than those anticipated by such imaginaries (Castañeda and Suchman, 2014: 316), which were cautiously reproduced even during the launch phase of the project under consideration. Consequently, the enthusiastic narratives surrounding artificial intelligence initially generate increased interest in these solutions but are quickly followed by disappointment (Vicsek, 2021).

> You need to be very motivated to log all the foods, really. As for lunch in the cafeteria, the foods were already listed [i.e., automatically uploaded by the company managing the employee cafeteria], but some were not recorded correctly. Then, for everything else – dinners, lunches . . . – it was difficult to track and enter the foods correctly.
>
> **[Man, 52 years old, Blue Organisation]**

Finally, the everyday context of the workers involved in the project often appears significantly more complex than the one embedded in the technological artefact (Akrich, 1992: 209). The mobile app requires users to input data continuously, meal by meal, based on which data analyses and recommendations are provided to guide them in managing their diet.

However, workers' daily lives are shaped by a complex network of pre-existing practices – work-related, family, and social – that, on the one hand, reduce the time available for data entry and, on the other, make it difficult to consistently adopt the dietary and exercise practices promoted by the project. The script of the technology – that is, the set of implicit and explicit instructions inscribed within it – was primarily followed by workers during the data entry phase, although not always within the timelines envisioned by the designers, and in receiving algorithm-generated analyses regarding whether or not they had met the project's goals. However, when it comes to how these goals can actually be achieved, technological support appears insufficient and poorly suited to dealing with the complexities of life (Gorm and Shklovski, 2019: 2513), making the app's recommendations seem generic and abstract.

5.5 Rearranging the Organised Textures of Practices Inside and Outside the Workplace

As seen so far, technology can be used in ways (such as the limited use of food diary or the discontinuous wearing of a wristband) and for purposes (to measure the divergence between one's lifestyle and the standards set by clinical guidelines) that differ from those envisioned by the designers and creators of the project. This section explores the efforts made by users, along with other actors present in their daily lives (e.g., counsellors, other workers involved in the project, as well as friends and family), to connect their use of technology with other practices, some pre-existing and others emerging in the context of the project.

> At the first meeting, I would arrive and ask them, first of all, how it went with the doctor. They would already tell me, 'Yes, I should lose weight,' 'I should be more physically active,' 'I should . . .' The app helped me . . . to better understand the context in which I was working, meaning what kind of eating habits this person had. . . . [For each worker] I asked, 'Can you show me? Can you show me how last week went? What did you eat?' And then you could see the screen displaying different weeks, where green indicated foods eaten in the right proportions and red indicated overconsumed foods. The colours were fundamental because I could see consumption patterns – how much red was present, meaning what was eaten in excess or what was missing.
>
> **[Counsellor]**

First and foremost, throughout the project, the use of *MyFitness* became integrated with counselling practices, serving as a support tool. The exclusive use of the app as an analytical instrument to clinically assess eating habits is interwoven with several factors, including the complexity of workers' lives, the disappointment users experienced when interacting with the app's 'intelligent' features, and, ultimately, the opportunity to engage with a human counsellor. Despite the limited number of counselling sessions available, for nearly all participants, the counsellor became the key figure with whom they shared the analyses generated by the mobile app and developed strategies to achieve the project's objectives. Thus, technology use and professional counselling practices developed in a mutually constitutive relationship, evolving through their interaction. On the one hand, counsellors acknowledged the technology's ability to generate detailed data on workers; on the other hand, possibly due to users' dissatisfaction with the app's 'intelligent' features, counsellors became the main reference point for negotiating lifestyle change strategies.

> At that time, my colleague also had the wristband, as well as another coworker. We would compete with each other, and every now and then, we'd challenge each other . . . to see who had the most active day – it was fun.
>
> **[Woman, 50 years old, Blue Organisation]**

> One of the things [about the app] that I would have liked to explore more were the weekly reports. At first, I didn't even know they existed [laughs], then I found out about them from my colleagues.
>
> **[Man, 32 years old, Blue Organisation]**

Second, within the considered organisations, individual users' technology-related practices are connected with collective practices, developed alongside colleagues, either to achieve project goals (as seen in the first excerpt) or to share knowledge about using the technology itself (as seen in the second excerpt). This occurred even though the mobile app and the project protocol were based on a behaviourist paradigm, which assumes that behaviours related to physical activity and nutrition are the result of individual choices, influenced by expert knowledge – whether provided through direct professional support or mediated by professionals (Cohn and Lynch, 2017). However, the excerpts provided earlier show that simply sharing the use of a technological device and workspaces fostered the emergence of collaborative and competitive dynamics that were inherently collective. For example, interactions with colleagues could lead to asynchronous physical activity, with subsequent comparison of results (e.g., steps and kilometres tracked by the wristband). Similarly, they could facilitate the exchange of experiences and knowledge about the technology, contributing to shaping the meaning-making processes surrounding it.

> [During lunch break] I try to follow my colleagues because I'm only here two days a week [the rest of the time I work remotely], so they already have their habits. . . . I try to avoid heavy foods, and I never eat desserts. I either have just a first course or a second with side dishes – if I choose a second, I go for steamed or oven-cooked vegetables without dressing.
>
> **[Woman, 49 years old, Red Organisation]**

> My son is very active, so sometimes we did things together – he would come for a walk with me. . . . The thing is, as a mom, after work, you pick up your child from school, do homework, and in the end, you're always sitting. So, the counsellor suggested: 'On nice days, why not go for a walk?' And we did – he would ride his bike, and I would walk beside him.
>
> **[Woman, 49 years old, Red Organisation]**

Finally, the use of *MyFitness* and its connected sensors led workers not only to integrate the app into their 'healthy' practices – whether previously negotiated with their counsellor or spontaneously emerging in daily life – but also to reflect on how to reconcile these practices with the other activities that shape their daily routines inside and outside the workplace. As previously observed, the complexity of participants' lives often led them to disregard the app's recommendations and turn to professionals – particularly counsellors – to define ways to achieve both the app's goals and the broader project objectives. In the cases presented earlier, interviewees sought to align technology-driven practices with their existing routines, such as having lunch with colleagues or spending time with their children after work. Under the supervision of the counsellor, the distinction between practices aimed at improving health and those related to family and work life blurred (see also Bønnelycke et al., 2019; Miele, 2022).

Thus, the organised texture of practices emerging around the technology and the broader project was shaped by direct interplay between users and the technological device, by dietary and physical activity habits influenced by the app and the project's guidelines, and, ultimately, by the work, family, and social practices that define each worker's daily life.

5.6 Final Remarks

The chapter is prompted by a deep dissatisfaction with the current debate about the ongoing relationships between stochastic technologies and their usages, grounding on qualitative research concerning two case studies in which working organisations have implemented a stochastic technology for changing workers' lifestyles. The sociological debate, mostly critical towards the implications of these technological objects on workforce, has conceived the agency of 'unwitten' (Morreale et al., 2024) and 'subsumed' (Atanasoski and Vora, 2019) workers principally in terms of acceptance or refusal of the stochastic technologies. The latter, labelled as *algoactivism* (Kellogg et al., 2020; Cobonpue et al., 2024), consists of tactics enacted by workers to resist the surveillance imposed by stochastic technologies. In this contribution, I choose to maintain the term 'algoactivism' – evocative for giving the idea that workers can maintain a proactive and non-passive attitude in front of new and imposing technologies – reconceptualising it. Grounding on the integration between the perspective of appropriation and enactment – both definable as constructionist approaches (Leonardi and Barley, 2010) – I proposed to see at algoactivism as *the set of practices through which workers and other actors in their daily lives engage with stochastic technologies, contributing to shaping their use and organising processes that incorporate them.* Now, to conclude, it is important to understand to what extent this more comprehensive perspective on algoactivism has helped us to understand how workers can become actively engaged in the use of stochastic technologies.

The first emerging topic concerns the interplay between algoactivism and surveillance dynamics. While previous literature has primarily interpreted algoactivism as a form of resistance, it has also highlighted how users engage with mobile apps to strike a balance between costs and benefits (see Malhotra, 2020; Pregenzer et al., 2021; Möhlmannn et al., 2023). Building on these studies, the escape from surveillance dynamics is always linked to conscious choices, where workers deliberately bypass platform instructions or manipulate the system to evade algorithmic surveillance. As shown in previous sections, this can occur, for example, when workers remove wearables to protect their privacy. However, at other times, workers may use stochastic technologies in ways not anticipated by designers or technology providers. Their motivations for doing so can vary: workers may hold personal beliefs about healthy living, become disillusioned with the actual performance of stochastic technologies, or find these tools inadequate for navigating the complexities of daily life. Some may also find it useful to combine algorithmic support with professional advice in unexpected ways. Appropriation generally occurs as users reshape new technologies to align with their social lives, personal needs, and beliefs (Minniti, 2020: 115–119). In doing so, they redefine both the meaning and the usage of stochastic technologies, reframing them as mere tools to support lifestyle changes and interactions with professionals. In this context, workers may escape the surveillance imposed by stochastic technologies and technology providers, though this outcome may be unintended from their perspective. So, workers can be 'unwitting' not only in their acceptance of stochastic technologies, inadvertently accepting to concede their data for training these systems (Morreale et al., 2024), but they can also become 'unwitting' opponents to the control exercised by them.

The second emerging issue concerns the hierarchies between humans and non-humans. The #Healthforall project initially was not characterised by a clear hierarchy among the human and non-human elements involved in the project. The latter was designed to enable cooperation among clinicians, the counsellor, digital technologies, and workers, with the final aim of improving the workers' health status. When the project started, workers together with involved professionals found new organisational arrangements, in which the considered stochastic technologies find peripheral roles and – at the same time – become embedded in the daily practices that characterise working and private lives of participants. In parallel, the figure of the counsellor gains centrality, since counselling practices become the main ways through which workers receive recommendations about their lifestyles. The emergence of an organised texture of practices in which non-humans have a mere role of keeping track of people's habits is strictly connected with appropriation dynamics and with the disillusionment of workers towards the 'intelligent' features of stochastic technologies. In line with an STS-grounded approach, the hierarchies and the asymmetries between human and non-human elements must be interpreted as the effect of a collective performance (Law, 2008: 147–148). Using Latour's (2005: 84) words, in the case discussed here, human actors tend to 'turn matter into a mere intermediary faithfully "transporting" or "reflecting" society's agency'. The discourses mobilised through the interviews can be interpreted as a part of this effort, aimed at representing the embrace of new health practices as a process in which the supremacy of the human over the non-human is reaffirmed once again.

The third, and last, issue concerns the connections between algoactivism and the durability of stochastic technologies in a specific context. As claimed many times in this chapter, algoactivism has often been conceived as a work 'against' algorithms, aimed at hindering or at least limiting their spread in the workplace. Grounding on appropriation and enactment perspectives, it is possible to see the human work – also when it takes power to stochastic technologies – as a way for favouring the permanence of these technologies in our societies. As seen in the previous pages, workers can use only some functions of a technology, choose not to use wearables for measuring their lifestyles, co-producing with other actors an organised texture of practices in which the new technology has a marginal role. This is a work of contextualisation that transforms algorithms into something suitable to act in a specific context (Bailey et al., 2020), coherently with the constraints, the beliefs, the personal needs, and the pre-existing habits that characterise workers' daily lives. The considered algorithmic technology has been adjusted to private lives and organisational settings, showing a certain flexibility that guarantees the durability of a technology in certain contexts; as is well known, something which is adjustable and polymorphic proves more durable than that which is rigid and robust (see de Laet and Mol, 2000).

The chapter, therefore, primarily aimed to provide a reconceptualisation of the concept of algoactivism, demonstrating how it serves as a valuable analytical tool for exploring workers' engagement in the implementation of stochastic technologies. As a main limitation, it is important to note that the organisational contexts considered in the study – public institutions located in northern Italy, with relatively stable contractual and working conditions – have undoubtedly played a significant role in enabling and shaping the forms of algoactivism adopted by workers. For future research on algoactivism, it may be valuable to return to the productive sectors generally examined in existing literature (e.g., logistics and food delivery), which focus on exploring workers' resistance to technologies. This would allow for an assessment of whether algoactivism in more 'challenging' contexts is primarily reduced to the outright rejection of algorithmic surveillance or whether it instead gives rise to usage practices in which technology is incorporated and employed, either adapting to or opposing the intentions of designers and adopters.

Notes

1 The names of the project and of the apps, as well as of the organisations and of the interviewee, are totally anonymised.

2 This paragraph, as well as paragraph 5, revisits the analysis presented in the article " Né passivi né resistenti: algoattivismo, tecnologie digitali e organizzazione. " published in the Italian journal *Poliarchie/Polyarchies* in 2022.

References

Akrich, M., 1992. The de-scription of technical objects. In *Shaping technology/building society: Studies in sociotechnical change*. Bijker, W. E. and Law, J. (Ed.), MA: MIT Press.

Armstrong, D., 1995. The rise of surveillance medicine. *Sociology of Health & Illness, 17*(3), pp. 393–404.

Atanasoski, N. and Vora, K., 2019. *Surrogate humanity: Race, robots, and the politics of technological futures*. Duke University Press.

Bailey, S., Pierides, D., Brisley, A., Weisshaar, C. and Blakeman, T., 2020. Dismembering organisation: The coordination of algorithmic work in healthcare. *Current Sociology, 68*(4), pp. 546–571.

Bonifacio, F., 2024. Imbricated to platforms: The (re) production of differences in food-delivery work. *Tecnoscienza–Italian Journal of Science & Technology Studies, 15*(1), pp. 21–38.

Bønnelycke, J., Sandholdt, C. T. and Jespersen, A. P., 2019. Household collectives: Resituating health promotion and physical activity. *Sociology of Health & Illness, 41*(3), pp. 533–548.

Bruni, A., 2025. Algorithmic management in Italy: Four perspectives. In *Diversity and inclusion in Italy* (pp. 663–683). Cham: Springer.

Bruni, E. A., Andrei, F. and Tirabeni, L., 2022. Engaging the body, appropriating a corporate wellness programme. *Qualitative Research in Organizations and Management: An International Journal, 17*(5), pp. 88–107.

Castañeda, C. and Suchman, L., 2014. Robot visions. *Social Studies of Science, 44*(3), pp. 315–341.

Cobonpue, J. S., Wurm, B. and Hess, T., 2024. *Fighting back the algorithm: A systematic literature review on algoactivism*. ICIS 2024 Proceedings, pp. 1–16.

Cohn, S. and Lynch, R., 2017. Posthuman perspectives: Relevance for a global public health. *Critical Public Health, 27*(3), pp. 285–292.

De Laet, M. and Mol, A., 2000. The Zimbabwe bush pump: Mechanics of a fluid technology. *Social Studies of Science, 30*(2), pp. 225–263.

Eglash, R. ed., 2004. *Appropriating technology: Vernacular science and social power*. MN: University of Minnesota Press.

Gherardi, S., 2010. Telemedicine: A practice-based approach to technology. *Human Relations, 63*(4), pp. 501–524.

Gorm, N. and Shklovski, I., 2019. Episodic use: Practices of care in self-tracking. *New Media & Society, 21*(11–12), pp. 2505–2521.

Issar, S. and Aneesh, A., 2022. What is algorithmic governance? *Sociology Compass, 16*(1), p. e12955.

Jiang, J., Alizadeh, A., Adam, M., Wiener, M. and Benlian, A., 2023. *How algorithmic control mechanisms influence workers' individual-level algoactivistic practices on online labor platforms*. AICS 23 Proceedings, pp. 1–14.

Kellogg, K. C., Valentine, M. A. and Christin, A., 2020. Algorithms at work: The new contested terrain of control. *Academy of Management Annals, 14*(1), pp. 366–410.

King, N., 1998. Template analysis. In *Qualitative methods and analysis in organisational research: A practical guide*. Symon, G. and Cassell, C. (Ed.), Sage.

Latour, B., 2005. *Reassembling the social: An introduction to actor-network-theory*. Oxford University Press.

Law, J., 2008. On sociology and STS. *The Sociological Review, 56*(4), pp. 623–649.

Leonardi, D., Murgia, A. and Armano, E., 2020. Piattaforme digitali e forme di resistenza della soggettività precaria: un'inchiesta sul lavoro gratuito e la mobilitazione dei riders di Foodora a Torino. *Culture, 208*, pp. 29–47.

Leonardi, P. M. and Barley, S. R., 2010. What's under construction here? Social action, materiality, and power in constructivist studies of technology and organizing. *The Academy of Management Annals*, 4(1), pp. 1–51.

Lupton, D., 2016. *The quantified self.* John Wiley & Sons.

Malhotra, A., 2020. Making the one-sided gig economy really two-sided: Implications for future of work. In *Handbook of digital innovation* (pp. 228–249). Edward Elgar Publishing.

Maltseva, K., 2020. Wearables in the workplace: The brave new world of employee engagement. *Business Horizons, 63*(4), pp. 493–505.

Miele, F., 2022. Né passivi né resistenti: algoattivismo, tecnologie digitali e organizzazione. *Poliarchie/Polyarchies, 5*(2), pp. 210–229.

Miele, F., 2023. On care infrastructures and health practices: How people in health promotion programmes try to change their everyday life. *Health, 27*(6), pp. 980–997.

Miele, F. and Tirabeni, L., 2020. Digital technologies and power dynamics in the organization: A conceptual review of remote working and wearable technologies at work. *Sociology Compass, 14*(6), p. e12795.

Miller, D., 1987. *Material culture and mass consumption*. Oxford: Basil Blackwell.

Minniti, S., 2020. Utilizzatori e tecnologie. In *Gli studi sociali sulla scienza e la tecnologia* (pp. 109–126). Il Mulino.

Möhlmannn, M., Alves de Lima Salge, C. and Marabelli, M., 2023. Algorithm sensemaking: How platform workers make sense of algorithmic management. *Journal of the Association for Information Systems*, 24(1), pp. 35–64.

Morreale, F., Bahmanteymouri, E., Burmester, B., Chen, A. and Thorp, M., 2024. The unwitting labourer: Extracting humanness in AI training. *AI & Society, 39*(5), pp. 2389–2399.

Nicolini, D. and Monteiro, P., 2017. The practice approach: For a praxeology of organisational and management studies. In *The SAGE handbook of process organization studies*. Langley, A. and Tsoukas, H. (Eds.), (pp. 110–126). London: SAGE Publications.

Nielsen, J. A., Andersen, K. N. and Danziger, J. N., 2016. The power reinforcement framework revisited: Mobile technology and management control in home care. *Information, Communication & Society, 19*(2), pp. 160–177.

Norris, D. F. and Reddick, C. G., 2013. Local e-government in the United States: Transformation or incremental change? *Public Administration Review, 73*(1), pp. 165–175.

O'Neill, C., 2017. Taylorism, the European science of work, and the quantified self at work. *Science, Technology, & Human Values, 42*(4), pp. 600–621.

Orlikowski, W. J., 2007. Sociomaterial practices: Exploring technology at work. *Organization studies, 28*(9), pp. 1435–1448.

Pitts, F. H., Jean, E. and Clarke, Y., 2020. Sonifying the quantified self: Rhythmanalysis and performance research in and against the reduction of life-time to labour-time. *Capital & Class, 44*(2), pp. 219–239.

Poole, M. S. and DeSanctis, G., 1990. Understanding the use of group decision support systems: The theory of adaptive structuration. *Organizations and Communication Technology, 173.*

Poscia, A., Moscato, U., La Milia, D. I., Milovanovic, S., Stojanovic, J., Borghini, A., Collamati, A., Ricciardi, W. and Magnavita, N., 2016. Workplace health promotion for older workers: A systematic literature review. *BMC Health Services Research, 16,* pp. 415–428.

Pregenzer, M., Wieser, F., Santiago Walser, R. and Remus, U., 2021. *Obscure oversight: Opacity drives sensemaking and resistance behavior in algorithmic management.* Proceedings of the 42nd International Conference on Information Systems, Austin, USA.

Rongen, A., Robroek, S. J., van Lenthe, F. J. and Burdorf, A., 2013. Workplace health promotion: A meta-analysis of effectiveness. *American Journal of Preventive Medicine, 44*(4), pp. 406–415.

Rossi, P., Miele, F. and Piras, E. M., 2022. The co-production of a workplace health promotion program: Expected benefits, contested boundaries. *Social Theory & Health, 21,* pp. 368–387.

Ruckenstein, M. and Schüll, N. D., 2017. The datafication of health. *Annual Review of Anthropology, 46,* pp. 261–278.

Schmidt, K., 1997, November. Of maps and scripts – the status of formal constructs in cooperative work. In *Proceedings of the 1997 ACM international conference on supporting group work* (pp. 138–147).

Seibt, D., Schaupp, S. and Meyer, U., 2019. Toward an analytical understanding of domination and emancipation in digitalizing industries. In *Digitalization in industry: Between domination and emancipation.* Meyer, U., Schaupp, S., and Seibt, D. (Eds.), (pp. 1–25). London and New York: Palgrave Macmillan Cham.

Suchman, L. A., 2007. *Human-machine reconfigurations: Plans and situated actions.* Cambridge: Cambridge University Press.

Vicsek, L., 2021. Artificial intelligence and the future of work–lessons from the sociology of expectations. *International Journal of Sociology and Social Policy, 41*(7–8), pp. 842–861.

Wilson, H. J., 2013. Wearables in the workplace. *Harvard Business Review, 91*(11), pp. 27–27.

Yu, Z., Treré, E. and Bonini, T., 2022. The emergence of algorithmic solidarity: Unveiling mutual aid practices and resistance among Chinese delivery workers. *Media International Australia, 183*(1), pp. 107–123.

Section 2

Political Economies and Fantasies of AI

6

AI in the Shadow of Big Other: Planning, Power, and the Locus of Control

Elham Bahmanteymouri

6.1 Introduction

In the history of capitalism, technological innovation has never been neutral. As Marx argued, each major technological advance, from the steam engine to industrial automation, emerged not merely from ingenuity but as capital's strategic response to crisis. When profit rates fall, markets saturate, or labour unrest grows costly, capitalism turns to technology to rationalise production, reduce labour costs, and open new frontiers for accumulation. Today, artificial intelligence (AI) represents the latest expression of this logic: what I have called the Cybernetic Capital Cycle (Bahmanteymouri, 2025).

The Cybernetic Capital Cycle refers to a recursive dynamic in which economic downturns and systemic contradictions are temporarily alleviated through technological innovation. Yet these innovations – AI, predictive analytics, algorithmic governance, and platform economies – do not resolve capitalism's crises; they reconfigure them. They extend commodification into every aspect of life, displace labour into precarity or invisibility, and shift value production from material goods to immaterial processes like data extraction, behavioural prediction, and affective capture.

This chapter argues that AI systems are not neutral tools but components of capitalism's fantasy structure, symbolic supports through which contradictions are managed, repressed, or displaced. As such, the inner world of AI operates not only at a technical level but within a broader socio-symbolic, institutional, and ideological matrix. It becomes part of the fantasy that capitalism can be perfected or made just through technological means.

A Lacanian post-Marxist lens helps illuminate how AI reanimates core elements of capitalist fantasy: the dream of total control, the illusion of perfectly functioning markets, and the promise of a frictionless world governed by predictive rationality. Central here are the Lacanian concepts of the (Big) Other, the symbolic order of institutions, law, language, and norms, and the

DOI: 10.1201/9781003480167-8

unconscious, which speaks through, rather than simply being shaped by ideology (Bahmanteymouri, 2023a). As Lacan asserts, 'the unconscious is the discourse of the Other' (Lacan, 2006, p. 10); the Other is the locus 'in which speech is constituted' (Lacan, 1993, p. 272).

The locus of the Other is not a fixed subject but an empty structural place that can be occupied by different discourses (Laclau, 2005). In our context, capitalism occupies this locus, appearing as the ultimate arbiter of coherence and mastery. AI functions as a fantasy support that helps mask capitalism's structural incompleteness. The Real, another Lacanian concept, refers to the fundamental impossibility or lack within any symbolic system, appearing here as capitalism's inherent contradictions. These tensions cannot be resolved by technology; rather, they are concealed through fantasies of total rationality and control. As Marx (1976 [1867]) and Feenberg (2002) argue, technological transformation can support social change only if rooted in a non-capitalist or democratically rearticulated discourse.

I explore this potential through a Lacanian post-Marxist analysis of AI and its role in either reinforcing or disrupting capitalist dynamics. I then turn to planning,[1] a discipline born to correct market failures, which now finds itself paradoxically aligned with capitalist logic. While planning aspires to rational order and public good, it often reproduces the very inequalities it seeks to address. The integration of AI intensifies these contradictions, positioning planners as divided subjects: agents of control facing algorithmic systems claiming epistemic authority. Simultaneously, planners risk losing technical agency while neglecting the ideological and philosophical complexities of their work.

This chapter critically engages with these tensions. It examines AI as both a threat to planning's institutional authority and a potential site for post-capitalist reimagination. Rather than treating AI as a technocratic fix, I frame it as a desiring practice embedded in capitalist discourse. I ask: Can AI be turned against the logic that gave rise to it? Can the algorithm, instead of saving us, reveal the limits of our current structures and open space for genuine transformation?

6.2 Two Approaches to AI: Fantasy and Emancipation

Technological systems emerge within discursive, institutional, and political formations that confer upon them not just function but meaning. AI, as the most recent expression of this long lineage, embodies the contradictions, desires, and fantasies of the world that gave rise to it. In this section, I develop two contrasting approaches to understanding AI, extending the theoretical foundation proposed in *Cities and Digital Platforms* (Bahmanteymouri, 2025):

1. Critical Approach: AI as Capitalism's Fantasy.
2. Emancipatory Horizons: Alternative Discourses and the Possibility of a Non-Capitalist AI.

These approaches are not simply binary but reflect the dialectical tension between capitalist hegemony and the possibility of its transformation. They draw on Lacanian post-Marxist theory, particularly the concepts of the Real, the Big Other, surplus enjoyment, and fantasy, as well as the political economy of digital platforms.

6.3 Critical Approach: AI as Capitalism's Fantasy

This section critically examines how AI operates as a fantasy of the Big Other. In this context, capitalism occupies the position of the Other: a symbolic authority that organises language, norms, ideologies, and institutions, shaping social reality and directing subjects to conform, often unconsciously, to its desires. Its hegemonic discourse appears in multiple guises, including neoliberalism, growth ideology, and technocratic rationality, and it presents itself as the natural order of things: unquestionable, complete, and necessary. As we have argued elsewhere (Bahmanteymouri & Mohammadzadeh, 2023), AI and other digital infrastructures function as symbolic and ideological artefacts that reproduce these hegemonic fantasies, align subjectivities, and reinforce the dominance of technocratic rationality under late capitalism.

Capitalism is haunted by its inherent contradictions, which a post-Marxist Lacanian theory calls its *logic of impossibilities* (Bahmanteymouri, 2016): overproduction, falling profit rates, alienation, the tension between use value and exchange value, and the division between accumulation and social reproduction. These contradictions correspond to the Lacanian concept of the Real, what is foreclosed by the symbolic order yet constantly returns to disrupt it. The Real is not merely a crisis event but a structural impossibility, the traumatic kernel that capitalist discourse attempts to cover over.

The Real can be understood, in discursive terms, as that which resists symbolisation – experiences that lie outside or beyond dominant discourses of social reality. Or as Žižek (2002, p. 6) puts it, the Real is 'the price to be paid for peeling off the deceptive layers of reality'. Economic crises, for instance, do not represent the Real itself but rather function as symptomatic eruptions – visible manifestations of the failures within the symbolic order. These crises make palpable the underlying impossibility that structures capitalist discourse. The Real remains *unsymbolisable*, yet its disruptive presence is registered through such events that signal the system's inability to fully secure coherence and closure. In Lacanian political discourse theory, every hegemonic symbolic system constructs fantasies precisely to cover over these symptomatic ruptures. These fantasies, sustained by the desire of the Other, operate to preserve the illusion of stability and completeness within an inherently incomplete order.

Technological advancement, in this framework, should not be understood as a response to capitalism's failures but as part of its fantasy structure. These are not neutral tools; they operate within the coordinates of desire and power. AI, in particular, helps sustain the fantasy of capitalist coherence, efficiency, innovation, optimisation, and control, while concealing the traumatic kernel at its core.

AI thus represents a condensation of fantasies: total knowledge and control without politics. It is presented not simply as a technical instrument but as a symbolic cure for systemic disorder. It appears to promise seamless coordination, frictionless efficiency, and apolitical governance, offering, in short, a fantasy of redemption.

The fantasmatic functions of AI under capitalism may include the following:

6.3.1 Fantasies of Labour and Automation

These fantasies frame AI as a liberating force for workers, suggesting that intelligent machines can eliminate the drudgery of labour while enhancing human flourishing. However, they obscure the persistence of alienation, the rise of precarious work, and the structural reorganisation of labour markets around hidden and unwitting forms of exploitation.

- **Automation without alienation** – The belief that machines can replace labour while improving life, even as precarity deepens. As shown in another research collaboration (Morreale et al., 2023), there are many cases of unwitting labourers involved in surplus value creation, labour that remains hidden, uncompensated, and difficult to categorise legally as exploitation or alienation.
- **Fantasy of autonomy** – The illusion that digital workers are self-managing and empowered, when in fact they are structurally subordinated to algorithmic optimisation, productivity feedback loops, and behavioural nudging. Neoliberal subjects appear free but are shaped by invisible ideological constraints.
- **Quantified subjectivity and enjoyment of optimisation** – Under technocapitalism, AI systems restructure subjectivity into data-driven feedback loops of self-monitoring, optimisation, and performance metrics. The subject's symbolic and libidinal life becomes flattened into quantifiable signals that align with the desire of the Other (capitalist accumulation and efficiency). Planners and workers alike unconsciously comply with the demand to optimise, not because they believe in its neutrality but because they enjoy being recognised within these regimes of valuation (Bahmanteymouri &

Mohammadzadeh, 2023). A sustaining fantasy of flawless optimisation underpins this complicity, concealing the structural incompleteness that drives the system.

6.3.2 Fantasies of Economic Optimisation and Post-Scarcity

This category captures fantasies that portray AI as a technocratic solution to scarcity, inefficiency, and inequality. These fantasies present digital technologies as engines of progress and abundance, while concealing the political contradictions of accumulation, distribution, and social reproduction.

- **Optimisation without contradiction** – The illusion that systemic inefficiencies (poverty, congestion, inequality) can be solved algorithmically, rather than structurally. This fantasy has deep historical roots and can be traced back to what Keynes (1930) envisioned as the fantasy *for the art of life* – a belief that compound interest, automation, and technical progress would ultimately resolve the 'economic problem' and free humanity to pursue leisure, creativity, and meaning. While humane in tone, this vision rests on a utopian faith in accumulation and technological progress, overlooking structural inequalities, alienation, and the contradictions inherent in capitalism. Today, a similar logic underpins contemporary AI discourse, where optimisation is imagined to replace economic-political struggle and social transformation with technical precision and computational foresight.
- **Accumulation without limit** – The belief that AI and digital platforms can extract limitless value from every aspect of life – attention, emotion, creativity – without exhaustion or systemic breakdown. It assumes an infinite capacity to commodify human and non-human inputs into surplus value. AI algorithms function as instruments of commodification, assigning market value to activities that were previously understood primarily in terms of use value. Everyday practices such as online research, learning, leisure activities, or listening to music are now marketed and reconstituted as exchange value (Morreale et al., 2023). As Birch and Bronson (2022) note, contemporary capitalism increasingly operates through assetisation, in which data, AI models, and digital infrastructures are treated as speculative financial instruments – intensifying value extraction and deepening the commodification of everyday life.

6.3.3 Fantasies of Control, Authority, and Epistemic Neutrality

These fantasies construct AI as a depoliticised, omniscient force that neutralises uncertainty, governs without accountability, and replaces contested knowledge with technical clarity (Stamboliev, 2023). They obscure the institutional, ideological, and power-laden nature of algorithmic governance, displacing political antagonism onto technical calculation.

- **Neutral prediction and unbiased decision-making** – The fantasy that the future can be anticipated and managed purely through data, bypassing ethical, social, and ideological deliberation. Prediction replaces planning, and statistical foresight is mistaken for structural reform.
- **Control without contingency** – At the heart of capitalist desire lies an impossible dream: to eliminate uncertainty and subjectivity by rendering the social fully calculable. This drive towards calculability reflects the need to monitor, manage, and target individuals and populations with ever-greater precision, thereby reinforcing control and extracting value. AI embodies this fantasy by promising to transform risk, complexity, and ambiguity into probabilistic models that predict and manage the future. As Žižek (1989) explains, fantasy serves precisely to conceal the impossibility at the core of the symbolic order; here, the promise that contingency can be tamed through data processing disavows the Real of structural antagonism.
- **Depoliticised governance** – The fantasy that AI systems can perform functions of authority, for example, allocation, regulation, moderation, and decision-making without the messiness of politics. Decision-making appears neutral and technocratic, bypassing democratic contestation or institutional responsibility. Through algorithmic management, governance appears technical, neutral, and objective, allowing the Other to present itself as coherent and self-regulating. This logic aligns with the broader fantasy structure of techno-capitalism, where planners and institutions operate in complicity with the desire of the Other, imagining themselves as facilitators of optimisation rather than political actors (Bahmanteymouri & Mohammadzadeh, 2023).
- **Epistemic purity and false transparency** – The fantasy of epistemic purity conceals the ideological work of data regimes: their framing, categorisation, and valuation processes remain deeply political, yet presented as natural and self-evident. AI explainability functions as a screen that offers comfort against the anxiety of systemic opacity while leaving power structures intact.

These fantasies are not generated by AI itself but are projected onto it by capitalism as the Other. AI functions as a fantasy machine, a mechanism through which capitalism reasserts its coherence precisely where it is most unstable. Its support is not only economic or logistical, as in the Cybernetic Capital Cycle, but also libidinal, ideological, and epistemological. At the subjective level, we are entangled in these fantasies – unconsciously accepting and reproducing them. This resounds with Zuboff's (2019) conception of surveillance capitalism, in which predictive analytics not only serve capital accumulation but also create a sense of epistemic control over the self and society, reproducing fantasies of omniscience and control. Rather than confronting the Real, the constitutive antagonisms and impossibilities of capitalism, we project our hopes onto intelligent machines, expecting them to deliver us from contradiction, limitation, and alienation.

In Lacanian terms, these fantasmatic operations are closely tied to the logic of *surplus enjoyment* – the subjective counterpart to *surplus value* – which sustains the desire of the Other (capitalism) despite its failures. This logic has been explored in my own work (Bahmanteymouri, 2021), where I examine how surplus-enjoyment at the subjective level parallels surplus-value at the objective level, together sustaining the neoliberal planning apparatus and its contradictory promises. The desire to complete the symbolic order, to fix its lack, is sustained by fantasies that promise redemption while actually reinforcing the authority of the Other. As Lacan (2006) explains, desire arises not from the subject alone but in relation to the perceived desire of the Other. Under capitalism, we unconsciously act in accordance with what we think the system wants from us: efficiency, innovation, and growth. This explains our complicity – we desire to please the Other, to conform, to be recognised, and in doing so, we sustain the very structures that produce our alienation. We are, in short, subjects of the Other. And because this Other remains hegemonic, incomplete, and unconscious, we cannot easily nominate a new symbolic authority to replace it. We are entrapped within its logic. Yet, this entrapment also marks a point of potential rupture. In the next section, I explore emancipatory approaches that do not pretend to replace the Other but instead work through its gaps, building new possibilities from within its breakdowns.

6.4 Emancipatory Horizons: Alternative Discourses and the Possibility of a Non-Capitalist AI

Despite AI's deep entanglement within capitalist logic, it is not inherently capitalist. Its design and deployment are dependent upon the discourses that occupy the locus of the Other. Here, I examine approaches that reveal the inherent rupture – the Real – within the hegemonic discourse of capitalism and consequently within the structure of AI. As such, the political task is to expose and address these capitalist fantasies rather than to disavow the Real – the contradictions of capitalism. In doing so, we can open a space where AI may become a site of counter-hegemonic intervention, fostering democratic participation, ethical discussion, and redistributive possibility.

Beginning with a review of Marx's labour theory and moral economy is both necessary and helpful. As Marx's early writings in *Grundrisse* and *Capital* emphasise, the forces of production, including technology, are not inherently capitalist but are shaped by prevailing social relations. In a post-capitalist context, these same forces could be reconfigured to enable liberation from alienation rather than deepen it. Central to this possibility is Marx's theory of value, which clarifies that only living labour produces surplus value, while technology – as 'dead labour' – merely transfers its pre-existing value to products (Marx, 1976 [1867], pp. 163–165). Ignoring this distinction sustains the fantasy of profit at the minimum cost of labour – a core fantasy of techno-capitalism.

While AI and automation may raise productivity, they cannot generate new value independently. Capitalism thus remains structurally dependent on labour, even as it fantasises about a frictionless, post-labour future. The myth that technology can replace labour while sustaining profit fundamentally misrecognises the true source of value. Apparent profits from AI-driven automation often reflect *fictitious capital* – perceived gains that do not arise from new surplus value but from speculative valuations, data commodification, or rent-seeking mechanisms (Perelman, 2008; Durand, 2017). AI intensifies surplus value extraction by managing, optimising, and surveilling labour, and by commodifying behavioural data, attention, and interaction (Zuboff, 2019). It does not replace labour's role in value creation but reorganises and obscures the conditions under which value is extracted, thereby covering over the incompleteness of the Other.

In contrast to mainstream economic logic, which celebrates profit from any source – whether derived from exploitation, rent, or speculation – a Marxian perspective clarifies that profit ultimately depends on surplus value extracted from labour. Even in accounting terms, value added as the basis of profit is primarily attributed to human labour (Mandel, 1962). Machines and AI merely transfer depreciated value, while productivity gains reflect increased labour output rather than autonomous value creation. Confronting the fantasy of profit without workers is thus essential for any emancipatory critique of AI. Recognising that liberation cannot emerge from machines alone but requires transforming the social relations governing their use remains a necessary precondition for imagining non-capitalist technological futures.

As Marcuse (2013 [1964], p. 23) argues, drawing on Marx, a genuine transformation of technology requires more than technical reorganisation; it demands a reconfiguration of the entire technological apparatus. In late capitalism, technology is not neutral but functions as the medium binding private and public life into a one-dimensional order, an ideological universe that suppresses contradictions and sustains control. Marcuse critiques advanced industrial and service-based societies – capitalist and communist alike – showing how technological rationality, mass media, and hierarchical management structures create 'false needs' and integrate individuals into systems of production and consumption. As a result, language, thought, and opposition are flattened: critical categories like 'freedom', 'truth', or 'alienation' lose meaning, and thinking becomes operational rather than reflective. Workers become alienated from their own productivity, and when all activity aligns with the system's logic, resistance appears irrational or unnecessary.

Yet, even within this pessimistic analysis, Marcuse leaves space for resistance through what he calls the 'great refusal' (Marcuse, 2004): acts that disrupt the system, expose its contradictions, and interrupt its narratives. Emancipation requires not merely reorganising production but transforming consciousness itself. However, Marcuse's hopes remain gestural and provisional rather than programmatic; he insists alternatives must be possible, though they cannot yet be clearly imagined because even our capacity to envision them has been colonised. Rather than offering a roadmap, he diagnoses the conditions making alternatives unthinkable, warning that we must recover the ability to think the impossible, to negate, and to refuse. Until then, we remain trapped in a one-dimensional world that neutralises opposition by satisfying false desires.

Building on this idea, Feenberg (2002, 2017) offers a critical theory of technology that, in line with much of Science and Technology Studies (e.g., Bijker et al., 1987), rejects determinism and stresses that technologies are socially shaped, embodying specific interests and values from inception. What distinguishes Feenberg's approach is his emphasis on the emancipatory potential of technology and the possibility of redirecting its development through democratic intervention and participatory design. While technology under capitalism often functions as an instrument of domination – organising labour, reinforcing hierarchies, and normalising control – Feenberg highlights how end-users and citizens can actively reshape technical systems to support human flourishing rather than automate obedience. Such transformation requires more than technical refinement; it demands a fundamental reordering of the symbolic and political frameworks that govern technological development. Reimagining AI, therefore, involves confronting the socio-political logics that define its goals, resisting the reduction of life to operational efficiency, and opening space for more humane and democratic futures.

An alternative philosophical orientation can be found in a strand of critical posthumanism that does not reject Enlightenment values such as universality or scientific rationality outright but critiques their appropriation within capitalist and colonial logics (Braidotti, 2013; Barad, 2007). Rather than viewing the human as sovereign – for example, as autonomous planners – posthumanist thinkers such as Haraway (2016), Latour (2005), Barad (2007), Braidotti (2013), and Wolfe (2010) reconceptualise the human as relational and co-constituted through entanglements with technological, ecological, and symbolic forces. This approach challenges fantasies of mastery and control, proposing instead an ontology attentive to contingency, interdependence, and shared ethical responsibility beyond anthropocentric boundaries. In planning and AI, this more-than-human approach means resisting the design of AI as a totalising or omniscient authority and instead situating it as one actor among many within a dynamic urban ecology. Such a perspective displaces capitalist fantasies of optimisation and utility, opening space for non-capitalist imaginaries where AI is embedded, partial, and fundamentally incomplete. As I have argued elsewhere (Bahmanteymouri, 2025), what is needed is a post-positivistic synthesis of universalism and particularism, recognising that the problem lies not in knowledge itself but in its appropriation by capital. Embracing this reframing invites us to accept the imperfection of the Other's discourse and to engage in open-ended discussions that confront the Real.

A confrontation with the Real – capitalism's contradictions – and a refusal to displace these contradictions onto technology is itself a political act. In a Lacanian approach, this confrontation corresponds to a rupture: a breakdown of the fantasy that sustains the coherence of the Other. Only when the subject ceases to seek surplus-enjoyment from capitalist fantasies that treat nature, knowledge, and subjectivity as domains to be optimised and commodified, and recognises the symbolic order as incomplete, can a non-capitalist mode of technology begin to emerge.

In considering AI's emancipatory potential, we must confront not only its economic and technical logics but also the ideological formations that sustain its appeal. As Žižek (1989) repeatedly emphasises, systems persist not because they function effectively, but because they are sustained through enjoyment, through the fantasies that keep subjects invested even in the face of failure. The challenge is therefore ideological. A genuinely critical approach to AI requires disinvestment from the fantasies of perfection that reflect not only capitalist rationalities but also deeper human drives towards control and excess. AI should be reimagined not as a totalising system of control but as a limited, contextual tool that supports collective decision-making. This resonates with Haraway's (1988) notion of 'situated knowledges' and with Barad's (2007) posthumanist account of relationality, both of which emphasise context-specific practices. The value of AI, in this view, lies in enabling democratic, agonistic, and materially grounded planning processes that embrace uncertainty and shared responsibility. Following Laclau and Mouffe's (1985) theory of hegemony, AI must not be seen as a fantasy resolution to planning's crisis but as a site where the Real persists: in contradiction, opacity, and undecidability.

6.5 Planning and AI: Early Hesitations and Political Challenges

While fields such as music composition, architectural design, and other creative industries have already begun integrating AI as a tool for augmentation and co-creation, planning remains far more tentative and exploratory. In these domains, AI is often seen as a creative collaborator (Pram & Morreale, 2025), expanding aesthetic possibilities without fundamentally challenging underlying political and social structures. In contrast, planning is deeply political and multidimensional, involving contested values and interests, collective futures, and community behaviours. Its entanglement with power, economic gain and interests, governance, and social justice makes integrating AI not only technically challenging but ethically and ideologically fraught.

Although AI is already used in planning for modelling, simulation, traffic optimisation, and risk assessment, these applications remain largely technical. Initial findings from my ongoing research on AI application, risks, and safety in planning[2] suggest we still lack a full understanding of how AI might shape human environments and social relations. At both objective and subjective levels, the planning field is increasingly concerned about its future authority and control: whether AI might take over the urban environment as a 'big market', substitute for future planning jobs and decision-making, or even replace planning itself. As both an academic and a practitioner, I have found that planning education and practice struggle with fundamental questions: not just how to use AI, but whether, and under what terms, it should be used at all. In the following section, I explore whether planning – historically tasked with correcting market failures – could become a space for reimagining technological futures, or whether it remains trapped within the very fantasies it seeks to contest.

6.6 Automating the Janus-Faced Discipline: AI's Promise and Peril in Planning

Planning and AI share important parallels: both are deeply entangled with and shaped by capitalist logic, yet neither is inherently capitalist.

6.6.1 Planning: A Discipline of Contradictions

Planning embodies a fundamental contradiction. It aspires to deliver justice, equity, and collective welfare yet often reproduces power structures and reinforces capitalist rationalities (Allmendinger, 2009; Bahmanteymouri, 2016, 2021; Flyvbjerg, 1998; Friedmann, 1987; Gunder, 2015; Lefebvre, 2003). Historically conceived to correct market failures and manage resources for the public good, planning frequently aligns with speculative logics that secure land value gains and enable private accumulation (Friedmann, 1987; Harvey, 1985). This tension reflects the conflict between use value (social needs) and exchange value (market-driven profit), positioning planning as both a tool for redistribution and a mechanism that perpetuates inequality.

Far from being a neutral technical practice, planning is deeply political and shaped by ideological fantasies that justify its contradictions (Bahmanteymouri & Mohammadzadeh, 2023; Gunder & Hillier, 2009). At a subjective level, drawing on Lacanian psychoanalysis, planning operates through desire and fantasy, sustaining an impossible ideal of a fully equitable urban order – what Lacan would call the 'lack' (Gunder & Hillier, 2009; Bahmanteymouri, 2021; Bahmanteymouri & Mohammadzadeh, 2025). Planners and institutions unconsciously reproduce this fantasmatic logic through visions and plans that promise resolution of problems but can never fully deliver.

This dynamic mirrors the homology between Marxian surplus-value and Lacanian surplus-enjoyment: just as surplus-value drives economic accumulation, surplus-enjoyment sustains the subject's investment in ideological fantasies (Žižek, 2002; Lacan, 2006; Bahmanteymouri, 2023b). The paradox deepens when contrasting planners as individual professionals – who may genuinely seek the public good – and planning as an institutional apparatus operating as a vehicle for control (Gunder, 2004; Flyvbjerg, 1998). Thus, planning stands as a Janus-faced discipline: promising justice while structurally tied to perpetuating inequality and speculative accumulation.

Theoretical interventions have sought to expose these contradictions. Some scholars use Lacanian analysis to reveal unconscious attachments underpinning planning (Gunder & Hillier, 2009; Bahmanteymouri & Mohammadzadeh, 2023), while others, drawing on poststructuralism, Foucault, and Deleuze and Guattari, critique planning as a technology of power rather than a benevolent public service (Flyvbjerg, 1998; Healey & Hillier, 2017; Hillier, 2023). Central to these critiques is a rejection of instrumental rationality – the notion that planning can be reduced to technical problem-solving divorced from politics and values (Allmendinger, 2009). Collaborative and participatory approaches attempt to democratise decision-making and foreground community voices, yet often remain limited by deeper structural and market constraints (Healey, 1997). Together, these theoretical strands reveal planning as a contested field, always oscillating between emancipatory ideals and complicity with domination.

6.6.2 AI in Planning: Between Emancipation and Domination

In recent literature, AI is increasingly portrayed as a substitute for human planners, promising precision, efficiency, and predictive foresight. For example, Wang et al. (2023) conceptualise planning as a generative AI task, akin to neural network–based image creation. Here, planning may be reduced to computational optimisation rather than a socio-political process, embodying a broader fantasy of depoliticised, frictionless governance in which the planner's authority is replaced by machinic intelligence.

Next, I categorise the main ways AI is envisioned in planning, paralleling the AI fantasies discussed previously.

- **Fantasies of Labour and Automation**
  - **AI as a co-planner:** AI is often framed as an assistant rather than a replacement, with human feedback iteratively refining outputs (American Planning Association, 2022). However, this view may reduce planners to mere functionaries who adjust parameters rather than shape visions, formalising social values into technical constraints.
  - **Generative rather than merely predictive:** AI models increasingly propose urban futures rather than merely forecast them (He et al., 2025), risking the transformation of planning into an abstract, technical exercise detached from conflict, negotiation, and context.
- **Fantasies of Economic Optimisation and Post-Scarcity**
  - **Planning as optimisation and reinforcement loops**: AI reframes planning as a multidimensional optimisation problem – minimising deviations while introducing controlled novelty (He et al., 2025; Wang et al., 2023; Jiang et al., 2025). Collaborative and participatory processes are increasingly channelled through AI-driven platforms (e.g., council chatbots, automated feedback systems). Reinforcement learning loops depend on continuous feedback, entrenching efficiency logics and prioritising smooth consensus over conflict and plurality (Boyco & Robinson, 2024).

    These trends reflect an 'efficiency ideology' that responds to critiques of planning as slow and obstructive to market operations. By promising to streamline approvals and eliminate 'human error', AI is framed as a technocratic fix rather than a democratic tool, reinforcing the fantasy that social conflicts and economic inequalities can be solved algorithmically without addressing structural roots. AI thus becomes a symbolic guarantee of perpetual optimisation, aligning with the capitalist fantasy of seamless urban growth and limitless accumulation.
- **Fantasies of Control, Authority, and Epistemic Neutrality**
  - Drawing on Cugurullo et al.'s (2023) concept of 'AI urbanism', which distinguishes instrumental, organic, and sentient modes, each mode advances fantasies of omniscient control. AI is positioned as a tool of the Other's desires, promising coherence while concealing uncertainty and conflict. From a Lacanian perspective, this sustains the illusion that urban complexity can be fully known and governed, disavowing contingency and antagonism.
  - Rather than neutral instruments, AI and urban systems are deeply entangled, co-evolving ecologies rather than objects of total mastery (Iapaolo & Lynch, 2025). While AI can support technical tasks,

> wholesale adoption risks transforming planning into an algorithmic domain, detached from ethical negotiation and collective life. Confronting these fantasies is crucial if planners are to envision AI as a genuinely democratic and pluralistic partner rather than a technocratic redeemer.

In light of these tensions, planning stands as a Janus-faced discipline: caught between emancipatory aspirations and complicity with capitalist and technocratic fantasies. AI, rather than transforming these structures, often merely automates and intensifies them. The next section explores how planning might reframe its relationship with AI to move beyond these entrenched limitations.

6.6.3 Beyond the Horizon: Reframing AI and Planning Futures

Contemporary urbanism is shaped by a technocratic rationality that treats cities as objects of optimisation, prediction, and control. Rooted in capitalist ideology, this logic cultivates fantasies of seamless governance and frictionless urban futures. Yet, as Marcuse (2013 [1964]) reminds us, genuine transformation demands more than technical refinement; it requires a radical reconfiguration of consciousness and social relations. Planning, in its contradictory role, stands precisely at this crossroads: aspiring to justice while often sustaining the very power structures it claims to contest.

A critical reframing of AI in planning must confront the fantasy of total control rather than perpetuate it. Inspired by Marcuse's idea of the 'great refusal', we must ask whether planning can ever achieve its emancipatory aims while embedded in capitalist logics that disavow contradiction and suppress conflict. Outsourcing 'market-aligned' (echoing von Hayek) planning tasks to AI may appear rational from an efficiency standpoint, but it risks cementing planning's role as a technical fixer for market operations – displacing its critical and democratic functions onto machinic processes that intensify social inequities.

Following posthumanist approaches in AI urbanism, I suggest viewing AI not as a sovereign planner or a masterful Other but as a co-constitutive actor within broader urban assemblages. Iapaolo and Lynch (2025) highlight this emergent, relational ontology, challenging mechanistic and technocratic fantasies. This perspective rejects the illusion of omniscient urban governance and instead embraces an ontology of incompleteness, relationality, cohabitation, and ethical entanglement. From this vantage point, AI becomes not a deterministic solver of urban crises but one tool among many in an open-ended, negotiated, and agonistic planning process.

Rather than replacing human deliberation with algorithmic certainty, AI could reveal hidden exclusions, visualise diverse scenarios, and provoke collective reflection – supporting pluralistic and context-sensitive urban imaginaries. A Marxian perspective sharpens this critique: while capitalism celebrates profit from any source – including speculative rents and

AI-mediated productivity – Marxian value theory insists that only living labour creates surplus value. Technologies like AI, as forms of 'dead labour', cannot autonomously generate value; they reorganise, intensify, and obscure exploitation. Recognising this exposes the fantasy of profit without workers and clarifies that true emancipation depends not on technological substitution but on transforming social relations.

From a Lacanian perspective, the persistence of these fantasies reflects our collective investment in the desire of the Other, capitalism as the symbolic authority promising coherence and mastery. As Žižek (1989) argues, systems persist not because they function well, but because they are enjoyed. Overcoming the fantasy of AI as a redemptive force requires symbolic disinvestment: accepting the limits of planning, the necessity of conflict, and the inescapable incompleteness of urban life. This confrontation with the Real – acknowledging what escapes prediction and control – is a political act, marking the possibility of rupture and transformation.

In confronting the Real – the contradictions, antagonisms, and contingencies inherent in urban life – we encounter what Lacan describes as a locus in the symbolic order: the structural void that no fantasy or technocratic apparatus, including AI, can fully close. This locus of control is precisely what AI fantasies seek to obscure, promising coherence where there is only contingency and conflict.

An alternative horizon thus emerges: a planning practice that does not seek to master the city through algorithms but embraces uncertainty as a constitutive feature of urban life. Rather than treating AI as a sovereign decision-maker, planners could engage it as a situated tool – one that maps complexities, generates reflective scenarios, and supports contested negotiations without foreclosing antagonism. Following Feenberg's call for democratic technology design, this vision demands that AI systems be embedded in participatory, pluralistic, and ethically accountable frameworks. Here, AI is not an endpoint of optimisation but a facilitator of orientation – a means to navigate, not resolve, the tensions of collective urban futures.

In this reframed approach, planning becomes a space of co-production rather than control, nurturing agonistic democracy rather than enforcing technocratic closure. By rejecting the fantasy of seamless mastery and embracing an ethic of care, cohabitation, and epistemic humility, we open the possibility for a genuinely emancipatory integration of AI – foregrounding social justice, shared responsibility, and the ongoing work of confronting the Real.

6.7 Conclusion

Ultimately, AI must be understood not as a neutral or technical tool but as a deeply political and economic apparatus – an embodiment of fantasies of control, optimisation, and technocratic, frictionless governance. Its deployment in planning risks reproducing and intensifying power structures and capitalist logics unless approached with deep critical thinking, theoretical consciousness, and collective reflexivity.

To engage with AI meaningfully, planners and scholars need more than semi-technical proficiency; they require critical thinking, philosophical awareness, and a deep understanding of the socio-political structures that shape – and are shaped by – technological systems. As echoed throughout this volume, such engagement demands embracing a philosophy of science that resists instrumental rationality and reclaims space for ethical, agonistic debate. It also includes developing sufficient technical literacy to understand how AI systems operate and encode social values.

While AI offers tools that can support modelling, visualisation, and scenario-building, its value lies not in its promise of total control but in its potential to help us navigate complexity, expose hidden dynamics, and provoke critical reflection. We must learn to read AI's 'inner world' that is its encoded ideologies, fantasies, and power relations, if we are to meaningfully reorient the 'outer world' of planning and institutional imaginaries.

This chapter calls for responsible optimism grounded in critical consciousness: a commitment to technical and beyond-technical expertise to include political-economic, philosophical, and ethical capacities. From a Lacanian perspective, we cannot transcend fantasy; we can only deconstruct prevailing fantasies, reveal their constitutive lacks, and create space for alternative discourses shaped by new desires and impossibilities. Accepting uncertainty and confronting the Real are not weaknesses to be overcome but essential conditions for reimagining planning futures with AI.

Notes

1 By planning in this chapter, I refer to urban planning, urban design, and regional planning.

2 The research project titled "Risk and Safety in Urban Digital Governance and AI-based Planning" (2024–2025), funded by Lloyd's Register Foundation as part of its 'Work Risk Poll into action' funding programme.

References

Allmendinger, P. (2009). *Planning Theory.* 2nd ed. Basingstoke: Palgrave Macmillan.

American Planning Association. (2022). *AI in Planning: Opportunities and Challenges and How to Prepare. White Paper.* Chicago: American Planning Association.

Bahmanteymouri, E. (2016). *An Ontological Investigation of Urban Growth Management Policies Under Neoliberalism*. PhD Thesis, The University of Auckland. ResearchSpace@Auckland.
Bahmanteymouri, E. (2021). A Lacanian Understanding of Urban Development Plans Under the Neoliberal Discourse. *Planning Theory, 20*(3), pp. 231–254. https://doi.org/10.1177/1473095220981118
Bahmanteymouri, E. (2023a). Big Other. In Van Assche, K., Beunen, R. and Duineveld, M. (Eds.), *Elgar Encyclopedia in Urban and Regional Planning and Design* (pp. 38–39). Edward Elgar Publishing Limited. https://doi.org/10.4337/9781800889002.000017
Bahmanteymouri, E. (2023b). Desire, Drive, Disavowal. In Van Assche, K., Beunen, R. and Duineveld, M. (Eds.), *Elgar Encyclopedia in Urban and Regional Planning and Design* (pp. 105–109). Edward Elgar Publishing Limited. https://doi.org/10.4337/9781800889002.000041
Bahmanteymouri, E. (2025). *Cities and Digital Platforms*. Taylor & Francis. https://doi.org/10.4324/9781003352273
Bahmanteymouri, E. and Mohammadzadeh, M. (2023). The Emerging Autonomous Smart City and Its Impacts on Planning and Power Relations in Late Capitalism. In Gunder, M., Grange, K. and Winkler, T. (Eds.), *Handbook on Planning and Power* (pp. 321–338). Edward Elgar Publishing. https://doi.org/10.4337/9781839109768.00029
Bahmanteymouri, E. and Mohammadzadeh, M. (2025). Commodifying Climate Solutions: A Critical Investigation of Circular Economy. *Journal of Environmental Policy & Planning*, pp. 1–13. https://doi.org/10.1080/1523908X.2025.2496818
Barad, K. (2007). *Meeting the Universe Halfway: Quantum Physics and the Entanglement of Matter and Meaning*. Durham: Duke University Press.
Bijker, W. E., Hughes, T. P. and Pinch, T. (Eds.). (1987). *The Social Construction of Technological Systems: New Directions in the Sociology and History of Technology*. Cambridge, MA: MIT Press.
Birch, K. and Bronson, K. (2022). Big Tech. *Science as Culture, 31*(1), pp. 1–14. https://doi.org/10.1080/09505431.2022.2036118
Boyco, M. and Robinson, P. (2024). *Artificial Intelligence: Its Potential and Ethics in the Practice of Public Participation*. SSRN 5015632. https://dx.doi.org/10.2139/ssrn.5015632
Braidotti, R. (2013). *The Posthuman*. Cambridge: Polity Press.
Cugurullo, F., Caprotti, F., Cook, M., Karvonen, A., McGuirk, P. and Marvin, S. (Eds.). (2023). *Artificial Intelligence and the City: Urbanistic Perspectives on AI*. Taylor & Francis.
Durand, C. (2017). *Fictitious Capital: How Finance is Appropriating Our Future*. London: Verso Books.
Feenberg, A. (2002). *Transforming Technology: A Critical Theory Revisited*. Oxford University Press.
Feenberg, A. (2017). Beyond One-Dimensionality. In Funke, P., Lamas, A. and Wolfson, T. (Eds.), *The Great Refusal: Herbert Marcuse and Contemporary Social Movements* (pp. 229–241). Philadelphia: Temple University Press.
Flyvbjerg, B. (1998). *Rationality and Power: Democracy in Practice*. Chicago: University of Chicago Press.
Friedmann, J. (1987). *Planning in the Public Domain: From Knowledge to Action*. Princeton: Princeton University Press.

Gunder, M. (2004). Shaping the Planner's Ego-Ideal: A Lacanian Interpretation of Planning Education. *Journal of Planning Education and Research, 23*(3), pp. 299–311.

Gunder, M. (2015). Planning's "Failure" to Ensure Efficient Market Delivery: A Lacanian Deconstruction of this Neoliberal Scapegoating Fantasy. *European Planning Studies, 24*(1), pp. 21–38. https://doi.org/10.1080/09654313.2015.1067291

Gunder, M. and Hillier, J. (2009). *Planning in Ten Words or Less: A Lacanian Entanglement with Spatial Planning*. Farnham: Ashgate.

Haraway, D. (1988). Situated Knowledges: The Science Question in Feminism and the Privilege of Partial Perspective. *Feminist Studies, 14*(3), pp. 575–599.

Haraway, D. (2016). *Staying with the Trouble: Making Kin in the Chthulucene*. Durham: Duke University Press.

Harvey, D. (1985). *The Urbanization of Capital: Studies in the History and Theory of Capitalist Urbanization*. Baltimore: Johns Hopkins University Press.

He, M., Liang, Y., Wang, S., Zheng, Y., Wang, Q., Zhuang, D., . . . Zhao, J. (2025). *Generative AI for Urban Design: A Stepwise Approach Integrating Human Expertise with Multimodal Diffusion Models*. arXiv preprint arXiv:2505.24260.

Healey, P. (1997). *Collaborative Planning: Shaping Places in Fragmented Societies*. Basingstoke: Macmillan.

Healey, P. and Hillier, J. (2017). *Contemporary Movements in Planning Theory: Critical Essays in Planning Theory*. Volume 3. Routledge.

Hillier, J. (2023). Deleuze, Guattari and Power. In Gunder, M., Grange, K. and Winkler, T. (Eds.), *Handbook on Planning and Power* (pp. 74–89). Edward Elgar Publishing. https://doi.org/10.4337/9781839109768.00012

Iapaolo, F. and Lynch, C. R. (2025). Rethinking Urban AI: A Critical Posthumanist Perspective on Intelligence, Autonomy, and Agency. *Urban Geography*, pp. 1–23. https://www.tandfonline.com/doi/full/10.1080/02723638.2025.2510812

Jiang, H., Li, M., Witte, P., Geertman, S. and Pan, H. (2025). Urban Chatter: Exploring the Potential of ChatGPT-Like and Generative AI in Enhancing Planning Support. *Cities, 158*, p. 105701.

Keynes, J. M. (1930). Economic Possibilities for Our Grandchildren. In *Essays in Persuasion* (pp. 321–332). London, UK: Palgrave Macmillan.

Lacan, J. (1993). *The Psychoses: The Seminar. Book III. 1955–56*. London: Routledge.

Lacan, J. (2006). *Ecrits*. New York: Norton.

Laclau, E. (2005). *On Populist Reason*. Verso.

Laclau, E. and Mouffe, S. (1985). *Hegemony and Socialist Strategy*. Verso.

Latour, B. (2005). *Reassembling the Social: An Introduction to Actor-Network Theory*. Oxford: Oxford University Press.

Lefebvre, H. (2003). *The Urban Revolution*. Translated by R. Bononno. Minneapolis: University of Minnesota Press.

Mandel, E. (1962). *Marxist Economic Theory*. London: Merlin Press.

Marcuse, H. (2004). *Technology, War and Fascism: Collected Papers of Herbert Marcuse*. Volume 1. Routledge.

Marcuse, H. (2013 [1964]). *One-Dimensional Man: Studies in the Ideology of Advanced Industrial Society*. Routledge.

Marx, K. (1976 [1867]). *Capital: A Critique of Political Economy*. Volume I. Translated by B. Fowkes. London: Penguin Books.

Morreale, F., Bahmanteymouri, E., Burmester, B., Chen, A. and Thorp, M. (2023). The Unwitting Labourer: Extracting Humanness in AI Training. *AI & Society*. https://doi.org/10.1007/s00146-023-01692-3

Perelman, M. (2008). *Fictitious Capital: How Finance is Appropriating Our Future*. Basingstoke: Palgrave Macmillan.
Pram, L. and Morreale, F. (2025). *Opening Musical Creativity? Embedded Ideologies in Generative-AI Music Systems*. arXiv preprint arXiv:2508.08805. Retrieved 21/9/2025 from https://arxiv.org/abs/2508.08805
Stamboliev, E. (2023). Proposing a Postcritical AI Literacy: Why We Should Worry Less About Algorithmic Transparency and More About Citizen Empowerment. *Media Theory*, 7(1), pp. 203–224.
Wang, D., Fu, Y., Liu, K., Chen, F., Wang, P. and Lu, C. T. (2023). Automated Urban Planning for Reimagining City Configuration Via Adversarial Learning: Quantification, Generation, and Evaluation. *ACM Transactions on Spatial Algorithms and Systems*, 9(1), pp. 1–24. https://doi.org/10.1145/3524302
Wolfe, C. (2010). *What is Posthumanism?* Minneapolis: University of Minnesota Press.
Žižek, S. (1989). *The Sublime Object of Ideology*. London: Vero.
Žižek, S. (2002). *Welcome to the desert of the real*! London: Verso.
Zuboff, S. (2019). *The Age of Surveillance Capitalism*. London: Profile Books.

7

Land for AI: Data Center Real Estate Markets

Dillon Mahmoudi and Alan Wiig

7.1 Introduction: Data Centers in the AI Era

The rapid growth of artificial intelligence (AI) tools – such as ChatGPT, Deepseek, Claude, Grok, Ernie, Llama, and other large language models (LLMs) – has profoundly impacted the market for globalized telecommunications infrastructure, driving an unprecedented demand for massive data storage and compute resources. This surge in demand is being met by the rapid expansion and development of data centers, which serve as the backbone for storing and processing digital information at scale. Data centers refer not just to warehouse-scale computing that is used for data storage but also to data processing, or "compute," centers for use in, for example, the training or use of AI models. AI technologies rely on processing and analyzing vast amounts of data, leading to an explosion in digital data generation and computation, therefore necessitating the expansion of data centers worldwide to store and process that data. This surge amplifies the need for material, digital telecommunication infrastructure while significantly increasing regional electricity consumption, water usage for cooling systems, and land for building data centers (Sayegh, 2024).

This transformation is not merely technical but deeply financial. Data center Real Estate Investment Trusts (REITs, which we discuss later in the chapter) exemplify the financialization of digital infrastructure: rentiership is increasingly based on control over power, land, and connectivity. Their financial strategies, operational models, and forms of rent extraction differ fundamentally from traditional REITs, a difference that reflects both the materiality of digital infrastructure and the imperatives of global capital. To clarify the distinct forms of value at stake, we use the terms *data rent* and *computational rent*. Data rent refers to the value extracted from controlling the storage and transmission of digital information – often realized through fees for colocation, bandwidth, or network proximity. Computational rent, by contrast, is the value derived from providing access to compute power, such as the processing capacity required for training and deploying AI models.

DOI: 10.1201/9781003480167-9

Both forms of rent are central to the business models of data center REITs and distinguish them from traditional real estate landlords.

The trajectory of AI infrastructure mirrors earlier industrial growth waves. The political scholar Herman Schwartz (2024), writing on industrial divides and new forms of production, characterizes the ICT wave of the late 20th century as a transformative era powered by general-purpose technologies such as flexible automation and cheaper computing, which reshaped production and consumption. Similarly, AI represents a rapidly diffusing general-purpose technology, spurring waves of investment and embedding digitalization into production and consumption patterns and subsequently urban and economic geographies. Yet, these industrial moments of growth are also subject to endogenous decay dynamics, limits that constrain technological and economic growth. In ICTs, for instance, the rising costs of semiconductor fabrication facilities and energy-intensive operations marked such constraints. AI infrastructure may encounter similar challenges as LLMs grow larger, requiring exponentially greater data inputs, compute power, and energy (Toczé et al., 2022). That is, innovative efficiency gains in data storage and computation are outpaced by the growth in demand and applications of LLMs.

The physical footprint of data centers is one such area where this growth and demand are outpacing efficiency gains, reshaping land and real estate markets. The footprint of facilities requires substantial space and is subsequently strategically located near urban centers to minimize latency and optimize performance (Wiessner et al., 2024). Northern Virginia's Data Center Alley exemplifies this phenomenon, leveraging proximity to Washington, D.C., alongside tax incentives and robust connectivity to become a global hub for digital infrastructure (Luitse, 2024; Rosati et al., 2023). Examining this region reveals how specific locations become pivotal for AI and how their growth impacts broader urban and economic development patterns.

This chapter explores these dynamics through analysis of white and grey literature, including financial filings and industry reports, to shed light on the interplay of AI, data centers, and land markets. Understanding these intersections is critical for navigating the future trajectories of digital urbanization. In line with infrastructural research methods (e.g., Mahmoudi et al., 2024; van Es and de Lange, 2020; Wiig, 2013), field observations via automobile and on foot in Northern Virginia were undertaken by the authors in November 2024 to photo-document and ground truth desk-based mapping research. Ultimately, we show that the AI economy's reliance on financialized land and data infrastructures transforms urban peripheries into pivotal nodes of digital capitalism, deepening logics of data colonialism and extractivism (Brodie, 2024; Thatcher et al., 2016). Following other work at the crucial intersection of technology and power (Albertus and Klaus, 2024; Graham and Marvin, 2001; Wiig et al., 2022), we argue that discussions of the inner workings of AI must also include discussions of land and the reshaping of spatial relationships that embed new forms of economic power into digitized landscapes.

7.2 The Geography of Data Centers

Understanding the current landscape of data centers requires a brief look back at the evolution of these networked computers as a key infrastructure of telecommunication and digital society. The development of these facilities can be traced to the 1990s, when early internet infrastructure and redistribution centers began to reshape the digital economy (Wiessner, 2025). These warehouse-scale facilities, precursors to today's hyperscale data centers, played a foundational role in the transformation of regional and suburban landscapes, laying the groundwork for the current wave of AI-driven expansion (Edwards et al., 2025). Warehouse-scale computing refers to the use of massive data centers that function as single, colossal computing units. These facilities consolidate thousands of servers alongside networking equipment under one roof, designed to operate at a scale where the entire data center is viewed as one large computer (Ranganathan and Hölzle, 2024). This concept grounds the discussion of data centers within the context of their spatial form as ICT warehouses due to their vast size and utilitarian design, emphasizing efficiency in space utilization, energy consumption, and cooling systems. The physical resemblance to warehouses is not merely aesthetic but integral to their operational philosophy.

7.2.1 Logics of Warehouse-Scale Computing

The historical development of warehouse-scale computing is closely tied to innovations by companies like Google in the early 2000s. Faced with the growing demands of its search engine, the growing use of cloud-based email, and development of other web services, Google pioneered custom-built data centers that could handle unprecedented levels of processing and storage. They implemented innovative cooling and energy management systems to improve efficiency, setting industry standards for large-scale data processing solutions. From a technical development perspective, warehouse-scale computing significantly impacted computing paradigms by affording a shift in industry practices toward cloud-based services and remote data processing (Ranganathan and Hölzle, 2024). It promoted the growth of software-as-a-service models and enabled economies of scale that reduced costs per unit of computing power. Third-party data center providers allowed companies to quickly scale by renting out access to server space within data centers. By consolidating resources, third-party providers can achieve reduced costs through enhanced energy efficiency and bulk management, making warehouse-scale computing both an economically and a technologically advantageous model. However, this efficiency doesn't necessarily reduce consumption (Toczé et al., 2022). Instead, it produces additional capacity – prompting new technologies that could leverage this newfound data storage capacity and computing power – contributing to the growth, demand, and proliferation of hosted and cloud-based technologies. Amazon, for example, sought to create efficiency in its distribution and geography of online shopping servers. In doing so, they were able to leverage that extra capacity for other consumer and convenience products such as streaming audio, streaming video, and personal data storage (Mahmoudi and Wiig, 2024).

Data centers are critical infrastructure that undergirds the global information and innovation economies that are concentrated in major urban areas. This infrastructure provides essential services such as cloud computing, e-commerce platforms, streaming services, and financial transactions. By facilitating real-time data processing and storage, data centers support the digital economy of cities and enable urban management systems, underscoring both the dependency of urban centers on these peripheral facilities for their daily operations and their role in driving demand in data center capacity (Toczé et al., 2022). The material and spatial dependency of the global information and innovation economies on peripheral facilities results in investment flows from urban tech companies to peripheral and peri-urban ICT infrastructure projects. This interconnectedness influences planning policies, prompting adjustments to accommodate data center needs, sometimes outside the direct urban area itself (Mahmoudi and Levenda, 2016). In peri-urban areas, development practices, energy policies, and zoning laws may be modified to allow for large-scale industrial facilities, and municipalities may provide infrastructure investments via the construction of access roads and utility hookups, and through this, the digital and physical connectivity required to network a facility into regional and global connectivity.

To appreciate the scale of these technical, economic, and material changes, it is helpful to clarify the concept of warehouse-scale computing. Warehouse-scale computing is critical for AI infrastructure because training and operating large AI models require immense, centralized processing resources. These facilities are designed not only for data storage but also for high-density compute tasks, enabling the rapid analysis and manipulation of vast datasets that underpin contemporary AI systems. The development and deployment of AI and LLMs amplify the reliance on, and scale of, warehouse-scale computing and data centers. These models require unprecedented levels of compute power and storage, necessitating hyperscale data centers capable of handling AI's massive processing demands. This dependency further entrenches the economic and spatial importance of data centers within global ICT infrastructures. As AI becomes central to global innovation economies, the proliferation of data centers sediments the flows between urban tech firms and peri-urban or rural data center hubs. The demand for reduced latency and increased processing power ensures that AI-centric workloads drive the clustering of data centers. At the same time, their form as warehouse-scale data centers contribute to the physical and economic landscapes traditionally dominated by suburban housing, retail, and warehouse distribution centers. The sheer scale and functional importance of these facilities reflect a shift in urbanization patterns, where the global innovation economy, with its urban hubs, drives the expansion of physical infrastructure in peri-urban areas (Mahmoudi and Levenda, 2016).

This shift consequently reshapes urban-peripheral relationships, as the demand for AI and its data centers reinforces the need for adaptable zoning laws, resource allocation, and infrastructure investments to sustain this computational ecosystem. Bringing these threads together, the explosive growth of AI technologies drives demand for data center capacity, which in turn accelerates the transformation of urban and peripheral landscapes. This feedback loop, where advances in AI spur data center expansion, and new infrastructure enables further AI development, then reshapes land markets, energy systems, and regional economies, reinforcing the centrality of digital infrastructure in contemporary urbanization.

7.2.2 The Financialization of Data Centers

Building on this theoretical foundation, it is important to recognize how the rise of data center infrastructure is deeply entangled with the logics of digital capitalism and the concentration of economic and social activities in cities. As digital platforms and AI applications proliferate, their infrastructural requirements are reshaping urban and peri-urban geographies, intensifying demands on land, energy, and public utilities, and generating new forms of environmental impact and spatial inequality. The financialization of data centers marks a fundamental shift in how these facilities are understood, valued, and integrated into the broader economy (Edwards et al., 2025). Once viewed as purely functional sites for data storage and processing, data centers have evolved into financialized assets capable of generating substantial long-term returns. This transformation has been driven by a growing trend of assetization (Kay and Tapp, 2022) and a growing need for capital to produce profit through the assetization of technology and data (Beauvisage and Mellet, 2020). Regarding data center economies, REITs specializing in data centers have emerged as a financialized intermediary that acquires, manages, and leases data center infrastructure to tech companies and cloud service providers (Citrome, 2014). By pooling capital from institutional and retail investors, REITs transform data centers into lucrative investment vehicles, aligning their operations with the imperatives of financialization and digital capitalism (Citrome, 2014; Greene, 2022).

Data center REITs, such as Digital Realty and Equinix, have been instrumental in embedding financial logic into the operation of data centers. These entities treat their holdings as financial assets rather than purely infrastructural nodes, decoupling the physical facilities from their operational functions and emphasizing their potential for capital appreciation and consistent revenue generation (Citrome, 2014). By leveraging both tangible elements, such as strategically located land, and intangible factors, like the demand for low-latency connectivity, these REITs amplify the economic significance of data centers. These locations are chosen not only for their affordability and proximity to major urban markets but also for their alignment with the operational needs of tech companies, ensuring seamless data transmission and service reliability (Greenstein and Fang, 2020; Sayegh, 2024). This dual value – combining real estate profitability with technological necessity – positions data center REITs as central players in the emergent, AI-centric digital economy.

REITs provide physical facilities equipped with power, cooling, and connectivity essential for data center operations. These spaces are leased not only by Amazon Web Services, Microsoft Azure, and Google Cloud but also by numerous other companies. By renting rather than owning, tech companies reduce capital expenditure and operational burdens, allowing them to focus on core business functions. This leasing model enables REITs to maintain predictable revenue streams through long-term contracts, which often include fixed monthly fees, additional charges for energy consumption, and premiums for enhanced connectivity or security. Some REITs also offer value-added services, such as interconnection, private cloud hosting, or disaster recovery solutions, further diversifying revenue sources. The exponential growth in data consumption, driven by cloud computing, and fueled by AI, has created a persistent demand-supply gap in storage and processing capabilities. REITs capitalize on this demand through continual expansion, investing in new facilities or upgrading existing ones to attract tenants. The strategic selection of locations near urban centers and critical network hubs allows REITs to command higher rents due to low latency and operational efficiencies. Major tech companies' reliance on third-party data centers for scalable solutions ensures a stable, long-term customer base, reinforcing REITs' financial viability (Citrome, 2014).

The financialization process also allows REITs to attract substantial investment by promising scalable and predictable revenue streams. Asset appreciation further enhances the value of data centers, particularly in strategic locations. As a recognized and growing segment of REITs, data center-focused investments attract significant institutional and retail capital, offering high dividends and exposure to the digital economy. The modular design of many data centers enables incremental expansion, ensuring cost-effective growth aligned with market trends. Beyond their function as revenue-generating infrastructure, data centers are fundamental to tech capital accumulation (Greene, 2022). While REITs earn income from leasing and asset appreciation, their infrastructure underpins the digital economy by enabling AI development, targeted advertising, and subscription models, without requiring tech companies to invest in real estate management. This dynamic positions REITs as both financial and infrastructural intermediaries, embedding data centers more deeply into the logic of financialized digital capitalism. By treating data centers as financial assets, REITs decouple the physical infrastructure from its operational role, instead focusing on – even isolating – potential for capital appreciation and revenue generation.

7.2.3 Space and Financialization

The financialization of data centers has significant spatial consequences, restructuring urban-peripheral dynamics and embedding financialized logics into the physical fabric of the digital economy. Though technologically advanced, data centers are immobile and capital-intensive, anchoring capital in specific locations to enable further accumulation. While data flows globally, the infrastructure supporting it is deeply rooted in specific geographies, generating distinct patterns of development and dependency tied to broader capitalist imperatives (Greenstein and Fang, 2020). The resulting clustering of data centers fosters agglomerative economies of place, where proximity among facilities creates efficiencies that drive down operational costs and enhance service reliability (Hogan, 2021). Shared infrastructure, such as cooling systems and energy grids, reduces per-unit expenses, while co-located facilities attract additional tenants and investment. These clusters amplify competitive advantages over time, creating self-reinforcing cycles of growth that integrate local economies into global digital infrastructure markets.

However, this spatial configuration also intensifies uneven development. Rural and peri-urban areas incorporated into global circuits of data center investment often experience rising land values and heightened resource pressures (Olivo and Neff, 2024). These dynamics are especially evident in the spatial and financial shifts triggered by AI. The rapid revaluation of land and real estate markets near major data center clusters illustrates how AI technologies, by demanding ever more compute power, make land with access to robust energy and connectivity infrastructure a prime asset, attracting speculative investment and driving up prices. Further, the energy and water demand of data centers can overwhelm local infrastructure, while financial capital disrupts traditional land uses and economic practices. The displacement of agricultural land and residential spaces by industrial-scale facilities further deepens peripheral regions' dependency on volatile global tech markets and financial systems, embedding vulnerabilities in local economies increasingly tied to the fortunes of data-driven capitalism (Greenstein and Fang, 2020).

The concept of "data gravity" – as defined by the data center REIT Digital Realty (Digital Realty, 2020) – further underscores the financialization of data centers, highlighting how the accumulation of data creates a gravitational pull that attracts additional infrastructure and investment by increasing the complexity and dependency of data exchange within a given region. As these facilities store and process ever-larger volumes of information, they contribute to the growth of a feedback loop that necessitates further capacity.

This loop reinforces concentrations of data centers in their central role in the global digital economy. This dynamic situates data centers at the nexus of technological ecosystems and financial markets, where they function as both operational infrastructure and speculative assets.

These transformations illustrate the broader dynamics of financialized digital capitalism, where infrastructure becomes both a productive site and a financialized asset class. The immobility of data centers locks capital into specific regions, fostering localized dependencies while sustaining global data flows, embedding financial logics into the landscapes they occupy, and perpetuating uneven development. The entanglement of geography, technology, and finance highlights the need for critical engagement with the socio-economic and environmental implications of data center expansion. The impact of REITs extends beyond the physical construction of data centers. By channeling investment into peri-urban areas, these entities influence uneven regional development patterns, from infrastructure upgrades to policy shifts. Local governments, eager to attract data center projects, often modify and capitulate to the zoning needs and financial incentives to ensure REIT profitability (Halper and O'Donovan, 2024; Olivo and Neff, 2024). This collaboration between public and private sectors exemplifies the broader trend of neoliberal urbanism, where market-driven solutions shape the trajectory of urban development.

7.3 Northern Virginia's Data Center Alley: Convergence of Land, Data, and Capital

Northern Virginia has emerged as a key node in the global digital economy, with 453 data centers operated by 61 providers (Baxtel, 2025), the most dominant being Amazon with over 150 data centers. Yet, over 250 of these data centers are concentrated in a small area known as Data Center Alley, with its extensive network of data centers that serve to provide a competitive advantage to local firms while also serving as a global backbone for ICT and AI infrastructure. Of these data centers, 52 belong to the region's four largest REITs – Digital Realty, Equinix, NTT, and QTS – which comprise nearly 800,000 square meters of built data centers in our estimate. Figure 7.1 shows a high concentration of data centers in Ashburn, VA, nestled among residential neighborhoods. The region's transformation has been shaped by a confluence of historical infrastructure, financial incentives, and strategic location near Washington, D.C. Scholars have highlighted how Northern Virginia's rise as a data hub is rooted in its deep connectivity to global networks, facilitated by dense fiber optic corridors and a reliable energy grid (Fard, 2024; Rosati et al., 2023). The interplay of local policies and real estate investment

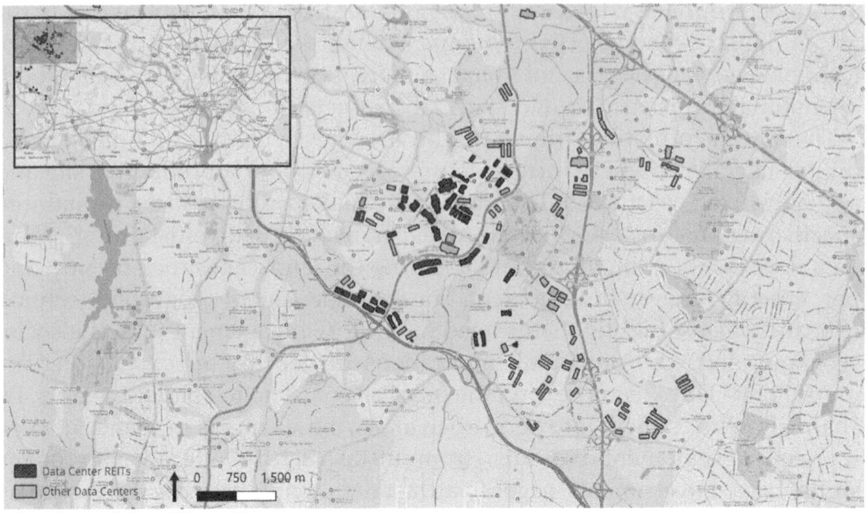

FIGURE 7.1
Data center REITs make up a significant portion of data centers in the Ashburn, Virginia area. Data compiled from Baxtel (2025), DataCenterMap.com (Data Center Map, 2025), and author fieldwork in November 2024.

has accelerated this growth, embedding data centers into the financial and spatial fabric of the region. As a result, the area has become an archetype of how financialized digital infrastructure reshapes peripheral urban geographies, creating new forms of economic dependency and spatial organization.

Fieldwork conducted over two days in November 2024 provided firsthand insights into the material presence and spatial impact of data centers in the region. The scale and security of these facilities stood in stark contrast to their surroundings. Unlike traditional suburban developments characterized by strip malls and residential communities, the region's data centers presented an aesthetic of industrial fortification: high fences, security checkpoints, and a conspicuous absence of human presence (see Figure 7.2). At one site, we were told we had to leave the premises after two security guards approached us, reinforcing the sense of restricted access and securitization that defines these infrastructures. The sheer number of ongoing construction projects indicated the rapid expansion of the industry, with cranes, excavators, and construction crews scattered across multiple locations (see Figure 7.3). Many data centers were built adjacent to new development projects by the same REITs, emphasizing the speculative nature of these investments and the expectation of continued demand.

Despite their utilitarian design, data centers are not isolated from the everyday spaces of suburban life. Observations revealed their adjacency to a variety of land uses, from apartment complexes and townhomes to entertainment districts and high-end residential developments. This juxtaposition

FIGURE 7.2
Data centers are heavily patrolled and securitized, some even with double fencing, as seen here from a data center in Northern Virginia. Picture taken by the authors.

FIGURE 7.3
Construction crews worked not just on building more data centers but also on the below surface infrastructure that they rely on. Picture taken by the authors.

FIGURE 7.4
Data and networking infrastructure are in high demand, as seen by signs posted throughout Northern Virginia stating, "We Buy Cisco, Ciena, Juniper," referring to the makers of data and networking hardware. Picture taken by the authors.

was particularly striking in the wealthier areas of Northern Virginia, where data centers coexisted with gated communities and highly manicured landscapes. Unlike lower-income urban neighborhoods in the mid-Atlantic where real estate speculation typically manifests in signs such as "We Buy Homes" or "We Pay Cash for Homes," suburban Northern Virginia featured a different kind of speculative economy – one marked by signs stating, "We Buy Cisco," referencing the secondary market for networking hardware (see Figure 7.4). This signage reflected the broader integration of data infrastructure into speculative financial circuits, where both real estate and technology assets are continually bought, sold, and repurposed.

The integration of data centers into suburban landscapes also raises questions about their environmental and infrastructural impact. The environmental and infrastructural consequences of data center growth are significant and increasingly visible. The expansion of data centers places substantial stress on public utilities and local infrastructure, often requiring major investments in energy supply, water cooling, and network connectivity. These costs are frequently socialized, with municipalities subsidizing electricity or permitting resource-intensive operations. Notable examples include the use of river water for cooling, increased CO_2 emissions, and experiments with alternative energy sources such as nuclear reactors by companies like Alphabet.

The relationship between AI computation, energy consumption, and efficiency is increasingly scrutinized, raising questions about the sustainability of current growth trajectories.

In our fieldwork, the noise from these facilities was a striking feature of the landscape; exhaust systems produced a constant hum that was especially loud near an apartment complex we visited, underscoring the ways in which these facilities alter the sensory experience of nearby residents. Roads surrounding the facilities were heavily trafficked with construction vehicles, and large swaths of land had been cleared for further expansion. These projects not only consume land at an unprecedented rate but also place significant strain on local energy and water resources. The visibility of Tesla Cybertrucks with stickers for electrical repair and networking services underscored the industry's reliance on specialized labor and technical expertise, reinforcing the entanglement between data infrastructure and broader supply chains of energy and digital services. Beyond environmental impacts, the social and economic effects on local communities also deserve attention. While data centers require relatively few on-site workers compared to other forms of real estate, their presence can reshape local labor markets and community relations. The influx of high-value infrastructure may generate limited direct employment but can have broader effects on housing, public services, and local economies, sometimes exacerbating inequalities or generating resistance from affected communities. The proliferation of data centers in the region is thus not simply an issue of land use but of resource allocation and environmental sustainability.

The presence of data centers in Northern Virginia has become a topic of public concern, as reflected in local news coverage and resident feedback (Halper and O'Donovan, 2024; Levy, 2025; Olivo and Neff, 2024). While proponents emphasize the economic benefits, including job creation in construction and maintenance, critics highlight the disruption to local communities and environmental risks. The securitization and spatial dominance of these facilities, coupled with their ever-expanding footprint, have led to increased scrutiny over zoning policies and corporate incentives, including development and revenue tax breaks (Mangum et al., 2020). Field observations confirmed the colocation (see Figure 7.5) and resulting tensions between the financial priorities driving data center expansion and the lived realities of those residing in their shadow. This ongoing transformation underscores the need for critical engagement with the socio-spatial consequences of financialized digital infrastructure, particularly as AI-driven demand accelerates the commodification of land and technological assets in peripheral regions.

While the expansion of data centers is framed as an economic win for host communities, the financial rewards flow primarily to REIT shareholders and tech companies rather than to local residents. Despite their proximity to these facilities, those living alongside data centers see little direct economic benefit, instead experiencing the downsides of industrial-scale infrastructure in their neighborhoods. The profits generated by these facilities are extracted from the land and funneled into global financial markets, reinforcing the

FIGURE 7.5
Apartment buildings near data centers with fencing and security visible. Picture taken by the authors.

disparities between capital accumulation at the corporate level and the material conditions of those who cohabitate with the data centers. This dynamic exemplifies the broader logic of financialized urbanization, where infrastructure serves as an asset for distant investors while shaping the lived experiences of those at the periphery of digital capitalism.

Although Northern Virginia serves as a leading example, it is important to recognize that similar dynamics are unfolding in global data center hubs such as Singapore (Neilson and Notley, 2019), Dublin (Brodie, 2024), and Amsterdam (Monstadt and Saltzman, 2025). Each region presents unique regulatory, infrastructural, and market conditions, but all reflect the growing centrality of digital infrastructure in urban and economic development.

7.4 Making Sense of Data Center REITs: Data Rent and Computational Rent

While data centers are not necessarily new, the scale and intensity of data and computation needs are unprecedented, fueling a data center boom that consumes vast tracts of land in peri-urban areas. As we've shown, Northern Virginia exemplifies this phenomenon, having transformed from a landscape of suburban residential neighborhoods and open farmland into a hub for hyperscale data centers. Our fieldwork revealed relentless construction activity, with cranes, bulldozers, and excavation equipment scattered across multiple sites, underscoring the urgency of expansion to accommodate AI-driven workloads. This surge in infrastructure development is not merely a technical necessity but also a reflection of broader financial dynamics.

Data center REITs have played a pivotal role in this transformation, turning data centers into financial instruments. By commodifying land and infrastructure, these financial entities fuel speculative investments, further embedding data centers into the circuits of digital capitalism. As a result, land that might once have been allocated to residential or commercial purposes is increasingly absorbed into the expansion of digital infrastructure, reinforcing the dominance of profit-driven real estate logics over long-term urban and environmental planning.

The rise of AI has dramatically reshaped the economic value of data and compute resources, introducing new forms of financialized rent generation that underpin the digital economy. The emergence of data rent – the revenue derived from storing, managing, and transmitting vast quantities of digital information – reflects the monetization of the infrastructure required to sustain AI's continuous extraction of data. Simultaneously, computational rent arises from the processing power necessary for AI platforms, such as LLMs, to function.

These forms of rent illustrate how AI has intensified the commodification of infrastructure, embedding digital activity into both the financial and physical landscape. This dynamic exemplifies how AI's infrastructural footprint is not just about technical capability but also about who captures the value produced by this expansion, deepening the inequalities embedded in digital capitalism.

TABLE 7.1

Summary of the Differences between Traditional Real Estate Rent, Data Rent, and Computational Rent

Type of Rent	Source of Value	Spatial Anchor	Key Actors	Example Mechanisms
Traditional Rent	Land/space	Urban, Residential, retail	Landlords, tenants	Lease agreements, zoning
Data Rent	Data storage/ transmission	Proximity to networks	REITs, tech firms	Colocation fees, connectivity
Computational Rent	Compute power	Near AI/cloud clusters	REITs, cloud providers	GPU leasing, power contracts

7.4.1 Data Rent, Computation Rent, and AI

Data rent capitalizes on the inherent value of storing and transmitting information, a cornerstone of AI operations. As AI platforms rely on ever-growing datasets to train and refine their models, the demand for reliable, scalable data storage has surged. Data centers have become the physical manifestation of this need, functioning as repositories for digital information that clients – from tech companies to governments – depend on. These centers charge for the space and services they provide, monetizing the act of storing and safeguarding data. This system thrives on centralization. Entities controlling data storage infrastructure wield significant power over digital capital flows, reinforcing their economic and strategic dominance. For example, data centers near major urban markets like Northern Virginia are positioned to minimize latency and enhance efficiency, making them prime sites for businesses reliant on real-time data access. These locations amplify the economic value of infrastructure, creating a concentrated geography of corporate wealth and influence.

Computational rent arises from the specialized processing power required to support AI systems. LLMs and other AI applications depend on hyperscale computing, including advanced GPUs and AI-specific hardware, to process trillions of parameters. This infrastructure incurs significant costs, from maintenance to energy consumption, which are passed on to AI companies and their clients. The scarcity of high-performance compute resources and the speculative scramble to meet demands ensure that providers can command premium prices, embedding computational rent as a core component of digital capitalism. The relationship between computational rent and data rent is spatially anchored in the clustering of data centers near AI training facilities. Proximity between massive datasets and the high-powered processors needed to train AI models reduces latency and improves overall system efficiency. As training AI models requires constant access to vast quantities of stored data, keeping storage and computation within the same physical region accelerates data retrieval, minimizes bandwidth constraints, and decreases operational lag. This is particularly critical for deep learning applications, where iterative adjustments to models depend on the rapid movement of data between storage and processing units. The closer the data is to the computation, the faster AI systems can be trained, refined, and deployed, making co-location a competitive advantage for tech firms and cloud providers.

The clustering of data centers in specific geographies is not merely a byproduct of financial speculation but a functional necessity for optimizing AI performance. As computational demand grows, so too does the need for land to house the infrastructure required to support AI training and deployment. The financialization of data centers transforms land into a strategic resource, attracting investment and reshaping peri-urban landscapes into hubs of digital production. This process drives up land values and reconfigures space, often at the expense of prior land uses, whether residential, agricultural, or commercial. AI's reliance on massive computational resources embeds digital capitalism into the physical environment, integrating financialized circuits of rent extraction directly into urban and regional development.

7.4.2 Feedback Loops between Data, Computation, Space, and Nature

The interdependence of data rent and computational rent creates reinforcing feedback loops that accelerate the expansion of digital infrastructure. As AI models grow more complex, they require increasingly large datasets for training, which in turn necessitates greater storage and processing capacity (Amvrosiadis et al., 2019). This cycle fuels exponential demand for data centers, embedding them further within global economic and technological circulations. Simultaneously, AI platforms generate new data through their operation, which not only refines existing models but also opens avenues for monetization through targeted advertising, predictive analytics, and other secondary uses (Citrome, 2014). The continuous production and consumption of data ensure that AI's infrastructure remains indispensable, further entrenching the demand for land and energy resources to sustain its expansion. Data and computational rents transform physical space into strategic assets, concentrating investment in locations where connectivity, energy availability, and urban proximity maximize efficiency (Lorenzo-Eiroa, 2023). These clusters reinforce the financialization of land, embedding data centers into the logic of real estate speculation and corporate asset management.

The financialization of data centers through REITs is not an abstract process; it materializes in specific locations, transforming landscapes and producing new spatial demands. Data and computational rent are not extracted in isolation but are embedded in physical land, where data centers require vast tracts of space for servers, cooling systems, and high-voltage connectivity. As data centers cluster in strategic locations, financial capital flows into these geographies, reshaping land markets and intensifying pressures on surrounding municipal and regional infrastructure. The financialization of digital infrastructure means that land itself becomes a speculative asset, as REITs acquire, develop, and lease properties not only for their immediate use-value but for their long-term investment potential. This process prioritizes profitability over local needs, often driving up land values, altering zoning laws, and increasing demands on energy and water resources. The clustering of data centers in regions like Northern Virginia reflects how digital capitalism does not simply operate in placeless networks but instead consolidates in specific urban-peripheral landscapes. As AI's appetite for computation grows, so too does the demand for land, embedding financial speculation directly into the built environment, where the logic of rent extraction extends beyond data and computation to the very ground on which these infrastructures stand.

The entrenchment of data and computational rent within digital capitalism reveals the material stakes of AI's expansion. The growing demand for computation is not just an abstract economic process but one that reshapes physical landscapes, restructures land markets, and prioritizes speculative investment over long-term urban and environmental planning. As AI models grow in complexity, the infrastructure supporting them becomes ever more indispensable, reinforcing the necessity of data centers while simultaneously deepening financial extraction from land, energy, and local resources. This dynamic not only accelerates the centralization of corporate wealth and influence but also underscores the uneven distribution of costs and benefits: while REITs and tech firms profit from AI's infrastructural footprint, local communities bear the burden of environmental strain, spatial disruption, and rising land values. In this way, the expansion of AI is inseparable from the financialization of the built environment, embedding digital capitalism into the urban periphery and cementing the centrality of rent extraction in the digital economy.

7.5 Conclusion: AI and the Future of Land and Urbanization

The restructuring of urban and suburban geographies to accommodate AI's infrastructure represents a profound shift in the organization of economic space. Just as postwar suburbanization was fueled by the decentralization of industrial and corporate employment away from city centers – facilitated by financial incentives, state-backed mortgages, and large-scale infrastructure projects (Ceruzzi, 2008; Garreau, 2011; Graham and Marvin, 2001; Wright, 1983) – contemporary data center expansion parallels this process in and for the digital economy. Rather than solely housing workers commuting to urban cores, today's suburban peripheries house the compute power required for the AI systems that increasingly shape urban life. The urban economy remains dependent on the infrastructure that lies beyond it, as AI-driven applications, cloud computing, and data-intensive services rely on the storage and processing capacities of these suburban digital enclaves. This division of space underscores how digital capitalism is not placeless; rather, it produces and relies on new spatial configurations that bind urban consumption to suburban and rural production (Brodie, 2024; Cugurullo et al., 2023; Fard, 2024).

Yet, unlike mid-century suburbanization, which was largely tied to homeownership and the expansion of consumerism, the financialization of AI infrastructure extracts profit through land and computation without necessarily redistributing wealth to the regions that host these developments. The economic benefits of data center expansion accrue to institutional investors and REIT shareholders rather than to the communities in which these massive facilities are built. This patchy topography of value extraction mirrors broader shifts in the contemporary economy, where infrastructure increasingly serves as an asset class rather than a public good (Furlong, 2020).

The spatial logics of AI urbanism also reinforce the broader processes of enclosure and privatization within digital capitalism (e.g., Cugurullo et al. 2023). As the AI economy continues to expand, its infrastructural footprint will further entrench existing disparities in land use, economic power, and detrimental environmental consequences. Already, this economy is remaking the suburban and exurban landscape, turning vast areas into securitized, privately controlled infrastructural spaces that primarily serve corporate clients. These dynamic raises critical questions: How will cities adapt to a model of urbanization shaped not by human labor but by the logistical needs of digital infrastructure? Unlike industrial parks or suburban office complexes, which were often integrated into municipal economies through employment or tax bases, data centers function with minimal labor and limited community interaction. Their economic significance is not measured by local productivity but by their ability to facilitate the profit-making processes of financial markets and distant corporate entities. This transformation further erodes the traditional relationship between infrastructure, place, and economic participation, embedding speculative investment into the material landscapes of AI urbanization. Through field observations and mapping from Northern Virginia's Data Center Alley, we've highlighted the tangible impacts of this transformation, from the reconfiguration of land use to the social and environmental tensions it generates. The role of REITs in driving these changes underscores the need for policymakers to reconcile the economic benefits of data center development with its broader implications. Addressing these challenges requires moving beyond a technical understanding of AI toward a deeper interrogation of how digital capitalism restructures space, governance, and economic participation. In sum, a comprehensive framework for scholars must consider the cascading effects of financialization and digital infrastructure on physical spaces. This includes prioritizing environmental resilience, ensuring community involvement in development decisions, and balancing short-term economic gains with long-term societal well-being. Only by addressing these challenges can the interplay between AI, land, and urbanization be managed to create inclusive and sustainable futures.

In sum, data center REITs stand as paradigmatic examples of the financialization of digital infrastructure. Their distinct forms of rentiership and financial strategies – shaped by the material demands of power, land, and connectivity – set them apart from traditional real estate models and underscore the profound influence of global capital on the built environment. As digital capitalism continues to evolve, the stakes of these infrastructural transformations will only intensify.

References

Albertus, M., Klaus, K., 2024. *Land and Politics*. https://doi.org/10.1146/annurev-polisci-040623-112955

Amvrosiadis, G., Butt, A. R., Tarasov, V., Zadok, E., Zhao, M., 2019. *Data Storage Research Vision 2025* (Report on NSF Visioning Workshop held May 30–June 1, 2018), 6.

Baxtel, 2025. Northern Virginia Data Center Market [WWW Document]. *Baxtel Advisory*. https://baxtel.com/data-center/northern-virginia (accessed 1.30.25).

Beauvisage, T., Mellet, K., 2020. Datassets: Assetizing and Marketizing Personal Data. In: Birch, K., Muniesa, F. (Eds.), *Assetization: Turning Things into Assets in Technoscientific Capitalism, Inside Technology*. The MIT Press, pp. 75–96.

Brodie, P., 2024. Smarter, Greener Extractivism: Digital Infrastructures and the Harnessing of New Resources. *Information, Communication & Society* 0, 1–20. https://doi.org/10.1080/1369118X.2024.2341013

Ceruzzi, P. E., 2008. *Internet Alley: High Technology in Tysons Corner, 1945–2005*, 1st ed. The MIT Press, Cambridge, MA.

Citrome, L. G., 2014. Data Centers and REITs: Is There Real Estate in the Cloud? Student Note. *N.Y.U. J.L. & Bus*. 11, 246.

Cugurullo, F., Caprotti, F., Cook, M., Karvonen, A., McGuirk, P., Marvin, S. (Eds.), 2023. *Artificial Intelligence and the City: Urbanistic Perspectives on AI*, 1st ed. Routledge.

Data Center Map, 2025. Data Center Map – Colocation, Cloud and Connectivity [WWW Document]. https://www.datacentermap.com/ (accessed 1.31.25).

Digital Realty, 2020. *DGX: Report Measuring the Intensity of Data Gravity and Its Effect on the Global 2000 Enterprises*. Digital Realty, Austin, TX.

Edwards, D., Cooper, Z. G. T., Hogan, M., 2025. The Making of Critical Data Center Studies. *Convergence: The International Journal of Research into New Media Technologies* 31, 429–446. https://doi.org/10.1177/13548565231224157

Fard, A., 2024. Platforms and Palimpsests: Urban Landscapes of Data in Northern Virginia. *Footprint* 17, 27–42. https://doi.org/10.59490/footprint.17.2.6726

Furlong, K., 2020. Geographies of Infrastructure 1: Economies. *Progress in Human Geography* 44, 572–582. https://doi.org/10.1177/0309132519850913

Garreau, J., 2011. *Edge City: Life on the New Frontier*, Reprint ed. Anchor.

Graham, S., Marvin, S., 2001. *Splintering Urbanism: Networked Infrastructures, Technological Mobilities and the Urban Condition*. Routledge.

Greene, D., 2022. Landlords of the Internet: Big Data and Big Real Estate. *Soc. Stud. Sci*. 52, 904–927. https://doi.org/10.1177/03063127221124943

Greenstein, S., Fang, T. P., 2020. *Where the Cloud Rests: The Economic Geography of Data Centers (Working Paper No. 21-042)*. Harvard Business School, Cambridge, MA.

Halper, E., O'Donovan, C., 2024. As Data Centers for AI Strain the Power Grid, Bills Rise for Everyday Customers. *Washington Post*.

Hogan, M., 2021. The Data Center Industrial Complex. In: Jue, M., Ruiz, R. (Eds.), *Saturation: An Elemental Politics*. Duke University Press, pp. 283–305. https://doi.org/10.1515/9781478013044-016

Kay, K., Tapp, R., 2022. Un/Making Assets: The Institutional Limits to Financialization. *Annals of the American Association of Geographers* 112, 1243–1259. https://doi.org/10.1080/24694452.2021.1960474

Levy, M., 2025. Big Tech Wants to Plug Data Centers Right into Power Plants. Utilities Say It's Not Fair. *Washington Post*.

Lorenzo-Eiroa, P., 2023. *Digital Signifiers in an Architecture of Information: From Big Data and Simulation to Artificial Intelligence*. Routledge.

Luitse, D., 2024. Platform Power in AI: The Evolution of Cloud Infrastructures in the Political Economy of Artificial Intelligence. *Internet Policy Review* 13(2), 1–44.

Mahmoudi, D., Levenda, A., 2016. Beyond the Screen: Uneven Geographies, Digital Labour, and the City of Cognitive-Cultural Capitalism. *tripleC: Communication, Capitalism & Critique. Open Access Journal for a Global Sustainable Information Society* 14, 99–120. https://doi.org/10.31269/triplec.v14i1.699

Mahmoudi, D., Levenda, A., Sabatino, A., 2024. The Urban-Tech Feedback Loop: A Surveillance and Development Data-Walk in South Lake Union. *Digital Geography and Society* 7, 100106. https://doi.org/10.1016/j.diggeo.2024.100106

Mahmoudi, D., Wiig, A., 2024. The Data Politics of Tech Corporations. *Buildings and Cities*. https://www.buildingsandcities.org/insights/commentaries/data-politics-tech-corporations.html

Mangum, A. F., Zorn, D., Arel, M., Driebe, K., 2020. *The Impact of Data Centers on the State and Local Economies of Virginia*. Northern Virginia Technology Council.

Monstadt, J., Saltzman, K., 2025. How Data Centers Have Come to Matter: Governing the Spatial and Environmental Footprint of the 'Digital Gateway to Europe.' *International Journal of Urban and Regional Research* 49, 757–778. https://doi.org/10.1111/1468-2427.13316

Neilson, B., Notley, T., 2019. Data Centres as Logistical Facilities: Singapore and the Emergence of Production Topologies. *Work Organisation, Labour & Globalisation* 13. https://doi.org/10.13169/workorgalaboglob.13.1.0015

Olivo, A., Neff, W., 2024. Our Digital Lives Need Massive Data Centers. What Goes on Inside Them? *Washington Post*.

Ranganathan, P., Hölzle, U., 2024. Twenty Five Years of Warehouse-Scale Computing. *IEEE Micro* 44, 11–22. https://doi.org/10.1109/MM.2024.3409469

Rosati, C., James, A., Metcalf, K., 2023. Data Plantation: Northern Virginia and the Territorialization of Digital Civilization in "the Internet Capital of the World." *Online Media and Global Communication* 2, 199–227. https://doi.org/10.1515/omgc-2023-0017

Sayegh, E., 2024. The Billion-Dollar AI Gamble: Data Centers as the New High-Stakes Game. *Forbes*.

Schwartz, H., 2024. Brave New World: A Third Industrial Divide? *Phenomenal World*. https://www.phenomenalworld.org/analysis/a-third-industrial-divide/ (accessed 1.21.26).

Thatcher, J., O'Sullivan, D., Mahmoudi, D., 2016. Data Colonialism through Accumulation by Dispossession: New Metaphors for Daily Data. *Environ Plan D* 34, 990–1006. https://doi.org/10.1177/0263775816633195

Toczé, K., Madon, M., Garcia, M., Lago, P., 2022. *The Dark Side of Cloud and Edge Computing: An Exploratory Study*. Presented at the Eighth Workshop on Computing within Limits 2022, LIMITS, Virtual. https://doi.org/10.21428/bf6fb269.9422c084

van Es, K., de Lange, M., 2020. Data with Its Boots on the Ground: Datawalking as Research Method. *European Journal of Communication* 35, 278–289. https://doi.org/10.1177/0267323120922087

Wiessner, M., 2025. Digital Construction Comes to the Pacific Northwest: Timber and the Landscapes of Automation. *IEEE Annals of the History of Computing* 1–14. https://doi.org/10.1109/MAHC.2025.3577940

Wiessner, M., Kellogg, S., Starosielski, N., 2024. The Visual Culture of 'Silicon Heartland': Architecting Agricultural Past as Infrastructural Future. *Journal of Visual Culture* 23, 156–167. https://doi.org/10.1177/14704129241274149

Wiig, A., 2013. Everyday Landmarks of Networked Urbanism: Cellular Antenna Sites and the Infrastructure of Mobile Communication in Philadelphia. *Journal of Urban Technology* 20, 21–37. https://doi.org/10.1080/01446193.2013.823051

Wiig, A., Karvonen, A., McFarlane, C., Rutherford, J., 2022. Splintering Urbanism at 20: Mapping Trajectories of Research on Urban Infrastructures. *Journal of Urban Technology* 0, 1–11. https://doi.org/10.1080/10630732.2021.2005930

Wright, G., 1983. *Building the Dream: A Social History of Housing in America*, Reprint ed. The MIT Press, Cambridge, MA.

8

Artificial Intelligence and Surveillance in the City: Implications for Urban Governance, Democracy, and Power

Shona Geoghegan and Federico Cugurullo

8.1 Introduction

As artificially intelligent technologies become increasingly embedded within our urban environments, the inevitability of implications for urban governance and democracy presents as vividly apparent. The dawn of urban artificial intelligence (AI) extends far beyond the evolution of the smart city and instead marks the emergence of a model fundamentally distinct in sophistication, materialisation, and complexity (Cugurullo, 2021; Caprotti et al., 2024). In this way, the emergence of AI technologies with the capability to act autonomously inevitably, in their obscure, ambiguous, and constantly evolving forms, poses novel challenges in navigating their role in the city (Cugurullo et al., 2024; Cugurullo, 2020). Whilst AI has shown great potential for enhancing the efficiency of urban activities, its negative externalities, particularly those associated with surveillance practices, cannot be overlooked (Makanadar, 2024; Catlett et al., 2023; Kitchin, 2023; Sherman, 2023; Zuboff, 2023). Such undesirable manifestations, including the erosion of privacy through pervasive data collection and the exacerbation of inequality through algorithmic bias, have presented as fundamental challenges for urban governance and regulation (Makanadar, 2024). This exacerbation of pre-existing power asymmetries is facilitated through the often unconscious provision of personal data by citizens to institutions and corporations via AI-driven analysis and surveillance (Zuboff, 2022). As a result, citizens are positioned with limited agency over how their information is used, creating concerns surrounding equality, autonomy, and democratic accountability (Kitchin, 2023).

As our urban populations continue to rise at an exponential rate (WBG, 2023), they become an increasingly favourable target of surveillance capitalist endeavours as the potential for monetising the daily activities of citizens

DOI: 10.1201/9781003480167-10

through AI appears infinite (Geoghegan and Cugurullo, 2025). This raises significant concerns about transparency, accountability, and the ethical implications of AI-collected data (Cugurullo and Xu, 2025), particularly when personal information is leveraged to inform policies or commercial strategies without explicit consent from the individuals involved (Jones, 2025; Makanadar, 2024; Sherman, 2023). In this way, our increasingly AI-centred world has created a fundamental need to reimage urban data governance so that human rights are upheld and the integrity of democratic institutions is safeguarded (Cugurullo et al., 2025; Jørgensen, 2019). The origins of the term 'democracy', which was etymologically derived from the ancient Greek concepts of *demos* (people) and *kratos* (power), offer a foundational lens for assessing its contemporary implementation (Jent, 1967). Although constrained by the social norms of the time, early critical engagements with democracy, most notably the Platonian interpretation of Athenian democracy, remain strikingly pertinent to modern conceptions of 'oligarchy, rule by the few' (Jent, 1967, p. 242). The notion of Platonism remains salient when discussing contemporary times as the caution exhibited towards prevailing oligarchical social structures (Jent, 1967) underscores the imperative for critical reflection on the governance of AI (Catlett et al., 2023; Cugurullo, 2024; Kitchin, 2023). In today's tech-driven landscape, figures like Elon Musk, whose influence over AI development and deployment extends beyond corporate spheres into political decision-making, mirror the very oligarchical power imbalances that Plato warned against centuries ago. Much like in the philosophy of Platonism (360 BCE; translated by Jowett, 2010), the confinements of current technological manifestations that limit our perspective must be reframed, so as to instead explore opportunities that serve the collective good. Therefore, the dominant role played by technology conglomerates in exerting 'oligopolistic control over most digital information and communication spaces, systems, and processes' (Zuboff, 2022, p. 1) must be challenged, so as to ensure that data power is not leveraged by society's elites to the detriment of the masses (Kitchin, 2023). By adopting a perspective that moves beyond the technocratic control currently characterising our cities in the way of corporate oligarchies, this chapter calls for a bold reimagining of urban spaces as inclusive data-driven democracies where human rights and collective wellbeing thrive in harmony with technological advancement.

This chapter begins with a critical engagement with the rise of AI-powered urban technocracy, examining its implications for governance, democracy, and power. The next section offers an exploration of the potential for AI to enhance democratic urban functioning, emphasising the need to strike a balance between technological efficiency and civic accountability. This is followed by a discussion on Barcelona as a case study of a city actively working to achieve this balance, offering an alternative model of AI-driven governance rooted in transparency and public participation. The chapter concludes by considering the future role of cities on the global stage, arguing that they must resist the erosion of democratic principles and take an active role in shaping responsible AI governance both within and beyond their immediate jurisdictions.

8.2 The Rise of AI-Powered Urban Technocracies

In the contemporary context, governance strategies have become increasingly reliant on the interplay between public and private actors alike in what Harvey (1989, p. 4) described as the 'shift towards entrepreneurialism'. In particular, this transition towards privatised amenities and services is most pronounced in urban centres as conditions of austerity led authorities to become dependent on private capital as a means of sustaining infrastructure and public services (Pollio, 2016). As a result, cities have emerged as primary hubs for private technological experimentation as dense populations provide a sufficient supply of users critical for accelerated innovation through data production (Cugurullo and Xu, 2025; Evans et al., 2016). From the introduction of predictive algorithms in security and policing to the implementation of advanced management systems for energy, transportation, and environmental monitoring, local authorities have become increasingly dependent on vast networks of AI sensors and data analytics tools, which promise to enhance the management of urban living (Cugurullo et al., 2025; Kitchin, 2023). However, this deepening reliance has encountered some strong criticism as the automation of decision-making processes reshapes urban governance, including claims of reduced democratic accountability, political deliberation, and citizens' rights (Jones, 2025; Catlett et al., 2023; Kitchin, 2023; Cugurullo, 2020). Ultimately, as the governance of cities and artificially intelligent services provided by private ventures become increasingly entangled, the relationship between the city and its citizenry will continue to radically transform (Yigitcanlar et al., 2024; Rosen and Alvarez León, 2022).

The idea that data acts as an important entity in governance has existed long before the rise of modern technology, with city administrators utilising methods such as censuses, surveys, and registrations as far back as the Enlightenment era (Kitchin, 2023). However, as our world becomes increasingly digitised by means of AI-driven surveillance systems, the rate at which data can now be collected has accelerated governments towards real-time analysis models (Kitchin, 2023). This novel approach to urban governance largely depends on management systems that are outsourced from corporations, which allows authorities to benefit from private capital and expertise. Nevertheless, this does not come without major trade-offs as access to vast datasets enables private actors to leverage their agendas and exert influence in the process of decision-making (Kitchin, 2023; Sadowski, 2019). In this way, a profound reconfiguration of power dynamics can be seen emerging as technology conglomerates gain disproportionate agency over socio-economic trajectories and consolidate their position as a 'new quasi-governing class' (Cupać et al., 2024, p. 901). With the continuous expansion of this ideology of tech solutionism, claims of administrative refinement possible through automation justify an imposed technocracy that promotes elitist rule rather than the governance of elected officials (Cugurullo, 2025; Knebel et al., 2022). As a result, such processes of urban governance and policy cultivation have been criticised for becoming increasingly technocratic (Cugurullo and Xu, 2025; Sherman, 2023; Xu et al., 2024) as algorithmic rationalities have been seen to overtake traditional democratic activities of deliberation and participation (Caprotti et al., 2024; Zuboff, 2023).

The aforementioned challenges to the proper functioning of democracy, which have arisen from the increasing influence of powerful private interests in urban governance, inevitably exert significant implications for human rights, namely equality and autonomy. The preservation of democracy is fundamental in the protection of human rights as it allows for institutional accountability, public deliberation, and legal transparency to safeguard basic freedoms (UN, 2025). In the urban context, these principles have been brought into question as private agendas dependent on the capture of large quantities of data from public spaces via AI sensors undermine the autonomy of citizens (Makanadar, 2024). This sees individuals stripped of data dignity and sovereignty (Makanadar, 2024) as they navigate digitised environments with little possibility to opt out of such exploitative services (Catlett et al., 2023). As a result, citizens are often subjected to a dual burden of financial contributions through taxation and/or service fees, as well as the collection and subsequent (re)distribution of their personal data and information (Catlett et al., 2023). Additionally, this dual burden raises concerns about transparency, accountability, and the ethical implications of data use (Cugurullo and Xu, 2025), particularly when personal information is leveraged to inform policies or commercial strategies without explicit consent from the individuals involved (Jones, 2025; Makanadar, 2024; Sherman, 2023). The commodification of personal data often exacerbates power imbalances, which enable institutions and corporations to consolidate influence while leaving citizens with limited agency over how their information is used (Kitchin, 2023). In this way, such dynamics, which see citizens monitored by big tech companies on behalf of their governmental clients, have led some critics to label current practices as a form of tech authoritarianism (Duberry, 2022). Despite being presented under the guise of efficiency, when the attention shifts beyond this narrative of innovation, the true extent of threats to democratic norms posed by AI technologies becomes strikingly apparent (Jones, 2025; Makanadar, 2024; Sherman, 2023).

The monopolistic distribution of control among technology conglomerates, facilitated by the surveillance systems they depend upon for capital accumulation, has begun shaping public life in a way that shows an inherent disregard for civil liberties in what Zuboff (2019, p. 26) described as 'the new frontier of power'. In this way, the technology being deployed across our urban centres must not be considered neutral or benign but rather laden with bias that assists it in the task of furthering its controllers' agenda (Knebel et al., 2022). This paternalistic prevalence of AI technology in the city reinforces a top-down system of governance whereby automated systems are seen to sideline human agency in the process of decision-making (Cupać et al., 2024). As a result, surveillant activities associated with urban AI have been considered one of the most ethically contentious (Saheb, 2023) as it makes protecting the rights of privacy and equality increasingly difficult in cities (Calzada, 2019). The means by which AI operates is 'to acquire information on the surrounding environment and make sense of it, in order to act rationally and autonomously even in uncertain situations' (Cugurullo, 2020, p. 3). However, whilst being trained on vast accumulations of data, AI algorithms inevitably absorb human biases which they then reproduce as they lack the capacity to assess the ethicality of their actions (Calzada, 2019). This has seen AI algorithms responsible for the exacerbation of social inequalities through increasingly obscure forms of systematic discrimination (Jørgensen, 2019). While critical scholarship has denounced these injustices as inevitable in an AI-driven world with limited opt-out options (Catlett et al., 2023), others argue that opting out exacerbates underrepresentation in digital decision-making (Jørgensen, 2019). This tension underscores the paradoxical nature that can occur with digital participation, as even with a choice between participation and withdrawal, citizens are faced with a lose–lose scenario. In this way, AI-driven governance threatens to reinforce structural inequalities, expand surveillance infrastructures, and erode the democratic legitimacy of municipal decision-making if meaningful action is not taken (Zuboff, 2022).

Moreover, the increasing reliance on automated methods of urban governmental management by means of predictive policing, surveillant sensors, and automated decision-making has inevitably blurred the line between governance and control. This has raised concerns regarding who truly possesses the power to determine developments in our cities and who is rendered largely invisible (Cugurullo et al., 2023). In this way, city authorities must take action to actively resist the concentration of power within technocratic and corporate systems by demanding transparency in AI decision-making that ensures citizens have meaningful agency in shaping how these technologies are deployed (Zuboff, 2022). This shift is not only a threat to individual autonomy and sovereignty but a direct assault on democratic urban governance as a whole. As previously discussed, these AI-powered tools need to be recognised as far from neutral and thus must be utilised in a way that negates the legitimisation of governance models that operate with minimal public deliberation or participation (Cugurullo, 2025; Knebel et al., 2022). Without urgent intervention, AI-driven urbanism risks deepening existing inequalities, expanding systems of control, and stripping away public agency under the guise of technological progress.

8.3 Striking the Balance for Data-Driven Democracies

Whilst the aforementioned materialisation of rapidly evolving technology may appear unruly and out-of-control (Cugurullo, 2024), the early stage within which this novel advancement currently occupies allows for a degree of malleability whereby the possibility of moving beyond this hegemonic model remains tangible (Lynch, 2020). As AI-driven urban governance characterised by hyper-surveillance and exclusionary policy-making continues to expand, the need for intervention continues to grow exponentially (Barns, 2021). However, with an increasing sense of awareness relating to technological risk, an opportunity presents for us to redefine the role of AI in our cities so as to ensure democratic governance is strengthened rather than compromised and eroded (Lynch, 2020; Ribera-Fumaz, 2019). It is important to note that the rejection of the current trajectory of technological advancement does not require the outright resistance of digital innovation but rather a proactive effort to uphold citizen sovereignty and dignity (Lynch, 2020). This calls for a collective shift away from the passive acceptance of highly opaque AI algorithms and data sharing policies in favour of urban environments that foster space for sovereignty, transparency, and engagement without compromised accountability (Fernandez-Monge et al., 2024). In this way, the issue at hand extends beyond the cultivation of regulation as the need to re-establish transparent strategies of urban governance requires a fundamental balancing of risks and benefits. Therefore, by harnessing AI in a responsible way, it can serve as a tool that assists with the equitable management of cities through establishing frameworks that prioritise public control over essential digital infrastructure and urban data (Fernandez-Monge et al., 2024; Pierri and Lüning, 2023; Bria, 2017).

One of the principal barriers to fully realising the potential of urban AI is the tension it creates with traditional conceptions of sovereignty (Makanadar, 2024). Although sovereignty has traditionally been linked to the nation-state (Calzada, 2018), advances in urban AI have conferred a heightened degree of power upon municipal governments, enabling them to leverage interconnected networked systems to extend their influence both within their locality and on the global stage (Manfredi-Sánchez, 2021). However, as governments increasingly outsource these services to private corporations, they cede significant authority to private elites who often possess interests that diverge from that of the wider citizenry. This has resulted in the emergence of debates surrounding who owns urban data and is responsible for how it is used and protected. The potential to cultivate vast datasets through AI-driven monitoring systems has created an abundance of information that can aid city authorities in predicting needs and allocating resources more effectively. In this way, local authorities must reclaim their agency from private corporations through implementing measures that ensure transparency and accountability throughout the process of collecting, storing, and sharing data (Pierri and Lüning, 2023). This can be achieved through striving to maintain the equilibrium between harnessing the AI-powered potential of private innovation and upholding the norms of human-centric democratic governance (Tomaževič et al., 2023). However, as noted by Slaughter (2024) at a discussion at the 'State of the Union', it is paramount that we negotiate novel ways of including tech companies in discussions in a legitimate way as they possess the expertise necessary for the transformation. By striking this balance, AI-driven cities can potentially serve as cornerstones of democracy, paving the way for futures defined by sovereignty, resiliency, and transparency.

Within the framework of democracy, one of the most pressing issues is the protection of human dignity, which can be understood as ensuring the inherent worth of every individual is upheld (Latonero, 2018). However, this has become a challenge amid contemporary AI developments as citizens' ability to self-protect has been significantly inhibited by opaque algorithms (Makanadar, 2024). The vast quantities of personal data now collected in our urban centres often operate in a reductive manner whereby the complexity of individuals' lived experiences becomes overshadowed by large corporate agendas (Yigitcanlar et al., 2023). This can leave citizens feeling stripped of their agency and dignity as unregulated monopolies exploit personal information in favour of capital gain. As a result, there is a growing need to ensure actions are taken that protect human dignity amid this mass expansion of technological advancements. In this way, cities that are successful in safeguarding their inhabitants are positioned to leverage many positive outcomes, including responsive public services and effective infrastructure. Whilst regulation plays a part in achieving this by ensuring data is managed in a way that benefits wider society, this alone will not be enough as the growing demand for alternative digital infrastructure necessitates a shift beyond technocratic control (Bria, 2024). The cultivation of an urban digital landscape characterised by conditions of transparency and accountability can be achieved by empowered citizens with the tools to understand how their information is used and to contest decisions they believe violate their rights (Makanadar, 2024). Therefore, urban areas can embrace the benefits of the digital age without compromising the individual dignity of citizens by placing the democratic principles of human worth and agency at the centre of AI-driven models.

8.4 Barcelona Case Study: Reclaiming Urban AI for Democracy

As aforementioned, a plethora of urban governments around the globe have attempted to implement AI-driven forms of governance, yielding a diverse range of both positive and negative externalities (Palmini and Cugurullo,

2023). The city of Barcelona, Spain, has emerged as a prominent leader in urban AI implementation precisely because its governance model is grounded in the inter-locking pillars of transparency, digital sovereignty, and participatory democracy (March and Ribera-Fumaz, 2018; Charnock et al., 2021; Monge et al., 2022). However, the evolution of AI-driven governance in Barcelona did not happen in isolation but rather is the product of a long period of experimentation (Monge et al., 2022). This began with the introduction of the 'smart city' initiative, which saw local authorities in Barcelona join forces with large corporations with a primary focus on improved urban efficiency (Monge et al., 2022). However, as attention began to grow relating to the implications of such technologies on privacy, citizen engagement, and social equality, the city of Barcelona began to embark on a reform of the *status quo* in data management in what became known as the 'New Data Deal' (Bria, 2018). In this way, a profound shift occurred in the digital governance strategy of Barcelona as civic engagement and democratic accountability began to take precedence over a top-down technocratic approach (Monge et al., 2022). Thus, Barcelona's integration of AI illustrates how open-source tools, participatory platforms, and ethical audits can operationalise democratic principles in practice.

A key element safeguarding the democratic integrity of Barcelona's urban AI strategy is its strong emphasis on upholding sovereignty as a fundamental principle (Smith and Martín, 2021). The adoption of the participatory platform 'Decidim' (translates from Catalan to English as 'we decide') can be seen as a key manifestation of the city's efforts towards such sovereign and democratic forms of data-driven governance (Monge et al., 2022). This open-source online platform enables collaborative policy-making as citizens are given the opportunity to propose ideas and offers transparent justifications when such proposals are rejected (Garcia et al., 2023). By embedding transparency and accountability into digital infrastructure, it fosters civic engagement while countering the opacity of algorithmic governance prevalent in many smart city initiatives. In this way, Barcelona's approach illustrates how digital sovereignty can be operationalised through municipal infrastructures that institutionalise citizen agency in AI governance. The integration of natural language processing (NLP) tools directly addresses algorithmic opacity and bias identified earlier in the chapter by making public reasoning legible and accountable (Monge et al., 2022). This aligns with broader theoretical arguments that rejecting the dominant trajectory of digital innovation does not require resistance to technology itself but rather a commitment to preserving citizen dignity and autonomy within digital systems (Lynch, 2020). Thus, Barcelona represents a real-world alternative to the passive acceptance of opaque AI and extractive data-sharing policies, instead creating urban digital environments rooted in transparency, participation, and democratic oversight (Fernandez-Monge et al., 2024).

In the case of Barcelona, the governance of data generated from AI operations in the city is grounded in the principles of transparency, accountability, and citizen control, emphasising the importance of open source systems (Smith and Martín, 2021). The city's collaborative ethos sees city officials, academic institutions, civil society, and technology experts collectively interact in the development of innovative urban projects (Cardullo et al., 2023). This interdisciplinary approach not only enriches the decision-making process but also ensures that AI-driven innovations align with human rights standards and democratic norms. A central component of this governance strategy is data transparency, as seen with the city's commitment to building public trust through open access to municipal data and decision-making processes. Through real-time data analysis, the city publishes dashboards under an open licence, allowing civil-society groups to scrutinise urban functioning as it exists (Makanadar, 2024). These dashboards ensure that alterations cannot be made without explicit citizen oversight, exemplifying democratic participation and the safeguarding of digital sovereignty (Makanadar, 2024). This approach directly responds to broader critiques around the lack of transparency, accountability, and ethical oversight in data use, particularly when personal information is employed to guide public policies or commercial strategies without informed consent (Jones, 2025; Makanadar, 2024; Sherman, 2023). In this way, open-data platforms are leveraged to further promote transparency and innovation, while citizen feedback is systematically incorporated into ongoing mobility improvements (Makanadar, 2024; cf. Cuppini et al., 2025).

The digital governance model of Barcelona places strong emphasis on citizen participation. As part of these efforts, the identification of existing disparities has been streamlined, allowing for reforms to be implemented at an expedited rate. This can be seen with the city's introduction of initiatives such as the digital literacy programmes, which aim to bridge the gap for various segments of the population, in particular the elderly, who struggle to adapt to the new digital services in the city (Agents TIC, 2025). These initiatives collectively operationalise a model of AI-driven governance rooted in equity, dignity, and shared control. Furthermore, independent algorithmic audits continue to monitor and remediate inequities in municipal AI systems (AdB, 2025), maintaining coherence across oversight mechanisms. Although processes of urban governance have been widely criticised for becoming increasingly technocratic, where algorithmic rationalities risk overtaking traditional democratic activities of deliberation and participation (Cugurullo and Xu, 2025; Sherman, 2023; Xu et al., 2024; Caprotti et al., 2024; Zuboff, 2023), Barcelona offers a counter-example. By embedding mechanisms for citizen input, redistributive digital programmes, and ongoing algorithmic accountability, the city resists the tendency towards decision-making becoming detached from public contestation and debate (Monge et al., 2024). Through independent oversight boards and formalised ethical frameworks, Barcelona works to lead the way in demonstrating that AI-driven governance can serve as a tool for social equity, rather than a mechanism for deepening existing inequalities.

The leadership exhibited by Barcelona in AI-driven urban governance offers a salient model for cities worldwide seeking to uphold democratic principles in the face of rapidly evolving technological landscapes. However, it must be noted that while the city highlights the positive contributions possible through technological innovation, it does not come without limitations, challenges, and errors (Garcia et al., 2023; Cancela and Goikoetxea, 2025). The emergence of factors such as political instability, low participation rates, and cost can inevitably hinder the agenda of democratised digital urban strategies (Garcia et al., 2023). Accordingly, Barcelona's progress should be regarded as contingent and ongoing, inviting continuous scrutiny rather than uncritical emulation (Ribera-Fumaz, 2019). With this in mind, the case of Barcelona still remains exemplary in the willingness of local authorities to actively engage with citizens instead of succumbing to the private agenda of corporations and technology elites (Garcia et al., 2023). By foregrounding transparency through open-data mandates, securing sovereignty via municipal data commons, and embedding citizen deliberation into every algorithmic workflow, Barcelona demonstrates how democratic principles can be translated into technical architectures (Monge et al., 2022).

8.5 Conclusions and Future Prospects

With the rapid implementation of AI-driven governance systems, local authorities have the capacity to harness these technologies to enhance urban functioning, optimise resource allocation, and foster more responsive public services. However, the task of achieving this requires the strategic combination of regulation, public–private partnership, and citizen engagement so as to ensure the risks and benefits are carefully balanced. The continuous refinement and adaptation of regulations and oversight mechanisms in parallel with technological developments is fundamental in ensuring urban AI infrastructures evolve in alignment with democratic principles and human rights. This feedback can be likened to the theory of the Red Queen, whereby self-reinforcing processes ensure that negative externalities remain stagnant or improve rather than worsen existing conditions (see Leigh, 1973). As a result, cities that strategically invest in ethical AI development can set normative precedents at both national and international levels, positioning themselves as leaders in responsible technological innovation, as seen in the case of Barcelona, Spain (Bria, 2019). As the implementation of AI-powered technologies is largely dependent on surveillance systems, authorities must maintain a sense of caution through recognising that advancements will inevitably introduce new risks and ethical dilemmas.

When socio-political factors are taken into account, the growing imperative for cities to assert themselves as pivotal global actors becomes increasingly apparent (Robin and Acuto, 2018). This comes as the variability in and between urban spaces underscores the likelihood for diverse expectations and interpretations of AI implementation, which necessitates nuanced strategies that respond to each city's unique institutional, cultural, and political landscape (Wood et al., 2020). In this way, cities must leverage technology to exert their influence as pivotal global actors and harness collective influence through international networks and alliances that transcend national borders (Robin and Acuto, 2018). By participating in a collaborative manner, urban governments hold the potential to shape policy frameworks that place transparency, civic engagement, and the protection of fundamental rights at the heart of AI implementation (Bria, 2019). Ultimately, through advocating for data sovereignty and algorithmic accountability, city-level authorities can serve as critical actors working against the erosion of democratic principles and influence responsible AI both within and beyond their immediate jurisdictions.

References

AdB. (2025). *The municipal algorithms and data strategy for an ethical promotion of artificial intelligence.* Accessed 8th February 2025 via; https://ajuntament.barcelona.cat/digital/en/technology-accessible-everyone/ethical-use-artificial/ethical-use-artificial-intelligence/municipal

Agents TIC. (2025). *Programa d'acompanyament presencial per a la tramitació digital.* Accessed 8th February 2025 via; https://bithabitat.barcelona/projectes/agents-tic-2/

Barns, S. (2021). Out of the loop? On the radical and the routine in urban big data. *Urban Studies, 58*(15), 3203–3210.

Bria, F. (2017). Public policies for digital sovereignty. In *Ours to hack and to own: The rise of platform cooperativism, a new vision for the future of work and a fairer internet* (1a ed. pp. 218–222). New York/London: OR Books.

Bria, F. (2018, April 5). Our data is valuable. Here's how we can take that value back. *The Guardian.* Accessed 8th February 2025 via; https://www.theguardian.com/commentisfree/2018/apr/05/data-valuable-citizens-silicon-valley-barcelona

Bria, F. (2019). *Building digital cities from the ground up based around data sovereignty and participatory democracy: The case of Barcelona.* Barcelona Centre for International Affairs.

Bria, F. (2024). *Tech diplomacy: International cooperation for sustainable digital – panel discussion.* Accessed 1st February 2025 via; https://www.youtube.com/watch?v=eYqxGN0a8VA

Calzada, I. (2018). 'Algorithmic nations': Seeing like a city-regional and techno-political conceptual assemblage. *Regional Studies, Regional Science, 5*(1), 267–289.

Calzada, I. (2019). Data spaces and democracy. *RSA Journal, 165*(2 (5578)), 40–43.

Cancela, E., & Goikoetxea, J. (2025). Spanish fake sovereignty: From privatising the nation-state to becoming a digital colony. *Ethnopolitics, 24*(1), 54–74.

Caprotti, F., Cugurullo, F., Cook, M., Karvonen, A., Marvin, S., McGuirk, P., & Valdez, A. M. (2024). Why does urban artificial intelligence (AI) matter for urban studies? Developing research directions in urban AI research. *Urban Geography*, 1–12.

Cardullo, P., Ribera-Fumaz, R., & González Gil, P. (2023). The Decidims' soft infrastructure': Democratic platforms and technological autonomy in Barcelona. *Computational Culture*, (9). http://computationalculture.net/the-decidim-soft-infrastructure/

Catlett, C., Portugali, J., & Venkatakrishnan, V. (2023). Privacy and trust in artificially intelligent cities. In Portugali, J. (Ed.). *The Crisis of Democracy in the Age of Cities* (pp. 167–183). Edward Elgar Publishing.

Charnock, G., March, H., & Ribera-Fumaz, R. (2021). From smart to rebel city? Worlding, provincialising and the Barcelona model. *Urban Studies*, *58*(3), 581–600.

Cugurullo, F. (2020). Urban artificial intelligence: From automation to autonomy in the smart city. *Frontiers in Sustainable Cities*, *2*, 38.

Cugurullo, F. (2021). *Frankenstein urbanism: Eco, smart and autonomous cities, artificial intelligence and the end of the city*. Routledge.

Cugurullo, F. (2024). The obscure politics of artificial intelligence: A Marxian sociotechnical critique of the AI alignment problem thesis. *AI and Ethics*, 1–13.

Cugurullo, F. (2025). AIdeology: Unpacking the ideology of artificial intelligence and its spaces. *Antipode*. https://doi.org/10.1111/anti.70065

Cugurullo, F., Caprotti, F., Cook, M., Karvonen, A., McGuirk, P., & Marvin, S. (Eds.). (2023). *Artificial intelligence and the city: Urbanistic perspectives on AI*. Routledge.

Cugurullo, F., Caprotti, F., Cook, M., Karvonen, A., McGuirk, P., & Marvin, S. (2024). The rise of AI urbanism in post-smart cities: A critical commentary on urban artificial intelligence. *Urban Studies*, *61*(6), 1168–1182.

Cugurullo, F., Caprotti, F., Day, J., Geoghegan, S., Lynch, C. R., Menga, F., Robinson, C., & Williams, J. (2025). The nature of AI: Metabolism, energy, water, labour, and justice in the urban political ecology of artificial intelligence. *Urban Political Ecology*. https://doi.org/10.1177/30497515251344495

Cugurullo, F., & Xu, Y. (2025). When AIs become oracles: Generative artificial intelligence, anticipatory urban governance, and the future of cities. *Policy and Society*, *44*(1), 98–115.

Cupać, J., Schopmans, H., & Tuncer-Ebetürk, İ. (2024). Democratization in the age of artificial intelligence: Introduction to the special issue. *Democratization*, *31*(5), 899–921.

Cuppini, N., Barns, S., Bignami, F., Brady, D., Chan, J. K. H., Cugurullo, F., & Hanakata, N. C. (2025). Towards an extended concept of citizenship in a digital urban environment. *Nature Cities*. https://doi.org/10.1038/s44284-025-00236-8

Duberry, J. (2022). Artificial intelligence and democracy: Risks and promises of AI-mediated citizens–government relations. In *Artificial intelligence and democracy*. Edward Elgar Publishing.

Evans, J., Karvonen, A., & Raven, R. (Eds.). (2016). *The experimental city*. Routledge.

Fernandez-Monge, F., Barns, S., Kattel, R., & Bria, F. (2024). Reclaiming data for improved city governance: Barcelona's new data deal. *Urban Studies*, *61*(7), 1291–1307.

Garcia, D. L., Calleja-López, A., & Linares-Lanzman, J. (2023). Collective intelligence and digital participatory platforms: Learnings from Barcelona's Decidim. In *The Routledge handbook of collective intelligence for democracy and governance* (pp. 326–338). Routledge.

Geoghegan, S., & Cugurullo, F. (2025). Beyond dystopian smart cities? Unlocking a progressive utopian future in smart urbanism. *Urban Geography*. https://doi.org/10.1080/02723638.2025.2496508

Harvey, D. (1989). From managerialism to entrepreneurialism: The transformation in urban governance in late capitalism. *Geografiska Annaler: Series B, Human Geography*, *71*(1), 3–17.

Jent, H. C. (1967). Demos Kratos: Democracy, old and new. *The Social Studies*, *58*(6), 242–245.

Jones, J. (2025). Don't fear artificial intelligence, question the business model: How surveillance capitalists use media to invade privacy, disrupt moral autonomy, and harm democracy. *Journal of Communication Inquiry*, *49*(1), 6–26.

Jørgensen, R. F. (2019). *Human rights in the age of platforms*. The MIT Press.

Kitchin, R. (2023). Urban data power: Capitalism, governance, ethics, and justice. *Data Power in Action*, *21*.

Knebel, N. M. P., Fornasier, M. D. O., & Borges, G. S. (2022). Political economy of smart cities and human rights: From corporative technocracy to sensibility. *Braz. J. Int'l L.*, *19*, 259.

Latonero, M. (2018). Governing artificial intelligence: Upholding human rights & dignity. *Data & Society*, *38*.

Leigh, V. V. (1973). A new evolutionary law. *Evol. Theory*, 1–30.

Lynch, C. R. (2020). Contesting digital futures: Urban politics, alternative economies, and the movement for technological sovereignty in Barcelona. *Antipode*, *52*(3), 660–680.

Makanadar, A. (2024). Digital surveillance capitalism and cities: Data, democracy and activism. *Humanities and Social Sciences Communications*, *11*(1), 1–7.

Manfredi-Sánchez, J. L. (2021). Urban diplomacy: A cosmopolitan outlook. *Brill Research Perspectives in Diplomacy and Foreign Policy*, *3*(4), 1–90.

March, H., & Ribera-Fumaz, R. (2018). Barcelona: From corporate smart city to technological sovereignty. In *Inside smart cities* (pp. 227–242). Routledge.

Monge, F., Barns, S., Kattel, R., & Bria, F. (2022). *A new data deal: The case of Barcelona*. UCL Institute for Innovation and Public Purpose. https://www.ucl.ac.uk/bartlett/publicpurpose/sites/bartlett_public_purpose/files/new_data_deal_barcelona_fernando_barns_kattel_and_bria_18_feb.pdf.

Palmini, O., & Cugurullo, F. (2023). Charting AI urbanism: Conceptual sources and spatial implications of urban artificial intelligence. *Discover Artificial Intelligence*, *3*(1), 15.

Pierri, P., & Lüning, E. C. (2023). Civic participation in the datafied society| a democratic approach to digital rights: Comparing perspectives on digital sovereignty on the city level. *International Journal of Communication*, *17*, 19.

Plato, B. (360 BCE). (2010). *The allegory of the cave*. Translated by Benjamin Jowett. Brea, CA, USA: P & L Publication.

Pollio, A. (2016). Technologies of austerity urbanism: The "smart city" agenda in Italy (2011–2013). *Urban Geography*, *37*(4), 514–534.

Ribera-Fumaz, R. (2019). Moving from smart citizens to technological sovereignty? In *The right to the smart city* (pp. 177–191). Emerald Publishing Limited.

Robin, E., & Acuto, M. (2018). Global urban policy and the geopolitics of urban data. *Political Geography*, *66*, 76–87.

Rosen, J., & Alvarez León, L. F. (2022). The digital growth machine: Urban change and the ideology of technology. *Annals of the American Association of Geographers*, *112*(8), 2248–2265.

Sadowski, J. (2019). When data is capital: Datafication, accumulation, and extraction. *Big Data & Society, 6*(1), 2053951718820549.

Saheb, T. (2023). Ethically contentious aspects of artificial intelligence surveillance: A social science perspective. *AI and Ethics, 3*(2), 369–379.

Sherman, S. (2023). The polyopticon: A diagram for urban artificial intelligences. *Ai & Society, 38*(3), 1209–1222.

Slaughter, A. (2024). *Tech diplomacy: International cooperation for sustainable digital – panel discussion.* Accessed 1st February 2025 via; https://www.youtube.com/watch?v=eYqxGN0a8VA

Smith, A., & Martín, P. P. (2021). Going beyond the smart city? Implementing technopolitical platforms for urban democracy in Madrid and Barcelona. *Journal of Urban Technology, 28*(1–2), 311–330.

Tomaževič, N., Ravšelj, D., & Aristovnik, A. (2023). *Artificial intelligence for human-centric society: The future is here.* European Liberal Forum.

UN. (2025). Peace, dignity and equality on planet earth: Democracy and human rights. *United Nations.* Accessed 2nd February via; https://www.un.org/en/global-issues/democracy

WBG. (2023). Urban development. *World Bank Group.* Accessed 2nd February 2025 via; https://www.worldbank.org/en/topic/urbandevelopment/overview

Wood, S., Stacie, H., McFadden, M., Akhiljeet, K., Sarongrat, W., Schoentgen, A., . . . Laura, W. (2020). *Digital sovereignty: The overlap and conflict between states, enterprises and citizens.* Plum Consulting.

Xu, Y., Cugurullo, F., Zhang, H., Gaio, A., & Zhang, W. (2024). The emergence of artificial intelligence in anticipatory urban governance: Multi-scalar evidence of China's transition to city brains. *Journal of Urban Technology*, 1–25.

Yigitcanlar, T., Agdas, D., & Degirmenci, K. (2023). Artificial intelligence in local governments: Perceptions of city managers on prospects, constraints and choices. *Ai & Society, 38*(3), 1135–1150.

Yigitcanlar, T., Senadheera, S., Marasinghe, R., Bibri, S. E., Sanchez, T., Cugurullo, F., & Sieber, R. (2024). Artificial intelligence and the local government: A five-decade scientometric analysis on the evolution, state-of-the-art, and emerging trends. *Cities, 152*, 105151.

Zuboff, S. (2019). Surveillance capitalism and the challenge of collective action. In *New labor Forum* (Vol. 28, No. 1, pp. 10–29). Sage CA: Los Angeles, CA: SAGE Publications.

Zuboff, S. (2022). Surveillance capitalism or democracy? The death match of institutional orders and the politics of knowledge in our information civilization. *Organization Theory, 3*(3), 26317877221129290.

Zuboff, S. (2023). The age of surveillance capitalism. In *Social theory re-wired* (pp. 203–213). Routledge.

9

Can Artificial Intelligence Facilitate Faster Development Assessment? The Case of an Early Adopter Programme

Wayne Williamson

9.1 Introduction

Artificial intelligence (AI) has recently evolved from a niche curiosity to a powerful tool with the potential to augment many labour-intensive human tasks. Similarly, the application of AI in urban and regional planning has the potential to bring about significant transformation. Moreover, Sanchez et al. (2023) observe that now is an opportune time for urban planners to consider the application of AI-related methods, given vast increases in data collection, increased processing speeds, and increased popularity and accessibility. Likewise, Fu (2024) notes there is an urgent need to collaborate with urban planners to understand how Natural Language Processing (NLP) could be adopted in planning practice, and Batty (2023) calls for a deeper examination of the implications of AI in urban settings.

This case study investigates the *AI in Planning Early Adopter* programme being pursued in the state of New South Wales (NSW), Australia. Drawing on interviews with staff from local government who were selected for the programme, this research investigates the following questions:

- Are there existing AI products that can be used in the development assessment process?
- What human labour is required to assemble specific planning data sets for AI solutions?
- What are the potential implications for existing management processes?

To these ends, by using a series of interviews with metropolitan and regional local government staff, this chapter explores what existing AI products can or may be used in the development assessment process, any human labour

DOI: 10.1201/9781003480167-11

required to assemble specific planning data sets for AI training purposes, and the potential implications for existing management processes. This chapter also engages with the ongoing narrative of using technology to streamline development assessment processes in a neoliberal planning system.

Urban planning is influenced by neoliberal ideology, emphasising economic performance, deregulation, and efficiency (Gleeson and Low, 2000; McGuirk, 2005). Planning reforms aim for faster, simpler systems but often prioritise market mechanisms over broader social and environmental goals (Inch, 2009; Williamson and McFarland, 2012; Gunn and Hillier, 2014). Planning reforms are pursued as a lever for improving economic efficiency (Ruming and Goodman, 2016). However, this is often met with concerns over reduced public participation and weakening environmental and social considerations. For example, in the pursuit of efficiency, the development assessment process is often targeted by process standardisation, the complete removal of referral requirements that would allow government agencies to provide feedback, and increasing private certification and planning panels that allow independent experts to make planning decisions that would otherwise be made by local government (Ruming and Goodman, 2016). Likewise, neoliberalism and AI share a focus on efficiency, market-driven systems, cost reduction, and streamlined services. This shift risks biases and commodifies technology as market products (Reynolds and Szerszynski, 2012). Given the synergies between urban planning, neoliberalism, and AI, we apply a critical neoliberal lens to the introduction of AI in urban planning through market-driven mechanisms. Specifically, this chapter explores contradictions between AI efficiency narratives and human labour requirements, how government funding opportunities commodify AI products and how data influences the nature of AI product usage.

This chapter begins by providing an overview of literature on AI use in urban planning, the case study, and discusses neoliberal influences in urban planning and AI. To present the case study, the results section is organised into three parts. The first section provides insights into existing AI products that could be implemented to support development assessment, the second section examines planning data requirements, and the third considers different approaches to change management. The chapter then discusses the diverse approaches to implementing AI products, concerns with data accuracy, and change management from a local government perspective.

9.2 AI in Urban Planning Practice

In recent years, there have been multiple surveys of planning practitioners that reported that planners either never use AI or that there is very low use of AI in their daily work practices (Sanchez et al., 2023; Daniel and Pettit, 2021; Daniel et al., 2023; Potts and Webb, 2023). Despite the low levels of AI knowledge and usage, many urban planners expect AI to 'have a significant impact on planning practice in the future' (Sanchez et al., 2023, p. 191). From a scholarly literature perspective, Sanchez et al. (2023) found a large amount of AI-based research focused on topics that are in the same domain and theoretically relevant to planners. However, this research tends to be highly technical and offers little acknowledgement of how it would be implemented in planning departments (Sanchez et al., 2023). Batty (2023) argues that the current application of AI in urban planning reflects the shift from the ambitious goals of *strong AI* to the more pragmatic *weak AI* approach, which is focused on analysing patterns and behaviours rather than replicating human cognitive processes. This shift highlights the importance of understanding the urban and/or regional context in which AI operates, as it can exacerbate existing issues or create new ones, particularly in the effectiveness of complex urban planning matters (Batty, 2023).

While there is no standardised definition of AI (Cugurullo, 2021; Son et al., 2023), AI can be defined as using computers to mimic human intelligence (Sanchez, 2023). There are various forms of AI. Othengrafen et al. (2025) categorise AI as analytical, functional, textual, visual, and interactive, where analytical and functional AI identify, interpret, and communicate meaningful patterns in data (Sarker, 2022). Textual and interactive AI covers textual analytics or NLP for text classification, speech-to-text conversion, machine translation, and content generation (Sarker, 2022). Visual AI can recognise, classify, and sort items, as well as convert images and videos. Textual AI can support internal administrative procedures and planning processes, for example, checking whether the documents required for a planning application are complete (Sarker, 2022).

The scholarly literature suggests there is an extensive range of prospective AI applications for urban planning, in domains as diverse as land use, zoning and permitting, environmental planning, and transportation (He and Chen, 2024; Yigitcanlar et al., 2024; Othengrafen et al., 2025). Many of these examples represent wicked problems within planning operations that, among other things, do not have agreed-upon rules, logic, or finite sets of outcomes (Sanchez et al., 2023). A broad study by Yigitcanlar et al. (2024) of local government adoption of AI in China, US, Canada, UK, Australia, Argentina, Sweden, and Singapore found that NLP and robotic process automation (automation of repetitive business processes) are the most prevalent AI technologies deployed for information management, back-office work, transportation, and traffic management (Yigitcanlar et al., 2024). Although Yigitcanlar et al. (2024) identified 262 AI service implementations, it is noted that only four were categorised as urban planning. Another systematic literature review by He and Chen (2024) notes that AI presents significant opportunities for improving urban planning processes but also introduces challenges such as data privacy and ethical concerns, and the need for interdisciplinary expertise. Moreover, Yigitcanlar et al. (2024) notes while AI has the potential to enhance government services, there are significant challenges for integration with legacy information systems, financial constraints, limited technical expertise, regulatory compliance, public trust, and diverse stakeholder interests.

Research on AI governance in public agencies is still emerging. While existing studies highlight both the potential benefits and risks of AI for society, there is limited understanding of how the public perceives the use of AI in local government service delivery (Selwyn and Gallo-Cordoba, 2021). Notwithstanding, AI is beginning to influence governance and policy making, as governments around the world adopt AI technologies (Sanchez, 2023). However, public agencies often face challenges in deploying and managing these systems due to a lack of data management skills among staff. Sanchez (2023) argues that data governance and management practices must extend beyond IT departments to include planning staff to better utilise data assets. Desouza et al. (2020) emphasise that the public sector must navigate a range of complex economic, societal, policy, and legal factors that may be avoided by the private sector. As a result, government AI initiatives must deliver more than just cost savings and operational efficiencies; they need to address the diverse and often conflicting needs of stakeholders. Transparency and fairness in decision-making are particularly critical, as government AI projects are funded by taxpayers and are subject to a level of scrutiny that does not apply to private sector initiatives (Desouza et al., 2020).

A prominent theme in the literature is the use of NLP in local government (Senadheera et al., 2024). Case studies for NLP often discuss the capabilities of NLP to remove language barriers and provide residents with a connection to local government services 24 hours a day and enhanced customer services (Senadheera et al., 2024). Fu et al. (2024) also note future research should investigate how to integrate NLP technologies more systematically into planning practice. The existing literature focuses on how all levels of government are using chatbots for citizen complaints and enquiries for a wide range of government services (Bright et al., 2019; Makasi et al., 2020). Furthermore, specialised urban planning chatbots may be beneficial for both citizens and city planners (Hasan et al., 2023). Othengrafen et al. (2025) suggest future AI systems will be highly specialised for processing specific planning tasks but will only make suggestions. Hence, AI will be regarded as a planning tool rather than a planning solution (Othengrafen et al., 2025). The existing literature on NLP is exploratory and fragmented and suggests future research should seek to benchmark different NLP techniques, particularly given the latest developments with large language models such as ChatGPT (Fu, 2024). To contribute to the literature, this chapter presents a case study that applies AI products in a real-world planning context.

9.3 The Case Study: AI in NSW Planning Programme and Its Context

The broad context for this case study is the Australian Commonwealth Government's National Housing Accord (Australian Government, 2022a). Under the Housing Accord agreement, all levels of government, institutional investors, and the construction industry will align with a shared ambition to increase market housing and affordable housing supply. The Housing Accord's aspirational target is to build 1.2 million new, well-located dwellings over five years from mid-2024 across Australia. Each state has agreed to a dwelling target, with NSW committed to building 377,000 new dwellings across the state by 2029 (DPHI, 2025).

The drivers for the Housing Accord assume that to improve Australia's productivity, home ownership must be increased, rental costs and vacancy rates reduced, and the supply of social and affordable housing increased (Australian Government, 2022b). The Housing Accord acknowledges that the residential construction industry is currently facing capacity constraints, including increasing costs of materials and skills shortages, which are exacerbating housing supply and affordability (Australian Government, 2022b). Given that the Housing Accord is based on built dwellings, part of the NSW Government's response has been to support local governments to improve development assessment timeframes. The NSW Government acknowledges that a collaborative approach is critical to enabling dwelling supply, as local government is responsible for determining 85 per cent of all new dwellings in NSW (Scully and Hoenig, 2024).

As part of the focus on local development assessment timeframes, the NSW Department of Planning, Housing and Infrastructure (Department) launched the *AI in NSW Planning* project in November 2023. The initial step was to undertake a process to identify ready-for-market AI products that create workflow efficiencies in the development assessment process, with a focus on the pre-lodgement stage (Scully, 2024a). The pre-lodgement focus was informed by engagement with municipalities and industry, which identified that the initial stages in the process are where issues with incomplete information can delay lodgement and assessment of applications (Scully, 2024b; DPHI, 2024). Therefore, the selection of AI providers targeted AI products that would help prospective applicants by identifying site-specific development requirements and conducting a self-assessment before lodgement of their application to address potential gaps in their documentation (Scully, 2024b). AI products that could aid local government assessment officers to identify non-compliant elements within an application and verify an applicant's documentation were also pursued (DPHI, 2024).

In December 2023, the Department formed the *AI Solutions Panel* (DPHI, 2024; Scully, 2024b), which sought to identify ready-for-market AI products.

The supplier selection process was based on the use cases described in Table 9.1. Three use cases concentrate on helping applicants to prepare better applications, and a fourth identifies the application lodgement and triage process as a potential step in the process to introduce AI products.

The AI Solutions Panel published the supplier list and associated use case(s) that each product can achieve in April 2024 and an updated version in October 2024 (Table 9.2).

The suppliers consist of two established products – Archistar and PropCode – and two emerging chatbot products. It is noted that the MyLot product was added to the supplier list after the first round of grant funding and may be involved in future funding rounds. All products were chosen by the

TABLE 9.1

AI Solutions Panel Use Cases (Source: DPHI, 2024)

Use case	Description
Pathways and requirements finder	Help prospective applicants identify site-specific development requirements.
Material self-assessment health check	Help applicants conduct a self-assessment before lodgement of their development application.
Risk-based triage	Identify non-compliant elements within an application so that the triage process is efficient.
Site-specific documentation support	Provide guidance on site-specific development application documentation.

TABLE 9.2

Suppliers Selected by AI Solutions Panel (Source: DPHI, 2024)

Supplier Name	Use Case(s)	Product Name and Type	Date Listed by Solutions Panel
ADAPTOVATE Consulting Pty Ltd	• Pathways and requirements finder • Material self-assessment health check	DAISY (chatbot)	April 2024
Archistar Pty Ltd	• Pathways and requirements finder	Archistar Platform (GIS, analysis tool, chatbot)	April 2024
PropCode Trading Pty Ltd	• Pathways and requirements finder • Risk-based triage	PropCode CDC (analysis tool, chatbot)	April 2024
Siena Planning Pty Ltd	• Site-specific documentation support	MyLot (chatbot)	October 2024

AI Solutions Panel based on their ability to identify planning pathways and site-specific requirements. These products can identify what types of development are permitted on a chosen piece of land based on current land use zoning and what documentation may be required for assessment, for example, heritage, flood, or bushfire studies.

The expression of interest, selection, and awarding of grant funding was done swiftly between April and July 2024. All 128 NSW municipalities were invited to express interest in participating in the grant funding that would require them to choose a product from the supplier list and conduct a 12-month trial to ascertain if the chosen AI product will expedite and enhance the pre-lodgement/lodgement stage of the development application process (DPHI, 2024). Sixteen municipalities were selected to participate in what became known as the *Early Adopter Programme* within the AI in NSW Planning project (Scully and Hoenig, 2024). Table 9.3 lists the successful local government areas.

The key messaging for the AI in NSW Planning project is to invest in AI to help reduce development assessment timeframes and deliver more housing (Scully, 2024a). This will be done using two approaches. First, providing public-facing AI products that can simplify and streamline the application process by identifying what documentation is required for a site-specific application (Scully, 2024a). Incomplete applications have been identified as a major issue for delivering housing. Hence, improved application quality will reduce development assessment processing timeframes (Scully, 2024a). Second, there is a focus on reducing the administrative workload of planners. Using AI to assist in the assessment of development applications is a critical way the NSW Government can support local governments to speed up development assessment times to better address the housing crisis (Scully and Hoenig, 2024). In all media communications released by the Department, there is a strong emphasis on using AI so local government 'can assess DAs faster, which helps to build more homes' (Scully, 2024a).

TABLE 9.3

Recipients of Early Adopter Grants (Source: Scully and Hoenig, 2024)

Metropolitan Municipalities	Regional Municipalities
Bayside	Cessnock City
Blacktown City	Co-applicants: City of Newcastle, Central Coast, Muswellbrook Shire
Burwood	Eurobodalla Shire
City of Canterbury Bankstown	Lake Macquarie City
Cumberland City	Wagga Wagga City
Hawkesbury City	Wingecarribee Shire
Inner West	
Randwick City	

9.4 Methods

The analysis in this chapter draws on six interviews with local government staff (Metropolitan: two, Regional: four). The Minister for Planning announced the municipalities selected for the early adopter programme (Scully and Hoenig, 2024) but did not provide any contract details. To recruit participants, we emailed an invitation to participate in a research interview to the municipalities' general contact email address and asked for the email to be forwarded to the relevant project manager(s). This approach was successful for 12 of the 16 local governments. Six declined to participate. Semi-structured interviews were conducted online and guided by open-ended questions regarding the AI product chosen and why, the data requirements, and any thoughts on the implications for future management. Interviewees were project managers and IT project officers. The interviews were transcribed and analysed thematically. The analysis was guided by a code sheet that was developed deductively, where interviewees' experiences within the AI Early Adopter programme were identified as themes under the broad research questions. The deductive approach was adopted as the research is grounded in pre-existing theories and ideologies, which guided the coding and theme development (Naeem et al., 2023). To analyse the themes in the data collected, we draw on neoliberal literature. Neoliberalism is considered an ideology based on a set of economic beliefs (Harvey, 2005). To this end, neoliberalism is characterised by a diverse suite of market reforms, including the privatisation of public services, deregulation, unrestricted financial and capital flows, and unfettered access to markets (Neubauer, 2011), which has resulted in a fundamental re-evaluation of how government services are delivered (Jobberns and Guihot, 2024).

9.4.1 Neoliberalism and Urban Planning

Urban planning has not been immune to neoliberal ideology. Reforms or changes to planning systems typically enact an effort to improve economic performance. These changes frequently form part of a broader shift towards neoliberal urban governance models, characterised by reduced state involvement, deregulation, an increased emphasis on market mechanisms and a push for speed and efficiencies, particularly regarding urban development (Gleeson and Low, 2000; McGuirk, 2005). Numerous international examples conclude that there is an almost universal desire for simpler, more efficient, and faster planning systems, which will deliver long-term economic performance (Inch, 2009; Gunn and Hillier, 2014). Urban planning straddles the divide between neoliberal imperatives and broader social and environmental agendas (Inch, 2009). Gurran and Phibbs (2014, p. 234) note that the 'pressure for planning reform tends to arise through political processes' and will 'particularly resonate during downturns in the building cycle, when a new government comes into power and/or when there is a new planning minister'. In the case of the AI in NSW Planning programme, there is a 'housing crisis' (Minns and Scully, 2023), a new government, and a new Planning Minister seeking to leverage AI (Scully, 2024a). Amati (2020) notes that the technical nature of digital planning research has been dominated by attempts to refine the technology without questioning whether it can deliver better planning outcomes. Moreover, the often-quoted benefits of digital planning, such as greater transparency and faster decision-making, cannot always coexist (Piracha et al., 2011; Williamson and McFarland, 2012; Amati, 2020).

9.4.2 Neoliberalism and AI

There is much debate about how neoliberalism and AI intersect, given that both have an emphasis on market-driven systems, privatisation, and competition. Sanchez et al. (2023) argue that the theory and creation of AI is developed within a paradigm of efficiency and neoliberal values. For government services, neoliberalism prioritises efficiency and cost reduction, which has led to a significant shift to the integration of AI-enabled technology to streamline operations and reduce financial costs (Jobberns and Guihot, 2024). This shift has moved some government services from human decision-makers to automated systems, which can process vast amounts of data more efficiently but may also introduce biases and inaccuracies inherent in the data used for training these models (Jobberns and Guihot, 2024). Reynolds and Szerszynski (2012) coined the term *commodification of technology* in reference to technological innovations, such as AI, being transformed into marketable products and services, which then dictate the direction and nature of technological development. Furthermore, Morozov (2023) introduces the concept of *adaptation bias*, where technology is seen to help organisations adapt to deteriorating conditions, for example, inadequate government services, rather than fixing those conditions. Morozov (2023) advocates for a balanced approach that critically assesses the promises of AI, while prioritising the strengthening of public institutions and addressing the root causes of public service issues.

Nonetheless, Yigitcanlar et al. (2024) emphasise several best practice lessons for governments when adopting AI, in particular, conducting pilot projects and implementing robust data governance. First, Yigitcanlar et al. (2024) advise conducting pilot projects is essential for gaining insights into the feasibility and potential impacts of AI. This approach will help to mitigate risks and optimise resource allocation (Yigitcanlar et al., 2024). Second, it is crucial to implement a data governance framework to ensure quality, integrity, and ethical use of data in AI initiatives (Yigitcanlar et al., 2024).

9.5 Results

The following section presents the findings from the interviews with local government staff participating in the early adopter programme within the

AI in NSW Planning project. By examining the experiences and insights, we aim to understand the practical applications of AI in planning processes. The results are categorised into three sections: the AI products that may be used in the development assessment process, the required human labour for assembling planning data sets for AI training, and the possible ramifications for existing management procedures.

9.5.1 What Existing AI Products Can or May Be Used in the Development Assessment Process

The local governments that were successful in their grant bids met with all the AI suppliers that were selected by the solutions panel. This process was a swift series of demonstrations and meetings; 'everything was so quick. That's the thing, everything was so quick' (Regional, 2024). This made the selection of a supplier unusual in that it forced a quick decision that saw at least 75 per cent of the early adopters choose the Archistar product. This was based on the product being capable of '3D generation and precinct mapping, we were actually looking at it across the board' (Metropolitan, 2024), not just the AI capabilities. The strong take-up of Archistar was for two reasons: in regional areas, there are fewer complying development certificates (CDC) issued due to environmental constraints, so these municipalities were restricted to selecting a product that can provide guidance on both CDC and Development Applications (DA). In the NSW jurisdiction, there are two distinct planning pathways: CDC, fast-tracked construction approvals issued by a building surveyor, and DA, merit-assessed planning approvals issued by an assessment officer. For metropolitan Sydney, the decision was based on 'it's a proven product' (Metropolitan, 2024), and the suppliers' experienced staff conducted 'strong product demonstrations and follow up meetings' (Metropolitan, 2024). The metropolitan municipalities were clear that they have high numbers of applications to process and are 'focused on delivery' (Metropolitan, 2024). Municipalities did attend a demonstration for the chatbot product, but most did not select the product for the trial. Some noted it was not supported by our IT department 'because of the set up and maintenance' (Regional, 2024). An interviewee further elaborated:

> Our IT person said there is no way they could support the man hours that would be potentially required and they were actually building that, it wasn't a proven system. You need to be relatively confident that the supplier can do what it says it can.
>
> **(Regional, 2024)**

Conversely, the municipalities that chose the chatbot product were clear that it is being trained on existing public-facing information only:

> The data set that the chatbot is using is limited to the factual council information that can be found on our website.
>
> **(Metropolitan, 2024)**

The announcement of the AI in the NSW Planning programme and subsequent early adopter funding caught both suppliers and local government unprepared. Some suggested that it 'would have been good to give suppliers 6 months to prepare themselves' (Regional, 2024). This was based on two observations. First, the small number of products identified by the solutions panel is emerging in the market and does not include all the required functionality that local governments were looking for. Second, although two products have functioning AI-based chatbots, another 'is trying to retrofit the chatbot into the product' (Regional, 2024) during the trial. One municipality suggested a 12-month lead-in for the trial would have been better:

> It would have been great for them [Department of Planning] to actually arrange a meeting 12 months before they did the funding and actually say hey just give you guys a heads up we are going to have so much funding coming up we'll give them a some time to develop your product before we call for tenders.
>
> **(Regional, 2024)**

The lack of preparation time was also highlighted by the products on the supplier list mostly being developed primarily for internal use by property developers; 'a lot of the things on the screen are because it's for a developer' (Regional, 2024). For instance, the products have tools to explore potential development sites to purchase, 'government and potential mum and dad applicants don't need this' (Regional, 2024). Early notice for the suppliers may have helped them adapt their products, before the trial started, rather than trying to do this during the trial period. There is a significant neoliberal theme to this aspect of the early adopter programme, where it is trying to use existing AI products in the marketplace to fix issues identified in development applications. Moreover, the majority of the existing AI products have been developed for and used by private property developers.

The initial round of the AI early adopter funding highlighted that there may only be a small number of AI products, in Australia at least, that are ready to be used in the development assessment process. Moreover, the products that have been identified either require modifications to be categorised as an AI product or include more functionality that covers a broader range of planning application types to make it worthwhile for local government to trial and implement.

9.5.2 The Human Labour Required to Assemble Specific Planning Data Sets for AI Training Purposes

When asked about the data requirements for the early adopter programme, some interviewees bluntly responded, 'This project is resource hungry' (Regional, 2024). There are two distinct data-related pathways for local government based on the type of product they chose. For the established analysis tools, the AI suppliers already have compiled databases with planning data; 'They have their own data. We don't give them anything' (Regional, 2024), with most of the data sourced from the Department's open data repository (DPHI, n.d.). Hence, the human labour required for this pathway is data validation between legacy land information systems and the trial AI product. This highlights a significant contradiction between the dominant narrative of improving efficiency to speed up development assessment times (Scully and Hoenig, 2024) and the reality of data validation that requires staff to manually enter property addresses into the trial product interface and check against existing systems; 'everyone is getting people to go through and do all of these data checks' (Regional, 2024; Metropolitan, 2024). This process resulted in conversations between municipalities about data validation issues; 'some of the other councils have been saying there's been a lot of data issues identified' (Metropolitan, 2024). To reduce human labour and speed up the data validation process, some municipalities requested data dumps from the suppliers to semi-automate data validation:

> [I]n reality I don't want to test their product as much but I want to test the data. . . . I wanna test they have got their data mapped correctly.
>
> **(Regional, 2024)**

Although some municipalities are pursuing data validation that requires significant human resources, some metropolitan municipalities with high volumes of development applications are relying on the accuracy of the supplier's data:

> Our AI experience at this point, in simple terms, is that we have purchased a largely off the shelf product using a grant . . . the data in this platform is collected and maintained by the vendor, so we haven't had involvement in that process.
>
> **(Metropolitan, 2024)**

For the municipalities that chose a chatbot product, they are taking a low-risk approach by restricting the training data to information that is currently available on their websites. Local governments have a large amount of planning information outlining the steps involved and required documentation to support planning applications on their websites in a mix of web pages and PDF documents. Using the public information would potentially cover the

Department's chatbot use cases to help prospective applicants identify development requirements and aid in self-assessment before lodgement:

> We believe we can provide use case 1 and 2 with mostly publicly available information.
>
> **(Regional, 2024)**

The chatbot supplier also advised that any data used for training purposes would 'undergo personal information scrubbing and redacting to ensure compliance with council standards' (Metropolitan, 2024), but the interviewee noted it 'doesn't matter as we are only providing publicly available information' (Regional, 2024). The chatbot supplier advised that data would be securely stored, and the municipalities' IT team could undertake any security checks they deemed necessary:

> They said any data we provide will be stored in a data centre with high levels of security. They suggested councils are welcome to perform penetration testing as required.
>
> **(Regional, 2024)**

A relevant concern for local government is the currency of data used by a chatbot and administrative processes to refresh training data. This is particularly relevant to planning where legislative changes routinely alter processes and material requirements for both the CDC and DA pathways. The chatbot supplier advised that they have change management processes that will cover this eventuation with minimal manual labour required by staff:

> The supplier said they can take the existing council documentation as the source files. When they are updated through council business processes, the index for their database will be updated without any extra administrative work from the council.
>
> **(Regional, 2024)**

Finally, municipalities raised the concern that the chatbot may suffer from hallucinations. The term hallucinations refers to the tendency for Large Language Models (LLM) to produce incorrect or nonsensical responses (Townsen Hicks et al., 2024) in both technical documentation (OpenAI, 2023) and the popular media (Weise and Metz, 2023). When a chatbot misinterprets a user's query or generates inaccurate information, the consequences can range from minor inconveniences to significant legal action (Migliorini, 2024), particularly in urban planning, where an applicant may rely upon information provided by the chatbot for a future application (Migliorini, 2024). To address hallucinations, 'They [supplier] have been talking about reducing the AI temperature to limit hallucinations' (Regional, 2024) and 'using succinct and explicit data will reduce the probability for AI hallucinations' (Regional, 2024). The temperature concept is a parameter that can be adjusted to control the randomness and creativity of a chatbot response; the lower the temperature, the more predictable and conservative the response (Prakash, 2025).

The interviews highlighted the resource-intensive nature of data validation, requiring significant human labour to ensure accuracy and compatibility with legacy systems. In this sense, the AI products have positioned themselves as products and services that are equipped with datasets sourced from government repositories and marketed as low-maintenance solutions. This is an example of a neoliberal process that transforms data traditionally held by local government into marketable products and services and will lead some municipalities into greater reliance on the AI supplier for data maintenance, which undermines their control over data accuracy (Reynolds and Szerszynski, 2012). Moreover, municipalities are seeking a low-risk approach by relying on publicly available information for training chatbots, although they still raise concerns about data quality and the risk of hallucinations. There was also an emphasis on the importance of keeping training data current due to legislative changes that affect planning processes, while AI suppliers indicated they have change management processes to alleviate administrative burdens. Overall, the discussion about assembling planning datasets for AI highlighted the complexities of adopting AI technologies in urban planning and stressed the need for effective data management and collaboration with suppliers to ensure accuracy.

9.5.3 The Potential Implications for Existing Management Processes

Future management of the AI products implemented will be progressively determined by how they are used. Different internal users complicate this situation – strategic planning teams who work on rezoning and precinct planning and assessment officers who assess and determine development applications. Then there are the needs of the external users, ranging from homeowners to property developers. All these users have different requirements:

> We look at what our internal guys, what they actually use it for in our strategic planning area, about future rezonings and things like that. We've got two different uses; a customer or rate payer user and we've got internal use. I think we definitely have to balance those. If I'm looking at assessment officers, they would probably like a hybrid.
>
> **(Regional, 2024)**

Some municipalities advised they are pursuing a *soft launch* strategy, where the AI product will be implemented in a production environment for a restricted audience to measure the product take up in the first instance:

> We could potentially do a soft launch because I really want to see the take up. Because the take up of it will be what guides us, if we get more internal use than external then its potential the wrong tool for us. . . . We may need to run two systems, one for the customer and one for staff.
>
> **(Regional, 2024)**

This goes to the original intent of the AI early adopter programme is this project about 'trying to increase the quality of DA applications' or just make 'it easier for mum/dad' (Regional, 2024) to find planning information. This fundamental question will become clearer as the product usage is monitored and analysed:

> We are focused on mapping the customer's possible journeys using the chatbot. Then our effort will be more about the continuous improvement going forward to improve the answers delivered by the chatbot.
>
> **(Regional, 2024)**

Conversely, others advised that they have prepared staff engagement strategies: 'Ensuring staff buy-in is crucial for operational success' (Regional, 2024) and change management programmes:

> We are implementing a change management strategy and staff engagement plan. This is mainly using workshops, training sessions and regular updates to involve staff. Staff seem genuinely interested in how the chatbot works and what data it uses.
>
> **(Regional, 2024)**

Although interviewees discussed different approaches to managing the introduction of AI products, implementation of technology is not solely about technology. There will be some level of cultural and business process change for those participating in the early adopter programme. Ongoing monitoring of usage will also determine the impacts on existing processes and usefulness for staff, industry experts, and the community.

9.6 Discussion

The objectives of this chapter were to explore existing AI products that can be implemented in urban planning processes, assess the labour required to assemble specific planning datasets, and consider potential implications for existing management processes. These questions have been explored within the context of an AI early adopter programme in the NSW planning system.

The use of technology has been a component of an ongoing narrative to create simpler, more efficient, and faster planning systems (Williamson and McFarland, 2012; Amati, 2020). The faster and more efficient planning system rhetoric has been amplified by the need for the NSW Planning system to address the current 'housing crisis' (Minns and Scully, 2023) by a government keen to leverage AI (Scully, 2024a). There are strong neoliberal narratives of speed and efficiency in the NSW Government's communications that repeatedly state, 'AI will accelerate the planning process' (Scully and Hoenig, 2024). The results reveal that only a small number of AI products in Australia can be readily used in the development assessment process in local governments, and they require modifications to make it worthwhile for local governments to implement them. Given the importance of accurate data for AI products, the AI suppliers are focused on data quality and the administrative burden of keeping data up to date. Meanwhile, local government is keen to explore low-risk implementations that only utilise publicly available data. To successfully implement their chosen AI product, most are acutely aware of managing change in their organisation and monitoring usage. It is acknowledged that this case study focuses on an early adopter programme, but early findings suggest that AI will not enable a simpler, faster planning system until usage by different stakeholders has been evaluated over the medium term. However, the early adopter programme will provide valuable lessons that will inform future implementations.

The implementation of AI products in local government is a multifaceted challenge that extends beyond technology integration. As highlighted earlier, the progressive management of AI products will be determined by their specific use cases for different internal and external stakeholders. These stakeholders represent diverse internal functions such as strategic planning and development assessment, and external users ranging from homeowners to property developers – each poses unique requirements and expectations, necessitating a careful approach to the deployment and operation of AI products. The management of various stakeholders reflects the findings of Desouza et al. (2020), that local government projects funded by taxpayers must navigate a complex maze of economic, social, and legal factors. One significant approach among the early adopters is the potential benefit of a soft launch strategy. This approach introduces the AI product to a limited audience with minimal communication and allows municipalities to gauge initial uptake and identify areas requiring adjustment. Such a strategy is particularly valuable in determining whether AI products will serve internal or external users, guiding further investment and development accordingly.

A key insight from the interviews was that the early adopter programme caught both local government and AI suppliers unprepared when it was announced and then progressed through a rapid expression of interest phase. While the grant funding process has been more successfully negotiated by established AI suppliers, there has been a significant burden for both municipalities and the AI suppliers. For municipalities, there has been an intense period of administrative burden to prepare for the implementation of their chosen AI product, as well as significant human labour to ensure compliance with existing data. This situation contradicts the dominant narratives of the early adopter programme that the market has off-the-shelf products ready for implementation in the development assessment process, and they will modernise 'the NSW planning system by making it more efficient' (Scully, 2024b). For the AI suppliers, some were required to retrofit AI functions to conform to the scope of the early adopter programme. The neoliberal era is often characterised by the promise of a high-tech, knowledge-based economy, but Reynolds and Szerszynski (2012) argue it has also led to technological stagnation. AI suppliers using early adopter programme funding to update their products to meet the programme's entry requirements suggest that these AI products are being developed more like speculative commodities linked to venture capital and government funding opportunities, rather than mature technologies. For Reynolds and Szerszynski (2012), this situation often sees speculative gains rather than substantial improvements in productivity.

Conversely, the AI products chosen by the early adopter municipalities are also potentially setting the AI direction for local government in two distinct ways. First, although local government legally holds land and planning information that planning activities rely upon, all the AI products listed by the solutions panel have compiled their own datasets, which concurs with Reynolds and Szerszynski's (2012) commodification of technology concept that sees marketable AI products begin to influence the direction and nature of their use. Second, there is a touch of irony in the use of existing AI products in the marketplace to fix issues identified in development applications from external applicants. Some of these AI products are being used by property developers, and if they were a proven product, the quality of development applications should have already improved. It would be wise to pursue Morozov's (2023) balanced approach of critically assessing the usefulness of existing AI products, while continuing to investigate the root cause of claims of inefficiencies in the development assessment process. In line with Yigitcanlar et al. (2024), the early adopter programme is conducting pilot projects to gain insights. However, data governance is more challenging, given the approach being taken by the AI suppliers.

9.7 Conclusions

The deployment of the early adopter programme in local government marks the next phase in the adoption of advanced technologies in urban and regional planning, although the neoliberal narratives of using technology to speed up the planning system and making it more efficient remain unchanged. As discussed, the multifaceted nature of the early adopter programme encompasses technological, cultural, and procedural dimensions, all of which must be closely scrutinised and managed. Ongoing monitoring and analysis will be crucial in evaluating the impact of these technologies on existing processes and their overall utility for various stakeholders. The experiences of early adopters will provide valuable lessons, paving the way for more informed and effective implementations in the future. This may lead to local governments harnessing the full potential of AI to improve planning service delivery.

References

Amati, M. (2020). 'Virtual borders in the online world: How e-planning helps and hinders communicative planning practice', in: W. Steele, T. Alizadeh, L. Eslami-Andargoli and S. Serrao-Neumann, eds. *Planning across borders in a climate of change*. Routledge, Oxford, pp. 205–217.

Australian Government. (2022a). *National housing accord 2022*. Available at: https://ministers.treasury.gov.au/sites/ministers.treasury.gov.au/files/2022-10/national-housing-accord-2022.pdf [Accessed 5 October 2024].

Australian Government. (2022b). *Improving housing supply and affordability: The Australian government's commitment to deliver more homes for Australians*. Available at: https://archive.budget.gov.au/2022-23-october/factsheets/download/factsheet_housing.pdf [Accessed 5 October 2024].

Batty, M. (2023). 'The emergence and evolution of urban AI', *AI & Society*, 38(3), pp. 1045–1048.

Bright, J., Ganesh, B. and Seidelin, C. (2019). *Data science for local government*. University of Oxford, Oxford.

Cugurullo, F. (2021). *Frankenstein urbanism: Eco, smart and autonomous cities, artificial intelligence and the end of the city*. Routledge, Oxford.

Daniel, C. and Pettit, C. (2021). 'Digital disruption and planning – use of data and digital technology by professional planners, and perceptions of change to planning work', *Australian Planner*, 57(1), pp. 50–64.

Daniel, C., Wentz, E., Hurtado, P., Yang, W. and Pettit, C. (2023). 'Digital technology use and future expectations: A multinational survey of professional planners', *Journal of the American Planning Association*, 90(3), pp. 405–420.

Department of Planning, Housing and Infrastructure (DPHI). (2024). *Artificial intelligence solutions panel supplier list*. Available at: https://www.planning.nsw.gov.au/sites/default/files/2024-04/ai-solutions-panel-supplier-list-april.pdf [Accessed 5 November 2024].

Department of Planning, Housing and Infrastructure (DPHI). (2025). *Housing targets*. Available at: https://www.planning.nsw.gov.au/policy-and-legislation/housing/housing-targets [Accessed 12 January 2025].

Department of Planning, Housing and Infrastructure (DPHI). (n.d.). *Datasets*. Available at: https://www.planningportal.nsw.gov.au/opendata/dataset/ [Accessed 5 November 2024].

Desouza, K., Dawson, G. and Chenok, D. (2020). 'Designing, developing, and deploying artificial intelligence systems: Lessons from and for the public sector', *Business Horizons*, 63, pp. 205–213.
Fu, X. (2024). 'Natural language processing in urban planning: A research agenda', *Journal of Planning Literature*, 39(3), pp. 395–407.
Fu, X., Brinkley, C., Sanchez, T. and Li, C. (2024). 'Text mining public feedback on urban densification plan change in Hamilton, New Zealand', *Environment and Planning B: Urban Analysis and City Science*. https://doi.org/10.1177/23998083241272097
Gleeson, B. and Low, N. (2000). 'Unfinished business: Neoliberal planning reform in Australia', *Urban Policy and Research*, 18(1), pp. 7–28.
Gunn, S. and Hillier, J. (2014). 'When certainty is interpreted as risk: An analysis of tensions relating to spatial planning reform in England', *Planning Practice and Research*, 29(1), pp. 56–74.
Gurran, N. and Phibbs, P. (2014). 'Evidence-free zone? Examining claims about planning performance and reform in New South Wales', *Australian Planner*, 51(3), pp. 232–242.
Harvey, D. (2005). *A brief history of neoliberalism*. Oxford University Press, Oxford.
Hasan, F., Jayasinghe, A. and Sathsarana, S. (2023). 'Specialized urban planning chatbot: A participatory approach for evaluating efficiency', *Bhúmi Planning Research Journal*, 10(2), pp. 3–16.
He, W. and Chen, M. (2024). 'Advancing urban life: A systematic review of emerging technologies and artificial intelligence in urban design and planning', *Buildings*, 14, p. 835.
Inch, A. (2009). 'Planning at the crossroads again: Re-evaluating street-level regulation of the contradictions in new labour's planning reforms', *Planning Practice and Research*, 24(1), pp. 83–101.
Jobberns, J. and Guihot, M. (2024). 'Digital governance and neoliberalism: The evolution of machine learning in Australian public policy', *Law, Technology and Humans*, 6(2), pp. 1–24.
Makasi, T., Nili, A., Desouza, K. and Tate, M. (2020). 'Chatbot-mediated public service delivery', *First Monday*, 25(12), pp. 1–22.
McGuirk, P. (2005). 'Neoliberalist planning? Re-thinking and re-casting Sydney's metropolitan planning', *Geographical Research*, 43(1), pp. 59–70.
Metropolitan. (2024). *Metropolitan municipality interviews with Wayne Williamson*. December 2024, online.
Migliorini, S. (2024). 'More than words: A legal approach to the risks of commercial chatbots powered by generative artificial intelligence', *European Journal of Risk Regulation*, 15(3), pp. 719–736.
Minns, C. and Scully, P. (2023). *A shared responsibility: The plan to begin addressing the housing crisis in NSW*. NSW Government, Sydney.
Morozov, E. (2023). *AI, neoliberalism's hip friend*. Voxeurop. Available at: https://voxeurop.eu/en/evgeny-morozov-ai-neoliberalism-hip-friend/ [Accessed 18 October 2024].
Naeem, M., Ozuem, W., Howell, K. and Ranfagni, S. (2023). 'A step-by-step process of thematic analysis to develop a conceptual model in qualitative research', *International Journal of Qualitative Methods*, 22, pp. 1–18.
Neubauer, R. (2011). 'Neoliberalism in the information age, or vice versa? Global citizenship, technology, and hegemonic ideology', *tripleC*, 9(2), pp. 195–230.
OpenAI. (2023). *GPT-4 technical report*. ArXiv Preprint arXiv:2303.08774v3.

Othengrafen, F., Sievers, L. and Reinecke, E. (2025). 'From vision to reality: The use of artificial intelligence in different urban planning phases', *Urban Planning*, 10, pp. 1–18.

Piracha, A., Williamson, W. and Parolin, B. (2011). 'e-Planning evolutions in Australia: A New South Wales perspective', *12th international conference on computers in urban planning and urban management proceedings*, 5–8 July. University of Calgary, Lake Louise, Canada.

Potts, R. and Webb, B. (2023). 'Digital planning practices: Benchmarking planners' use of information and communication technologies (ICTs)', *Planning Practice & Research*, 38(4), pp. 520–540.

Prakash, P. (2025). *Understanding temperature in AI: Balancing creativity and precision*. Medium. Available at: https://medium.com/@alokpand885148/understanding-temperature-in-ai-balancing-creativity-and-precision-ddd192690792 [Accessed 27 May 2025].

Regional. (2024). *Regional municipality interviews with Wayne Williamson*. November–December 2024, online.

Reynolds, L. and Szerszynski, B. (2012). 'Neoliberalism and technology: Perpetual innovation or perpetual crisis?', in: L. Pellizzoni and M. Farnham, eds. *Neoliberalism and technoscience: Critical assessments*. Ashgate, Surrey, pp. 27–46.

Ruming, K. and Goodman, R. (2016). 'Planning system reform and economic development: Unpacking policy rhetoric and trajectories in Victoria and New South Wales', *Built Environment*, 42(1), pp. 72–89.

Sanchez, T. (2023). 'Planning on the verge of AI, or AI on the verge of planning', *Urban Science*, 7(3), pp. 1–13.

Sanchez, T., Shumway, H., Gordner, T. and Lim, T. (2023). 'The prospects of artificial intelligence in urban planning', *International Journal of Urban Sciences*, 27(2), pp. 179–194.

Sarker, I. (2022). 'AI based modeling: Techniques, applications and research issues towards automation, intelligent and smart systems', *SN Computer Science*, 3, p. 158.

Scully, P. (2024a). *NSW planning wants AI product solutions to make faster development assessments*. NSW Government, Sydney.

Scully, P. (2024b). *The NSW government is bringing planning into the 21st century*. NSW Government, Sydney.

Scully, P. and Hoenig, R. (2024). *Artificial intelligence trial to speed up local planning systems*. NSW Government, Sydney.

Selwyn, N. and Gallo-Cordoba, B. (2021). 'Australian public understandings of artificial intelligence', *AI & Society*, 37, pp. 1645–1662.

Senadheera, S., Yigitcanlar, T., Desouza, K. C., Mossberger, K., Corchado, J., Mehmood, R., Yi Man Li, R. and Cheong, P. (2024). 'Understanding chatbot adoption in local governments: A review and framework', *Journal of Urban Technology*. https://doi.org/10.1080/10630732.2023.2297665

Son, T., Weedon, Z., Yigitcanlar, T., Sanchez, T., Corchado, J. and Mehmood, R. (2023). 'Algorithmic urban planning for smart and sustainable development: Systematic review of the literature', *Sustainable Cities and Society*, 94, p. 104562.

Townsen Hicks, M., Humphries, J. and Slater, J. (2024). 'ChatGPT is bullshit', *Ethics and Information Technology*, 26(38), pp. 1–10.

Weise, K. and Metz, C. (2023). When AI chatbots hallucinate. *New York Times*. Available at: https://www.nytimes.com/2023/05/01/business/ai-chatbots-hallucination.html [Accessed 10 January 2025].

Williamson, W. and McFarland, P. (2012). 'Investigating the role of electronic planning within planning reform', *International Journal of E-Planning Research*, 1(2), pp. 65–78.

Yigitcanlar, T., David, A., Li, W., Fookes, C., Elias Bibri, S. and Ye, X. (2024). 'Unlocking artificial intelligence adoption in local governments: Best practice lessons from real-world implementations', *Smart Cities*, 7(4), pp. 1576–1625.

10

AI and the Governance of Risk: Fantasies, Safety, and Situated Futures

Elham Bahmanteymouri and Mohsen Mohammadzadeh

10.1 Introduction

Artificial intelligence (AI) is increasingly positioned at the centre of contemporary governance debates, celebrated for its capacity to generate efficiencies, reduce uncertainty, and provide technical solutions to complex economic and social challenges. Yet its adoption in urban governance and planning[1] raises profound questions about how power, legitimacy, and authority are being reshaped. How do planners, policymakers, and private actors interpret and negotiate the risks and opportunities of AI? What forms of knowledge and authority are privileged when algorithms are embedded in decision-making? What factors shape its legitimacy – and what should shape it? And how might these dynamics reveal both the fantasies of optimisation that sustain technological enthusiasm and the situated possibilities for more democratic and context-specific forms of AI governance?

In other chapters of this section, Bahmanteymouri (2026) conceptualises AI as a *fantasy of the Big Other*, sustaining capitalist logics of accumulation and control while masking the structural incompleteness of the system, the *Real*. Mohammadzadeh (2026) examines how urban AI is represented symbolically and imaginatively, revealing the repression of the *Real* in planning discourse and the ways in which governance is staged through ideological narratives. Together, these contributions show that AI cannot be understood as a neutral technical apparatus but as a site where ideology, fantasy, and power intersect.

This chapter builds on those insights and grounds them in empirical evidence. Drawing on a Lloyd's Register Foundation–funded project on AI governance in Aotearoa New Zealand[2] it presents selected findings from surveys and interviews with planners, policymakers, and AI service providers across the country's major cities. In doing so, it bridges theory and practice, examining how the fantasies that sustain AI's appeal are reflected in professional discourses of risk and safety, and how these discourses

DOI: 10.1201/9781003480167-12

shape the possibilities for using AI ethically and effectively in planning and governance.

Our research reveals that awareness of AI in planning and urban governance is currently low, professional preparedness limited, and institutional trust fragile. Survey data show that only around one-third of respondents were aware of AI-based tools used in planning (Figure 10.1), while confidence in AI's ability to interpret zoning and planning laws was weak: more than half rated themselves 'not at all' or 'slightly' confident, and fewer than one in five expressed higher levels of confidence (Figure 10.2). At the same time, participants conveyed cautious optimism about AI's potential to improve efficiency, forecasting, and data analysis yet voiced persistent concerns about bias, transparency, data sovereignty, and cultural alignment. These findings highlight the contradictions of contemporary AI governance: enthusiasm for its promises coexists with scepticism about its neutrality and distrust in the institutions responsible for its oversight.

In framing these results, we argue that discourses of risk and safety operate ideologically, sustaining the fantasies that render AI attractive to policymakers and planners. As Žižek (1989) repeatedly emphasises, systems

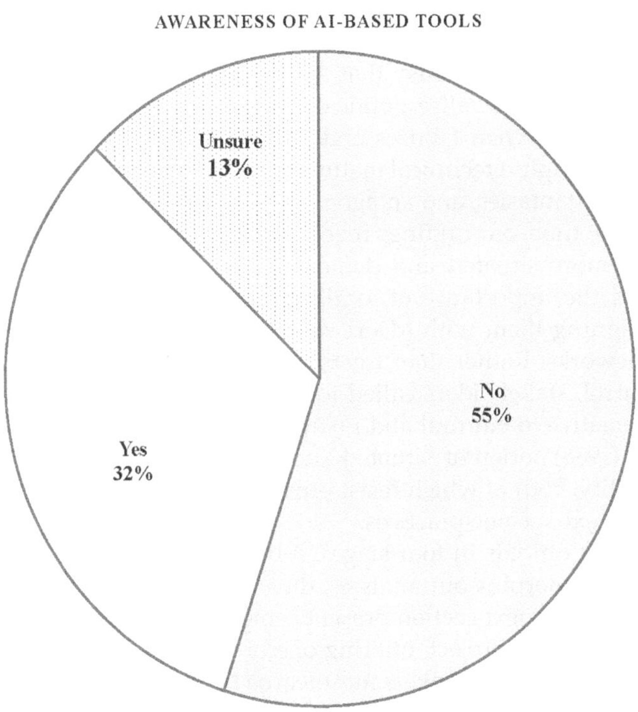

FIGURE 10.1
Awareness of AI-based tools (by authors).

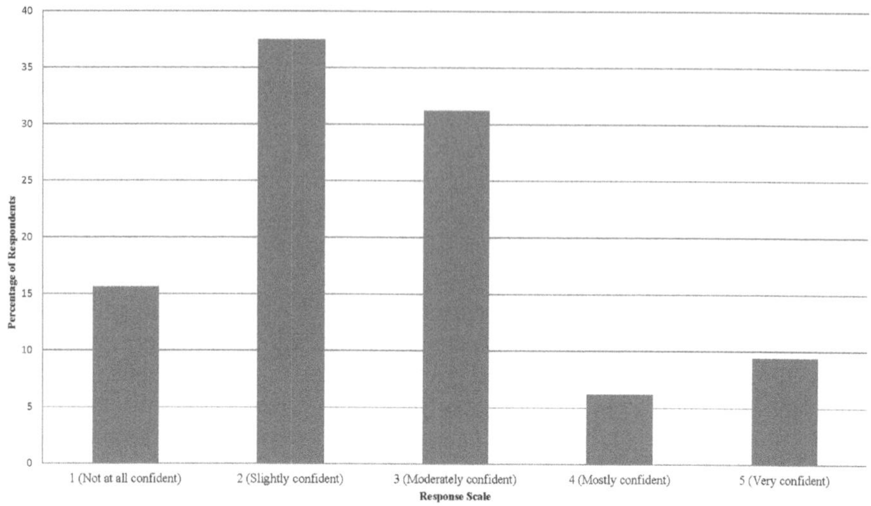

FIGURE 10.2
Confidence in AI interpreting zoning and planning laws (by authors).

persist not because they function effectively, but because they are sustained through enjoyment, through the fantasies that keep subjects invested even in the face of failure. The fantasy that AI can discipline uncertainty, optimise performance, and neutralise political antagonism maintains investment in its adoption even when failures and risks are evident. Risk governance is therefore not simply a technical matter of safeguards but a political terrain in which desires, fantasies, and antagonisms are continually negotiated.

At the same time, our findings reveal opportunities for rethinking AI governance in more situated and democratic terms. Respondents repeatedly emphasised the importance of localising AI systems to the New Zealand context, aligning them with Māori values, Treaty obligations, and national legal frameworks. Rather than treating AI as a universal or totalising system of control, stakeholders called for tools that are accountable, transparent, and sensitive to cultural and institutional contexts. This resonates with Haraway's (1988) notion of 'situated knowledges' and Barad's (2007) account of relationality, both of which resist universalising claims and highlight the need for context-specific practices.

This chapter unfolds in four stages. It begins by outlining the theoretical framing that underpins our analysis, then turns to the research design and methodology. The next section presents empirical findings from the Lloyd's Register Foundation project, offering one of the first systematic accounts of how planners and policymakers in Aotearoa New Zealand perceive the risks and safety of AI. The discussion interprets these findings through the lens of fantasy, risk, and institutional politics, exposing the contradictions and contested meanings of safety within digital planning and AI governance. Finally, the chapter concludes by advancing its central argument: that AI governance is a site of political struggle where the task is not to eliminate uncertainty but to embrace contingency, foster democratic participation, and imagine situated futures that resist the reduction of life to operational efficiency.

10.2 Theoretical Framing

Understanding AI governance and its application in planning requires moving beyond the view of algorithms as neutral instruments of efficiency. AI systems are embedded in symbolic, ideological, and institutional frameworks that shape both their design and reception. As other chapters in this volume have shown, AI is not merely computational but a site where fantasies of order, optimisation, and neutrality intersect with political and economic structures. In this section, we weave together insights from our contributions (Bahmanteymouri, 2026; Mohammadzadeh, 2026; Morreale, 2026) through Lacanian critical theory, post-Marxist discourse, and science and technology studies (STS) to develop a framework for interpreting the empirical findings presented later.

Bahmanteymouri (2026) conceptualises AI as a *fantasy of the Big Other*: a symbolic authority that promises coherence, order, and control within capitalist society. Capitalism presents itself as the natural order, structuring desires for growth, profit, and innovation while disavowing its contradictions and the fundamental lack – the Real – at the heart of its fantasy of perfect market operation. This fantasy of perfection is, as Cassidy (2010) shows, central to the myth of self-correcting markets, while Wolff (2013) aptly calls 'pure' capitalism a fantasy that exists only in ideology or as a utopian theory, never in practice. Within this frame, AI embodies fantasies of control and neutrality, sustaining the belief that uncertainty can be eliminated and the social made fully calculable. Discourses of risk and safety must therefore be read as ideological projections: they imagine the possibility of perfect technical governance in which failures are anticipated and eliminated, even though such completeness is structurally impossible. This contradiction reveals how fantasies of the Big Other obscure the Real, the structural limits of governance that sustain expectations of technical perfection.

Mohammadzadeh (2026) examines how AI in planning is represented symbolically and imaginatively, showing how the Real is repressed in governance discourse. The symbolic order – law, professional norms, regulatory language – frames AI as rational and technical, while the imaginary dimension reflects collective desires for efficiency and foresight. What is excluded in both is the Real: the conflicts, contradictions, and structural antagonisms that generate economic deficiencies in the first place. AI cannot magically resolve these issues, yet discourses of risk and safety legitimise technocratic authority by presenting them as matters of technical calculation rather than political struggle. This logic reveals how fantasies obscure the Real, allowing structural contradictions to be misrecognised as technical shortcomings.

Morreale (2026) extends this critique by showing how AI systems depend on processes of primitive accumulation and hidden data labour. Training datasets are built from human contributions that are often uncompensated, invisible, or extracted without consent, exemplifying the exploitative logics of digital capitalism. These practices turn creativity, attention, and affect into surplus value, embedding dispossession at the core of AI infrastructures. Fantasies of control and neutrality therefore rest on material exploitation as much as on discourse. Yet, as our findings indicate, professionals rarely acknowledged this dimension. Survey respondents emphasised risks of bias, transparency, and data sovereignty but said little about the labour conditions underpinning AI systems. This silence reflects another form of repression: visible risks are debated, while the exploitative foundations of dataset production remain obscured. Fantasies of control and neutrality therefore rest on material exploitation as much as on discourse, an entanglement that sustains the illusion of safe and neutral governance.

Following Laclau and Mouffe (1985), we treat AI governance as a hegemonic project: fantasies of safety and neutrality temporarily stabilise antagonisms, even as contradictions persist. Within this frame, critical approaches such as Feenberg's (2002, 2017) highlight how technologies, far from being autonomous, are socially shaped and can be redirected through *democratic intervention* and *participatory design*. The key challenge, therefore, is to ensure that AI does not bypass or weaken democratic processes but instead strengthens accountability and collective decision-making.

Beck's (1992) theory of the *risk society* extends this argument by showing how struggles over governance are also struggles over how risks are defined. Modern societies generate systemic risks as a by-product of their own development, producing uncertainties that institutions struggle to control. AI exemplifies this dynamic; it is framed simultaneously as a solution to risk and as a risk in itself.

Critical feminist and posthumanist perspectives underscore the importance of situatedness. Haraway's (1988) notion of *situated knowledges* and Barad's (2007) relational ontology challenge universalist claims, insisting that technologies must be understood within context. From this perspective, localisation, culturally grounded obligations, and Indigenous principle – such as Māori data sovereignty – become central. In this framing, safe AI is not simply transparent or efficient in the abstract but aligned with specific cultural, legal, and institutional contexts.

In synthesis, these perspectives show how fantasies, symbolic representations, and exploitative practices shape professional understandings of AI's risks and promises. They clarify the central tensions of AI governance, optimism alongside mistrust, ethical commitment alongside low preparedness, and localisation within globalised systems, framing risk and safety not as technical matters but as contested political constructs.

10.3 Research Design and Methods

The study employed a mixed-methods design to capture how professionals in Aotearoa New Zealand perceive AI's promises and perils in planning and governance.

The first phase involved an online survey of planners, policymakers, and AI service providers in Auckland, Wellington, Christchurch, and Hamilton, generating 67 responses. Questions explored awareness, preparedness, and confidence in AI, as well as ethical and institutional concerns such as data privacy, bias, transparency, trust, job displacement, and alignment with *Te Tiriti o Waitangi*. Recruitment drew on professional networks, including the New Zealand Planning Institute (NZPI), council distribution lists, and targeted outreach across sectors.

The second phase comprised 29 semi-structured interviews with planners, policymakers, council officers, and service providers from public, private, and community sectors. These interviews probed more deeply into themes from the survey, focusing on risks and opportunities, institutional readiness, ethical principles, and expectations around localisation and cultural legitimacy. Survey data were analysed using descriptive statistics in Excel to identify levels of awareness, preparedness, and trust, among other factors such as perceived risks and concerns. These results also provide a basis for further quantitative exploration, such as correlations between awareness, confidence, and institutional trust. Interview transcripts were examined through discourse analysis, focusing on how risk and safety were articulated and what these framings revealed about deeper ideological and political logics.

The survey and interviews were structured around six key areas that form the basis of the analysis presented in the following section: (1) practical encounters with AI tools; (2) risks and opportunities as ideological constructs; (3) institutional capacity, trust, and public–private antagonisms; (4) democratic and ethical governance: accountability, fairness, and the limits of practice; (5) localisation, Te Tiriti o Waitangi, and cultural legitimacy; and (6) AI education, literacy and training. These themes generated rich narratives that provided valuable insights derived from the analysis of the collected data.

10.4 Analysis and Findings

10.4.1 Practical Encounters with AI Tools: Between Neutrality and Limits

This study revealed uneven awareness of AI applications in urban planning among New Zealand professionals. Only 34 per cent of survey respondents reported being aware of AI tools in use, while a majority (57 per cent) indicated they were not aware, and a further 9 per cent were unsure (Figure 10.1). Despite the prominence of AI in policy and media debates, its penetration into professional practice remains partial and fragmented.

Interviews provided a more nuanced picture. Many participants described using AI tools such as ChatGPT or Microsoft Copilot for drafting emails, preparing documents, or exploring ideas. These tools were generally regarded as helpful assistants that could facilitate routine tasks and improve efficiency. Many senior planners and managers described AI in similar terms, referring to it as a 'smart intern' that could assist in organising tasks, summarising information, and managing workflows. Rather than viewing AI as an autonomous decision-maker, they saw it as an intelligent assistant capable of speeding up administrative and analytical processes, enhancing productivity while leaving professional judgement intact.

At the same time, interviewees stressed that such applications could not capture the complexity of planning and policymaking. As one planner explained, 'AI can save time with the paperwork, but it won't make the hard calls – planning is still about judgement and negotiation'. This illustrates an important distinction; AI is welcomed as a supportive tool but not as a substitute for professional expertise.

Interviews and survey responses indicated that workshops and briefings could help close existing gaps by introducing planners and policymakers to more systematic evidence about risks and safety. Several council representatives remarked that participating in the survey and interviews themselves provided a 'first real opportunity' to reflect on AI beyond informal conversations. The shift from niche awareness to a recognised governance concern illustrates how knowledge mobilisation can be as important as technical literacy in shaping preparedness.

Theoretically, these findings illustrate how fantasy structures professional engagement with AI. On the one hand, planners and policymakers enjoy using AI as an assistant – a tool that makes paperwork faster or drafting easier. On the other hand, they firmly reject the idea that AI could resolve the deeper complexities of planning and governance. This coexistence of everyday reliance and strategic distancing shows how ideology works: AI is embraced for its conveniences while its structural conditions – exploitative data labour, institutional contradictions, and the political stakes of governance – remain out of sight. Fantasies of control and neutrality thus persist, enabling professionals to take pleasure in AI's surface efficiencies without confronting the antagonisms that define its role in governance.

10.4.2 Risks and Opportunities as Ideological Constructs

While much of the discourse around AI focused on risks, participants also identified several perceived opportunities. In the survey, the highest-rated opportunity was data analysis (mean = 3.54), followed by cost savings (3.2) and decision-support capabilities (3.1). Bias reduction, however, scored lower (2.6), suggesting limited awareness of how ethical design might be integrated into AI systems (Figure 10.3). Interviews reinforced these themes: planners described AI as useful for forecasting infrastructure demand, improving responsiveness in consent processes, and supporting real-time decision-making. As one council officer observed, 'AI can help us keep up with data in ways we never could manually – it's about efficiency and responsiveness'.

Yet these perceived opportunities were consistently articulated alongside concerns. Bias, automation risks, privacy, and transparency all scored highly as risks (mean > 3.7), and job displacement emerged as a recurring fear. As Figure 10.3 illustrates, concerns about bias, security, and transparency consistently outscored perceived opportunities, even as professionals emphasised efficiency gains and decision support, a pattern reflecting the contradictory coexistence of technocratic optimism and scepticism.

These tensions were particularly visible across sectors. Private-sector participants tended to emphasise efficiency, cost savings, and the risks of *non-adoption*, framing government caution as a barrier. Public-sector actors, by contrast, stressed accountability, safeguards, and the dangers of premature adoption, while community added a further dimension by emphasising cultural legitimacy and alignment with *Te Tiriti o Waitangi*.

From a theoretical perspective, these findings reveal what might be called *technocratic optimism*. Professionals enjoy the fantasy that AI can optimise planning, even while distrusting its institutional governance. This enjoyment

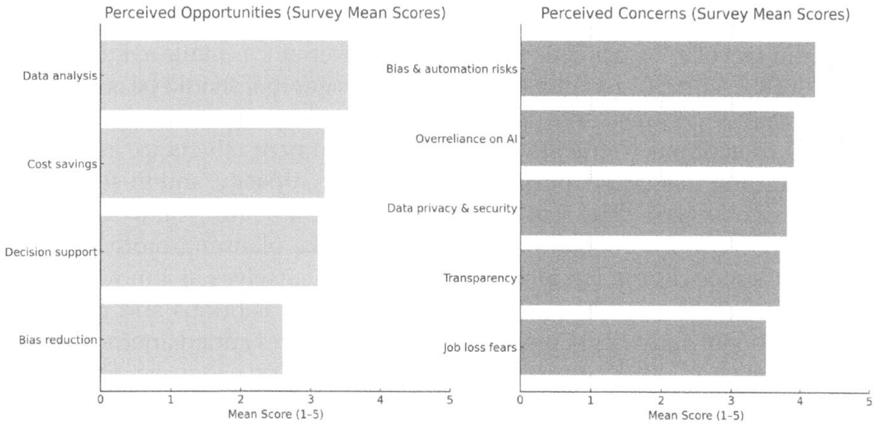

FIGURE 10.3
Contradictory perceptions of AI: opportunities and risks in planning practice (by authors).

sustains investment in AI as a solution to inefficiency, while masking structural antagonisms over authority, legitimacy, and, as Morreale (2026) reminds us, the hidden labour of dataset accumulation.

While most professionals viewed AI as an adjunct to planning practice, very few expressed more extreme views, criticising the planning profession as an inefficient bureaucracy and envisioning AI as a replacement for human planners altogether. This perspective aligns with what Gunder (2015) identifies as the neoliberal 'scapegoating fantasy', in which planning is blamed for inefficiency and market failure. Here, AI is imagined not only as a tool for optimisation but as a corrective to the supposed irrationalities or inefficiencies of the planning profession itself. Such views expose the ideological dimension of AI optimism – where fantasies of automation converge with longstanding critiques of planning as bureaucratic and obstructive.

10.4.3 Institutional Readiness and Public–Private Antagonisms

Survey data revealed strikingly low levels of preparedness among professionals, with an average score of 2.4/5 (Figure 10.4a) – one of the lowest ratings across all indicators. Interviewees described a profession 'playing catch-up' with technologies advancing faster than both regulatory frameworks and educational provision. While councils and professional bodies have begun to recognise AI's importance, regulatory systems remain hesitant to adapt, and planning education has yet to embed digital literacy engagement with AI into curricula. This combination of institutional inertia and professional uncertainty has produced what participants described as a culture of risk aversion: councils emphasise caution and accountability but hesitate to experiment, fearing the political consequences of failure.

At the institutional level, this fragility was evident in the survey results. Councils were rated at 2.6/5 for readiness to govern AI; NZPI scored slightly higher at 3.23/5 (Figure 10.4a). Qualitative accounts expressed doubts about the ability of councils to safeguard data, manage cybersecurity, and apply ethical frameworks in practice. Participants noted that AI governance entails a multilayered set of legal, technical, and organisational challenges that should be considered.

This caution contrasts sharply with private-sector perspectives. AI developers and consultants frequently described government reluctance as a risk in itself, arguing that delays perpetuate inefficiency, opacity, and mistrust. One developer observed, 'The real harm is government holding on to discretionary authority and refusing tools that could make planning more transparent'. In these accounts, developers positioned themselves as innovative and solutions-oriented, while councils appeared overly cautious and protective of institutional authority. Community representatives added another dimension, emphasising that cultural legitimacy and *Te Tiriti o Waitangi* obligations define the conditions of safe and acceptable AI adoption (Figure 10.4b).

These divergences reflect what Laclau and Mouffe (1985) describe as antagonism: irreconcilable contestation over meaning within hegemonic projects. For the public sector, risk was imagined as harm caused by premature adoption; for the private sector, as harm caused by inaction; and for communities, as harm caused by cultural erasure. From a theoretical perspective, this reveals the limits of symbolic assurances of safety. Fantasies of optimisation and control stabilise governance only temporarily, while the deeper struggle – between market efficiency, state authority, and cultural legitimacy – remains unresolved.

Figures 10.4a and 10.4b depict governance readiness indicators (survey mean scores, n≈67) and contrasting stakeholder perspectives on AI governance (qualitative coded references). Together, these figures illustrate the

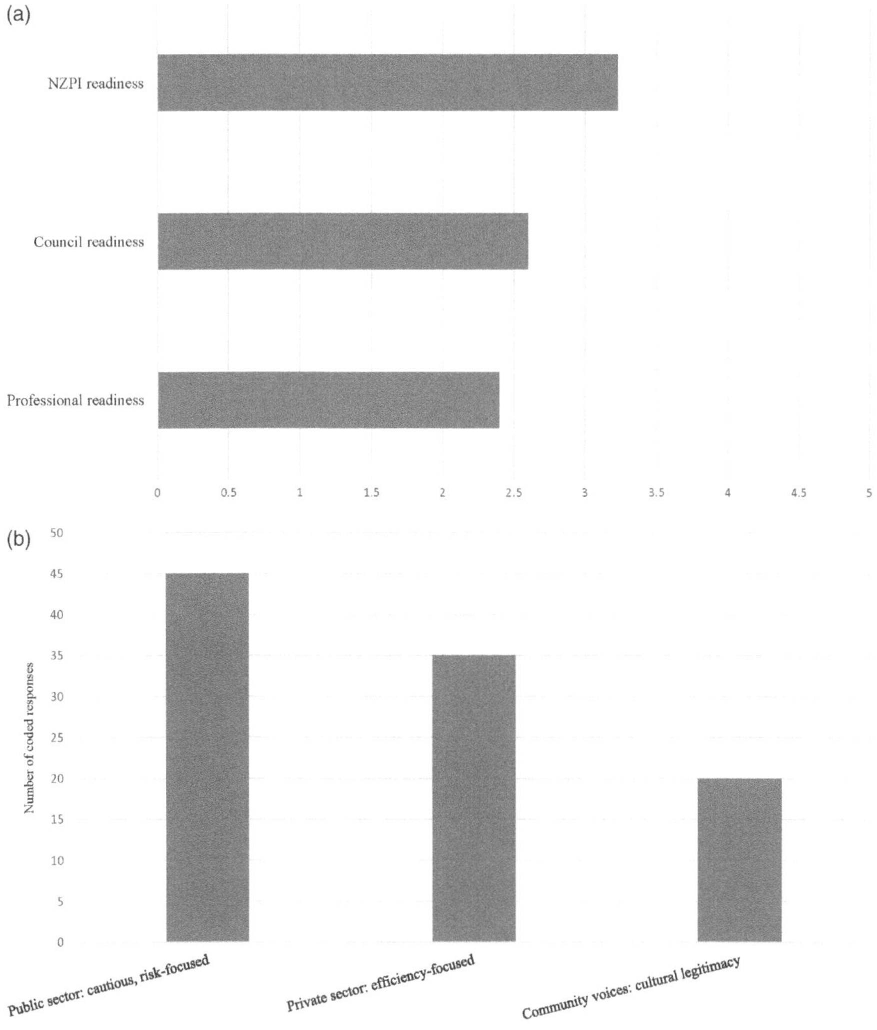

FIGURE 10.4 A-B
Institutional readiness and stakeholder perspectives on AI governance in planning Likert-scale responses (n=64) (by authors).

low institutional preparedness of councils and professional bodies, and the divergent framings of risk by public, private, and community actors.

10.4.4 Democratic and Ethical Governance: Accountability, Transparency, and the Limits of Practice

Survey findings revealed strong support for embedding democratic and regulatory principles in AI governance. Respondents rated the importance of public involvement and community engagement in AI-related decision-making highly, with mean scores above 3.6 on a five-point scale, reflecting widespread recognition that legitimacy depends on transparency, accountability, and participation. Equally, respondents emphasised that AI systems should be able to interpret and apply the principles of local planning regulations such as the Resource Management Act (RMA), assigning a mean score of 3.7 (Figure 10.5) – one of the highest across all indicators. These results suggest that planners and policymakers perceive governance not merely as a technical or ethical matter but as a democratic concern; decisions about AI must remain open to scrutiny and aligned with New Zealand's legal and institutional frameworks.

However, the findings also highlight the fragility of institutional capacity. Confidence in New Zealand's existing regulatory frameworks for governing AI was modest (mean ≈ 3.2), and perceptions of the NZPI's preparedness to provide ethical guidance were low (mean ≈ 2.4) (see Figure 10.5). This

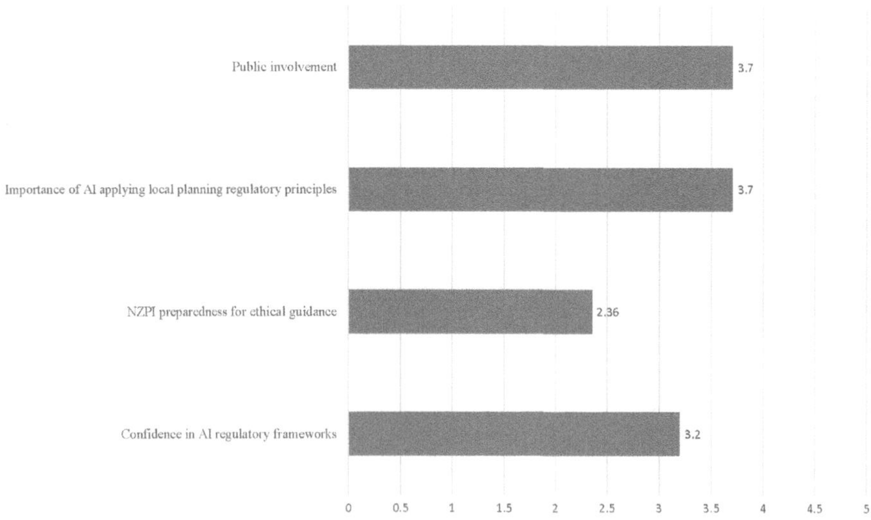

FIGURE 10.5
Perceptions of democratic and ethical governance dimensions of AI in planning (by authors).

gap between normative commitment and institutional readiness illustrates the contradictions of contemporary AI governance, where aspirations for accountability and fairness coexist with insufficient infrastructure and limited professional resources to deliver them.

Interview participants reinforced these themes. Many described the need for participatory structures that ensure transparency and public understanding. As one policymaker observed, 'It's not just about whether the system works; it's about whether people can understand how decisions are being made and whether they can trust them'. This reflects a broader anxiety about legitimacy: AI's authority is acceptable only when it remains open to contestation and embedded within democratic oversight.

Respondents consistently identified fairness, transparency, and responsibility as essential principles for any AI governance framework, yet their practical enactment remained elusive. While professionals expressed strong normative commitments to these values, preparedness among institutions and councils was limited, with average confidence scores of 2.4–2.6. This disparity suggests that ethical principles often function discursively – signalling good intentions rather than ensuring material change. As Morreale's (2026) analysis of dataset labour reminds us, ethics debates frequently focus on visible harms such as bias or exclusion, while ignoring the hidden, exploitative conditions that sustain digital infrastructures. In this sense, ethics can operate as a fantasy of safety and responsibility that masks the deeper political–economic antagonisms structuring urban governance.

Based on these findings, our project proposes translating these principles into practice through the development of an AI governance framework for councils, embedding key principles such as transparency, accountability, and compliance with regulatory and ethical standards. We recommend that future workshops and dialogues with councils and the NZPI be established to refine and co-design such a framework. These collaborative processes would provide structured spaces for professionals to engage with AI as a practical governance concern rather than an abstract technological issue, ensuring that ethical and democratic principles are meaningfully integrated into institutional practice.

Theoretically, these findings resonate with Feenberg's (2002, 2017) critical theory of technology, which emphasises participatory design and democratic intervention. They also align with Mohammadzadeh's (2026) analysis of the symbolic staging of governance, where legitimacy is produced discursively by making technology a collective concern. Together, these insights suggest that professionals do not primarily demand technical mastery but rather insist on participatory processes that allow them to shape how AI is developed and applied. Governance, in this sense, is not only about safeguards but about maintaining open, deliberative forums where algorithms can be held accountable and collective agency can be exercised.

10.4.5 Localisation, Te Tiriti, and Cultural Legitimacy

A recurring theme across both survey and interview data was the importance of localising AI systems to Aotearoa New Zealand's cultural, legal, and institutional context. Respondents expressed a strong preference for locally developed AI tools, with a mean score of 4.1/5 – one of the highest ratings recorded in the survey (see Figure 10.6). Legitimacy in AI governance, in other words, was tied not only to technical performance but also to cultural alignment and sovereignty.

A recurring theme across both survey and interview data was the importance of localising AI systems to Aotearoa New Zealand's cultural, legal, and institutional context. Respondents expressed a strong preference for locally developed AI tools, with a mean score of 4.1/5, the highest recorded in the survey (see Figure 10.6). Legitimacy in AI governance, in other words, was tied not only to technical performance but also to cultural alignment, sovereignty, and recognition of *Te Tiriti o Waitangi.*

Interviewees elaborated on this point, often contrasting the risks of imported models with the value of tools grounded in local realities. Imported AI was described as culturally misaligned, inattentive to Māori values, and likely to undermine data sovereignty. As one planner explained, 'We need AI systems that understand *mana whenua* and *te taiao.* Imported tools don't speak our language, culturally or legally'. This sentiment reflects a strong desire to embed AI within New Zealand's distinctive planning system, which integrates democratic accountability, Treaty obligations, and Indigenous perspectives.

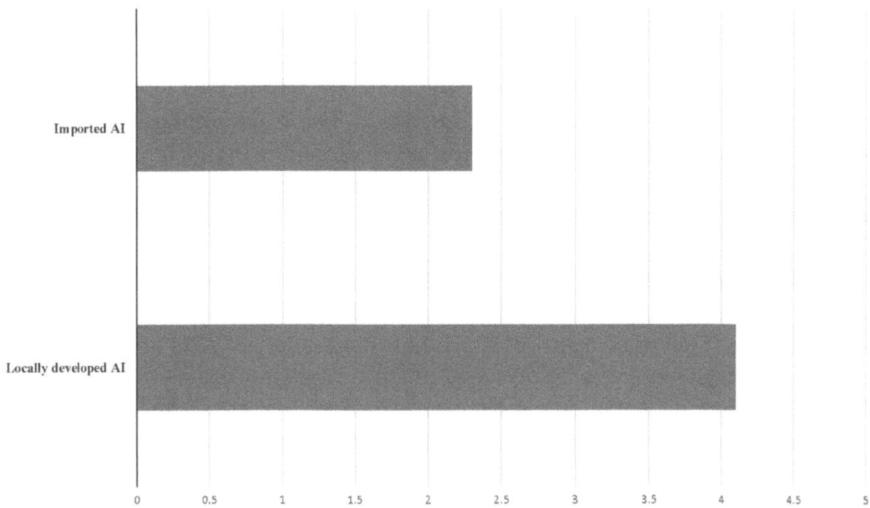

FIGURE 10.6
Preference for local versus imported AI systems in planning Likert-scale responses (n=57) (by authors).

At the same time, cultural legitimacy was not uncontested. While some participants expressed optimism that AI could enhance environmental stewardship and Māori values (average rating ≈ 3.5), others voiced deep scepticism, with confidence scores falling as low as 1 or 2 out of 5. This divergence underscores that localisation is not merely a technical adjustment but a political demand, reflecting wider struggles over sovereignty, recognition, and legitimacy in digital governance.

Theoretically, these findings resonate with Haraway's (1988) notion of *situated knowledges* and Barad's (2007) account of relational entanglement. Rather than treating AI as a universal technical fix, professionals stressed that safe and legitimate systems must be embedded in their specific cultural and institutional context. This also echoes Bahmanteymouri's (2026) critique of fantasies of universality: safety cannot be guaranteed by imported models that erase local antagonisms. Instead, governance must engage directly with the *Real* of cultural and political conflict – a terrain that no algorithm can resolve through neutrality alone.

10.4.6 AI Education, Literacy, and Training

Education emerged as one of the most critical yet neglected dimensions of AI governance. While planners and policymakers across Aotearoa New Zealand demonstrated low awareness and preparedness, universities and professional programmes have not yet responded with systematic curricula or training initiatives on AI in planning. Despite the rapid technological transformation of practice, higher education remains largely disconnected from it, offering few courses, research pathways, or capacity-building programmes addressing digital literacy, algorithmic governance, or ethical design. This institutional lag is striking, given the profession's clear recognition of its own knowledge gaps.

Survey results confirmed the gap between awareness and action. As Figure 10.7 shows, around 54 per cent of respondents rated AI training as *not or only slightly important*, 31 per cent as *moderately important*, and only about 15 per cent as *highly important*. This modest prioritisation, coupled with limited institutional provision, may underscore a clear contradiction: professionals recognise the need for digital and ethical literacy but lack access to structured learning pathways and institutional support to develop them.

Interviewees repeatedly described this condition as one of trial and error, a reactive effort to keep pace with fast-moving technologies. One senior planner noted, 'We don't need to become coders, but we must understand what's behind the dashboard'. This reflects a wider professional uncertainty about where education should lead: whether towards technical proficiency, critical literacy, or ethical governance.

Addressing this gap requires universities and professional institutes to take proactive leadership in defining the educational foundations of AI

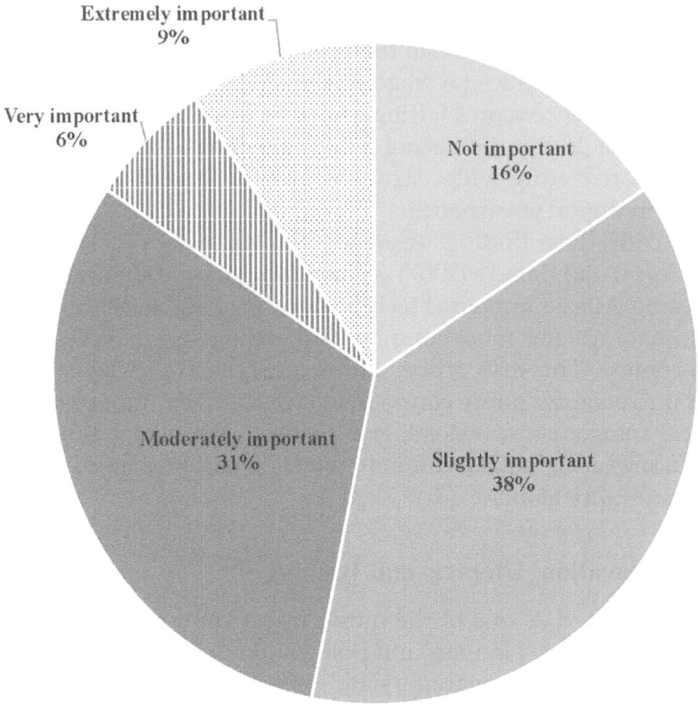

FIGURE 10.7
Importance of AI training (by authors).

governance. Universities, in particular, must lead rather than follow the profession, developing research-informed curricula that equip future planners to navigate not only the technical but also the social, ethical, and political dimensions of AI. Without such intervention, planning risks remaining reactive to technological change rather than shaping it through critical and democratic engagement.

10.5 Discussion and Conclusion: The Fantasies of Risk Governance

This chapter set out to examine how AI's promises and perils are understood within planning and urban governance in Aotearoa New Zealand, and how these understandings are shaped by fantasies of control, optimisation, and neutrality. Empirically, our survey and interviews revealed four intertwined patterns: (1) pragmatic uptake of AI as an assistant ('smart intern') alongside a refusal to treat it as a substitute for professional judgement; (2) simultaneous technocratic optimism and scepticism, with efficiency gains prized even as concerns about bias, transparency, and privacy remain high; (3) low institutional capacity and uneven trust in regulatory readiness; and (4) a strong preference for localisation, including alignment with *Te Tiriti o Waitangi*, local planning regulatory principles, and Māori data sovereignty. Together, these findings show that the governance of AI is not merely technical; it is a *deeply political* arena in which legitimacy is negotiated through claims to ethics, participation, and cultural alignment.

The divergence of approaches to risk and safety reflects the competing interests and power dynamics that structure AI governance, most visibly in the divide between public- and private-sector perspectives. Public-sector caution framed risk as harm arising from premature adoption, while private-sector enthusiasm redefined risk as harm stemming from non-adoption. In both cases, fantasies of safety and optimisation underpin how risk is conceptualised and managed. These dynamics echo Beck's (1992) theory of the risk society, in which modernity generates systemic risks that are both produced by and resistant to technological management. AI epitomises this duality; it is framed simultaneously as a solution to risk and as a source of new dangers. Planners and policymakers recognise its potential to enhance efficiency and forecasting, yet also fear bias, opacity, and job loss. Private AI developers warn that delaying adoption perpetuates inefficiency and mistrust, while public institutions stress caution and accountability. The category of 'risk' is therefore not neutral or technical but politically constructed – a site of antagonism where authority, legitimacy, and discretion are continually contested.

From the philosophical point of view, our results affirm the argument developed earlier in this volume: AI operates as a fantasy of the Big Other, promising coherence and calculability while disavowing the Real, the structural incompleteness, antagonisms, and contradictions of capitalist urban governance. Professionals' everyday embrace of AI for routine tasks sits alongside a strategic distancing from its imagined authority; they welcome assistance but resist automation of judgement. This coexistence of reliance and refusal reflects the ideological domination of the satisfaction derived from economic efficiencies and the pursuit of incessant added value that sustain capitalist rationalities while concealing exploitative data labour, institutional contradictions, and the political stakes of governance. The discourse of 'risk and safety' stabilises this terrain by projecting an image of perfect technical governance – anticipation, mitigation, elimination – despite the structural impossibility of such completeness within a capitalist market economy.

At the same time, the empirical emphasis on democratic process and localisation points towards possible departures from this technocratic fantasy. High importance is placed on public involvement and community engagement, and on the capacity of AI to interpret and apply the planning regulations, signals that legitimacy is tied to transparency, accountability, and cultural grounding. Respondents' strong preference for locally developed systems (mean ≈ 4.1/5) highlights that 'safety' is not simply a feature of code but a relational achievement rooted in *Te Tiriti o Waitangi*, data sovereignty, and the institutional ecologies of New Zealand cities. This critical yet constructive orientation reflects what Haraway (1988) calls situated knowledges and Barad (2007) terms relational entanglement, as well as Marcuse's notion of the *Great Refusal*: a refusal to accept technological domination as inevitable. In this sense, New Zealand's planners and policymakers exhibit both critical awareness and pragmatic optimism, recognising that robust governance emerges only when systems are designed for – and accountable to – their local contexts.

Yet a persistent contradiction remains: strong normative commitments to fairness, transparency, and responsibility coexist with low preparedness among professionals and institutions (≈2.4–2.6/5), and only modest confidence in broader regulatory readiness (≈3.2/5). Ethics, in this light, risks functioning as an ideological screen, signalling responsibility while leaving untouched the political–economic conditions that generate both digital infrastructures and urban inequalities. Following Gunder's critique of neoliberal scapegoating, we caution against the disavowal of the Real, the structural contradictions, and its fantasies that cast AI as a corrective to 'inefficient' planning. Such frames displace political judgement onto technical systems and invite the erasure of democratic deliberation under the banner of optimisation.

Empirically, we provide one of the first systematic portraits of New Zealand planning professionals' attitudes to AI, identifying the tension between enthusiasm for efficiency and demands for democratic accountability and localisation. Practically, our analysis supports a co-designed governance framework for councils that embeds:

1. **Participatory design and scrutiny**: Structured forums for public involvement, professional deliberation, and transparent decision-making;
2. **Contextual alignment**: Ensuring AI systems reflect *Te Tiriti o Waitangi*, local planning regulations, and Māori and Indigenous data sovereignty principles;
3. **Institutional capacity-building and education**: Embedding digital literacy, algorithmic accountability, and AI ethics in planning curricula, supported by ongoing professional development through NZPI-led workshops, accreditation standards, and training across councils;
4. **Accountability across the data lifecycle**: Maintaining visibility of dataset labour, provenance, consent, and continuous auditing of bias and harms;

5. **Role clarity for AI in planning**: Affirming AI as an assistive rather than substitutive tool, with decision rights retained within democratic and professional institutions.

Our dataset (n≈67 survey; 29 interviews) provides indicative, not exhaustive, coverage and is situated within the New Zealand context. In essence, AI in planning must be understood not as a neutral instrument but as a *site of political struggle* in which fantasies of control meet the Real of urban conflict. The task is not to eliminate uncertainty but to *govern it democratically*: to design situated systems, disclose their conditions of production, and sustain forums where algorithms are accountable to people, law, and place. Only then can AI support planning without subordinating it to the false promise of frictionless optimisation.

Notes

1 By planning in this chapter, I refer to urban planning, urban design, and regional planning.

2 The authors conducted the research on the project titled "Risk and Safety in Urban Digital Governance and AI-based Planning" (2024–2025), funded by Lloyd's Register Foundation as part of its 'Work Risk Poll into action' funding programme.

References

Bahmanteymouri, E. (2026). AI in the Shadow of Big Other: Planning, Power, and the Locus of Control. In E. Bahmanteymouri, M. Mohammadzadeh & F. Morreale (Eds.), *Inner World of Artificial Intelligence* (pp. 89–107). Melbourne: Routledge. DOI: 10.1201/9781003480167-8 *89*.

Barad, K. (2007). *Meeting the Universe Halfway: Quantum Physics and the Entanglement of Matter and Meaning*. Durham: Duke University Press.

Beck, U. (1992). *Risk Society: Towards a New Modernity*. London: SAGE Publications.

Cassidy, J. (2010). *How Markets Fail: The Logic of Economic Calamities*. New York: Picado.

Feenberg, A. (2002). *Transforming Technology: A Critical Theory Revisited*. Oxford University Press.

Feenberg, A. (2017). Beyond One-Dimensionality. In P. Funke, A. Lamas & T. Wolfson (Eds.), *The Great Refusal: Herbert Marcuse and Contemporary Social Movements* (pp. 229–241). Philadelphia: Temple University Press.

Gunder, M. (2015). Planning's "Failure" to Ensure Efficient Market Delivery: A Lacanian Deconstruction of This Neoliberal Scapegoating Fantasy. *European Planning Studies*, 24(1), pp. 21–38. https://doi.org/10.1080/09654313.2015.1067291

Haraway, D. (1988). Situated Knowledges: The Science Question in Feminism and the Privilege of Partial Perspective. *Feminist Studies*, 14(3), pp. 575–599.
Laclau, E. & Mouffe, S. (1985). *Hegemony and Socialist Strategy*. London: Verso.
Mohammadzadeh, M. (2026). Urban Artificial Intelligence and Planning: Symbolic and Imaginary Representations and the Repressed Real. In E. Bahmanteymouri, M. Mohammadzadeh & F. Morreale (Eds.), *Inner World of Artificial Intelligence* (pp. 185–204). Melbourne: Routledge. DOI: 10.1201/9781003480167-14 *185*.
Morreale, F. (2026). Human Subsumption in Training Datasets for Music Generation. In E. Bahmanteymouri, M. Mohammadzadeh & F. Morreale (Eds.), *Inner World of Artificial Intelligence* (pp. 13–31). Melbourne: Routledge. DOI: 10.1201/9781003480167-3 *13*.
Wolff, R. (2013). "Pure" Capitalism is Pure Fantasy. *Truthout Webpage*. Access 10/10/2025 https://truthout.org/articles/pure-capitalism-is-pure-fantasy/
Žižek, S. (1989). *The Sublime Object of Ideology*. London: Vero.

Section 3

AI, Urban Knowledge, and the Repressed Real

11

Urban Artificial Intelligence and Planning: Symbolic and Imaginary Representations and the Repressed Real

Mohsen Mohammadzadeh

11.1 Introduction

This chapter contributes to *The Inner World of Artificial Intelligence* by asking: what is the inner psychic infrastructure that underpins Urban Artificial Intelligence's rise? How does it reshape planning's Imaginary, Symbolic, and Real? And what happens to the possibilities for alternative urban futures when planners' inner worlds are increasingly sutured to an algorithmic order that systematically represses the messy, conflictual Real of urban life? To answer these questions, Artificial Intelligence (AI) is considered not merely a technical tool but a deeply political and ideological force that pervasively reshapes our everyday lives and critically, our cities. The development, testing, and deployment of AI are intrinsically urban processes, with cities acting as primary sites of experimentation and implementation (Xia et al., 2025; Sanchez et al., 2023). Yet, AI is not a new technology. Batty (2023: 1045) reminds us that it 'emerged alongside the development of the digital computer more than 80 years ago during the Second World War', setting in motion a vision to simulate human cognition algorithmically (Dyson, 2012). For all its historical lineage, AI today remains elusive in its meaning and manifestations (Crawford, 2021), yet few would dispute its transformative reach. Although there is no single, stable definition of AI. Sanchez et al. (2023: 180) push this further, arguing that AI is fundamentally 'developed largely within a paradigm of efficiency and neoliberal values'. This ideological embedding matters profoundly for cities, which increasingly host AI as an infrastructural layer shaping how urban life is perceived, managed, and governed (Caprotti et al., 2024). Crawford (2021: 20) rightly cautions, 'we are at a critical juncture, one that requires us to ask hard questions about the way AI is produced and adopted'.

DOI: 10.1201/9781003480167-14

Urban scholars now speak of Urban Artificial Intelligence (UAI) to name this entanglement: the relational interweaving of AI systems and urban spaces, infrastructures, and everyday practices. Cugurullo et al. (2023: 4) observe that the emergence of AI urbanism 'is neither a linear nor an atemporal process, but rather a multiform and geographically sensitive phenomenon ... destabilising the material and immaterial fabric of cities'. The UAI exceeds the smart city discourse; it signals an epistemic and ontological rupture – an algorithmic urbanism that is anticipatory, self-regulating, and increasingly non-human in its logics (Cugurullo, 2024). In this sense, Cugurullo (2021: 152) notably contends, 'Artificial intelligence is intangible software: a soul without a body. AI finds in cities numerous bodies'. Yet UAI's implications extend far beyond technical efficiency. While applications such as Urban Digital Twins (UDTs), IoT networks, and AI-based urban agents promise more data-driven insight, they also produce powerful symbolic and discursive frames through which urban futures are imagined and governed.

Batty (2023) argues that AI has long been envisaged as a planning aid, promising to help planners navigate urban complexity. But this promise remains constrained; planners rarely incorporate AI into everyday practice (Sanchez et al., 2023; Daniel et al., 2023; Potts & Webb, 2023). Batty (2023: 1045) echoes that today's 'weak AI' often remains focused on finding patterns in vast urban datasets, offering only limited predictive possibilities. Still, the technocratic appeal persists. Kitchin et al. (2019) argue that smart urbanism and now UAI foster a new urban technocracy rooted in what Mattern (2021) terms instrumental rationality – a logic that Morozov (2013) critiques as 'solutionism'. This instrumental rationality, embedded in AI applications, increasingly automates what can be seen and known: Urban Digital Twins duplicate cities in real time; sensors and IoT infrastructures feed constant streams of urban big data; Large Language Models (LLMs) generate planning scenarios and policy scripts (Cugurullo, 2020; Elliott, 2019; Palmini & Cugurullo, 2023). This, as Allmendinger (2009: 54) puts it, offers planners 'a simple and highly structured view of the world', abstracting lived complexity into calculable forms. Critically, drawing on Lefebvre, Savini and Raco (2019) show how such abstractions 'trap' social and political relations within models, foreclosing more plural and contested ways of knowing space. Gunder and Hillier (2009) remind us that technocratic planning knowledge is inherently unable to grasp the full, complicated reality of urban everyday life. As planning becomes ever more mediated by UAI, its risk of becoming an automated technocratic discipline grows – drifting further from its normative, critical possibilities (Bahmanteymouri & Mohammadzadeh, 2023; Raco & Savini, 2019). Marcuse (2013 [1958–1959]) famously warned that 'technological rationality' operates as a mode of domination, reinforcing systems of control. Delanty and Harris (2021) resonate this idea, arguing that technological rationality, rooted in industrial capitalism, privileges efficiency and standardisation at the cost of uniqueness and critical thought. Bridle (2018: 2) succinctly argues that 'we ourselves are utterly enmeshed in technological systems, which shape in turn how we act and how we think'. What remains underexplored, however, is how UAI operates at the level of the planner's subjectivity – the psychic attachments and ideological fantasies that sustain its promise of control.

In what follows, I use Lacan's concepts – Imaginary, Symbolic, and Real – to investigate the psychic mechanism of planning under UAI. I argue that urban automation and the pervasive deployment of AI amplify the tension between the allure of abstraction and the lived, contested realities that always escape its grasp. In so doing, I show how the extensive utilisation of UAI risks limiting planning knowledge – foreclosing its capacity to imagine and shape alternative urban space.

11.2 Spatial Planning as a Technocratic Discipline

In this section, I use 'planning' specifically to refer to spatial interventions – what is formalised as spatial planning. In its broadest sense, planning has long accompanied the historical evolution of human settlement. From the earliest urban formations along the Nile, Indus, and Tigris–Euphrates rivers, spatial organisation has never been neutral; it has always operated as a performative expression of power, knowledge, ideology, and cultural imaginaries. Yet, planning as a professionalised discipline is relatively modern – forged in response to the adverse environmental, economic, and socio-spatial consequences of industrial capitalism. It was conceived as a mechanism of spatial rationalisation: an instrument to impose order on the disorder of rapid urbanisation and to address the environmental, social, and sanitary crises of the industrial city. Gunder and Hillier (2009) note that the foundations of planning were laid at the intersection of architectural artistry and engineering science. From the outset, planning aligned itself with the modernist project – a rationalist and normative endeavour that Friedmann (1987: 53) famously described as 'a technique for guiding social progress'. Rooted in Enlightenment reason and the epistemology of scientific objectivity, early planning assumed that space and society could be analysed and managed through scientific empirical analysis and technical interventions. Its faith lies in rationalisation; its ontology was that of malleable plans, policies, and regulations, amenable to expert design.

The technocratic rationality legacy continues to dominate planning. Despite paradigm shifts and theoretical ruptures, the planning discipline remains deeply tethered to its technocratic genealogy – sustained by a persistent faith in prediction, control, and linear problem-solving. Hebbert (2019: 26) contends, 'technocracy shaped institutions and institutions shaped the contemporary city: in a direct and physical sense the built environment bequeathed to us by the later twentieth century embodies the values and solutions of its knowledge-providers'. Faludi (1973: 1) encapsulated this ethos: planning as 'the application of scientific method – however crude – to policymaking'. Within this frame, instrumental rationality became the discipline's foundational logic: planners were positioned as technicians of efficiency, tasked with selecting optimal means to realise pre-defined ends. Such positivist assumptions long masqueraded as value-neutral, yet critical theorists have shown how they mask powerful ideological commitments. The social and economic crises and political upheavals of the 1970s exposed the contradictions at the heart of the modernist planning project. The grand narratives of the post-war welfare state faltered under the pressures of stagflation, austerity, and the rising tide of neoliberal governance, while grassroots movements and urban uprisings challenged the legitimacy of top-down, technocratic interventions. In response, the emergence of bottom-up theories and practices – notably collaborative and communicative planning – sought to open planning to more inclusive, dialogical processes grounded in local knowledge and collective problem-solving (Healey, 1997; Innes & Booher, 2003; Forester, 1999). Yet despite these shifts, the epistemic grip of technocratic rationality has remained remarkably robust. It has not withered but has instead been rearticulated through the discourses and infrastructures of digital governance. In the contemporary age of algorithmic planning, smart city systems, and Urban Artificial Intelligence, the logics of prediction, optimisation, and control have not vanished; rather, they have been recalibrated and amplified within the circuits of computational rationality.

Some urban scholars, including Kitchin et al. (2019), Savini and Raco (2019), and Bahmanteymouri and Mohammadzadeh (2023), caution that we are witnessing the rise of a new urban technocracy – a computational regime that masks political and ideological norms, values, and interests beneath layers of algorithmic abstraction. Cities, long recognised as sites of agonistic struggle and cultural, social, economic, and political contestation, are increasingly recoded as 'urban labs': calculable terrains of data flows, programmable efficiencies, and technical 'solutions'. This technocratic lens, as Putnam (1977) foresaw decades ago, systematically excludes conflict, dissent, and pluralism, recasting social alternatives as inefficiencies to be optimised away. Within this regime, planners' subjectivities – their desires, knowledge practices, and professional self-understandings – are (re)constituted through their ever-deepening entanglement with technologies such as UAI and the algorithmic circulation of digital information.

Heidegger (1977: 4) famously warned that 'we are delivered over to [technology] in the worst possible way when we regard it as something neutral'. For him, technology is never merely an ensemble of tools; it is a mode of revealing – enframing beings as standing-reserve, raw inputs for instrumental use. Building on this conception, Feenberg (1999, 2002, 2017) rejects the idea that technocracy is somehow inherent to technology itself. Instead, he sees technocracy as the historical expression of dominant socio-political configurations. His theory of instrumentalisation distinguishes between a primary level, where phenomena are extracted and decontextualised, and a secondary level, where meanings are re-inscribed within social contexts. In this sense, technology is always saturated with power, intention, and interpretation. Marcuse (2013 [1958–1959]) likewise argued that technological rationality becomes political rationality – subordinating its emancipatory promise to the imperatives of capital accumulation and social control. As the Frankfurt School recognised, what appears liberatory often functions as a mechanism of domination. Delanty and Harris (2021) argue that technological rationality forecloses the very imagination of alternatives; it becomes not merely a means but an ideology – a horizon that limits what can be fantasised. Feenberg (2002: 8) argues, 'technology is not simply a means but has become an environment and a way of life'.

Lacan's psychoanalytic theory adds a crucial ontological and epistemological dimension to this critique. For Lacan, technocratic knowledge aligns with the 'discourse of the university', where knowledge serves the Master's desire by masking power through the language of neutrality and expertise. UAI, in this frame, produces technocratic knowledge positioned as neutral and rational, yet serving to sustain dominant ideological structures and fantasies of control. Scientific reason, far from liberatory, thus becomes a vehicle for reproducing desire, exclusion, and closure. Mohammadzadeh (2023) contends that technocratic planning is never purely procedural; it is ideological, suturing hegemonic fantasies to spatial order while obscuring the Real – that traumatic kernel which resists symbolisation and calculation. Planning, under this regime of technocratic rationality, performs an act of closure: reproducing the very exclusions it claims to overcome.

Planning, therefore, is – and has always been – deeply political and ideological. As Allmendinger (2009: 54) reminds us, technocratic planning projects 'a simple and highly structured view of the world', obscuring its embedded ideological commitments. Harvey (1978: 231) similarly notes that the 'ideology of harmony within the capitalist social order' remains the pivot around which planning's contradictions turn. Planning does not stand apart from power; it is historically entangled with the dominant social and economic logics of its time. The allure of Urban Artificial Intelligence today intensifies this tension. Scholars such as Kitchin et al. (2019) and Bahmanteymouri and Mohammadzadeh (2023) caution that smart technologies risk deepening instrumental rationality, narrowing spaces for contestation, and foreclosing alternative imaginaries – echoing Weber's 'iron cage' (Bauman, 2000) in which the world is ever more enclosed by procedural logics. Yet others, including Allam et al. (2022) and Yigitcanlar et al. (2018), suggest that, deployed critically, UAI might free planners from routine tasks, making room for more collaborative and relational practice. Feenberg (2002: v) aptly insists, 'The real issue is not technology or progress per se but the variety of possible technologies and paths of progress among which we must choose'. Technology itself is never neutral; its meaning is shaped by the political and ideological conditions in which it is embedded. Gunder and Hillier (2009) argue that technocratic knowledge – presented as neutral and rational – often functions as an ideological apparatus, reproducing dominant capitalist logics while disavowing their exclusions. The development and deployment of UAI thus remain deeply bound to these hegemonic structures – or what Suarez-Villa (2009) names technocapitalism: a regime in which technological innovation and knowledge are appropriated to serve the imperatives of market expansion and managerial control. In Lacanian terms, such technocratic fantasies sustain planning's illusion of coherence while systematically repressing the messy, conflictual Real that continually resists capture.

In late capitalism, this ideological enclosure tightens as technocratic reason is re-inscribed through Urban Artificial Intelligence. The fantasy of control sustains the planner's subjectivity yet always fails to contain the ruptures of the urban Real – those ungovernable dimensions of city life that resist capture by code. To grasp why this fantasy persists, we must turn to Lacan's psychoanalytic framework. It reveals the unconscious logics that bind planning to illusions of mastery while masking the city's inherent messiness and antagonisms. The Lacanian triad of the Imaginary, the Symbolic, and the Real offers a critical lens for understanding how UAI reshapes planning knowledge and forecloses what inevitably exceeds its grasp.

11.3 A Brief Introduction to the Lacanian Psychoanalytical Approach

This chapter undertakes a critical investigation of UAI through the lens of Lacanian psychoanalysis, employing Lacan's triadic schema of the Imaginary, the Symbolic, and the Real to explore how AI reconfigures planning knowledge and practice. These transformations are not merely technical in nature; they are profoundly ideological. UAI alters the conditions under which planners, policymakers, and communities perceive, narrate, and engage with space. Technologies such as sensors, Internet of Things (IoT) networks, City Brains, Urban Digital Twins, and Large Language Models (LLMs) do more than collect and process data – they intervene in the very structures through which space, everyday life, and the built environment are imagined, governed, and symbolically elucidated.

Jacques Lacan (1901–1981) – a French psychoanalyst, post-Freudian theorist, neo-structuralist, and arguably one of the most provocative intellectual figures of the twentieth century – offers a complex but invaluable conceptual toolkit for this inquiry (Mohammadzadeh, 2021). Bahmanteymouri (2023a: 211) argues, 'The Lacanian approach to psychoanalysis provides a useful but complex mechanism or system of analysis that seeks to understand the complexity of the world and its social and political relations'. Lacanian psychoanalysis enables a deep interrogation of ideology, subject formation, and symbolic systems – making it particularly well-suited for unpacking the psychic and political dimensions of contemporary urbanism (Stavrakakis, 2002; Pohl & Swyngedouw, 2023), including investigating the inner world of UAI.

At the heart of Lacan's thought lies a radical conception of the subject – not as a stable, autonomous ego but as a split subject constituted through unconscious processes. 'For Lacan, the true subject is the subject of the unconscious, not to be confused with the ego, which functions in consciousness as a structure of identification' (Muller, 2000: 44). In mapping the terrain of the subject, Lacan articulated a tripartite structure of the psyche: the Imaginary, the Symbolic, and the Real (Homer, 2005). These realms are not discrete but interdependent; as Wolfreys (2004: 108) remarks, 'The principal difficulty even in beginning to speak of the imaginary – [the] symbolic – [the] real, is that one cannot address any one term with any efficiency without speaking of the others' (Figure 11.1).

Through this triadic schema, Lacan conceptualised the dynamics of subject formation, the operation of desire, and the constitution of meaning. These concepts have since been taken up across political theory, sociology, critical planning, and architectural discourse to examine the psychic infrastructure of ideology under late capitalism (Bahmanteymouri, 2023b; Mohammadzadeh, 2023). Drawing on these Lacanian concepts enables a critical interrogation of how UAI reinforces the discursive dominance of technocratic knowledge and algorithmic rationality in planning – not only through its structuring of the material-symbolic governance of urban space but also through its suturing of the planner's subjectivity to fantasies of coherence, mastery, and control. These fantasies operate within the Imaginary and Symbolic registers, concealing the constitutive lack at the heart of planning knowledge and disavowing the disruptive presence of the urban Real.

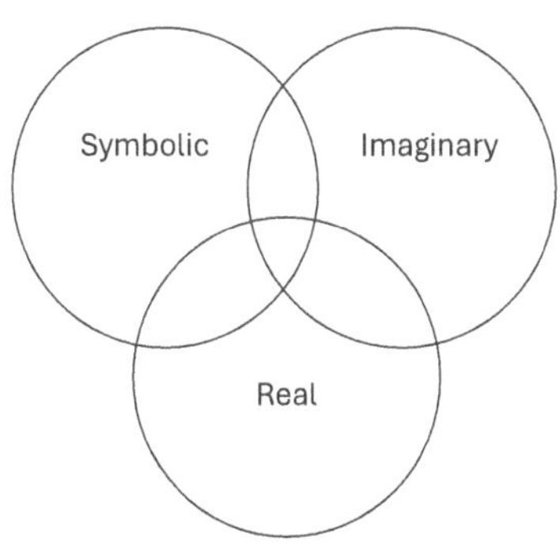

FIGURE 11.1
The Lacanian tripartite structure of the psyche: the Imaginary, the Symbolic, and the Real (by author).

11.4 AI-Driven Urban Digital Twin as the Urban Imaginary Realm

This chapter thus engages with UAI not as a neutral toolkit but as an ideological formation. It examines how emerging AI technologies displace the planner's role from critical mediator to data custodian, how they rewrite urban imaginaries with glossy simulations, and how they suppress or misrecognise the messy, contested Real of urban life. Through a Lacanian framework, we can move beyond celebratory or instrumental views of UAI to probe its unconscious effects on planning knowledge, subjectivity, and urban reality.

The Imaginary marks the historical and conceptual starting point for Lacan's psychoanalytic theory. In his seminal essay on the Mirror Stage, Lacan describes the moment when the infant first recognises its own reflected image – a formative experience that inaugurates the ego and sets subjectivity in motion (Homer, 2005). In this visual capture, the child misrecognises the mirror image as a unified, coherent self, in stark contrast to its lived sense of bodily fragmentation. As Homer (2005: 24) puts it, 'the mirror image . . . provides the first explication of unity for the child, sculpting a bridge between the chaotic experiences of movement and motor (in)coordination and the static surface of the image presented'. This identification with an external image – what Lacan calls the Gestalt – constitutes the ego as a fictional totality, formed not in inner coherence but in alienation (Evans, 2010). The ego, in Lacan's terms, is not an inner truth but an imaginary function sustained through images and illusions. Alienation, therefore, is intrinsic to ego formation: the subject becomes sutured to an image that is both reassuring and deceptive, a mirage of mastery that masks the fragmentation beneath.

This constitutive misrecognition – *méconnaissance* – structures the Imaginary order. The ego is never an authentic core of being but a defensive identification that displaces the Real. As Lacan (2006: 76) writes in Écrits, 'the total form of his body, by which the subject anticipates the maturation of his power in a mirage, is given to him only as a Gestalt, that is, in an exteriority'. This insight unsettles the Cartesian idea of a self-knowing subject; as Sarup and Raja (2005) argue, Lacan's analysis of the mirror phase disrupted conventional assumptions about self-consciousness. The Imaginary, then, is the register where fragmented sensations are synthesised into the illusion of wholeness. It 'turns out fantasies that proceed from a fragmented image of the body' to 'a form of its totality' (Lacan, 2006: 97).

At its heart is *Lack* – not merely the absence of something but an ontological void. Lacan (1988: 223) names this 'the lack of being, properly speaking', a constitutive emptiness that stimulates the subject's emergence. Desire, then, arises not as a drive to obtain some final object but as an endless movement to fill this structural lack – 'the metonymy of the want-to-be' (Lacan, 2006: 623). Crucially, it is not the object but the fantasy that sustains desire. Fantasy, Lacan writes, is 'the means by which the subject maintains himself at the level of his vanishing desire'

(Lacan, 2006: 637); it does not fulfil desire but perpetuates it, staging scenarios that keep the subject attached to an impossible wholeness. Glynos (2001) calls fantasy the infrastructure of desire itself, while Žižek (1989) argues that fantasy does not simply show what to desire but teaches how to desire. In this way, fantasy sustains the illusion of coherence, masking the lack at the core of being – an absence that, though impossible to fill, continually animates the subject's relations to self, others, and the social world (Jabareen, 2017). This foundational alienation reverberates well beyond the psyche. It illuminates how broader ideological formations – including technocratic planning – rely on Imaginary constructs of coherence, legibility, and control to stabilise an otherwise contested and conflictual political-symbolic field.

In the Lacanian psychoanalytic frame, the Mirror Stage illustrates how the subject's ego is formed through misrecognition: the child mistakes the reflected image – an exterior Gestalt of unity – for its fragmented, incoherent bodily reality. This psychic mechanism finds a striking parallel in how planners and urban technocrats deploy maps, models, and digital twins. As Wood (1992: 6) observes, 'maps don't just show the world, they shape it'. Planners generate spatial maps and images not only to make sense of urban complexity but also, unwittingly, to shape what counts as the city itself. Planning's visual and textual artefacts (plans, maps, renderings, policy narratives) help shaping the planner's Imaginary identification with mastery and order, while fantasy works to conceal the constitutive gaps and antagonisms of the urban Real by projecting an image of coherence and governability (Gunder & Hillier, 2024). In this sense, maps function as mirrors – reflecting not the unruly messiness of urban life but an idealised abstraction that planners misrecognise as reality. This seductive coherence is never neutral; it is an ideological construct that sustains fantasies of legibility, mastery, and control. As Harley (1989: 13) famously argues, 'maps are never value-free images: they are embedded in relations of power'. They do not simply record spatial reality; they actively produce it through selective abstraction, suppression, and symbolic representation. Crampton and Krygier (2006: 12) reinforce this point: 'Maps are texts of power . . . they create spatial realities rather than merely reflecting them'. In this way, the map becomes a mirror that sutures over gaps and contradictions, offering the planner an illusory sense of certainty. This reading echoes Lefebvre's spatial triad, especially his notion of representations of space (*l'espace conçu*), which impose conceptual coherence on the contradictions of lived urban life: 'Representations of space . . . identify what is lived and what is perceived with what is conceived' (Lefebvre, 1991: 38). Here, mapping operates as a Lacanian Imaginary: a fantasy construct that conceals the fractured urban Real, reproducing the technocratic subject's desire for order, predictability, and mastery.

Urban Digital Twins (UDTs), as AI-driven, real-time digital replicas of the city, epitomise what Lacan would call a mirror of urban space – a seductive Gestalt that masks the city's inherent contradictions. These systems promise 'total visibility' and seamless prediction by constantly synchronising sensor data, IoT networks, and machine-learning models. Yet, Gunder and Hillier (2009: 54) remind us that planning is always structured by fantasy: 'planners are seduced by images of spatial coherence that function as Imaginary constructs, suturing over the disorder of the urban Real'. In this way, the UDT becomes a psychoanalytic mirror – a real-time image that planners and policymakers misrecognise as the city itself. Recent critical urban AI scholarship reinforces this point. Kitchin et al. (2019) warn that the proliferation of AI-driven representations and real-time dashboards fosters an 'algorithmic technocracy' that privileges calculative rationality while displacing more plural, contested ways of knowing the city. Savini and Raco (2019: 10) similarly argue that these systems 'trap social, economic and political relations by positioning abstract representations as the fundamental basis for urban transformation'. Cugurullo (2020: 3) observes that AI-driven Urban Digital Twins 'are far from neutral . . . they are governed by algorithmic governance logics that can depoliticise planning discourse while embedding hidden biases and exclusions'.

For planners, these digital images operate at the level of the Imaginary. They offer a fantasy of wholeness, legibility, and control – mirroring the fragmented complexity of urban life back to the planner as if it were a coherent, governable object. Kitchin (2021: 6) reminds us that 'Urban Digital Twins are political technologies that encode assumptions about what counts as valid knowledge, who controls it, and how it should be used'. From a Lacanian perspective, these systems function precisely as mirrors that sustain the technocratic planner's desire for mastery over the city's messy Real. They transform the city into an abstract data object, promising that every movement, transaction, and social interaction can be rendered visible and programmable – what Savini and Raco (2019) call 'the rise of a new urban technocracy'. As Lacan (2006: 97) writes, the mirror image 'turns out fantasies that proceed from a fragmented image . . . to a form of its totality'. Yet this totality is always a misrecognition: a fantasy that forecloses more radical, relational, and contested understandings of urban space.

This section has shown how Urban Artificial Intelligence – and especially AI-driven Urban Digital Twins – operate not as neutral mirrors of urban reality but as seductive *Gestalts* in the Lacanian sense: fantasies of coherence that planners and policymakers misrecognise as the urban reality. These visual and computational abstractions often reinforce the technocratic desire for mastery and control, obscuring the messy, contested, and conflict-ridden nature of the urban Real. However, as we shift from the realm of images to the realm of language and discourse, it becomes clear that the power of UAI does not end with its capacity to mirror the city; it also profoundly reshapes how the city is named, narrated, and symbolically ordered. If the Imaginary realm sutures over fragmentation through captivating representations, the Symbolic realm structures what can be said, thought, and governed through the operations of language, codes, and algorithmic discourse. The next section, therefore, turns to the Urban Symbolic to examine how AI rewrites the discursive fabric of planning – embedding technocratic logics deeper into the language of policy, regulation, and knowledge production, while simultaneously foreclosing other ways of imagining and articulating urban life.

11.5 Urban Artificial Intelligence as the Urban Symbolic Realm

Having outlined the Imaginary, we now turn to the Symbolic realm – the register through which Lacan locates the subject within the field of language, law, and social structures. In his seminal 1953 lecture 'The Function and Field of Speech and Language in Psychoanalysis', Lacan (2006) famously asserts that 'the unconscious is structured like a language' (Homer, 2005: 33). For Lacan, the Symbolic is the domain of signifiers: the codes, discourses, and institutional logics that bind subjects into networks of meaning and power. While often misread as merely structuralist, Lacan's perspective is better understood as neo-structuralist (Sturrock, 2003), since he draws on Saussurean linguistics and Lévi-Strauss's structural anthropology while radically reframing their implications. As he writes, 'psychoanalysis as a science will be structuralist, to the point of recognising in science a refusal of the subject' (Lacan, 1987: 113).

This Symbolic order is not an inert backdrop; it actively shapes what subjects know, say, and imagine about themselves and the world. Roudinesco (1999: 211) argues that for Lacan 'symbols are more real than what they symbolise'. In the context of planning, this means that AI systems, big data taxonomies, and algorithmic policy scripts become more than neutral technical languages – they are Symbolic mechanisms that dominate how urban life is discursively produced and legitimised. Kitchin (2014, 2021) and Cugurullo (2020) remind us that the data infrastructures underpinning UAI carry the authority of what appears scientific, objective, and comprehensive, yet they encode powerful assumptions about who counts, what counts as knowledge, and how urban realities are to be ordered. Lacan (2006: 229) stressed, 'It is the world of words that creates the world of things . . . by giving its concrete being to their essence'. Under UAI, planners are not merely working with technology; they are enmeshed in Symbolic regimes that reinforce technical rationality, naturalise algorithmic rationality, and rearticulate urban governance as a question of calculable certainty – foreclosing other, more contested and plural vocabularies of the urban Real.

Urban Artificial Intelligence generates new forms of knowledge about cities and how they should be governed in the future. This Symbolic order – the discursive field of codes, categories, and technical terms – is increasingly formulated and channelled by algorithmic systems that embed and automate planning logics. UAI does not merely visualise the city's Imaginary coherence; it actively codifies and symbolises governance through sensors, IoT infrastructures, and Large Language Models (LLMs) that generate programmable rules, predictive models, and policy scenarios. As Allmendinger (2009: 54) observes, this Symbolic regime offers planners 'a simple and highly structured view of the world', smoothing away contradiction in favour of technocratic certainty. Zoning algorithms, regulatory bots, and policy-generating LLMs all re-script planning discourse to align with what Kitchin (2019) calls 'algorithmic governance' – an epistemology that privileges rule-based rationality as the only legitimate basis for decision-making. Yet, as Lacan warns, the Symbolic is always haunted by what it cannot contain: the Real – those unruly, traumatic, or opaque aspects of urban life that resist total symbolisation. If planners mistake AI-generated discourse for the city's truth, they risk what Gunder (2010) calls a fantasy suturing – a technocratic discourse detached from the messy, conflictual realities it claims to know and control. In this sense, the Symbolic order produced by UAI simultaneously structures, delimits, and disavows what can be thought, said, or planned – sustaining a fantasy of rational urban management while repressing the political and the plural that inevitably exceed the algorithm's code.

Sanchez et al. (2023: 2) argue that artificial intelligence – designed to perform tasks typically requiring human intelligence – is 'developed largely within a paradigm of efficiency and neoliberal values'. This orientation is far from neutral; it profoundly shapes how UAI, particularly through the deployment of Large Language Models (LLMs), reorganises the Symbolic order of planning. Kitchin (2014: 2) likewise contends that 'data-driven urbanism is profoundly shaped by the political economy and epistemology of neoliberalism', privileging optimisation, prediction, and control. In practice, LLMs trained on vast internet corpora reproduce dominant discourses – official narratives, institutional policies, and corporate vocabularies – while marginalising voices that are local, subaltern, or resistant to digitisation. Zuboff (2019: 8) warns that 'the goal is to automate us', translating human experience and subjectivity into data streams that feed algorithmic rationality. This, in turn, reinforces what Allmendinger (2009) calls 'a simple and highly structured view of the world', reducing urban complexity to programmable outputs. Yet as Eubanks (2018: 17) shows, these systems often 'punish the poor and marginalised precisely because they systematically overlook forms of knowledge, speech, and experience that are not easily machine-readable'. From a Lacanian perspective, the algorithmic Symbolic does not merely reflect technocratic rationality – it enforces it. It forecloses alternative discourses, situated knowledges, and plural ways of being that remain outside the machine-readable field. In doing so, UAI extends what Beer (2019: 27) describes as a 'government through abstraction', tightening the grip of an ideological order that disavows the unruly Real – that which resists codification, refuses capture, and insists on returning.

Crucially, planners' knowledge, norms, and professional desires are never purely independent or autonomous; they are constituted within this Symbolic field. As Gunder and Hillier (2009) contend, planning is not a neutral technical practice but an ideological formation sustained by fantasies of coherence and control. Urban AI now functions as a powerful extension of this Symbolic order, mediating how planners perceive the city, frame problems, and imagine possible futures. Through daily interactions with dashboards, zoning algorithms, or LLM-generated policy scripts, planners become interpellated – to borrow Althusser's term – into a technocratic discourse that increasingly defines what counts as legitimate knowledge or urban reality. In Lacanian terms, the planner's subjectivity is sutured to the promise of mastery that these algorithmic systems hold out, even as they structure desire in ways that reproduce hegemonic norms. As Hillier (2007: 294) reminds us, 'planning knowledge, like the subject, is never fully sovereign'; it is always partial and fantasmatic, masking its constitutive lack. The more planners rely on UAI, the more they risk mistaking algorithmic signifiers for the urban Real, displacing critical judgement with calculative certainty. Gunder (2010) goes further, arguing that planners' self-understanding is shaped by 'the ideological practice that constructs and reproduces hegemonic understandings of what space should be and how it should be used' (p. 299). Urban AI intensifies this dynamic by embedding planning within a Symbolic infrastructure that privileges what is machine-readable and efficient, while systematically repressing what is conflictual, ambiguous, or locally situated. In this way, the planner's norms, desires, and sense of self become increasingly entangled with an algorithmic Symbolic order – one that promises seamless urban governance while concealing its own exclusions and contradictions.

Yet for all its seductive coherence, the Symbolic order of UAI can never fully contain the contradictions, ruptures, and unrepresentable excesses of urban life – what Lacan calls the Real: that which stubbornly escapes signification, resists algorithmic capture, and returns as the reminder that the city can never be fully planned, predicted, or mastered.

11.6 Urban Reality as the Real

Having traced how Urban Artificial Intelligence reconfigures the Imaginary and Symbolic dimensions of planning, we now confront the third – and most elusive – of Lacan's registers: the Real. Lacan first introduced this term in the 1930s, but its meaning evolved profoundly throughout his work (Evans, 2010). Together, the Imaginary, Symbolic, and Real shape how the human subject apprehends the world – yet the Real remains fundamentally resistant to representation. The Real stands 'outside of any means of presentation by image and symbolism' (Gunder & Hillier, 2009: 67). It is not just what is 'out there', but what exceeds and disrupts the coherence produced by the Imaginary and the order imposed by the Symbolic. Gunder (2008: 195) captures it succinctly: the Real is 'an un-definable un-thought outside of language, imagination and signification, an unattainable and un-definable void that we desire to fill – but cannot'.

Within urban life, the Real is encountered in the city's inherent social, political, economic, and cultural contradictions – and in the emotional, embodied experiences of residents that defy neat abstraction. Even the most advanced UAI systems, with their predictive dashboards and digital twins, cannot fully capture the reality of urban phenomena (Gunder & Hillier, 2009). Rather, they attempt to repress this complex excess beneath a fantasy of hyper-rationalised order. Žižek (2001: 166) contends that 'the ultimate experience of the Real is not that of "reality" which shatters illusions, but that of an "illusion" which "irrationally" persists against the pressure of reality'. In *Welcome to the Desert of the Real,* he adds that the Real emerges with force when the comforting Symbolic layers are peeled away, revealing the violence, trauma, or unruly surplus that cannot be symbolised (Žižek, 2002). To glimpse what UAI cannot contain – the ruptures it disavows yet inevitably encounters – is to see the city not as a closed system but as a field of irreducible antagonisms and unscripted possibilities. It is precisely here that the planner's fantasy of control falters and the Real insists on returning.

This is not merely theoretical. The Real appears when predictive systems fail: when riots erupt despite 'social sentiment' models, when pandemics expose the fragility of algorithmic governance, or when algorithmic zoning collides with the messy reality of marginalised communities. Hillier (2003: 45) warns that any 'attempts to describe the Real are destined to simply distort it', yet its disruptive presence is always felt when the city refuses to be governed by the abstractions that planners or AI models impose. Graham and Marvin's (2001) classic work reminds us that cities are always 'splintering urbanisms' – riven by infrastructural breakdowns, disconnections, and local contingencies that elude centralised control. Kitchin et al. (2019) similarly show that the promise of seamless algorithmic governance inevitably collides with the unpredictability of lived urban life. Eubanks (2018) powerfully documents how automated systems often fail precisely when they confront the complex circumstances of people's real lives – deepening injustice rather than resolving it. As Mattern (2021) writes in A City is Not a Computer, 'No matter how many dashboards we build, there are parts of urban life that resist being rendered computational'.

The urban Real, then, is not some hidden 'truth' behind the system but the disruptive excess that unsettles our most carefully coded illusions – what Žižek (2001) calls the traumatic kernel that insists the city is always more than its data. To recognise the Real is to accept that urban life will always exceed the technocratic rationality of seamless automation. It calls planners back to the ethical and political work of engaging with conflicts, contradictions, and the impossible gaps in our maps, models, and discourses – what Gunder (2006) so aptly describes as planning's constitutive fantasy and its inevitable failure.

Conclusion

This chapter has argued that Urban Artificial Intelligence is not simply a technical apparatus but a deeply ideological formation that reshapes planning knowledge, subjectivity, and urban imaginaries. By reading UAI through Lacan's triadic registers – the Imaginary, the Symbolic, and the Real – this chapter examines how this technology potentially shapes planners' knowledge, understanding, and desire for control to an illusion of seamless urban order that is always, at its core, a misrecognition.

Maps are never neutral reflections but ideological constructs that produce spatial realities and legitimise power relations (Harley, 1989; Crampton & Krygier, 2006). In the Lacanian Imaginary, Urban Digital Twins, maps, and city replicas function like the mirror stage: they generate what Lacan called a Gestalt – a seductive image of coherence that planners mistake for urban reality. Hillier and Gunder (2003) argue that such images 'mask contradictions in the urban Real with fantasies of coherence' (p. 42), sustaining a fantasy of legibility while obscuring urban complexity. AI-driven UDTs amplify this by generating real-time replicas based on pre-set algorithms, which planners may wrongly accept as objective. As Harley (1989) reminds us, 'maps are embedded in relations of power', while Crampton and Krygier (2006) emphasise that 'maps are texts of power that reflect and reproduce social relations'. Over-reliance on UAI risks narrowing planners' imagination, subtly steering how urban futures are seen, governed, and constrained.

Within the Symbolic realm, Urban Artificial Intelligence does not merely extend what planning can do; it recodes what planning can say and know, embedding technocratic rationality in new algorithmic architectures that appear neutral yet are deeply ideological. As Kitchin (2014: 2) warns, 'data-driven urbanism is profoundly shaped by the political economy and epistemology of neoliberalism', privileging prediction and optimisation while systematically disavowing conflict and ambiguity. Zuboff (2019: 8) makes the danger plain: 'the goal is to automate us', reducing human experience to data streams that serve the logic of control. Feenberg (2002: 8) names this a 'technological environment' – a way of life that seeps into everyday practice and belief. Planners, through daily interactions with dashboards and AI-generated policy scripts, risk becoming, as Gunder (2010) puts it, agents of an 'ideological practice that constructs and reproduces hegemonic understandings of what space should be' (p. 299). This Symbolic order scripts the city as a rational object of calculation while systematically silencing what is unruly, agonistic, and resistant – the urban Real that always escapes the code.

The Real reminds us that this fantasy of seamless control is always haunted by its own impossibility. As Lacan (2006) contends, the Real stands 'outside of any means of presentation by image and symbolism' (Gunder & Hillier, 2009: 67). It erupts where the algorithm fails – in informal settlements that resist eviction, in street protests that block 'smart' traffic flows, in the mundane ruptures of daily urban life that refuse computational capture. Mattern (2021) puts it plainly: 'No matter how many dashboards we build, there are parts of urban life that resist being rendered computational'. Or, as Žižek (2001: 166) provocatively reminds us, 'the ultimate experience of the Real is not that of 'reality' which shatters illusions, but that of an 'illusion' which irrationally persists against the pressure of reality'.

This is the paradox at the heart of technocratic urbanism: the more we fantasise about mastering the city through code, the more we foreclose the Real that planning must engage if it is to remain genuinely democratic, ethical, and just. As Gunder (2006) puts it, planners must confront 'planning's constitutive fantasy and its inevitable failure'. To do so, as Feenberg (2002: v) insists, 'we must invent a politics of technological transformation' – one that does not confuse the map for the territory or the algorithm for the city's living pulse. What does this mean for practice? It means refusing to let UAI become a closed epistemic horizon. It means cultivating the critical capacity to 'stay with the trouble' (to borrow Haraway's phrase) of conflict, ambiguity, and excess. It means recognising that while 'technology is not simply a means but has become an environment and a way of life' (Feenberg, 2002: 8), we are not its passive subjects. Planners, as situated political actors, still have the capacity to question what urban intelligence means, whose voices it encodes, and which imaginaries it forecloses.

Ultimately, the challenge is to hold open the possibility that cities are never fully calculable and reducible to their digital images. It is here, in the messy, conflictual, and contradictory spaces, that planning's emancipatory potential might still be found.

References

Allam, Z., Bibri, S. E., Jones, D. S., Chabaud, D., & Moreno, C. (2022). Unpacking the '15-minute city' via 6G, IoT, and digital twins: Towards a new narrative for increasing urban efficiency, resilience, and sustainability. *Sensors*, 22(4), 1369. https://doi.org/10.3390/s22041369

Allmendinger, P. (2009). *Planning theory* (2nd ed.). Palgrave Macmillan.

Bahmanteymouri, E. (2023a). A Lacanian approach to spatial planning: Fantasy, ideology and desire. In E. Bahmanteymouri, J. Hillier, & M. Gunder (Eds.), *Planning and psychoanalysis: Lacanian perspectives on spatial planning* (pp. 210–229). Routledge.

Bahmanteymouri, E. (2023b). *Lacanian approaches to planning. In Elgar Encyclopedia in Urban and Regional Planning and Design* by Van Assche, K., Beunen, R. and Duineveld, M. (1st ed.). pp. 211–213. Edward Elgar Publishing Limited. https://doi.org/10.4337/9781800889002.000074

Bahmanteymouri, E., & Mohammadzadeh, M. (2023). Urban artificial intelligence and the new urban technocracy. In *Planning and knowledge*. Policy Press.
Batty, M. (2023). Artificial intelligence and cities: New technologies for new worlds. *Urban Studies*, 60(5–6), 1045–1063.
Bauman, Z. (2000). *Liquid modernity*. Polity Press.
Beer, D. (2019). *The data gaze: Capitalism, power and perception*. Sage.
Bridle, J. (2018). *New dark age: Technology and the end of the future*. Verso.
Caprotti, F., Cowley, R., & Datta, A. (2024). Algorithmic governance and urban futures: The politics of smart cities and artificial intelligence. *Urban Geography*, 45(6), 880–893.
Crampton, J. W., & Krygier, J. (2006). An introduction to critical cartography. *ACME: An International Journal for Critical Geographies*, 4(1), 11–33.
Crawford, K. (2021). *Atlas of AI: Power, politics, and the planetary costs of artificial intelligence*. Yale University Press.
Cugurullo, F. (2020). Urban artificial intelligence: From automation to autonomy in the smart city. *Frontiers in Sustainable Cities*, 2, 38. https://doi.org/10.3389/frsc.2020.00038
Cugurullo, F. (2021). *Frankenstein urbanism: Artificial intelligence, urban planning and cities*. Routledge.
Cugurullo, F. (2024). The AI-city: Post-smart urbanism and the logic of artificial intelligence. In T. Yigitcanlar, F. Cugurullo, & R. Corchado (Eds.), *Urban artificial intelligence* (pp. 12–27). Routledge.
Cugurullo, F., Palmini, C., & Caprotti, F. (2023). Urban artificial intelligence and the post-anthropocentric city. *Urban Studies*, 60(5–6), 1005–1022.
Daniel, T., Caprotti, F., & Cowley, R. (2023). Planners, smart city technologies and urban governance: New insights from practice. *Urban Studies*, 60(5–6), 1079–1095.
Delanty, G., & Harris, P. (2021). *The post-Western condition: Between cosmopolitanism and empire*. Cambridge Scholars Publishing.
Dyson, G. (2012). *Turing's cathedral: The origins of the digital universe*. Penguin Books.
Elliott, A. (2019). *The culture of AI: Everyday life and the digital revolution*. Routledge.
Eubanks, V. (2018). *Automating inequality: How high-tech tools profile, police, and punish the poor*. St. Martin's Press.
Evans, D. (2010). *An introductory dictionary of Lacanian psychoanalysis* (2nd ed.). Routledge.
Faludi, A. (1973). *Planning theory*. Pergamon Press.
Feenberg, A. (1999). *Questioning technology*. Routledge.
Feenberg, A. (2002). *Transforming technology: A critical theory revisited*. Oxford University Press.
Feenberg, A. (2017). *Technosystem: The social life of reason*. Harvard University Press.
Forester, J. (1999). *The deliberative practitioner: Encouraging participatory planning processes*. MIT Press.
Friedmann, J. (1987). *Planning in the public domain: From knowledge to action*. Princeton University Press.
Glynos, J. (2001). The grip of ideology: A Lacanian approach to the theory of ideology. *Journal of Political Ideologies*, 6(2), 191–214.
Graham, S., & Marvin, S. (2001). *Splintering urbanism: Networked infrastructures, technological mobilities and the urban condition*. Routledge.

Gunder, M. (2006). Sustainability: Planning's saving grace or road to perdition? *Journal of Planning Education and Research*, 26(2), 208–221.

Gunder, M. (2008). Ideologies of certainty in a risk society: The politics of fear and the suppression of plural debate in the planning profession. *Planning Theory*, 7(2), 186–206.

Gunder, M. (2010). Planning as the ideology of (neoliberal) space. *Planning Theory*, 9(4), 298–314.

Gunder, M., & Hillier, J. (2004). Conforming to the expectations of the profession: A Lacanian perspective on planning practice, norms and values. *Planning Theory & Practice*, 5(2), 217–235.

Gunder, M., & Hillier, J. (2009). *Planning in ten words or less: A Lacanian entanglement with spatial planning*. Routledge.

Harley, J. B. (1989). Deconstructing the map. *Cartographica: The International Journal for Geographic Information and Geovisualization*, 26(2), 1–20.

Harvey, D. (1978). The urban process under capitalism: A framework for analysis. *International Journal of Urban and Regional Research*, 2(1–4), 101–131.

Healey, P. (1997). *Collaborative planning: Shaping places in fragmented societies*. Macmillan.

Hebbert, M. (2019). Technocracy and the city: Urban theory in the late twentieth century. In M. Gunder, J. Hillier, & E. Bahmanteymouri (Eds.), *Planning and psychoanalysis* (pp. 20–35). Routledge.

Heidegger, M. (1977). *The question concerning technology and other essays*. Harper & Row.

Hillier, J. (2003). Agon'izing over consensus: Why Habermasian ideals cannot be 'real'. *Planning Theory*, 2(1), 37–59.

Hillier, J. (2007). *Stretching beyond the horizon: A multiplanar theory of spatial planning and governance*. Ashgate.

Homer, S. (2005). *Jacques Lacan*. Routledge.

Innes, J. E., & Booher, D. E. (2003). Collaborative policymaking: Governance through dialogue. In *Deliberative policy analysis* (pp. 33–59). Cambridge University Press.

Jabareen, Y. (2017). The dialectics of urban planning: Theoretical and methodological challenges. *Urban Studies*, 54(5), 1131–1146.

Kitchin, R. (2014). *The data revolution: Big data, open data, data infrastructures and their consequences*. Sage.

Kitchin, R. (2019). *The right to the smart city*. Emerald Publishing.

Kitchin, R. (2021). *Data lives: How data are made and shape our world*. Policy Press.

Kitchin, R., Coletta, C., Evans, L., & Heaphy, L. (2019). Smart cities, algorithmic technocracy and new urban technocrats. In M. Raco & F. Savini (Eds.), *Planning and knowledge* (pp. 199–212). Policy Press.

Lacan, J. (1987). *The seminar. Book I: Freud's papers on technique*. Cambridge University Press.

Lacan, J. (1988). *The seminar of Jacques Lacan: Book II: The ego in Freud's theory and in the technique of psychoanalysis, 1954–1955* (J.-A. Miller, Ed.; S. Tomaselli, Trans.). W. W. Norton & Company

Lacan, J. (2006). *Écrits: The first complete edition in English* (B. Fink, Trans.). W. W. Norton & Company.

Lefebvre, H. (1991). *The Production of Space* (Donald Nicholson-Smith, Trans.). Blackwell. (Original publication 1974)

Marcuse, H. (2013). *Technology, war and fascism* (Vol. 1). Routledge. (Original works 1958–1959)

Mattern, S. (2021). *A city is not a computer: Other urban intelligences*. Princeton University Press.

Mohammadzadeh, M. (2021). A Lacanian understanding of the southern planning theorists' identification under the hegemony of western philosophy. *plaNext–Next Generation Planning*, 11, 62–80.

Mohammadzadeh, M. (2023). *Lacan's Four discourses in planning. In Elgar encyclopedia in urban and regional planning and design* by Van Assche, K., Beunen, R. and Duineveld, M. (1st ed.). pp. 206–210. Edward Elgar Publishing Limited. https://doi.org/10(9781800889002),000073

Morozov, E. (2013). *To save everything, click here: The folly of technological solutionism*. PublicAffairs.

Muller, J. P. (2000). *Beyond the psychoanalytic dyad: Developmental semiotics in Freud, Peirce, and Lacan*. Routledge.

Palmini, O., & Cugurullo, F. (2023). Charting AI urbanism: Conceptual sources and spatial implications of urban artificial intelligence. *Discover Artificial Intelligence*, 3(1), 15. https://doi.org/10.1007/s44163-023-00060-w

Pohl, L., & Swyngedouw, E. (2023). 'What does not work in the world': The specter of Lacan in critical political thought. *Distinktion: Journal of Social Theory*, 24(1), 1–19.

Potts, R., & Webb, S. (2023). Artificial intelligence and the future of planning: A critical review. *Urban Planning*, 8(1), 120–133.

Putnam, R. D. (1977). *Elite transformation in advanced industrial societies*. Princeton University Press.

Raco, M., & Savini, F. (2019). *Planning and knowledge: How new forms of technocracy are shaping contemporary cities*. Policy Press.

Roudinesco, E. (1999). *Jacques Lacan: An outline of a life and history of a system of thought* (B. Bray, Trans.). Polity Press.

Sanchez, T. W., Son, T. H., Weedon, Z., Yigitcanlar, T., Corchado, J. M., & Mehmood, R. (2023). Planning on the verge of AI, or AI on the verge of planning. *Urban Science*, 7(3), 70.

Sarup, M., & Raja, T. (2005). *Identity, culture and the postmodern world*. Edinburgh University Press.

Savini, F., & Raco, M. (2019). The rise of a new urban technocracy. In M. Raco & F. Savini (Eds.), *Planning and knowledge* (pp. 3–18). Policy Press.

Stavrakakis, Y. (2002). *Lacan and the political*. Routledge.

Sturrock, J. (2003). *Structuralism and since: From Lévi-Strauss to Derrida* (2nd ed.). Oxford University Press.

Suarez-Villa, L. (2009). *Technocapitalism: A critical perspective on technological innovation and corporatism*. Temple University Press.

Wolfreys, J. (2004). *Critical keyword in literary and cultural theory*. Palgrave Macmillan.

Wood, D. (1992). *The power of maps*. Routledge.

Xia, Y., Qu, A., Zheng, Y., Tang, Y., Zhuang, D., Liang, Y., Shenhao, W., Wu, C., Sun, L., Zimmermann, R., & Zhao, J. (2025). *Reimagining urban science: Scaling causal inference with large language models*. arXiv preprint arXiv:2504.12345.

Yigitcanlar, T., Kamruzzaman, M., & Corchado, J. M. (2018). Understanding smart cities: Intertwining development drivers with desired outcomes in a multidimensional framework. *Cities*, 81, 145–160.

Žižek, S. (1989). *The sublime object of ideology*. Verso.

Žižek, S. (2001). *Did somebody say totalitarianism? Five interventions in the (mis)use of a notion*. Verso.

Žižek, S. (2002). *Welcome to the desert of the real*. Verso.

Zuboff, S. (2019). *The age of surveillance capitalism: The fight for a human future at the new frontier of power*. Profile Books.

12

From Urban Surveillance to Urban Care: Care-Full Justice in the Age of AI

Udipta Boro, Fran Meissner, and Karin Pfeffer

12.1 Introduction

In 2018, the Indian Government initiated the Safe City Projects (SCPs) following public outcry over the Nirbhaya Rape Case that had happened in New Delhi (Bakshi, 2017; Ministry of Home Affairs, 2018). This case led to widespread protests across the country demanding safety and care for women (Rana, 2020). The initiation of the SCPs responded to such demands by introducing AI-powered urban video surveillance systems (henceforth, AI surveillance) for women's safety (Press Information Bureau, 2019).

Such use of surveillance technologies is often justified with the notion of the caring watcher 'who not only watches but also "looks out for"' the public (Andrejevic et al., 2021, p. 569). Walsh (2010, p. 128) argues that surveillance, beyond its harmful potential, can construct 'counter geographies of hope', challenging control and creating a sense of care for those in need. With the automation in surveillance technologies powered by artificial intelligence (AI), the question arises whether such a sense of care still holds true. In relation to other AI systems, scholars such as Maalsen (2023) argue that AI algorithms hold the potential to be agents of care. But considering the harmful potential of surveillance and AI (Koskela, 2000; Costanza-Chock, 2018), it is pertinent to ask if similar arguments would also hold for AI-powered urban video surveillance technologies.

While AI surveillance is popularised with promises of better protection against crimes and increased safety (Whittaker, 2021), AI-fuelled automation poses risks, like automating biases, shifting the nature of power imbalances in society, and perpetuating control and discrimination (Costanza-Chock, 2018; Waelen and Wieczorek, 2022). Despite these concerns, cities worldwide are implementing AI surveillance. But as Bauman and Lyon (2013, p. 84) ask, 'can [AI-powered] surveillance technologies be tuned to the key of care'?

Care, in relation to technology, has been studied from different angles, ranging from health and environmental care to urban planning and critical data

DOI: 10.1201/9781003480167-15

studies (Rossitto et al., 2022; Binet et al., 2023; Goldberg et al., 2024; Zakharova and Jarke, 2024). We specifically focus on urban care. While there is yet to be an agreed-upon definition of urban care in the literature (Gabauer et al., 2022), we draw on scholarly work from feminist care ethics and urban studies (Williams, 2017; Power and Williams, 2019; Gabauer et al., 2022). Such authors evoke urban care as both socio-technical and relational. This begs to extend Bauman and Lyon's (2013) question to: how can we (if at all) reimagine AI-powered urban video surveillance systems as infrastructure of urban care? The terms 'socio-technical' and 'relational' are intertwined here. AI algorithms work 'through the relations of selves to selves, and selves to others' (Amoore, 2020, p. 8). 'Others' here can be understood as technology and people within the socio-technical entanglement of the city (Van Kleunen et al., 2021).

To do so, we analyse a set of technical literature that describes and justifies the development of AI surveillance in the Indian context. India, apart from being one of the most heavily surveilled countries (Mahapatra, 2021), is also planning and partly implementing the SCPs. We designed this study against the backdrop of India's SCPs and the use of AI within its video surveillance system. Focusing on the Indian context further allows us to contribute to the larger debates from India in the fields of critical data studies and surveillance studies (Henne, 2019; Rathi and Tandon, 2020; Vila-Seoane, 2021; Narayan, 2023).

We first explore the current development priorities for AI surveillance as explained in the technical literature. We evaluate these priorities using a feminist lens of care-full[1] justice (Williams, 2017). Conversing with other feminist works on surveillance studies, critical data studies, and science and technology studies (STS), we further explore interventions that would help us reimagine AI surveillance that upholds care-full justice. In doing so, this chapter advances current discussions surrounding technology and care by critiquing and challenging current understandings of care in the technical domain (Haraway, 2016; Powell et al., 2022; Jarke and Büchner, 2024).

12.2 A Caring City from AI Surveillance Perspectives

Scholarly work discusses care in relation to surveillance, cities, and AI. Despite the criticisms against surveillance for its harmful potential (Koskela, 2002; Monahan, 2009; Narayan, 2023) and the seeming contradiction between surveillance and care, Richardson et al. (2017, p. 110) state that surveillance and care are two concepts that are 'neither oxymoron nor tautology'. Walsh's (2010) work highlights that, departing from a social justice standpoint, activist groups in the southern USA have adopted surveillance technologies to practice care in the form of protecting and assisting migrants on the move, challenging state control through surveillance. Andrejevic et al. (2021) argue that a form of social surveillance by and of the public helped them enact mutual care during the Covid-19 pandemic in Australia. Surveillance is considered caring in these cases because 'the interests and well-being of watcher and watched [reportedly] coincide' (Andrejevic et al., 2021, p. 569). However, one must question the actions and principles of those in power to evaluate how care through surveillance is enacted in practice. (Stoddart, 2012).

Research has also discussed care in relation to cities. Gabauer et al. (2022) show that institutional caring (or uncaring) practices shape urban spaces, rendering them (un)caring for urban residents. Alam and Houston (2020) focus on non-institutional urban care spaces, where non-normative caring practices create caring cities. A caring city is one where the safety of its residents, especially those more vulnerable, is ensured (Bednarczyk, 2022). Bednarczyk (2022, p. 66) shows that by implementing caring practices for and with each other, women in Córdoba, Argentina, ensure their safety and 'redefine their presence in urban spaces' while striving to transform urban spaces into an empowering experience. In doing so, these women are reclaiming their rights to everyday life and to the city (Beebeejaun, 2016). In addition to safety, a caring city also facilitates inclusion and accessibility. Marchigiani (2022) similarly argues that an environment of care produces urban spaces that support everyday practices of urban residents and provide them with just and equal access to daily services and commodities. In these cases, urban quotidian constellations facilitate the protection of rights, freedoms, and justice to be considered caring.

Another group of scholars have explored the entanglement between AI and care. Maalsen (2023) calls for viewing AI algorithms as things that enhance our ability to care. She argues that such a view would help shift discussions from AI's threats to its potential to 'protect and reassure' (Maalsen, 2023, p. 204). McLean (2024) similarly argues that incorporating a care perspective is important while developing AI to challenge possible threats. However, AI's caring potential must be critically evaluated against the question of whether AI, rather than caring, may amplify the exercise of power within a surveillance system and automate social control.

These three strands – surveillance, cities, and AI – highlight the need for critically examining the power dynamics and the everyday enactment of care. With the proliferation of AI surveillance in cities as the 'caring watcher' (Andrejevic et al., 2021, p. 569), it is getting increasingly important to examine these three strands together.

To do so, we adopt a care-full justice framework (Williams, 2017) to better understand the interplay of care and AI surveillance in an urban setting. This framework enables critical exploration of the everyday city through the ideals of social justice and ethics of care, challenging prevalent power imbalances. In this chapter, we adopt Williams' thinking to theorise socio-technical entanglements in cities, specifically those that arise from AI-powered surveillance systems.

In developing care-full justice, Williams departs from a social justice perspective and argues for incorporating ethics of care in the discussions of socially just cities. In doing so, Williams disrupts the binary idea of care being private and justice being public while grounding both care and justice in the everyday urban setting. Williams develops four premises upon which the concept of care-full justice is built. These premises advocate that (i) 'care and justice are approached through a relational social ontology', (ii) 'care and justice need to be approached as distinct yet interdependent practices', (iii) 'care and justice [need to] be practised and understood in contextually dependent ways', and (iv) 'care and justice can be practised in everyday spaces and through mediated encounters and relationships' (Williams, 2017, p. 827). We use these premises to evaluate AI surveillance systems to assess their potential for care. An explanation of how we do so follows in the next section.

12.3 Methodology

To examine the interplay between care and AI surveillance, we first explore the current development priorities behind AI surveillance systems. To do so, we conduct a scoping review (Arksey and O'Malley, 2005) of technical literature proposing new AI surveillance systems. While scoping reviews do not produce generalisable results, they are suitable for mapping the nature and range of a particular topic and providing a detailed summary of it (Arksey and O'Malley, 2005). As such, a scoping review is suitable for an initial understanding of the development priorities behind AI surveillance systems.

The review focuses on how, in the technical domain, developing AI surveillance is justified and if and how this is done by alluding to surveillance systems as caring agents, given our wider research interests, particularly focusing on the Indian context (Boro et al., 2026). Including solely India-focused work may exclude international perspectives. However, examining a subsample of the articles included before applying the India-focused exclusion criterion suggests that narratives around justifying AI surveillance align with those we identify in our analysis.

The technical literature we review comes from the IEEE (Institute of Electrical and Electronics Engineers) Xplore Database. IEEE is the 'world's largest technical professional organisation' that advances 'technology for humanity' through 'highly cited publications, conferences, technology standards, and professional and educational activities' (IEEE, 2025; 'About' section). With the aim of understanding technological choices and claims, focusing on IEEE, which exclusively contains technical literature, allows for a targeted and feasible approach for the scoping review. However, this focus on IEEE leaves out other databases and more critical research on this topic. Moreover, having only one database could mean the representation of a particular research paradigm or particular contents of the articles. While for the scope of this paper, the IEEE database provides sufficient insight, future research can encompass a broader literature base for a systematic review.

We conducted the literature search, keeping an open timeframe until June 2024 (time of this research). We did so to account for not only recent but also early-stage work on AI surveillance technologies. We searched for writings that explicitly discussed AI-powered urban surveillance systems for or developed in an Indian context. The search terms and exclusion criteria were based on this objective. We used the following search string.

("All Metadata":surveillance OR "All Metadata":cctv) AND ("All Metadata":"artificial intelligence" OR "All Metadata":AI) AND ("All Metadata":urban OR "All Metadata":cit*) AND ("All Metadata":india OR "All Metadata":indian); where Metadata includes abstract, title and indexing terms.

The following were the exclusion criteria:

1. Paper does not discuss surveillance systems.
2. Surveillance systems discussed are not AI-powered.
3. AI-powered surveillance systems discussed are not for urban domain.
4. AI-powered urban surveillance system is not trained, developed, or tested out in/for Indian cities.

This search and exclusion strategy resulted in 29 articles. Table 12.1 contains the distribution of analysed articles by year. The table shows that interest and efforts on this topic have recently spiked. Figure 12.1 displays the literature collection process, including the search terms, exclusion criteria, and the number of literature included/excluded.

To interpret nuances, complexities, and context in the scoping review, content analysis was used (Hecker and Kalpokas, 2023). Content analysis is helpful while navigating large volumes of textual data to identify patterns, themes, and biases (Hecker and Kalpokas, 2023). Following Vila-Henninger et al. (2024), we operationalised this analysis through abductive coding. This provided us with an anchor point from which to start the analysis while generating new codes as the analysis proceeded. The following questions were used as departure points for the analysis:

TABLE 12.1

Distribution of Articles per Year

Publication Year	Count of Publication Year
2016	1
2019	1
2020	1
2021	4
2022	8
2023	10
2024	4
Grand Total	**29**

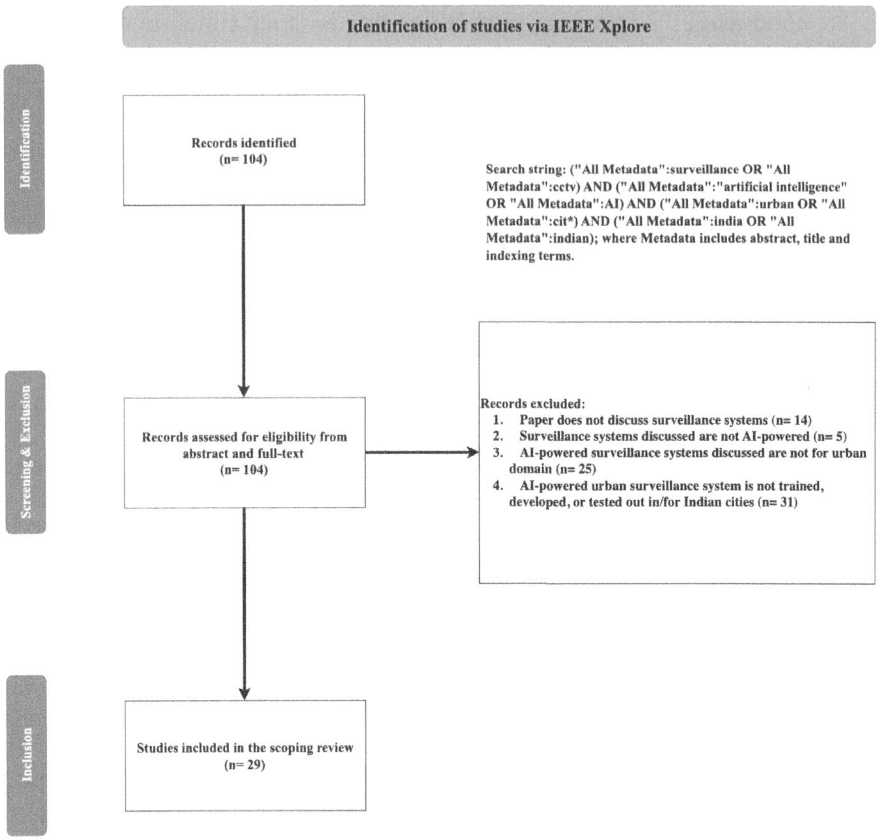

FIGURE 12.1
Collection of literature for review in different steps (adapted from PRISMA).[2]

i) Why is the AI-powered surveillance system being developed?
ii) Who is the system for?
iii) What does the system do?
iv) Who does the system target?

These questions relate to care-full justice as they seek to unveil the principles behind and the everyday operation of the developed AI surveillance systems. Asking these questions also provided a systematic start to the coding and analysis process. We developed the initial main codes based on these four questions. With the progress in analysis, more codes were generated, which were placed under the initial main codes. After three iterations of coding, the subcodes and their place within the initial main codes, as well as the associated groups, were finalised. Table 12.2 shows the final coding scheme.

TABLE 12.2

Coding Scheme

Guiding Question	Initial Main Codes	Sub Codes	Associated Groups of Sub Codes
Why is the AI-powered surveillance system being developed?	AI system development reasoning	accident prevention	prevention
		crime prevention	
		disease prevention	
		littering prevention	
		crowd management	management
		disaster and emergency management	
		energy management	
		traffic management	
		protecting environment	protection
		protecting people and property	
		enforcing law	law and order
		penalty for violators	
Who is the system for?	AI system intended users	municipalities	n.a.
		traffic authorities	
		security authorities	
		general public	
What does the system do?	AI system qualities and functionalities	accuracy	qualities
		effectiveness	
		efficiency	
		reliability	
		accident detection	functionalities
		crime detection	
		behaviour detection	
		emotion detection	
		face recognition	
		location detection	
		mask detection	
		object detection	
Who does the system target?	AI system target group	general public	n.a.
		rule breakers	

Next, we link these findings to the SCPs' development, as evidenced in official and journalistic articles on the SCPs, to show the empirical manifestation of these technological developments. Finally, we turn to Williams' (2017) care-full justice framework to critically discuss the results.

While doing a review may be influenced by one's subjectivity (Suri, 2020), we try to address that by being transparent and systematic about the analysis process. Further, when referring to reviewed technical literature, we use ID numbers to distinguish them from the other literature we draw on in the chapter. By doing so, we also attempt to keep a certain level of anonymity of the authors and avoid stigmatising individuals or groups of researchers, as we did not explicitly ask for their consent to analyse their scholarly work.

12.4 AI Surveillance in the City: Care versus Control

In analysing the technical literature, we found that AI-powered surveillance systems are developed with the overarching aim of helping to maintain a safer and healthier society where residents are actively discouraged from breaking the law for the greater good. The analysed articles can broadly be distinguished by their core goals as shown in Figure 12.2. The figure also shows the intended users of these systems and the relative frequency and interlinkages of each goal and intended main user. Only one article discusses surveillance that is meant to be used by the public for their safety on the road. We observe in the figure that caring is mostly understood as institutional practices (Gabauer et al., 2022), where municipalities, traffic, and security authorities attempt to care through different measures. The intended use of these systems for such purposes carries a caring undertone as they are

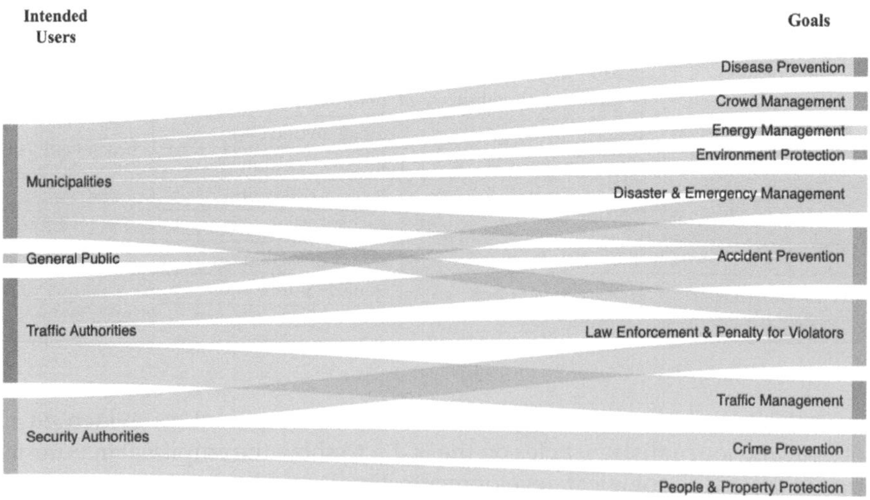

FIGURE 12.2
Reported goals of the developed systems and the intended users to achieve that goal (created by authors).

meant to help build a world where people can live 'as well as possible' (Fisher and Tronto, 1990, p. 40). However, care-full justice postulates that caring is more than facilitating living as well as possible (Williams, 2017). Next, we evaluate these reported caring practices through the lens of care-full justice.

The first premise of care-full justice is about a relational social ontology that posits that all beings rely on and are connected to each other for their well-being. This ontology facilitates understanding of our responsibilities towards each other as part of society. Williams offers two ways in which adopting a relational social ontology activates care-full justice thinking. Drawing on Massey (2004), Williams first argues that recognising these interconnected relationships enables us to see the relational connection and the making of urban spaces where care-full justice comes into being. Then, she highlights the sites where meaningful encounters or connections facilitate caring actions. Although Williams' work does not engage with AI surveillance, this first premise can help us examine the potential of AI surveillance to facilitate meaningful encounters in cities and the exercise of responsibilities towards each other.

In the analysed technical literature, we observe that AI surveillance technologies are portrayed as effective tools for exercising punitive measures. For example, Paper 22 suggests using AI-enhanced cameras with facial recognition capabilities to detect the faces of traffic law violators and display them on billboards for public humiliation. The assumption is that such shaming measures will reduce law violations. The reported caring aspect in this case is about increasing 'overall safety and compliance with traffic rules in urban areas' (Paper 22, p. 1128). However, applying punitive measures, such as public shaming with surveillance technologies for forced compliance with rules, creates imbalanced power relationships in urban spaces between the watcher and the watched, as often criticised by scholars (Akbari, 2019; Narayan, 2023). Such forced compliance does not facilitate caring actions. Such ideas may rather create an atmosphere of fear and forced obedience, where meaningful encounters between people and between people and technologies are hindered.

In the second premise, Williams explains that the distinctness and interdependence between care and justice help us work towards justice that is fair, attentive to others' needs, and sensitive to socio-political factors producing injustice. Similarly, it would help us work towards care that is attuned to the inequalities between carers and those being cared for. To examine AI surveillance based on this premise, Macnish's (2014) work on just surveillance shows us a way. His work guides us to ask questions regarding the reasons for the implementation of surveillance, the authority, and where it lies. Asking these questions can help us relate surveillance to the principles of fairness and attentiveness, as well as to challenging the oppressive nature of care practices (Macnish, 2014).

Our analysis highlights the challenges AI surveillance may face in being fair, attentive, and attuned to inequalities. Paper 2 proposes a crime prediction model that enables security authorities to care for society by ensuring public safety in cities. The system detects suspicious behaviour and potential criminals to predict crimes. Such predictive analytics primarily rely on anonymous and/or less sensitive data left by others or aggregated data from other sources to predict sensitive information about other (often disadvantaged) groups or individuals (Mühlhoff, 2021). While ensuring public safety could be a caring action, predictive analysis through AI surveillance violates the right to privacy as sensitive information is often predicted without the knowledge of those who are surveilled (Mühlhoff, 2021). Moreover, these technologies may define acceptable behaviour in public spaces without situating the behaviours within specific contexts. Such technological rationales, when translated into social domains, exacerbate inequalities as they unfairly enable authorities to care for the greater good while limiting people's agency by controlling their behaviour. Furthermore, depending on the specific socio-political context in which the system is used, the latter can expedite discrimination against vulnerable groups while sidelining the goal of ensuring safety, for example, through the use of biased offender databases that already disproportionally include images of overpoliced minorities (Boro et al., 2026).

The third premise of care-full justice draws on the idea that care and justice only hold meaning through people's actions and practices in specific contexts. This means that different socio-political, spatial, or economic contexts shape different kinds of carelessness and injustice. It is these contexts of carelessness and injustice that dictate how care and justice can be practised. For example, the reviewed Paper 19 proposes to develop a crowd monitoring surveillance system for city authorities to keep the public safe. This system monitors crowd behaviour as well as crowd density and alerts authorities if any anomaly in the crowd is detected. The paper argues that automated crowd management through CCTV surveillance reduces the chances of mishaps in crowded areas and upholds urban security – a caring goal. However, the politics of urban crowd management is more than just urban securitisation (Nishiyama, 2018). Depending on specific socio-political and spatial contexts, AI surveillance can codify normal and abnormal crowd conditions and behaviours, where abnormality is filtered out to keep the crowd normal (Nishiyama, 2018). However, what city authorities consider normal in certain contexts may not be normal in other contexts (Amoore, 2013). As such, people's actions and practices can be severely hampered, limiting the exercise of care-full justice.

Finally, the fourth premise of care-full justice postulates that care and justice should be practised in everyday, mundane settings. Williams (2017, p. 834) argues that the everyday practices of care and justice should allow us to exercise our collective responsibilities towards the 'near and distant others'. While Williams' idea of 'near and distant' revolves around physical proximity, for our research, we adopt a rather different idea of proximity: proximity to the centre of power. The ones closest to the centre are more privileged, while the distant ones are more marginalised. Ample research has highlighted that the benefits of AI technologies are primarily concentrated among those more privileged/least marginalised (Costanza-Chock, 2018; D'Ignazio and Klein, 2020).

Our analysis so far shows how AI surveillance risks further marginalising vulnerable groups while benefiting more privileged groups. Further, AI surveillance can also limit the mundane everyday practice of care-full justice. For example, Paper 3 develops a face-mask detection system for city authorities. The system aims to 'get individuals to avoid breaking the laws that are necessary to stop the spread of the coronavirus' (p. 5). While disease prevention is a caring goal, these developments fail to consider that technologies developed with the rationale of criminalising individuals based on what they wear have far-reaching consequences. For example, Rathi and Tandon's (2020) work on India's New Delhi and Akbari's (2019) work in Iran show that surveillance technologies can be used to place normative expectations on women regarding their daily clothing and movements. Automating these issues further restricts the freedom of vulnerable groups while enabling those in power to dictate everyday norms.

But how do such rationales for AI surveillance systems empirically manifest? Bringing back the example of India's Safe City Projects (SCPs), we observe that authorities of Bengaluru and Chennai SCPs view that the presence of any group of men close to a woman in public places can be suspicious (MTC Chennai, 2020; Bengaluru City Police, 2021). Moreover, the Bengaluru SCP conceptualises public places as inherently dangerous for women and in need of constant AI camera surveillance (Bengaluru City Police, 2021). To address these issues, these SCPs opt for predictive policing and crowd monitoring (MTC Chennai, 2020; Bengaluru City Police, 2021).

Further, the Lucknow SCP aims to implement emotion recognition by analysing facial expressions and suspicious activity recognition for better women's safety in the city (-Rakshit, 2021; Sur, 2021). Such developments may enable forced compliance with codified normal behaviours and daily encounters with emotion-recognising technologies. Following another rape case in India's Kolkata in 2024, a medical college issued a safety advisory to its women employees and students, asking them to be 'emotionally composed'[3] and gracious while interacting with the public (Purkayastha, 2024). Women victims of sexual violence in India often get blamed for their clothes and their participation in public places during risky hours (such as night-time) (Damania and Singh, 2022). With an emotion-recognising system in place, victims may be further blamed for not being *emotionally composed*.

Drawing on our analysis, we argue that the current development priorities for AI surveillance in India portray a caring appearance. But these systems fail to care in practice and cannot hold up to the four care-full justice premises. These systems simultaneously care for the powerful while pushing the more vulnerable to bear injustice and carelessness. Is it then possible to address these issues to uphold care-full justice in cities through AI surveillance systems?

12.5 Reimagining Surveillance for Care

In the previous discussion, evaluating William's first premise for urban care showed that AI surveillance may create an environment of fear, restricting meaningful encounters between people and technologies. Exploring the second premise showed us how AI surveillance potentially exacerbates inequality and limits people's agency. Looking at the third premise helped us discuss the inability of AI surveillance to respond to specific contextual needs. The fourth premise helped show that AI surveillance restricts the day-to-day practice of care-full justice, specifically for vulnerable populations. Overall, our analysis proposed that new surveillance systems did not show that these systems will be able to overcome problems with AI surveillance reproducing power imbalances, where powerful groups benefit at the cost of vulnerable groups.

In exploring alternative approaches, 'Protective Optimisation Technologies' (POTs) could present alternative ways forward (Kulynych et al., 2020). POTs empower those affected by technology-mediated harms and provide them with 'avenues for political contestation' (p. 1). What sets POTs apart is that they do not require service providers' cooperation to expose and address the harms posed by AI-powered systems. POTs operate with the assumption that those experiencing techno-mediated harm have better knowledge of the system's negative impacts and that they better understand the social utility of the system than the system providers do.

Kulynych et al. (2020) classify camouflaging and wearing items such as eyeglasses as POTs to evade face detection from surveillance cameras. Kazansky (2021) has discussed anticipatory data practices as a form of resistance to surveillance by affected groups, which also upholds the agency of the latter, as posited by William's second premise. Building on the idea of contesting and resisting harm, DeVrio et al. (2024) argue that affected groups' responses to algorithmic harm could be about protecting and strengthening their power to resist and contest harmful algorithmic systems and pressuring and attempting to gain power over authorities. Such actions could create a way for contestable AI surveillance systems by constantly engaging and intervening with the latter from the design to post-implementation phases (Alfrink et al., 2023). POTs, in this way, may instil meaningful encounters between people and technologies and allow for mutual caring actions among people. However, local laws and people's intersectional positions in society could impact how POTs are implemented and how successful they are.

Expanding on the idea of contestability inherent to POTs, co-designed contestable systems may be placed most effectively to shift the onus of ensuring care-full justice from public to broader sets of stakeholders. Co-design facilitates strong interactions between developers and stakeholders, including the public, during the development timeframe, addressing the power imbalance between them (Rittenbruch et al., 2022). It seeks to bring to the fore and, thus, empower the voices of those being marginalised (King et al., 2022). While co-designing contestable systems does not necessarily guarantee a harm-free system, by being made contestable, the system would leave room for being responsive to disputes/needs. As such, co-design can respond to specific contextual needs as postulated by care-full justice. However, co-design is criticised for being unclear in defining who can participate in the co-design process and who holds the ultimate decision-making power (Del Gaudio et al., 2020). This means that co-design may end up exacerbating inequality and limiting marginalised groups' agency, again restricting care-full justice.

The discussion shows that despite upholding certain aspects of care-full justice, the proposed interventions cannot truly create AI surveillance for care-full justice. We, therefore, argue that AI surveillance, despite claims to being caring, cannot be caring if evaluated through the four premises of care-full justice. Instead of reimagining AI surveillance, perhaps it is more useful to reimagine a caring city without such invasive and harmful systems. Krysztoforska et al. (2023, p. 13) suggest reimagining technology systems by removing one or more of their key properties, which 'forces us to reorganise knowledge, opening the door for new insights and for designing these objects differently in the future'. Taking their suggestion as a cue, and one by one removing system features that obstruct the possibility of care-full justice in the city, given our analysis, may result in stripping the system of all of its component parts. Doing so would leave us at a point where we should not call for reimagining the system to make it care, but reimagining cities that work without harmful and invasive AI surveillance systems while fostering care-full justice.

12.6 Conclusion

We started this chapter with the aim of reimagining AI-powered urban video surveillance systems as infrastructures of urban care. We did so by first examining the development priorities for AI surveillance in Indian cities by analysing a set of technical literature through the lens of care-full justice. We highlighted that AI surveillance is fundamentally not compatible with care-full justice as it risks disproportionately affecting vulnerable populations. We discussed interventions such as POTs and co-design, which also reiterated AI surveillance's incompatibility with care-full justice. Hence, we argued that AI surveillance systems cannot be infrastructures of urban care when examined using a care-full justice lens. Therefore, we finally called for reimagining cities without AI surveillance rather than attempting the seemingly impossible task of making AI surveillance arbiters of care-full justice in cities. However, we acknowledge that reimagining cities or technologies requires transdisciplinary collaborations and cannot be achieved through research alone.

With this chapter, we expect to kick-start dialogue among city authorities and surveillance technology developers on how their *caring projects* may fail to care for all. While there are city regulations aiming at transparency and fairness of their AI-based projects (City of Helsinki, 2025; Gemeente Amsterdam, 2025), this chapter brings focus to considering care for such regulatory frameworks. Further, this research can help spread citizen awareness by highlighting the importance of rights and agency in a society that is getting increasingly techno-dependent (Wessels, 2013; Pangrazio and Sefton-Green, 2021).

The scoping review in this chapter is based on a limited set of literature and a specific Indian context. While the review provided us with rich insights regarding urban care narratives and AI surveillance, future research can broaden the study by focusing on a wider setting with a larger literature base. Specifically, future research can explore how care-full justice (or the lack thereof) is experienced on the ground where such technologies are at play. Moreover, a complete removal of AI surveillance is a political decision. Such a decision would require the government's willingness and strong public narratives against such systems that, at least in part, are also viewed as necessary by different urban dwellers (Rathi and Tandon, 2020). Commenting on the feasibility of such a decision is beyond the scope of this chapter. Future research can thus also explore pathways to such feasibility as well as emerging interest in more-than-human relationalities (Williams, 2017). Each relevant to what such an imaginary of future cities would look like and which alternative technological mediation of cities it would entail.

12.7 Supplementary Materials

List of articles and conference proceedings analysed in this chapter: https://doi.org/10.17026/SS/AX2LWO

Notes

1 Scholars use both care-full and care-ful as spellings to denote the same concepts. As we follow a framework developed by Williams (2017), we have used her spelling of care-full.

2 https://www.prisma-statement.org/prisma-2020-flow-diagram (Accessed: 9 April 2025).
3 The advisory did not define what being emotionally composed would mean.

References

Akbari, A. (2019) 'Spatial|data justice: Mapping and digitised strolling against moral police in Iran', *SSRN Electronic Journal* [Preprint]. Available at: https://doi.org/10.2139/SSRN.3460224.

Alam, A. and Houston, D. (2019 July/2020) 'Rethinking care as alternate infrastructure', *Cities*, 100, p. 102662. Available at: https://doi.org/10.1016/j.cities.2020.102662.

Alfrink, K. et al. (2023) 'Contestable AI by design: Towards a framework', *Minds and Machines*, 33(4), pp. 613–639. Available at: https://doi.org/10.1007/s11023-022-09611-z.

Amoore, L. (2013) *The Politics of Possibility*. Duke University Press. Available at: https://doi.org/10.2307/j.ctv11sms8s.

Amoore, L. (2020) 'Politics and ethics in the age of algorithms', in *Cloud Ethics: Algorithms and the Attributes of Ourselves and Others*. 1st edn. Durham and London: Duke University Press, pp. 1–28.

Andrejevic, M. et al. (2021) 'Situating "careful surveillance"', *International Journal of Cultural Studies*, 24(4), pp. 567–583. Available at: https://doi.org/10.1177/1367877921997450.

Arksey, H. and O'Malley, L. (2005) 'Scoping studies: Towards a methodological framework', *International Journal of Social Research Methodology*, 8(1), pp. 19–32. Available at: https://doi.org/10.1080/1364557032000119616.

Bakshi, G. (2017) 'The "Nirbhaya" movement: An Indian feminist revolution', *GNOVIS Journal*, 17(2), pp. 43–55.

Bauman, Z. and Lyon, D. (2013) *Liquid Surveillance A Conversation*. 1st edn. Cambridge: Polity Press.

Bednarczyk, A. (2022) '"We are here to care": Gendered urban safety in Argentina"', in A. Gabauer et al. (eds) *Care and the City: Encounters with Urban Studies*. 1st edn. New York: Routledge, pp. 65–74. Available at: https://doi.org/10.4324/9781003031536-9.

Beebeejaun, Y. (2016) 'Gender, urban space, and the right to everyday life', *Journal of Urban Affairs*, 39(3), pp. 323–334. Available at: https://doi.org/10.1080/07352166.2016.1255526.

Bengaluru City Police. (2021) 'Request for proposal for selection of service provider for design, implementation and maintenance of Bengaluru safe city project E-procurement tender document', *Bengaluru City Police*, pp. 1–482. Available at: https://www.tendersontime.com/india/details/rfp-selection-service-provider-design-implementation-and-maintenance-bengaluru-safe-city-34b20f7/#.

Binet, A. et al. (2023) 'The urban infrastructure of care', *Journal of the American Planning Association*, 89(3), pp. 282–294. Available at: https://doi.org/10.1080/01944363.2022.2099955.

Boro, U., Meissner, F. and Pfeffer, K. (2026) 'Safety and the techno-mediated city: Lessons from Bengaluru's AI-powered CCTV network', *Journal of Urban Technology*, pp 1–26. Available at: https://doi.org/10.1080/10630732.2025.2583882.

City of Helsinki. (2025) *Artificial Intelligence Systems of Helsinki.* Available at: https://ai.hel.fi/en/ai-register/ (Accessed: 17 April 2025).

Costanza-Chock, S. (2018) 'Design justice, A.I., and escape from the matrix of domination', *Journal of Design and Science* [Preprint]. Available at: https://doi.org/10.21428/96c8d426.

Damania, M. H. and Singh, R. M. (2022) 'An exploratory qualitative analysis of rape myths in India', *Analysis of Social Issues and Public Policy*, 22(3), pp. 989–1016. Available at: https://doi.org/10.1111/asap.12323.

Del Gaudio, C., Franzato, C. and de Oliveira, A. J. (2020) 'Co-design for democratising and its risks for democracy', *CoDesign*, 16(3), pp. 202–219. Available at: https://doi.org/10.1080/15710882.2018.1557693.

DeVrio, A., Eslami, M. and Holstein, K. (2024) 'Building, shifting, & employing power: A taxonomy of responses from below to algorithmic harm', in *Proceedings of the 2024 ACM Conference on Fairness, Accountability, and Transparency.* New York, NY, USA: ACM, pp. 1093–1106. Available at: https://doi.org/10.1145/3630106.3658958.

D'Ignazio, C. and Klein, L. F. (2020) *Data Feminism.* 1st edn. Cambridge, MA: MIT Press.

Fisher, B. and Tronto, J. (1990) 'Toward a feminist theory of caring', in E. E. Abel and M. Nelson (eds) *Circles of Care: Work and Identity in Women's Lives.* Albany: State University New York Press, pp. 35–62.

Gabauer, A. et al. (2022) 'Care, uncare, and the city', in A. Gabauer et al. (eds) *Care and the City: Encounters with Urban Studies*. 1st edn. New York: Routledge. Available at: https://doi.org/10.4324/9781003031536.

Gemeente Amsterdam. (2025) *Het Algoritmeregister van de Nederlandse overheid.* Available at: https://algoritmes.overheid.nl/nl/organisatie/gemeente-amsterdam (Accessed: 17 April 2025).

Goldberg, C. B. et al. (2024) 'To do no harm – and the most good – with AI in health care', *Nature Medicine*, 30(3), pp. 623–627. Available at: https://doi.org/10.1038/s41591-024-02853-7.

Haraway, D. J. (2016) *Staying with the Trouble: Making Kin in the Chthulucene.* 1st edn. Durham and London: Duke University Press.

Hecker, J. and Kalpokas, N. (2023) 'The ultimate guide to qualitative research – part 2: Handling qualitative data', *Atlas.ti.* Available at: https://atlasti.com/guides/qualitative-research-guide-part-2.

Henne, K. (2019) 'Surveillance in the name of governance: Aadhaar as a fix for leaking systems in India', in B. Haggart, K. Henne and N. Tusikov (eds) *International Political Economy Series.* 1st edn. Palgrave Macmillan, pp. 223–245. Available at: https://doi.org/10.1007/978-3-030-14540-8_11.

IEEE. (2025) *IEEE Advancing Technology for Humanity.* Available at: https://www.ieee.org/about/index.html (Accessed: 10 April 2025).

Jarke, J. and Büchner, S. (2024) 'Who cares about data? Data care arrangements in everyday organisational practice', *Information, Communication & Society*, 27(4), pp. 702–718. Available at: https://doi.org/10.1080/1369118X.2024.2320917.

Kazansky, B. (2021) '"It depends on your threat model": The anticipatory dimensions of resistance to data-driven surveillance', *Big Data & Society*, 8(1). Available at: https://doi.org/10.1177/2053951720985557.

King, P. T. et al. (2021 August/2022) 'Co-design for indigenous and other children and young people from priority social groups: A systematic review', *SSM – Population Health*, 18, p. 101077. Available at: https://doi.org/10.1016/j.ssmph.2022.101077.

Koskela, H. (2000) '"The gaze without eyes": Video-surveillance and the changing nature of urban space', *Progress in Human Geography*, 24(2), pp. 243–265. Available at: https://doi.org/10.1191/030913200668791096.

Koskela, H. (2002) 'Video surveillance, gender, and the safety of public urban space: "Peeping Tom" goes high tech?', *Urban Geography*, 23(3), pp. 257–278. Available at: https://doi.org/10.2747/0272-3638.23.3.257.

Krysztoforska, M., Docherty, N. and Biega, A. J. (2023) 'Integrative objects in sociotechnical contexts: Constructing digital well-being with generic epistemology', in *Proceedings of the 2023 CHI Conference on Human Factors in Computing Systems*. New York, NY, USA: ACM, pp. 1–17. Available at: https://doi.org/10.1145/3544548.3580717.

Kulynych, B. et al. (2020) 'POTs: Protective optimization technologies', in *Proceedings of the 2020 ACM Conference on Fairness, Accountability, and Transparency*. New York, NY, USA: ACM, pp. 177–188. Available at: https://doi.org/10.1145/3351095.3372853.

Maalsen, S. (2023) 'Algorithmic epistemologies and methodologies: Algorithmic harm, algorithmic care and situated algorithmic knowledges', *Progress in Human Geography*, 47(2), pp. 197–214. Available at: https://doi.org/10.1177/03091325221149439.

Macnish, K. (2014) 'Just surveillance? Towards a normative theory of surveillance', *Surveillance and Society*, 12(1), pp. 142–153. Available at: https://doi.org/10.24908/ss.v12i1.4515.

Mahapatra, S. (2021) *Digital Surveillance and the Threat to Civil Liberties in India, GIGA Focus|Asia, 3*. Hamburg. Available at: https://nbn-resolving.org/urn:nbn:de:0168-ssoar-73130-3.

Marchigiani, E. (2022) 'Healthy and caring cities: Accessibility for all and the role of urban spaces in re-activating capabilities', in A. Gabauer et al. (eds) *Care and the City: Encounters with Urban Studies*. 1st edn. New York: Routledge, pp. 75–87. Available at: https://doi.org/10.4324/9781003031536-10.

Massey, D. (2004) 'Geographies of responsibility', *Geografiska Annaler: Series B, Human Geography*, 86(1), pp. 5–18. Available at: https://www.jstor.org/stable/3554456.

McLean, J. (2024) 'Responsibility, care and repair in/of AI: Extinction threats and more-than-real worlds', *Environment and Planning F*, 3(1–2), pp. 3–16. Available at: https://doi.org/10.1177/26349825241228586.

Ministry of Home Affairs. (2018) *Safe City Framework Guidelines*. Available at: https://safecity.mha.gov.in/Employee/images/Safe_City_Framework_Guideline_OM_Sept2018.pdf (Accessed: 2 July 2022).

Monahan, T. (2009) 'Dreams of control at a distance: Gender, surveillance, and social control', *Cultural Studies ↔ Critical Methodologies*, 9, pp. 286–305. Available at: https://doi.org/10.1177/1532708608321481.

MTC Chennai. (2020) *Request for Proposal for Selection of System Integrator to "Design, Supply, Implement, Commission, Operate & Manage the Safe City Solution" as a Part of Nirbhaya Safe City Project for Metropolitan Transport Corporation*. Available at: https://mtcbus.tn.gov.in/asset/tenders/Volume_2_-_MTC.pdf (Accessed: 30 July 2022).

Mühlhoff, R. (2021) 'Predictive privacy: Towards an applied ethics of data analytics', *Ethics and Information Technology*, 23(4), pp. 675–690. Available at: https://doi.org/10.1007/s10676-021-09606-x.

Narayan, S. (2023) 'CCTVs and the criminal city', *Surveillance and Society*, 21(4), pp. 363–374. Available at: https://doi.org/10.24908/ss.v21i4.15779.

Nishiyama, H. (2018) 'Crowd surveillance: The (in)securitization of the urban body', *Security Dialogue*, 49(3), pp. 200–216. Available at: https://doi.org/10.1177/0967010617741436.

Pangrazio, L. and Sefton-Green, J. (2021) 'Digital rights, digital citizenship and digital literacy: What's the difference?', *Journal of New Approaches in Educational Research*, 10(1), pp. 15–27. Available at: https://doi.org/10.7821/naer.2021.1.616.

Powell, A. B. et al. (2022) 'Addressing ethical gaps in "technology for good": Foregrounding care and capabilities', *Big Data and Society*, 9(2), pp. 1–12. Available at: https://doi.org/10.1177/20539517221113774.

Power, E. R. and Williams, M. J. (2019) 'Cities of care: A platform for urban geographical care research', *Geography Compass*, 14(1), pp. 1–11. Available at: https://doi.org/10.1111/gec3.12474.

Press Information Bureau. (2019) *Safe City Project, Government of India*. Available at: https://pib.gov.in/newsite/PrintRelease.aspx?relid=188078 (Accessed: 10 February 2022).

Purkayastha, B. K. (2024) 'Avoid roaming alone on campus at night, SMCH issues advisory to female doctors after Kolkata incident, faces backlash', *Hindustan Times*. Available at: https://www.hindustantimes.com/education/news/avoid-roaming-alone-on-campus-at-night-smch-issues-advisory-to-female-doctors-after-kolkata-incident-faces-backlash-101723603902410.html (Accessed: 2 October 2024).

Rakshit, D. (2021) 'Lucknow will use facial expression--recognition cameras to spot women in danger, report to police-', *The Swaddle*. Available at: https://www.theswaddle.com/lucknow-will-use-facial-expression-recognition-cameras-to-watch-for-women-in-danger-report-to-police (Accessed: 23 June 2023).

Rana, S. (2020) 'Visualizing the semiotics of protest: The "Nirbhaya" rape case:', *Indian Journal of Gender Studies*, 27(1), pp. 141–153. Available at: https://doi.org/10.1177/0971521519891482.

Rathi, A. and Tandon, A. (2020) *Capturing Gender and Class Inequities The CCTVisation of Delhi, Digital Development Working Paper Series The Urban Data Justice Case Study Collection*. Available at: https://doi.org/10.2139/ssrn.3705563.

Richardson, I. et al. (2017) 'Careful Surveillance at Play: Human-Animal Relations and Mobile Media in the Home', in E. G. Cruz, S. Sumartojo and S. Pink (eds) *Refiguring Techniques in Digital Visual Research*. Melbourne: Palgrave Macmillan, pp. 105–116. Available at: https://doi.org/10.1007/978-3-319-61222-5_9.

Rittenbruch, M. et al. (2022) 'Co-Designing Planning Support Systems in Urban Science: The Questions They Answer and the Questions They Raise', *Journal of Urban Technology*, 29(2), pp. 7–32. Available at: https://doi.org/10.1080/10630732.2021.1980319.

Rossitto, C. et al. (2022) 'Towards Digital Environmental Stewardship: The Work of Caring for the Environment in Waste Management', in *CHI Conference on Human Factors in Computing Systems*. New York, NY, USA: ACM, pp. 1–16. Available at: https://doi.org/10.1145/3491102.3517679.

Stoddart, E. (2012) 'A surveillance of care Evaluating surveillance ethically', in K. Ball, K. Haggerty and D. Lyon (eds) *Routledge Handbook of Surveillance Studies*. 1st edn. London: Routledge, pp. 369–376.

Sur, A. (2021) 'Lucknow safe city project: Uttar Pradesh to deploy facial recognition, 'label' faces of suspects', *Medianama*. Available at: https://www.medianama.com/2021/08/223-lucknow-safe-city-project-uttar-pradesh-facial-recognition/ (Accessed: 19 April 2022).

Suri, H. (2020) 'Ethical considerations of conducting systematic reviews in educational research', in O. Zawacki-Richter et al. (eds) *Systematic Reviews in Educational Research*. 1st edn. Wiesbaden: Springer Fachmedien Wiesbaden, pp. 41–54. Available at: https://doi.org/10.1007/978-3-658-27602-7_3.

Van Kleunen, L., Muller, B. and Voida, S. (2021) '"Wiring a city": A sociotechnical perspective on deploying urban sensor networks', *Proceedings of the ACM on Human-Computer Interaction*, 5(CSCW1), pp. 1–22. Available at: https://doi.org/10.1145/3449252.

Vila-Henninger, L. et al. (2024) 'Abductive coding: Theory building and qualitative (re)analysis', *Sociological Methods and Research*, 53(2), pp. 968–1001. Available at: https://doi.org/10.1177/00491241211067508.

Vila-Seoane, M. F. (2021) 'Data securitisation: The challenges of data sovereignty in India', *Third World Quarterly*, 42(8), pp. 1733–1750. Available at: https://doi.org/10.1080/01436597.2021.1915122.

Waelen, R. and Wieczorek, M. (2022) 'The struggle for AI's recognition: Understanding the normative implications of gender bias in AI with Honneth's theory of recognition', *Philosophy & Technology*, 35(2), pp. 1–17. Available at: https://doi.org/10.1007/s13347-022-00548-w.

Walsh, J. P. (2010) 'From border control to border care: The political and ethical potential of surveillance', *Surveillance and Society*, 8(2), pp. 113–130. Available at: https://doi.org/10.24908/ss.v8i2.3481.

Wessels, B. (2013) 'Exploring human agency and digital systems', *Information, Communication & Society*, 16(10), pp. 1533–1552. Available at: https://doi.org/10.1080/1369118X.2012.715666.

Whittaker, D. (2021) 'Why AI CCTV is the future of security and surveillance in public spaces', *Security Magazine*. Available at: https://www.securitymagazine.com/articles/96719-why-ai-cctv-is-the-future-of-security-and-surveillance-in-public-spaces (Accessed: 16 March 2022).

Williams, M. J. (2017) 'Care-full Justice in the city', *Antipode*, 49(3), pp. 821–839. Available at: https://doi.org/10.1111/anti.12279.

Zakharova, I. and Jarke, J. (2024) 'Care-ful data studies: Or, what do we see, when we look at datafied societies through the lens of care?', *Information Communication and Society*, 27(4), pp. 651–664. Available at: https://doi.org/10.1080/1369118X.2024.2316758.

13

Tackling the Bias Problem at the Design Stage: Empirical Evidence from the CommuniCity Project

Kristina Khutsishvili

13.1 Introduction

The CommuniCity project (2022–2025), funded by the Horizon Europe programme, in its proposal adopted a needs-based approach to digital innovation. The idea of the project – to conduct 100 technological, mostly AI-based, pilots through three rounds of open-calls in response to the existing needs of the European cities and communities – was accompanied by the complexity of having vulnerable and disadvantaged groups in focus.

Rather than imposing top-down solutions, the project aimed to facilitate processes in which municipalities, community members, associations (intermediary organisations with established contacts with target communities), researchers, and technological providers collaborate to address existing challenges by means of technology. Such a challenge-driven model is aimed at ensuring that technological innovations, including those involving artificial intelligence, are created in response to existing needs as opposed to being developed in isolation from the real-world contexts and societal demands. The importance of technological and social innovations to be viewed not in silos but as intertwined had been articulated in the CommuniCity academic proceedings (Khutsishvili et al. 2024).

The results of the project, which started with the core cities of Amsterdam, Porto, and Helsinki and then involved multiple and diverse European cities, demonstrated the potential of incremental, ethically guided experimentation aimed at creating replicable yet locally grounded technological solutions addressing the particular needs of given cities and communities (Combé & Pavicic 2024; Khutsishvili 2024).

The 'Fair AI' concept had several perspectives in the project. First, the need-based articulation of challenges by the cities was seen as reflecting a 'fair'

DOI: 10.1201/9781003480167-16

perspective of developing AI solutions in response to the problem, aimed at social good. Second, co-creation – as one of the non-negotiable elements of piloting and a requirement for the winning teams (technological providers in partnership with associations, with the latter aimed at sharing knowledge about the target group and facilitating connection) – made it feasible to explore the possibilities of 'fair by design' technological solutions. Third, the project contained a specific work package aimed at providing interoperable solutions for the cities. This work package included the development and testing of a special Minimal Interoperability Mechanism (MIM) entitled 'Fair AI' (Open and Agile Smart Cities 2025).

The chapter proceeds as follows: it begins with a theoretical exploration of fairness in AI, drawing on philosophical frameworks such as Rawlsian and recognition theories; it then moves to the technological domain, discussing how current toolkits for bias detection and mitigation operationalise these ideals in practice. Building on these insights, the analysis turns to the CommuniCity project's own technical developments, focusing on the Minimal Interoperability Mechanism 5 (MIM5; Open and Agile Smart Cities 2022) – 'Fair AI' as a concrete attempt to embed fairness. This technical perspective opens into a broader reflection on co-creation, treated here as an ethical and epistemic practice that redefines whose knowledge and values shape smart city innovation. The chapter culminates in a synthesis of empirical lessons from experimentation, showing how these experiences collectively inform context-aware and ethically grounded approaches to AI design.

13.2 The Theory behind Fairness

Definitions of 'Fair AI' may vary across different knowledge areas and contexts. It may be understood as a system that treats individuals in a just, impartial, and unbiased manner; as 'probabilistic decision support that prevents disparate harm (or benefit) to different subgroups' (Barocas & Selbst 2016; Barocas et al. 2019); as a framework that incorporates pre-defined sensitive attributes – such as race, gender, or disability – to ensure these do not lead to discriminatory outcomes (Hardt et al. 2016; Feuerriegel et al. 2020); or as the principle that 'similarly situated individuals should be treated in a similar way' (Dwork et al. 2012). These conceptualisations are not confined to the domain of artificial intelligence and machine learning but are rooted in broader philosophical, legal, and socio-technical discourses. The inherently normative and emotionally charged nature of fairness adds further complexity: what is considered 'fair' by one stakeholder may be perceived differently by another. In the context of AI, this complexity is compounded by the need for genuine interdisciplinary engagement.

The Rawlsian view on fairness (Rawls 1999) can be applied to algorithmic decision-making processes. For example, fairness metrics in AI can be understood as institutional rules that govern who receives resources, opportunities, or scrutiny – translating the role that institutions play in Rawls' theory. Designing technological solutions from a 'veil of ignorance' perspective implies considering outcomes from the standpoint of the most vulnerable or disadvantaged users and ensuring that no group systematically bears disproportionate burdens or enjoys excessive benefits.

However, translating Rawlsian justice into machine learning systems is a challenge. First, Rawls' principles are abstract and assume ideal conditions, while algorithmic systems operate in real-world contexts characterised by multiple layers of complexity, including historical bias and power imbalances. Second, operationalising concepts such as the 'least advantaged' or 'equality of opportunity' in mathematical terms often demands serious simplifications and reductions that risk erasing their substantive meaning. Third, Rawls' framework is primarily focused on distributive justice, which may not fully capture the *procedural* dimensions or *aspects of recognition* – for example, being heard, understood, or respected. The latter limitation, however, may be partially addressed through co-creation, which can facilitate the recognition crucial for positive identitarian processes (Taylor 1992).

Rawls' arguments centre on justice within the *nation-state,* while many AI systems operate transnationally, and are developed by private entities, with many of their challenges deriving from globally oriented, top-down forms of governance (Michailidis et al. 2024). This raises the critical questions: who is behind the veil when decisions are embedded in systems created by corporations? Can fairness be achieved by technological means alone, or does it require political participation and contestation? Indeed, many of the difficulties confronting AI systems today stem from this global, centralised governance structure.

As such, importing Rawlsian fairness into AI systems involves complex ethical aspirations that are accompanied by epistemological and institutional limitations. Thus, defining and designing *Fair AI* is not merely a matter of selecting an appropriate fairness metric but a deeply normative project that must engage with foundational questions about the kind of society we want AI systems to help create.

13.3 Technological Approach to Bias Detection and Mitigation

While social and institutional factors underpin many of the biases found in artificial intelligence, technological interventions still play a crucial role in mitigating them. In recent years, the open-source ecosystem has seen the emergence of multiple libraries and toolkits designed to support fairness in machine learning models. The following is an overview of some of the most prominent tools currently available, grouped according to their primary focus. These tools, though varied in scope and methodology, share the goal of promoting algorithmic fairness, achieved through the application of specialised fairness metrics, bias diagnostics, and mitigation techniques.

Among the most prominent tools is FairML, an open-source Python library designed primarily for fairness diagnostics (Adebayo 2025). Its approach centres on quantifying the influence of input features on model predictions through sensitivity analysis. The interpretability-driven framework enables researchers and practitioners to identify potential sources of bias by highlighting which features disproportionately affect model outputs. However, FairML's capabilities are largely diagnostic and interpretative rather than prescriptive, focusing on post-hoc analysis without direct intervention mechanisms to correct bias.

In contrast, IBM's AI Fairness 360 (AIF360) offers a more comprehensive solution, encompassing over 70 fairness metrics together with a set of bias mitigation algorithms applicable at various stages of the machine learning pipeline (Bellamy et al. 2018). Such breadth allows for greater flexibility in addressing bias, depending on the specific context and model architecture. At the same time, the careful selection of appropriate fairness metrics remains essential to leveraging AIF360 effectively.

Aequitas, developed by the University of Chicago's Center for Data Science and Public Policy, is a tool specialised in auditing bias within public sector decision-making (Saleiro et al. 2019). It provides subgroup fairness reports along with visualisations that clearly communicate results to non-technical audiences. This focus aligns well with *policy-driven applications*, where transparent communication of fairness assessments to stakeholders is *essential*. Nevertheless, *Aequitas primarily performs an auditing function and places less emphasis on direct bias-mitigation strategies.*

Microsoft's Fairlearn focuses on fairness-aware learning algorithms that enable model training under explicit fairness constraints (Weerts et al. 2023). Its methods include reduction-based techniques and post-processing adjustments, aiming to balance predictive accuracy with equitable treatment across groups. The toolkit is particularly strong in addressing group fairness concerns, though it offers less coverage of individual fairness concepts.

The relationship between fairness, privacy, and robustness is increasingly recognised as integral to responsible AI development. The IBM Adversarial Robustness Toolbox (ART) exemplifies this by addressing the vulnerability of machine learning models to adversarial attacks, which can amplify existing biases, while also incorporating tools for bias evaluation and privacy testing (Nicolae et al. 2019). Similarly, privacy-preserving libraries such as OpenDP (OpenDP Project 2020) and TensorFlow Privacy (TensorFlow 2024) implement differential privacy mechanisms, protecting sensitive data without compromising the utility of trained models. These privacy safeguards are particularly relevant in domains such as healthcare, where fairness and confidentiality must be upheld simultaneously.

Interpretable machine learning tools constitute another important dimension of the fairness ecosystem. Libraries such as InterpretML (Nori et al. 2019), LIME (Ribeiro et al. 2016), SHAP (Lundberg & Lee 2017), and Alibi Explain (Klaise et al. 2021) provide methods to elucidate the decision-making processes of complex models. By generating both local and global explanations, these frameworks help stakeholders understand model behaviour and identify potential ethical concerns, thereby complementing existing bias detection and mitigation efforts. Among these, SHAP stands out for its theoretically grounded approach based on Shapley values.

13.4 An Overview of the Toolkits Discussed

I. *These toolkits aim to evaluate and reduce unfair outcomes across different demographic groups, often using fairness metrics and reweighting or resampling techniques:*

Aequitas (Saleiro et al. 2019)

Developed by the Center for Data Science and Public Policy at the University of Chicago, Aequitas is a bias audit toolkit designed specifically for public sector decision-making contexts. It aims to provide user-friendly visualisations and detailed subgroup fairness reports.

Fairlearn (Weerts et al. 2023)

A Python library that focuses on fairness-aware learning, allowing users to train models under fairness constraints or analyse existing models for group-level disparities. It supports several mitigation techniques, including reduction-based methods and post-processing adjustments.

FairML (Adebayo 2025)

An open-source Python library that supports fairness diagnostics by quantifying the relative influence of input features on model predictions. It provides interpretability through sensitivity analysis, helping practitioners uncover potential sources of bias.

IBM AI Fairness 360 (AIF360, *Bellamy et al. 2018***)**

A comprehensive toolkit developed by IBM Research for assessing and mitigating bias in AI systems. It includes over 70 fairness metrics and a suite of mitigation algorithms applicable at pre-processing, in-processing, and post-processing stages. The library also features tutorials and educational resources.

II. *These libraries are designed to improve the reliability of AI systems under adversarial conditions, including attacks that can exacerbate bias or exploit vulnerabilities:*

IBM Adversarial Robustness Toolbox (ART, *Nicolae et al. 2019*)

A Python toolkit for evaluating and enhancing the robustness of machine learning models against adversarial attacks. ART also includes tools for bias evaluation and privacy testing, making it suitable for fairness-sensitive contexts.

III. *Privacy is often intertwined with fairness, especially in sensitive domains such as healthcare or social services. These tools implement differential privacy and related techniques to protect the user data:*

OpenDP (OpenDP 2020)

An initiative led by Harvard University and supported by the broader differential privacy community, OpenDP provides modular building blocks for privacy-preserving statistical analysis. It supports end-to-end privacy guarantees and promotes transparent governance.

TensorFlow Privacy (TensorFlow 2024)

A library that integrates differential privacy mechanisms into TensorFlow training pipelines. It allows developers to train machine learning models that maintain rigorous privacy guarantees while still achieving high performance.

IV. *Understanding how AI systems make decisions is crucial for identifying and correcting the bias. The following libraries provide methods to interpret the models:*

Alibi Explain (*Klaise et al. 2021)*

A library developed by Seldon for advanced model diagnostics. It includes techniques such as counterfactual explanations, anchor explanations, and adversarial testing. Its modular design makes it ideal for integration into enterprise-grade machine learning workflows.

InterpretML (Nori et al. 2019)

A unified framework for interpretable machine learning, InterpretML supports both glass-box models (e.g., Generalised Additive Models) and black-box explainers (e.g., SHAP, LIME). It helps stakeholders understand model behaviour and surface potential ethical issues.

LIME (Local Interpretable Model-Agnostic Explanations, Ribeiro et al. 2016)

A widely used toolkit that generates local approximations of model behaviour, helping users interpret individual predictions. It is particularly effective for black-box models and widely adopted in both research and industry.

SHAP (SHapley Additive exPlanations, Lundberg & Lee 2017)

Based on game theory, SHAP attributes feature importance scores to model predictions using Shapley values. It is considered one of the most theoretically grounded interpretability methods and offers strong visualisations for model insights.

These tools represent the state of the art in technical fairness interventions. However, it is important to emphasise that such *tools alone may not guarantee 'fair' outcomes.* Yet, when they constitute part of a technical toolkit that accompanies ethical and participatory design processes – such as co-creation – and align with broader institutional commitments to equity, transparency, and accountability, the problem can be addressed more holistically and in proportion to its complexity. In this sense, technological debiasing is not a substitute for societal awareness but a complement to it.

13.5 Technological Developments of the Project

Minimal Interoperability Mechanism (MIM 5) – 'Fair AI' was tested within the CommuniCity project. The idea of MIMs originates from the Open and Agile Smart Cities (OASC) network, which has coordinated the consortium of partners. According to the OASC network (Open and Agile Smart Cities 2025), 'The minimal interoperability mechanisms emerged to enable a minimal but sufficient level of interoperability for data, systems, and services specifically in the context of smart city solutions'. Another definition states that 'Minimal Interoperability Mechanisms (MIM) are a universal tool for achieving interoperability of data, systems, and services between cities and suppliers around the world. They are based on an inclusive list of baselines and references, which takes into account the different backgrounds of cities and communities and allows cities to achieve interoperability based on a minimal common ground', states one of the definitions (Open and Agile Smart Cities 2023, slide 3).

The goal of MIM 5 is articulated as providing the technical capabilities 'required to check that the algorithmic systems offered by suppliers comply with the requirements for fairness, trustworthiness and transparency' (Open and Agile Smart Cities 2023, slide 6).

The MIM5 working group, headed by Martino Maggio (CommuniCity partner – *Engineering Group*, Italy), developed this proposition:

Category: Fairness

Capabilities: Ensuring that the algorithmic system does not systematically disadvantage, show bias against, or even discriminate against, different social groups and demographics.

Requirements: The algorithmic system should use publicly available and validated datasets to train/develop the model. The algorithmic system should be validated against specific test cases created to validate bias, discrimination, and in general the outcomes of the algorithm.

Category: Context

Capabilities: The assessment of fairness depends on facts, events, and goals, and therefore has to be understood as situation or task-specific and necessarily addressed within the scope of practice. For instance, there may be an explicit goal to address a historic imbalance, where positive discrimination is considered appropriate. Here, the aspect of 'fairness' needs to be seen in the wider context.

Requirements: The algorithmic system must be contextually aware and capable of recognising the specific facts, events, and goals relevant to the task. The algorithmic system should support customizable fairness metrics that can be tailored to the specific situation or task. The algorithmic system should adhere to a set of ethical guidelines that prioritise fairness and equitable outcomes.

The development and testing of MIM5 – 'Fair AI' – within the CommuniCity project made it an illustrative case of how technical approaches to Fair AI can be incorporated into a co-creation-oriented initiative. MIM5 obviously reflects the recognition that ethical principles – such as fairness, transparency, and trustworthiness – need to be addressed not only normatively but also technically, through the infrastructures of smart city solutions.

The proposition developed by the MIM5 working group, led by Martino Maggio, reflects an attempt to 'embody' fairness through a structured set of technical capabilities and requirements. This approach assumes fairness to be a measurable and verifiable attribute of algorithmic systems. The requirement to use publicly validated datasets and bias-sensitive test cases exemplifies a shift from theoretical ethical considerations to actionable system-design constraints, which can be systematically evaluated and compared. Yet, it is precisely in this attempt at operationalisation that the limitations of purely technical approaches to ethics become evident.

Notably, MIM5 includes a dedicated category addressing *context*. This recognition of the 'situatedness' of fairness – its dependence on socio-economic, political, and historical circumstances – represents an important theoretical move towards acknowledging the socio-technical nature of AI systems. By emphasising contextual awareness and the incorporation of task-specific fairness metrics, the MIM5 framework reflects a pluralistic understanding of fairness, recognising the specificity of local challenges and conditions.

At the same time, the very ambition of defining *minimal* interoperability mechanisms raises epistemological and practical questions. What constitutes a 'minimal' yet 'sufficient' threshold for fairness in algorithmic systems? How are trade-offs negotiated between generalisability and specificity? These questions become particularly salient when MIM5 is implemented across diverse municipalities, each with its own context and resource constraints. From a critical perspective, MIM5 can be seen as a site where governance, ethics, and technology converge – and where tensions between them are actively negotiated. In general, the development and testing of MIM5 within the CommuniCity project provides a case study of how interoperability mechanisms may function not only as enablers of data and service integration but also as *ethical infrastructures* aimed at translating normative commitments into the technical requirements of smart city initiatives.

13.6 Co-Creation of Technological Solutions

While co-creation has emerged as an endorsed paradigm in both academic discourse and policy frameworks, its application in the context of AI development remains insufficiently theorised. At the same time, valuable lessons can be derived from co-creation cases situated within smart cities and communities context (e.g., Rill & Hämäläinen, 2018; Hoffecker, 2018).

In technological domains, discussions of bias often focus on computational artefacts – such as biased datasets, algorithms, and inequitable outputs. In this way, the problem tends to be perceived as mainly statistical and computational rather than epistemic. Co-creation, when genuinely implemented, functions as a mechanism not only for 'inclusive design' but also for epistemic re-design. It creates opportunities to broaden the knowledge sources that inform and shape the system – sources that are often absent from or marginalised within dominant innovation processes and structures.

Epistemic pluralism is particularly evident in contexts such as *CommuniCity,* where digital solutions are developed in partnership with underserved communities. In this context, co-creation is not intended as a procedural or image-focused checkbox but as a normative commitment to rebalancing voice and power within innovation processes (Khutsishvili 2024). It entails a move towards reciprocity (Khutsishvili 2025) – from consultation to collaboration, and from developing *for* to developing *with.*

Importantly, this co-creative process is neither linear nor frictionless. It is iterative, relational, and often uncomfortable – yet it is precisely in this discomfort that ethical reflection deepens. The challenge lies not only in generating more inclusive outputs but also in reshaping the very processes of technological innovation. Co-creation then can be understood as an ethical practice that seeks to democratise technological development by acknowledging and addressing asymmetries of knowledge, access, and power.

In *CommuniCity*, co-creation was understood within a broader framework of *incremental improvement* (Combé & Pavicic, 2024). Rather than viewing co-creation as a static method in a toolkit, it was treated as a dynamic practice continually shaped by experimentation, reflection, and learning. Each co-creation instance generated lessons aimed to be useful in subsequent instances, possibly in other cities and communities. Importantly, co-creation within *CommuniCity* did not assume the elimination of bias or the attainment of perfect equity. Rather, it aspired for experimentation and creating the space where bias can be incrementally addressed.

13.7 Empirical Synthesis

13.7.1 Lessons Learnt

In the context of the CommuniCity project, the Municipality of Amsterdam conducted analysis of the main 'bottlenecks' of the process of matching the needs of communities with the solutions coming from technological providers (Combé & Pavicic 2024):

1. **Technology is not yet sufficiently recognised as a solution to the social challenges faced by marginalised groups.**

   Technology remains insufficiently recognised as a viable solution to the complex social challenges faced by marginalised groups. Its development continues to be predominantly driven by commercial interests, with limited awareness of its potential to effect social transformation. This gap in recognition spans across civil society organisations (CSOs), public institutions, technological providers, and marginalised communities themselves.
2. **Due to insufficient understanding of marginalised groups and the challenges they face, technological solutions are often poorly aligned with their needs.**

   The limited understanding of disadvantaged communities and the specific challenges they encounter often results in technological solutions that are poorly fit. While a growing number of technological providers are expressing willingness to contribute to societal good, this ambition seldom translates into genuine, participatory co-creation with end users. As a result, insufficient investment is made in building equitable, trust-based relationships with these communities. There remains a pervasive lack of insight into their socio-economic contexts, the barriers they face, and their digital competencies. This disconnect leads to minimal involvement of these groups in design processes, producing tools that neither reflect their needs nor gain meaningful traction or adoption.

3. **Limited familiarity with technology poses challenges for civil society organisations/'associations' in the implementation and maintenance of technological tools.**

   CSOs, which often work most closely with marginalised groups, face distinct challenges in leveraging technology to meet community needs. The integration of digital tools remains far from standard practice, constrained not only by a general lack of awareness but also by limited access to technical expertise, time, and financial resources – factors that are deeply intertwined. Many organisations lack the foundational digital knowledge to make informed decisions regarding technology, including areas such as cybersecurity or the reliability of service providers. In parallel, the absence of sustainable funding mechanisms hampers long-term investments in technological infrastructure, training, and maintenance, further limiting the role of technology in social interventions.

4. **The development of technological solutions is often financially inaccessible for marginalised groups and civil society organisations.**

   The financial realities of disadvantaged communities and the organisations that serve them further compound this issue. Vulnerable communities often represent a small, resource-constrained market, which limits the commercial attractiveness of tailored technological solutions. CSOs, frequently operating within tight budgets and reliant on project-based external funding, struggle to allocate capital towards technological innovation. Their non-profit orientation precludes the accumulation of financial surpluses that could support such investments. At the individual level, members of marginalised communities often lack the disposable income required to access digital tools or subscription services, reinforcing a cycle of technological exclusion.

The specific points of complexity reflected in the CommuniCity project include the following (Khutsishvili 2024):

- **Technologies per se:** The unknowns they bring, their dynamic nature, their role as both drivers of change and markers of difference.
- **Communities brought to the centre:** No longer peripheral, they are made key participants in shaping direction and outcomes.
- **Conditions of vulnerability and marginalisation:** The project operates with an aspiration to bring about positive change, but also

with a consciousness – and cautiousness – not to worsen existing conditions.

- **Geographical diversity:** Starting with three cities in three different countries – Porto, Helsinki, Amsterdam – each with distinct national legal frameworks, with an intention to translate insights across further cities and contexts. Similarly, the consortium includes partners from varied institutional and personal backgrounds – municipalities, universities, applied academic institutions, think tanks, NGOs.
- **Multiplicity of mentalities and perspectives** within the 'applicant' ecosystem: Technological providers, associations, communities – each with its own view. This requires collaboration, mutual respect, and a willingness to listen.
- **Scale of the project:** Operating across several countries with around 100 planned partners, which inevitably introduces a degree of bureaucratisation.
- **Short duration of pilots:** Winners of the open calls are given six months to develop their projects. What happens after that remained open.

Trust is the cornerstone of successful co-creation. Building trust takes time – and 'rushing' the design phase risks overlooking the nuances of the problem. This reality limits the types of challenges that can be effectively addressed within short pilot cycles. Yet, even within these constraints, thoughtful and well-facilitated engagement can lead to meaningful insights and set the scene for longer-term impact.

13.8 Experimentation and Replicability

One of the distinctive contributions of the CommuniCity project lies in its use of inductive experimentation across diverse urban contexts. The project did not begin with a universal framework for fairness or co-creation. Instead, it built such a framework incrementally – by learning from practice, from one round of open calls to another, reflecting on real-world co-creation processes, and gradually refining approaches through replication.

Each city in the CommuniCity project served as a site of experimentation: once completed, the lessons from the pilot – both technical and social – were translated and adapted in a replicator city. The second-round pilots were not copies; they were contextual reinterpretations, shaped by new stakeholders and local needs. This recursive loop of experimentation, reflection, and adaptation constituted a form of grounded theorising – a bottom-up, inductive method for building not only better technologies but more just innovation processes.

The project's aspiration was not merely to build good enough solutions for single-use cases but to foster interoperable and scalable practices that other cities and communities can meaningfully adopt. Interoperability here has two layers:

Technical interoperability. Ensuring that systems, data formats, and APIs are standardised enough to enable transfer across contexts. This is where the Minimal Interoperability Mechanism (MIM5 for Fair AI) comes into play, offering structured requirements for fairness, contextual awareness, and transparency.

Social and ethical interoperability. Ensuring that design processes, fairness criteria, and engagement strategies are sufficiently modular, narrated, and adaptable so that they can be translated across social worlds without erasing local specificity.

In this model, interoperability is not about one-size-fits-all but about building flexible, transferable knowledge infrastructures. Just as open-source code must be documented and legible to others, co-creation practices need to be articulated in forms that others can understand, critique, and build upon.

A central risk in scaling technological solutions is the loss of nuance – flattening rich, situated knowledge into oversimplified generalisations. The CommuniCity approach aimed to counter this by embedding reflexivity into the process: each pilot is not only a solution but also a research site. What worked? What failed? What ethical tensions emerged? How were power asymmetries addressed? This reflexivity is documented and shared, as the goal was not to scale tools alone but to scale the capacity for ethical co-creation.

An inductive, practice-led approach has clear strengths: it ensures responsiveness to local realities, centres lived experience, and avoids top-down universalism. However, it also faces limits. Inductive knowledge is always partial and contingent. What works in Amsterdam may not work in Manchester. Cultural differences, political structures, and infrastructural inequalities can constrain transferability.

Recognising these limits is not a weakness; it is part of the ethical commitment. Interoperability needs to remain a goal, but not an imposed standard. Scalability needs to remain sensitive to context, not driven by efficiency alone.

13.9 Conclusion

Co-creation of technological solutions with members of target communities exemplifies a bottom-up design approach, in which community-generated data can support efforts towards Fair AI and help address the problem of bias. At the same time, community involvement – particularly when working with vulnerable groups – requires a strong commitment to the 'do no harm' principle and a careful, context-sensitive ethical stance.

This contribution proposes co-creation as a means of tackling bias and developing fair-by-design technological solutions for cities and communities. The best and 'good-enough' practices of co-creating technological solutions with community members may take different forms – whether as formalised tools accessible to more technically inclined audiences or as narrative guidelines grounded in empirical evidence from experimentation and subsequent analysis. Such practices not only align with the principles of 'AI for social good' but also foster knowledge sharing, replication, and interoperability across diverse urban and regional contexts worldwide.

13.10 Acknowledgements

The author was supported by the European Union's Horizon Europe research and innovation programme under grant agreement no. 101070325, as part of the CommuniCity project: *Innovative Solutions Responding to the Needs of Cities and Communities*, while serving as a work package leader of the project and working at the Informatics Institute, University of Amsterdam.

References

Adebayo, J. (2025). *FairML: Toolbox for Diagnosing Bias in Predictive Modeling*. GitHub. https://github.com/adebayoj/fairml

Barocas, S., Hardt. M., and Narayanan, A. (2019). *Fairness and Machine Learning. Limitations and Opportunities*. https://fairmlbook.org/pdf/fairmlbook.pdf

Barocas, S., and Selbst, A. (2016). Big Data's Disparate Impact. *California Law Review*, 104(1), 671–729.

Bellamy, R. K. E., Dey, K., Hind, M., Hoffman, S. C., Houde, S., Kannan, K., Lohia, P., Martino, J., Mehta, S., Mojsilovic, A., Nagar, S., Natesan Ramamurthy, K., Richards, J., Saha, D., Sattigeri, P., Singh, M., Varshney, K. R., and Zhang, Y. (2018). *AI Fairness 360: An Extensible Toolkit for Detecting, Understanding, and Mitigating Unwanted Algorithmic Bias*. GitHub. https://arxiv.org/abs/1810.01943; https://github.com/Trusted-AI/AIF360

Combé, M., and Pavicic, N. (2024). *Deliverable 2.2. A Process for Incremental Improvement and Matching Needs of Local Citizens and Communities to Solutions Offered by Technology Providers*. CommuniCity Horizon Europe. https://zenodo.org/records/14066072

CommuniCity Horizon Europe: Innovative Solutions Responding to the Needs of Cities and Communities. (2022-2025). https://cordis.europa.eu/project/id/101070325; https://communicity-project.eu

Dwork, C., Hardt, M., Pitassi, T., Reingold, O., and Zemel, R. (2012). *Fairness through Awareness*. Proceedings of the Third Innovations in Theoretical Computer Science Conference, 214–226. https://www.cs.toronto.edu/~toni/Papers/awareness.pdf

Engineering Group. https://www.eng.it/en

Feuerriegel, S., Dolata, M., and Schwabe, G. (2020). Fair AI. *Business and Information Systems Engineering*, 62(4), 379–384. https://link.springer.com/article/10.1007/s12599-020-00650-3

Hardt, M., Price, E., and Srebro, N. (2016). *Equality of Opportunity in Supervised Learning*. https://arxiv.org/abs/1610.02413

Hoffecker, E. 2018. *Local Innovation: What It is and Why It Matters for Developing Economies. D-Lab Working Papers: NDIR. Working Paper 01*. MIT D-Lab. https://d-lab.mit.edu/sites/default/files/inline-files/Local%20Innovation%20Working%20Paper%2001.pdf

Khutsishvili, K. (2024). *Guidelines for Translating Frameworks, Methods, Tools and Principles of Local Innovations for Marginalised and Vulnerable Communities – 2023*. Open Research Europe. https://open-research-europe.ec.europa.eu/articles/4-36

Khutsishvili, K. (2025). From a Smart City to Wise Citizens – Smart Empowering with Artificial Intelligence. In Zaidan, E., Ibrahim, I. A., and Azar, E. (Eds.), *Smart Cities to Smart Societies*, 51–63. Routledge.

Khutsishvili, K., Pavicic, N., and Combé, M. (2024). The Challenge of Co-Creation: How to Connect Technologies and Communities in an Ethical Way. In Pelegrín-Borondo, J., Arias-Oliva, M., Murata, K., and Romero, M. S. (Eds.), *The Leading Role of Smart Ethics in the Digital World*. https://dialnet.unirioja.es/servlet/articulo?codigo=9537215

Klaise, J., van Looveren, A., Vacanti, G., and Coca, A. (2021). Alibi Explain: Algorithms for Explaining Machine Learning Models. *Journal of Machine Learning Research*, 22(1), 1–7. GitHub. https://jmlr.csail.mit.edu/papers/volume22/21-0017/21-0017.pdf; https://github.com/SeldonIO/alibi

Lundberg, S. M., and Lee, S.-I. (2017). A Unified Approach to Interpreting Model Predictions. In *Advances in Neural Information Processing Systems* (Vol. 30). Github. https://proceedings.neurips.cc/paper_files/paper/2017/file/8a20a8621978632d76c43dfd28b67767-Paper.pdf; https://github.com/shap/shap

Michailidis, D., Khutsishvili, K., Konstantis, K., Tympas, A., Ibrahim, I. A., and Ghebreab, S. (2024). Enabling Inclusive Urban Transport Planning Through Civic Artificial Intelligence. In Keseru, I., Basu, S., Ryghaug, M., and Skjølsvold, T. M. (Eds.), *Strengthening European Mobility Policy*. Palgrave Macmillan. https://doi.org/10.1007/978-3-031-67936-0_9

Nicolae, M.-I., Sinn, M., Tran, M. N., Buesser, B., Rawat, A., Wistuba, M., Zantedeschi, V., Baracaldo, N., Chen, B., Ludwig, H., Molloy, I. M., and Edwards, B. (2019). *Adversarial Robustness Toolbox v1.0.0*. Github. https://arxiv.org/abs/1807.01069; https://github.com/Trusted-AI/adversarial-robustness-toolbox

Nori, H., Jenkins, S., Koch, P., and Caruana, R. (2019). *InterpretML: A Unified Framework for Machine Learning Interpretability*. GitHub. https://arxiv.org/abs/1909.09223; https://github.com/interpretml/interpret

Open and Agile Smart Cities. (2022). *OASC MIM5*. GitHub. https://github.com/oasc/oasc-mims/tree/master/mims/oasc-mim5-transparency

Open and Agile Smart Cities. (2023). *MIM5 – Fair AI Workshop. Presentation*. https://public-buyers-community.ec.europa.eu/communities/procurement-ai/resources/mim5-fair-ai-workshop

Open and Agile Smart Cities. (2025). *Minimal Interoperability Mechanisms*. https://oascities.org/minimal-interoperability-mechanisms/

OpenDP Project. (2020). *The OpenDP White Paper*. Harvard University, GitHub. https://projects.iq.harvard.edu/files/opendp/files/opendp_white_paper_11may2020.pdf; https://opendp.org; https://github.com/opendp/opendp

Rawls, J. (1999). *A Theory of Justice: Revised Edition*. Harvard University Press.

Ribeiro, M. T., Singh, S., and Guestrin, C. (2016). "Why Should I Trust You?": Explaining the Predictions of any Classifier. In *Proceedings of the 22nd ACM SIGKDD International Conference on Knowledge Discovery and Data Mining*, 1135–1144. GitHub. https://dl.acm.org/doi/10.1145/2939672.2939778; https://github.com/marcotcr/lime

Rill, B. R., and Hämäläinen, M. M. (2018). *The Art of Co-Creation: A Guidebook for Practitioners*. Palgrave Macmillan.

Saleiro, P., Kuester, B., Hinkson, L., London, J., Stevens, A., Anisfeld, A., Rodolfa, K. T., and Ghani, R. (2019). *Aequitas: A Bias and Fairness Audit Toolkit*. GitHub. https://arxiv.org/abs/1811.05577; https://github.com/dssg/aequitas

Taylor, C. (1992). *The Politics of Recognition*. http://fs2.american.edu/dfagel/www/Class%20Readings/Taylor/multiculturalism.pdf

TensorFlow. (2024). *TensorFlow Privacy*. GitHub. https://www.tensorflow.org/responsible_ai/privacy/tutorials/classification_privacy; https://github.com/tensorflow/privacy

Weerts, H., Dudík, M., Edgar, R., Jalali, A., Lutz, R., and Madaio, M. (2023). *Fairlearn: Assessing and Improving Fairness of AI Systems*. GitHub. https://arxiv.org/abs/2303.16626; https://fairlearn.org; https://github.com/fairlearn/fairlearn

14

Machine Learning–Driven Framework for SDG-Based Impact Assessment of Transport Infrastructure Projects

Mohammed Ali Berawi, Dio Reyhan Fardizsa, Mustika Sari, Bambang Susantono, and Suci Indah Susilowati

14.1 Introduction

Indonesia and many other countries are racing against time to achieve the Sustainable Development Goals (SDGs) by 2030. Despite substantial investments in transport infrastructure, progress remains slow, especially because many projects are not aligned with sustainability principles (Nasikhin et al., 2022). Transportation infrastructure has a significant impact on society and the economy since it enables access and participation (Palei, 2015). However, Thacker et al. (2019) found that only 45% of the total 169 SDG targets are directly connected to infrastructure. This limited coverage highlights the need for a structured evaluation framework that measures how infrastructure contributes to the SDGs at the project level.

The SDGs promote social, economic, environmental, and institutional progress based on equity and human rights (Morton et al., 2017). Infrastructure influences many of these goals, particularly SDG 3 (health), SDG 6 (water), SDG 7 (energy), SDG 9 (industry and innovation), and SDG 11 (sustainable cities). In Indonesia, rapid infrastructure expansion without consistent sustainability assessment could weaken long-term development outcomes. Therefore, an SDG-based impact assessment framework is necessary to connect infrastructure performance with national sustainability objectives.

Existing sustainability rating systems, such as ENVISION (Oluwalaiye & Ozbek, 2019), Greenroads (Anderson & Muench, 2013), GreenLITES (Gudmundsson et al., 2016), Infrastructure Voluntary Evaluation Sustainability Tool (INVEST) (Behr & Sekyere, 2017), and CEEQUAL (Diaz-Sarachaga et al., 2016), provide structured indicators for infrastructure evaluation. However, these systems are limited by static criteria, context insensitivity, and

DOI: 10.1201/9781003480167-17

the absence of predictive capabilities. They focus on design or construction stages and rarely assess the long-term influence of projects on broader SDG outcomes. Moreover, they were designed for developed countries and do not reflect local development priorities in Indonesia. To address these issues, this research introduces a dynamic framework that integrates SDG indicators with digital analysis through machine learning (ML).

This study develops an SDG-based framework to assess the sustainability impact of transport infrastructure. The framework integrates measurable indicators from four SDG pillars of social, environmental, economic, and institutional into a data-driven classification system that evaluates project performance. It introduces a Sustainable Development Goals Index (SDI) that distinguishes projects by impact level and supports evidence-based assessment through ML techniques. The framework is designed to strengthen decision-making for infrastructure planning and prioritization in line with national sustainability targets.

The proposed framework contributes academically and practically. Academically, it bridges the gap between traditional sustainability rating systems and data-driven evaluation methods. It also advances infrastructure assessment by integrating expert-based weighting with predictive classification. Practically, it introduces a deployable tool consisting of a dashboard, a simulator, and performance interfaces. These tools help policymakers and planners screen, prioritize, and monitor infrastructure projects based on their SDG alignment.

This study contributes to closing the gap between existing rating systems and data-driven sustainability evaluation. It introduces a framework that integrates SDG-based indicators with ML to produce a structured and adaptive assessment tool suited to Indonesia's infrastructure context. The framework aims to help decision-makers evaluate project alignment with sustainability principles and guide investment prioritization toward achieving national SDG targets.

The remaining sections are organized as follows. Section 14.2 describes the research methodology, including indicator identification, data collection, and model development. Section 14.3 presents the results and discussion, and Section 14.4 concludes with recommendations for policy and future research.

14.2 Methods

This study has two main research objectives (ROs): the first (RO1) aims to identify SDG-based indicators for transport infrastructure impact assessment, while the second (RO2) focuses on developing an ML model for the impact assessment framework. There are five stages conducted to obtain these two ROs.

14.2.1 Stage 1: Indicator Identification and Data Collection

A literature study was conducted to identify relevant SDGs and targets for transport infrastructure. A benchmark study of existing project assessment tools and frameworks was also carried out to extract relevant SDG-based indicators. After determining the indicators, data collection combined secondary data from actual transportation infrastructure projects and synthetic data constructed to expand the training dataset. The dataset included 61 airport projects and 39 seaport projects distributed across America, Europe, and Asia, with most seaport data from Europe.

Synthetic data were necessary due to the limited availability of standardized project-level information, which affects ML model accuracy (Long et al., 2025; Sari et al., 2022). The missing indicator values were generated to maintain dataset completeness and balance across impact categories. The process began with identifying indicators that lacked complete information. For each indicator, statistical parameters were estimated by calculating the mean and standard deviation from the available real data after trimming outliers using the interquartile range (IQR) method. Synthetic values were then generated from normal distributions centered on these means, bounded by the observed minimum and maximum values to maintain realistic variability. Relationships among indicators were preserved based on empirical correlations observed in the real dataset.

For instance, projects with higher renewable energy (RE) use generally exhibited lower emission levels, and this relationship was reflected by proportionally adjusting the corresponding synthetic values. All generated records were manually reviewed to confirm that they represented plausible real-world conditions, and unrealistic entries, such as negative percentages or implausible emission intensities, were resampled or removed. Finally, the inclusion of synthetic records was adjusted to achieve an approximately balanced dataset across the three impact categories of low, medium, and high, which improved the representativeness and reliability of the ML model. A summary of the primary data sources used for real project records is provided in Table 14.1.

14.2.2 Stage 2: Expert Weighting Using AHP

A pairwise comparison questionnaire was distributed to experts to assign weights to the sustainability indicators identified in the previous stage. Respondents evaluated the relative importance of each indicator using Saaty's one-to-nine scale. The Analytic Hierarchy Process (AHP) was applied to calculate normalized weights, which were later used in constructing the SDI.

Experts were selected based on their experience and relevance to sustainable transport infrastructure (Table 14.2). Although the sample consisted of four experts, AHP prioritizes judgment consistency and expertise rather than large sample size (Kuo & Chen, 2023; Ramík, 2020).

TABLE 14.1
Data Sources

No.	Data Type	Source Name	Indicators	References
1	Project-level report	Hartsfield-Jackson International Airport	V.5, E.1, E.2, E.3	(ACI World, 2020; FAA, 2021; Pickard & Gençsü, 2021)
2	Project-level report	Heathrow Airport	V.5, E.1, E.2, E.3	(Acuity Analysis, 2020; CAA, 2021, 2022)
3	Annual Report	Freeport of Riga	E.1, E.3	(Freeport of Riga, 2022)
4	Project-level report	Port of Valencia	E.1, E.3	(DataPorts, 2020)
5	Port Authority Annual Report	Port of Bilbao	E.1	(Bilbao Port Authority, 2021)
6	Academic Source	Port of Koper	E.3	(Jittrapirom, 2013)
7	Academic Source	Belfast Harbour	E.3	(Albatross, 2022)
8	Port Authority Report	Port of Klaipeda	E.3	(Burskyte et al., 2011; Klaipėda Port Authority, 2012)
9	Institutional Database	International Council on Clean Transportation	V.5	(DataPorts, 2020)
10	Institutional Database	Federal Aviation Administration (FAA)	E.2, E.3	(FAA, 2021)
11	Institutional Database	Civil Aviation Authority (UK)	E.2, E.3	(CAA, 2021, 2022)

TABLE 14.2
The List of Experts

No.	Profession	Education	Work Experience
1	Transportation Research Group, Universitas Indonesia	Doctorate	>20 years
2	Indonesian Transportation Society (MTI)	Doctorate	11–20 years
3	Technical Director of Transportation, AECOM Indonesia	Master's	>20 years
4	National Advisor for Transport and Climate Change	Master's	<10 years

Experts compared indicators two at a time using the nine-point scale. Individual matrices were aggregated with the geometric mean method (Mu & Pereyra-Rojas, 2018). Each column was normalized, and the row averages produced the final weight vector. Consistency Ratios (CR) were calculated for each sustainability pillar following Saaty's threshold (CR < 0.10) to assess the coherence of expert judgments.

14.2.3 Stage 3: Sustainable Development Goals Index (SDI) Development

Following the weighting process, a sustainability scoring system was developed to evaluate the overall SDG performance of transport infrastructure projects. This evaluation was operationalized through the construction of an SDI, which aggregates weighted indicator scores across four key sustainability pillars.

The calculation of the SDI follows a multi-step process. First, each indicator value is normalized using min-max scaling to ensure all indicators are on a comparable 0–1 scale, as shown in Equations (14.1) and (14.2), as the normalization formula differs based on the direction of the impact:

$$\text{Positive impact}\left(\text{higher values are better}\right)\quad y_t^i = \frac{x_t^i - \min\left(x_t^i\right)}{\max\left(x_t^i\right) - \min\left(x_t^i\right)} \tag{14.1}$$

$$\text{Negative impact}\left(\text{lower values are better}\right)\quad y_t^i = \frac{x_t^i - \max\left(x_t^i\right)}{\min\left(x_t^i\right) - \max\left(x_t^i\right)} \tag{14.2}$$

where,
y_t^i is the normalized score of indicators *i* at time *t*
x_t^i is the original value of indicator *i*
$\min\left(x_t^i\right)$ and $\max\left(x_t^i\right)$ are the minimum and maximum values across the dataset for indicator *i*

Subsequently, the weighted indicator score (I) was calculated by multiplying the normalized score by its corresponding AHP-derived weight, as shown in Equation (14.3):

$$\text{Indicator score}: \mathrm{I} = \sum_{\mathrm{i}=x}^{\mathrm{n}} \left(\mathrm{W_i} \times Y_\mathrm{i}\right) \tag{14.3}$$

where,
$\mathrm{W_i}$ is the relative weight of indicator *i*
Y_i is the normalized value of indicator *i*

The project-level SDI was computed using Equation (14.4).

$$\text{Indicator score} \ : \text{SDI} = \sum_{1}^{15} \text{I} \tag{14.4}$$

Projects were classified with equal-interval cut-points on the normalized SDI: Low 0.00–0.33, Medium 0.34–0.66, High 0.67–1.00. These intervals were chosen to maintain balanced segmentation across normalized SDI scores. After identifying and validating the indicators, the final list of SDG-based indicators was organized into four sustainability dimensions: social, environmental, economic, and institutional.

14.2.4 Stage 4. Data Preparation and ML Model Development

Stage 4 focuses on developing and validating the ML model that assesses the impact level of transport infrastructure projects on SDG attainment. It included data compilation, preprocessing, model training, and validation.

The first step was to compile a comprehensive dataset necessary for the accurate evaluation and performance of the model in answering the research objective (Berawi et al., 2021). The dataset combined 61 real project records (airports and seaports) and 39 synthetic records that were generated based on statistical patterns described in Stage 1. All indicator values were normalized using the min–max scaling method to standardize units and ranges. Each project was assigned a classification label of Low, Medium, or High, based on its SDI score calculated in Stage 3, which served as the classification target.

Model development was carried out using RapidMiner Studio version 10.1, with integrated modules for classification, regression, clustering, and anomaly detection. The Auto Model function was applied for classification tasks to streamline data evaluation, algorithm selection, and performance comparison (Dawangi & Budiyanto, 2021; Sari et al., 2023).

Three supervised learning algorithms were trained and evaluated:

1. Naïve Bayes, chosen for its simplicity and computational efficiency (Testas, 2023),
2. Decision Tree, selected for interpretability and non-linear relationship handling (Thomas et al., 2020).
3. Deep Learning/Artificial Neural Network (DL/ANN), selected for its ability to model complex, multidimensional datasets (Sabbaghi & Tabatabaei, 2023).

The DL/ANN architecture comprised three hidden layers with 32, 16, and 8 neurons, respectively. The ReLU activation function was applied in hidden

TABLE 14.3
Confusion Matrix for Multi-Class Classification

	Predicted Class I	Predicted Class II	Predicted Class III
Actual Class I	a	b	c
Actual Class II	d	e	f
Actual Class III	g	h	i

layers and a Softmax function in the output layer. The Adam optimizer was used with a learning rate of 0.001 and a maximum of 50 epochs. Early stopping was employed if validation loss did not improve over five consecutive epochs.

To minimize bias and enhance generalization, a ten-fold cross-validation was implemented, ranked by the "real/synthetic" flag to ensure that each fold contained a proportional mix of real and synthetic data. A robustness analysis was also performed by training the DL/ANN model on real-only data and testing it on the mixed dataset.

To evaluate classification performance, a Confusion Matrix was used to compare actual and predicted impact categories. For multi-class classification involving Low, Medium, and High categories, a 3×3 matrix was applied. Each cell in the matrix represents a specific outcome of classification, where diagonal cells ("a," "e," "i") indicate correct predictions, and off-diagonal cells represent misclassifications (Table 14.3).

Model performance was measured using precision, recall, and F-measure (Sarker et al., 2019). Precision quantifies the ratio of correctly predicted positives to total predicted positives. Recall measures the share of actual positives that were correctly identified. F-measure represents the harmonic mean of precision and recall to balance accuracy and completeness. Equations (14.5), (14.6), and (14.7) show these metrics:

$$\text{Precision} \ : \frac{TP}{TP+FP} \tag{14.5}$$

$$\text{Recall}: \frac{TP}{TP+FN} \tag{14.6}$$

$$\text{F-Measure}: F-Measure = 2\times\frac{Precision\times Recall}{Precision+Recall} \tag{14.7}$$

This integrated workflow of data generation, weighting, and supervised learning produced a reliable foundation for developing the predictive SDG-based impact assessment framework. Figure 14.1 presents the complete process.

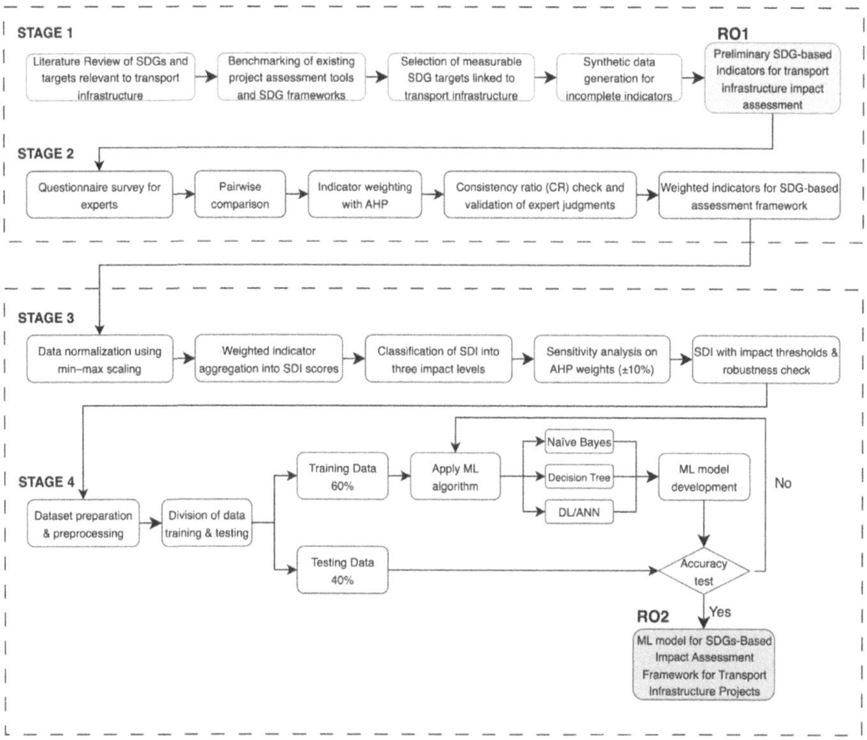

FIGURE 14.1
Research framework.

14.3 Results and Discussion

14.3.1 Identifying and Validating SDG-based Indicators for Transport Infrastructure Impact Assessment

14.3.1.1 Alignment of SDG-Based Indicators with Transport Infrastructure Projects

The selection of relevant indicators that reflect the alignment between transport infrastructure projects and the SDGs was conducted through a structured literature study. The process referenced Thacker et al. (2019), who identified 25 SDG targets with potential relevance to transport infrastructure. However, not all targets were directly measurable or contextually applicable to project-level assessments, particularly for large-scale transport facilities such as airports and seaports.

To refine this initial list, each target was evaluated based on three main criteria: (1) the existence of a direct and measurable relationship between transport infrastructure and the SDG target, (2) the availability of quantifiable data at the project level, and (3) contextual relevance to the Indonesian infrastructure landscape. Targets that depend primarily on broader network or social systems, such as healthcare access or poverty reduction, were excluded because their effects could not be directly attributed to an individual infrastructure project.

A comprehensive screening of 169 SDG targets resulted in the identification of 12 SDGs that exhibit a clear and traceable linkage to transport infrastructure development. These include SDGs 6, 7, 8, 9, 10, 11, 12, 13, 14, 15, 16, and 17. The retained targets cover employment, energy efficiency, climate action, resource management, and institutional transparency. The selected targets were translated into 15 measurable indicators, each mapped to its corresponding SDG targets, with specified measurement direction (↑ or ↓) and units, as summarized in Table 14.4.

14.3.1.2 AHP-Based Weighting and Expert Validation of SDG Indicators

To determine the relative importance of each SDG-based indicator, the AHP was applied. The method uses pairwise comparisons to evaluate how much more one indicator contributes to sustainability than another. The expert panel completed a structured questionnaire comparing the significance of the 15 indicators identified in Section 14.3.1.1. All consistency ratio (CR) values were below 0.10, which confirms that the expert judgments were coherent and met the AHP reliability standard (see Table 14.5).

The results of the AHP analysis are presented in Table 14.6. Five indicators received the highest weights: (S.1) percentage of workers with disabilities (8.08%), (S.2) average monthly income of workers (7.84%), (V.3) number of components that reduce energy and water requirements (7.40%), (V.4) percentage of green open area in the project (7.34%), and (V.1) share of RE used (7.12%). These weights demonstrate that social inclusion and environmental performance are the most influential aspects of transport infrastructure sustainability.

14.3.1.2.1 Indicator-Level Interpretation

Indicator S.1, which focuses on the percentage of workers with disabilities, emphasizes equity in the workforce and aligns with SDG 10.2. This indicator is supported by national regulations, particularly Indonesia's Law No. 8 of 2016, which obligates public institutions to employ at least 2% and private companies at least 1% of persons with disabilities, while also requiring equal pay for equal work. Indicator S.2 reflects SDG 8.5 because it considers whether wages in infrastructure projects exceed regional minimum standards. This serves as an indication of decent work conditions and improvements in workers' livelihoods (Sobieralski, 2021).

TABLE 14.4

SDG-Based Impact Assessment Framework for Transport Infrastructure Projects with Indicator Measurement Direction and Units

Dimension	Code	SDG Targets	Indicators	Measurement Direction	Units
Social	S.1	8.5, 10.2	Percentage of workers with disabilities	↑ Positive	% of total workforce
	S.2	8.5	The average income of workers per month	↑ Positive	USD/month per worker
Environmental	V.1	7.2, 12.a	Percentage of RE used	↑ Positive	% of total energy use
	V.2	7.3	Energy intensity estimation	↓ Negative	kWh/unit output or passenger
	V.3	6.4, 7.3, 9.4, 17.7	Number of components that reduce energy and water requirements	↑ Positive	Count of installed components
	V.4	11.7, 15.1	Percentage of green open area in the project	↑ Positive	% of total land area
	V.5	11.6, 13.2	Estimated annual greenhouse gas emissions	↓ Negative	tCO_2e/year
	V.6	11.6, 12.4, 12.5, 14.1	Percentage of recycled waste	↑ Positive	% of total waste recycled
Economic	E.1	8.3, 8.5, 8.6	Number of jobs produced	↑ Positive	Persons employed
	E.2	9.1, 11.2	Passenger volume per year	↑ Positive	Passengers/year
	E.3	9.1	Cargo volume (tons/year)	↑ Positive	Tons/year
Institutional	I.1	12.8, 13.3	Number of initiatives implemented for sustainability awareness or education	↑ Positive	Programs per year
	I.2	16.6, 16.10	Availability of publicly accessible information	↑ Positive	Binary (1 = available; 0 = not available)
	I.3	17.1	Various sources of income	↑ Positive	Count of distinct funding sources
	I.4	16.6, 16.7	Number of complaints filed by the local community	↓ Negative	Cases per year

TABLE 14.5

AHP Consistency Ratio Results

SDG Pillar	No. of Indicators	Average CR	Remarks
Social	2	0.06	Acceptable
Environmental	6	0.07	Acceptable
Economic	3	0.05	Acceptable
Institutional	4	0.08	Acceptable

TABLE 14.6

Weights of SDG-Based Indicators for Transport Infrastructure Projects

Social		Environmental		Economic		Institutional	
Code	Weight	Code	Weight	Code	Weight	Code	Weight
S.1	8.08%	V.1	7.12%	E.1	6.56%	I.1	5.96%
S.2	7.84%	V.2	6.93%	E.2	6.12%	I.2	5.70%
		V.3	7.40%	E.3	6.01%	I.3	5.52%
		V.4	7.34%			I.4	5.30%
		V.5	7.13%			I.1	5.96%
		V.6	6.98%				

In the environmental dimension, V.3 supports SDG targets 6.4, 7.3, 9.4, and 17.7 because it captures the application of eco-friendly technologies that aim to reduce energy and water use. This aligns with Indonesia's national energy policies (IEA, 2023). V.4, which measures the proportion of green open space, contributes to SDG 11.7 and SDG 15.1. Projects such as Forest Valley at Changi Airport and Waterfront Park at the Port of Seattle show how urban greenery can offer ecological benefits and public access to inclusive, healthy spaces (ARUP, 2014). V.1, which focuses on the share of RE used in project operations, reflects SDG 7.2 (Wei et al., 2019). This is illustrated by infrastructure examples such as Athens International Airport using solar power (Vourdoubas, 2024), the Port of Naples adopting wave energy (Contestabile et al., 2016), and the Port of Marseille using geothermal systems (Sdoukopoulos et al., 2019).

14.3.1.2.2 Dimension-Level Synthesis

The weight distribution from the AHP analysis places the highest priority on the social dimension, followed by environmental, economic, and institutional aspects. This result is consistent with findings from Mensah (2021) and Vijayakumar et al. (2022), who emphasize the central importance of social equity and human development when assessing the sustainability of infrastructure projects.

The social dimension emerged as the most influential, followed by environmental, economic, and institutional dimensions. This hierarchy indicates that transport infrastructure sustainability in Indonesia prioritizes inclusivity and decent employment, aligning with national policy on equitable growth. Similar patterns have been observed in comparative studies such as Rodríguez-Rosa et al. (2017), which found that higher-income regions tend to focus on social well-being once economic foundations are established. In Indonesia, this balance reflects the dual emphasis on social opportunity and environmental protection within ongoing infrastructure expansion.

14.3.1.2.3 Robustness Test of AHP Weights

A sensitivity analysis was conducted by varying each indicator's AHP weight by ±10% to evaluate the stability of the SDI. The results in Table 14.7 show minimal variation across all cases, which confirms the robustness of the indicator weighting structure.

The test confirms that modest fluctuations in weighting values do not materially affect SDI outcomes and indicate a consistent and reliable AHP structure derived from expert judgment within this framework.

14.3.2 Developing and Validating the ML Model for SDG-Based Impact Assessment

This section outlines the development of an ML model to support the SDG-based impact assessment of transport infrastructure projects. The objective is to classify infrastructure projects by their sustainability impact levels of low, medium, or high, derived from the weighted SDG indicators established earlier.

14.3.2.1 Data Composition and Preprocessing

The finalized dataset prepared for model training contained 100 project records representing airport and seaport infrastructure across multiple

TABLE 14.7

Sensitivity Test of SDI under ±10 % AHP Weight Variation

Scenario	Average SDI Variation (%)	Effect on Project Classification
+10% on social indicators	1.6	No change in SDI class
+10% on environmental indicators	1.2	No change in SDI class
−10% on economic indicators	1.8	1 project reclassified from High to Medium
−10% on institutional indicators	1.5	No change in SDI class

global regions. Each record included 15 validated SDG-based indicators derived from the identification and weighting processes described in Section 14.2.

All indicator values were normalized between 0 and 1 using the min–max scaling method to standardize the data range and remove unit inconsistencies. This step was essential to prepare heterogeneous variables such as energy intensity, employment generation, and emission levels for use in ML algorithms. Each project record was assigned an SDI-based classification label of Low, Medium, or High impact according to the thresholds defined earlier. This label served as the target variable for supervised learning.

14.3.2.2 ML Model Development and Configuration

Model training was conducted using the compiled dataset of 100 transport infrastructure projects. The RapidMiner Auto Model feature produced multiple candidate classifiers under identical training conditions with a 60:40 data split for model calibration and validation.

Among the three algorithms tested, the Decision Tree and Naïve Bayes models reached acceptable accuracy but showed limited differentiation between medium- and high-impact categories, which indicated reduced sensitivity to mid-range SDI values. In contrast, the DL/ANN achieved more consistent classification results and demonstrated greater adaptability to the data distribution.

The final DL/ANN configuration consisted of three hidden layers and converged within 35 epochs. Validation loss stabilized at epoch 28, after which early stopping was activated. This model produced balanced prediction rates across all three impact categories and minimized overfitting that appeared in preliminary runs. Figure 14.2 illustrates the finalized DL/ANN model workflow in RapidMiner and shows that the data flow from normalized indicators to predicted impact classes.

14.3.2.3 Data Quality and Validation

The dataset quality was verified through three statistical diagnostics: ID-ness, stability, and missing values. These metrics provided evidence of distinct project characteristics, sufficient variability, and complete data coverage across all 15 indicators. As shown in Table 14.8, all indicators recorded zero missing values, which demonstrates that the dataset was complete. Indicators such as S.2 (monthly income) and E.2 (passenger volume) recorded 100% ID-ness because their values were unique to each project, which is typical for project-level data. Indicator I.2 (publicly available information) recorded the highest stability at 50.5% due to its binary form, which restricted variation across projects. Overall, the dataset exhibited both completeness and variability suitable for reliable ML analysis.

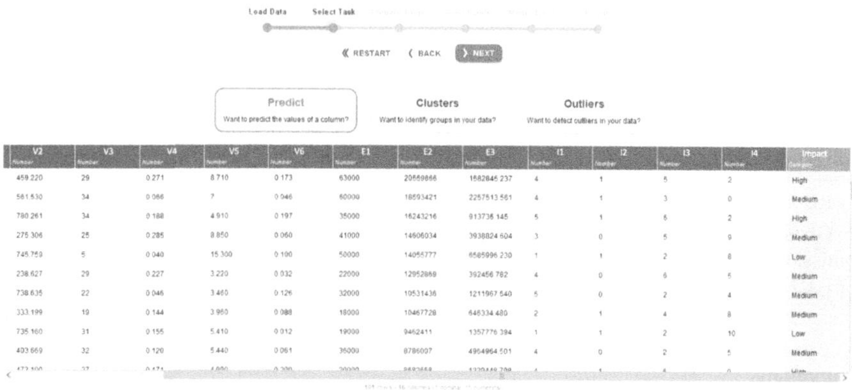

FIGURE 14.2
ML model task selection.

TABLE 14.8
Data Quality

Indicator Code	ID-ness (%)	Stability (%)	Missing (%)
S.1	0.99	9.90	0.00
S.2	100.00	0.99	0.00
V.1	0.00	1.98	0.00
V.2	0.00	1.98	0.00
V.3	33.66	7.92	0.00
V.4	0.00	1.98	0.00
V.5	2.97	2.97	0.00
V.6	0.00	2.97	0.00
E.1	73.27	3.96	0.00
E.2	100.00	0.99	0.00
E.3	72.28	1.98	0.00
I.1	5.94	23.76	0.00
I.2	1.98	50.50	0.00
I.3	5.94	28.71	0.00
I.4	10.89	14.85	0.00

Statistical checks confirmed that the synthetic records were consistent with the real project data. Descriptive analysis verified that all generated values were within three standard deviations of the real data means and maintained comparable mean–variance patterns. Pairwise correlation analysis using Pearson's r compared indicator relationships in the synthetic and real datasets. The difference in correlation coefficients was below ±0.05 for all major variable pairs. The negative association between RE use (V.1) and greenhouse

TABLE 14.9

Comparison of Real and Synthetic Data Statistics for Selected Indicators

Indicator	Mean (Real)	SD (Real)	Mean (Synthetic)	SD (Synthetic)	Δ Mean	Δ r (Correlation Difference)
V.1 RE share	32.4	5.6	33.1	5.8	+0.7	0.03
V.5 GHG emissions	75.2	10.9	74.7	11.1	−0.5	0.02
E.1 Jobs created	415	130	420	125	+5	0.01
E.2 Passenger volume	8.6M	3.2M	8.5M	3.3M	−0.1M	0.04
I.3 Funding sources	3.2	1.1	3.3	1.0	+0.1	0.02

gas emissions (V.5) remained consistent in both datasets, which shows that the statistical integrity of inter-indicator relationships was preserved.

The results in Table 14.9 show that the synthetic data closely matched the statistical properties of the real dataset. Differences in mean values and standard deviations remained within acceptable limits, and the correlation structures were nearly identical. These findings confirm that the synthetic dataset preserved the variability and interdependence of the real-world indicators.

Model robustness was also examined through a stratified ten-fold cross-validation that included proportional mixes of real and synthetic data. The DL/ANN model was then trained exclusively on real data and tested on the mixed dataset. The resulting classification accuracy was 88.5%, compared with 90.1% for the model trained on the full mixed dataset. The 1.6% difference confirms that the inclusion of synthetic records did not bias the model or reduce generalization performance. These results demonstrate that the dataset was statistically coherent, free from missing entries, and representative of real-world project conditions. This confirms that the dataset formed a reliable foundation for evaluating model performance in the subsequent section.

14.3.2.4 Model Performance and Robustness Analysis

The ML model was developed to classify transport infrastructure projects based on their contribution to the SDGs. The model's performance was evaluated through three standard classification metrics: precision, recall, and F-measure. Among the three tested algorithms, the DL/ANN model delivered the highest overall accuracy at 86.7%. This performance surpassed that of the Decision Tree (75.3%) and Naïve Bayes (64.7%) models. The Decision Tree recorded moderate accuracy but showed signs of overfitting when

TABLE 14.10

Error Value, Accuracy, and Runtime of Each ML Model

Algorithm	Classification Error (%)	Accuracy (%)	Runtime (seconds)
Naïve Bayes	35.3	13.3	8
DL/ANN	13.3	86.7	3
Decision Tree	24.7	75.3	2

TABLE 14.11

Results of the Confusion Matrix for the ML Model

	Precision			Recall			F-Measure		
Model	High (%)	Medium (%)	Low (%)	High (%)	Medium (%)	Low (%)	High (%)	Medium (%)	Low (%)
Naïve Bayes	0	58.33	100	0	100	50	0	73.7	66.7
DL/ANN	90	90.91	75	100	76.92	85.71	94.7	83.3	79.9
Decision Tree	90	68.42	0	100	92.86	0	94.7	78.8	0

processing indicators with limited variability. The Naïve Bayes model performed least effectively because it assumes independence among features, a condition that does not apply to transport infrastructure datasets, where several indicators are interrelated. The comparative results are presented in Table 14.10.

The confusion matrix analysis provides further insight into the performance of each algorithm. The DL/ANN model showed strong capability in identifying high-impact projects, achieving 90% precision and 100% recall. This result indicates that nearly all high-impact projects were correctly recognized with very few false positives. The Decision Tree model achieved good performance for high- and medium-impact projects but had difficulty with the low-impact category because of class imbalance. The Naïve Bayes model showed poor performance for high-impact projects, with zero precision and recall in that category. The detailed classification metrics are presented in Table 14.11.

14.3.2.5 Model Misclassification Analysis

The misclassification analysis examines where and why the tested algorithms produced errors when classifying transport infrastructure projects based on SDG impact levels. The errors mainly occurred in the low-impact category, which had fewer samples and lower indicator variability compared with the other classes (see Table 14.12).

TABLE 14.12
Summary of Misclassification Patterns across ML Algorithms

Algorithm	Most Misclassified Category	Primary Cause of Error	Example of Affected Indicators	Interpretation
Decision Tree	Low-impact projects	Limited variability and overlapping indicator ranges	V.1 RE Share, V.6 Waste Recycling Rate	Threshold-based splits failed to separate adjacent classes (Breiman et al., 2017; Kerdprasop & Kerdprasop, 2011).
Naïve Bayes	Low- and high-impact projects	Violation of feature independence assumption	V.2 Energy Intensity, V.5 GHG Emissions	Correlated variables distorted probability estimates (Frank et al., 2003).
DL/ANN	Medium-impact projects (minor error)	Limited training samples and residual noise	E.1 Jobs Created, I.3 Funding Sources	The model generalized effectively but showed a slight bias toward dominant classes (Goodfellow et al., 2016).

The Decision Tree model showed the highest rate of false classification for low-impact projects. Most of these cases were incorrectly assigned to the medium-impact group. This result reflects the model's dependence on threshold-based splits that perform poorly when input variables display narrow value ranges. Indicators such as RE share (V.1) and waste recycling rate (V.6) exhibited small spreads, which caused ambiguous boundary definitions between adjacent classes. The hierarchical structure of Decision Tree algorithms also increases sensitivity to fluctuations in small subsets of data, which reduces their ability to generalize when class distributions are uneven.

The Naïve Bayes model recorded systematic errors in both the low- and high-impact categories. Its statistical framework assumes independence among input features, a condition that was not met in this dataset. Several indicators, including energy intensity (V.2) and greenhouse gas emissions (V.5), were negatively correlated, which distorted the conditional probability calculations. This problem led to incorrect class assignments for projects that exhibited extreme values. The limited number of high-impact samples further reduced the reliability of probabilistic estimation within this model.

In contrast, the DL/ANN model performed more consistently across all categories. Its multi-layered structure captured nonlinear interactions among

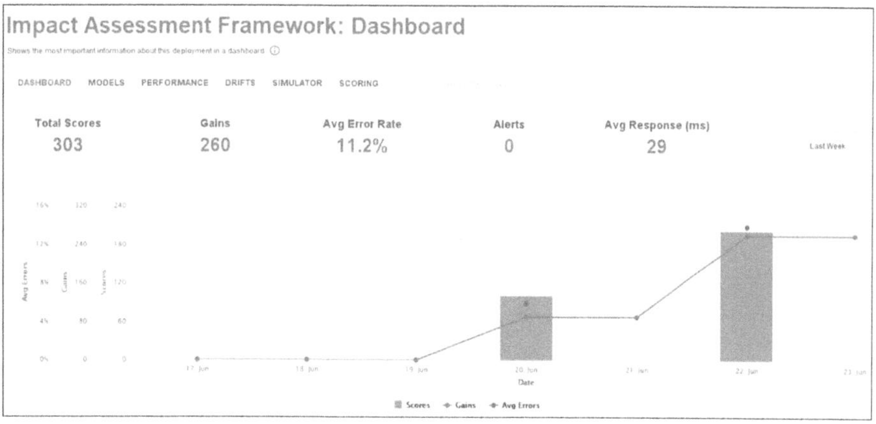

FIGURE 14.3
Dashboard of ML-based impact assessment framework.

correlated indicators, which produced balanced classification results. Minor misclassifications in the medium-impact group were attributed to limited training examples rather than structural limitations of the model.

Quantitatively, the Decision Tree model recorded 0% precision and recall for the low-impact class, while the Naïve Bayes model recorded 0% precision and recall for the high-impact class (Table 14.12). These results confirm that the observed misclassification patterns are supported by measurable performance differences derived from the confusion matrix. The DL/ANN model, which achieved 90% precision and 100% recall for high-impact projects, exhibited only minor deviations, which further validates its robustness compared with the other algorithms.

14.3.2.6 Deployment and Real-Case Demonstration of the DL/ANN Model

The DL/ANN model, which achieved the highest classification accuracy, was deployed as the core engine of the SDG-based impact assessment framework. The deployment produced an interactive web-based interface designed to support users in evaluating infrastructure projects through accessible visualization and scenario testing. The platform consists of three key components: the Dashboard, the Simulator, and the Performance pages, each serving a distinct analytical purpose.

The Dashboard page (Figure 14.3) summarizes the overall performance of the deployed model. It presents the number of evaluated records, average classification accuracy, and processing time. This page helps users gain a quick understanding of how projects align with SDG targets and how consistently the system performs across datasets. It also functions as a control panel for institutional users to monitor data updates and system reliability.

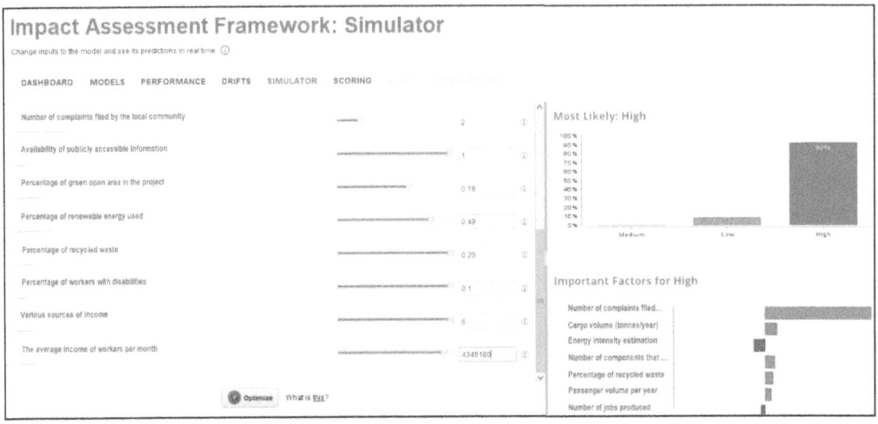

FIGURE 14.4
Simulator page of ML-based impact assessment framework.

The Simulator page (Figure 14.4) serves as an interactive environment for testing project scenarios. It allows users to manually adjust the 15 SDG-based indicators through the input panel and observe how these adjustments affect the project's predicted SDG impact level. To demonstrate its functionality, a representative dataset was entered to reflect the characteristics of a large-scale transport project with balanced social, environmental, and economic attributes. The simulation resulted in a High Impact classification, consistent with expectations for projects that emphasize renewable energy integration, employment generation, and transparent governance. This example shows that the deployed model can generate interpretable and stable outcomes under varying input conditions.

The Performance page (Figure 14.5) provides detailed information about model validation results, including confusion matrix outputs, accuracy rates, and comparison statistics for the three algorithms. This section allows technical users to review the model's reliability and assess any deviations from expected accuracy. The page also documents runtime efficiency and error distribution, which are critical for future model optimization and independent audits.

The deployment of the DL/ANN-based platform demonstrates that the proposed SDG impact assessment framework can function as a practical decision-support system. It allows institutional planners and analysts to identify infrastructure projects with strong sustainability potential and to replicate the workflow for other infrastructure categories. The integrated design also supports transparency, as users can trace the influence of each indicator on the predicted impact level.

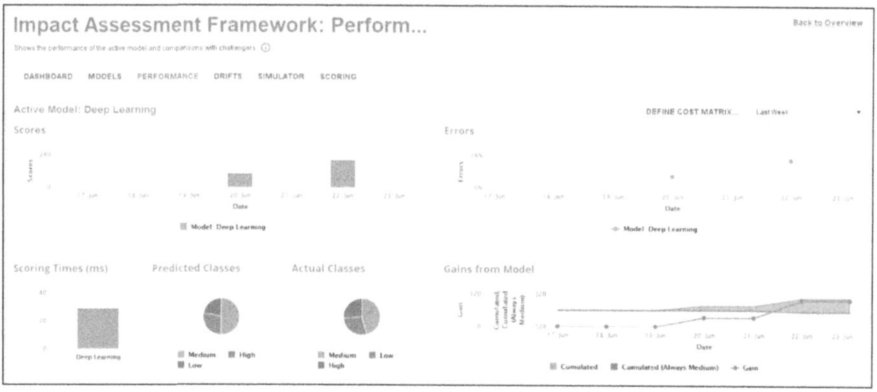

FIGURE 14.5
Performance page.

14.3.3 Discussion

ML has been applied in sustainability evaluation, as shown by Castaneda et al. (2021), who used supervised algorithms to assess freight transport projects in Europe, with SVM achieving 98% accuracy. Antunes et al. (2023) combined multiple-criteria decision-making (MCDM) and ML for road transport in China, which reported comparable accuracy across SVM, k-Nearest Neighbors (k-NN), and Multinomial Logistic Regression (MLR). While both studies demonstrated the usefulness of ML, their focus was limited to environmental and operational indicators.

The proposed framework advances this approach by integrating four SDG pillars into a unified model for transport infrastructure. Unlike existing tools such as ENVISION, INVEST, and CEEQUAL, which rely on static scoring and qualitative evaluation, this model applies expert-derived weighting through AHP and predictive analysis using a DL/ANN algorithm. The process quantifies sustainability alignment and produces transparent, data-driven classifications of project impact.

The integration of SDG indicators with machine learning prediction also improves applicability across infrastructure sectors. The dashboard supports monitoring of SDG alignment, the simulator allows scenario testing for new projects, and the performance page provides traceable evaluation records. Indicators can be adapted for other transport systems, such as substituting passenger or cargo volume with traffic flow or ridership in road or transit projects. This adaptability and predictive capability make the framework a practical and transferable decision-support tool that complements ENVISION, INVEST, and CEEQUAL through quantitative SDG-oriented assessment.

14.4 Conclusion

This study proposed a machine learning-based framework to evaluate the contribution of transport infrastructure projects to the Sustainable Development Goals (SDGs). The framework integrates structured indicator identification, expert weighting, and predictive modeling to provide a transparent and quantitative assessment method. Fifteen indicators were defined across social, environmental, economic, and institutional dimensions, with five emerging as most influential: the percentage of workers with disabilities, average monthly income, renewable energy use, energy intensity, and the number of components that reduce energy and water consumption. These indicators capture the multidimensional nature of sustainability at the project level.

Among the algorithms tested, the Deep Learning/Artificial Neural Network (DL/ANN) model demonstrated the highest accuracy in classifying project impacts. Its stability was confirmed through sensitivity and robustness analyses, which showed consistent predictive results under moderate variations in parameter and weight settings. The findings indicate that the proposed model can serve as a reliable decision-support tool for prioritizing infrastructure projects that advance SDG targets.

Despite these strengths, the framework has several limitations. The model was developed mainly from aviation and maritime datasets, which constrain its generalization to other transport modes or infrastructure types. The inclusion of synthetic data, although necessary to address data scarcity, may affect transferability to different regional contexts. Future research should validate the framework with larger, multimodal datasets and integrate real-time monitoring and stakeholder feedback to enhance adaptability and long-term relevance for SDG-aligned infrastructure planning.

References

ACI World. (2020). *Annual World Airport Traffic Report, 2020*. https://store.aci.aero/product/annual-world-airport-traffic-report-2020/

Acuity Analysis. (2020). *Economic and Social Importance of the UK's Regional Airports*. https://www.unitetheunion.org/media/3098/regional-airports-data.pdf

Albatross. (2022). *Belfast Harbour/Port*. https://albatrossshipping.co.uk/belfast-harbour-port/

Anderson, J., & Muench, S. (2013). Sustainability Trends Measured by the Greenroads Rating System. *Transportation Research Record*, 2357. https://doi.org/10.3141/2357-03

Antunes, J., Tan, Y., Wanke, P., & Jabbour, C. J. C. (2023). Impact of R&D and Innovation in Chinese Road Transportation Sustainability Performance: A Novel Trigonometric Envelopment Analysis for Ideal Solutions (TEA-IS). *Socio-Economic Planning Sciences*, 87. https://doi.org/10.1016/j.seps.2023.101544

ARUP. (2014). *Cities Alive: Rethinking Green Infrastructure*. ARUP.
Behr, C., & Sekyere, E. (2017). *Challenges and Opportunities in Evaluating Sustainable Infrastructure (Issue March)*. http://repository.hsrc.ac.za/handle/20.500.11910/11051
Berawi, M. A., Leviäkangas, P., Siahaan, S. A. O., Hafidza, A., Sari, M., Miraj, P., Harwahyu, R., & Saroji, G. (2021). Increasing Disaster Victim Survival Rate: SaveMyLife Mobile Application Development. *International Journal of Disaster Risk Reduction*, 60. https://doi.org/10.1016/j.ijdrr.2021.102290
Bilbao Port Authority. (2021). Economic Impact. *Bilbao Port*. https://www.bilbaoport.eus/en/corporate-social-responsibility-csr/economic-impact/
Breiman, L., Friedman, J. H., Olshen, R. A., & Stone, C. J. (2017). *Classification and Regression Trees*. CRC Press. https://doi.org/10.1201/9781315139470
Burskyte, V., Belous, O., & Stasiskiene, Z. (2011). Sustainable Development of Deep-Water Seaport: The Case of Lithuania. *Environmental Science and Pollution Research*, 18(5). https://doi.org/10.1007/s11356-010-0415-y
CAA. (2021). *Size of Reporting Airports 2021 Comparison with 2016*. https://www.caa.co.uk/Documents/Download/9115/8cce8a5d-a76b-4652-8fab-41ae2288f104/4631
CAA. (2022). *Freight 2011–2021 Tonnes*. https://www.caa.co.uk/Documents/Download/9115/8cce8a5d-a76b-4652-8fab-41ae2288f104/4665
Castaneda, J., Cardona, J. F., Martins, L. D. C., & Juan, A. A. (2021). Supervised Machine Learning Algorithms for Measuring and Promoting Sustainable Transportation and Green Logistics. *Transportation Research Procedia*, 58. https://doi.org/10.1016/j.trpro.2021.11.061
Contestabile, P., Ferrante, V., Di Lauro, E., & Vicinanza, D. (2016, January). *Prototype Overtopping Breakwater for Wave Energy Conversion at Port of Naples*. Proceedings of the International Offshore and Polar Engineering Conference.
DataPorts. (2020). *Port of Valencia*. https://dataports-project.eu/port-of-valencia/
Dawangi, I. D., & Budiyanto, M. A. (2021). Ship Energy Efficiency Management Plan Development Using Machine Learning: Case Study of CO2 Emissions of Ship Activities at Container Port. *International Journal of Technology*, 12(5). https://doi.org/10.14716/ijtech.v12i5.5183
Diaz-Sarachaga, J. M., Jato-Espino, D., Alsulami, B., & Castro-Fresno, D. (2016). Evaluation of Existing Sustainable Infrastructure Rating Systems for Their Application in Developing Countries. *Ecological Indicators*, 71. https://doi.org/10.1016/j.ecolind.2016.07.033
FAA. (2021, August 11). *CY 2020 All-Cargo Landed Weight Percentage Change from CY19*.
Frank, E. T., Hall, M. A., & Pfahringer, B. (2003). Locally Weighted Naive Bayes. In U. Kjaerulff & C. Meek (Eds.), *Proceedings of the 19th Conference on Uncertainty in Artificial Intelligence*. Elsevier Science Ltd. https://doi.org/10.48550/arXiv.1301.4606
Freeport of Riga. (2022). *Information Booklet 2022*. https://rop.lv/sites/default/files/2022-05/Buklets%20ROP%202022%20EN.pdf
Goodfellow, I., Courville, A., & Bengio, Y. (2016). Deep Learning. In *Request Exam Copy View Preview Adaptive Computation and Machine Learning Series*. The MIT Press. https://mitpress.mit.edu/9780262035613/deep-learning/
Gudmundsson, H., Hall, R. P., Marsden, G., & Zietsman, J. (2016). New York's GreenLITES Rating Systems. In *Sustainable Transportation* (pp. 251–276). Springer, Berlin, Heidelberg. https://doi.org/10.1007/978-3-662-46924-8_10
IEA. (2023). *Indonesia – Countries & Regions*. https://www.iea.org/countries/indonesia/efficiency-demand

Jittrapirom, P. (2013). *Port Koper, a Green Gateway to Europe.* http://www.marinetraffic.com/ais/details/ports/126

Kerdprasop, N., & Kerdprasop, K. (2011). The Development of Discrete Decision Tree Induction for Categorical Data. *International Journal of Mathematics and Computers in Simulations*, 5(6), 499–509.

Klaipėda Port Authority. (2012). *About the Port of Klaipėda.* https://portofklaipeda.lt/en/port/about-the-port-of-klaipeda/

Kuo, T., & Chen, M. H. (2023). On Using Pairwise Comparison in the Analytic Hierarchy Process: Validity is Goal While Consistency is Means. *Information Sciences*, 648. https://doi.org/10.1016/j.ins.2023.119630

Long, Y., Kroeger, S., Zaeh, M. F., & Brintrup, A. (2025). Leveraging Synthetic Data to Tackle Machine Learning Challenges in Supply Chains: Challenges, Methods, Applications, and Research Opportunities. *International Journal of Production Research.* https://doi.org/10.1080/00207543.2024.2447927

Mensah, J. (2021). Social Sustainability: A Dwarf Among Giants in the Sustainable Development Pillars? *Asian Journal of Management.* https://doi.org/10.52711/2321-5763.2021.00019

Morton, S., Pencheon, D., & Squires, N. (2017). Sustainable Development Goals (SDGs), and Their Implementation: A National Global Framework for Health, Development and Equity Needs a Systems Approach at Every Level. *British Medical Bulletin*, 124(1). https://doi.org/10.1093/bmb/ldx031

Mu, E., & Pereyra-Rojas, M. (2018). *Group Decision-Making in AHP* (pp. 81–89). https://doi.org/10.1007/978-3-319-68369-0_8

Nasikhin, R., Akib, M., & Triono, A. (2022). Sustainable Development Goals and Environmentally Sound Infrastructure Development in Indonesia. *Asian Journal of Legal Studies*, 1(1). https://doi.org/10.53402/ajls.v1i1.68

Oluwalaiye, O., & Ozbek, M. E. (2019). Consistency between Infrastructure Rating Systems in Measuring Sustainability. *Infrastructures*, 4(1). https://doi.org/10.3390/infrastructures4010009

Palei, T. (2015). Assessing the Impact of Infrastructure on Economic Growth and Global Competitiveness. *Procedia Economics and Finance*, 23, 168–175. https://doi.org/10.1016/s2212-5671(15)00322-6

Pickard, S., & Gençsü, I. (2021). *The Airport Tracker: Uncovering Aviation Emissions.* https://odi.org/en/publications/the-airport-tracker-uncovering-aviation-emissions/

Ramík, J. (2020). Applications in Decision-Making: Analytic Hierarchy Process – AHP Revisited. In *Lecture Notes in Economics and Mathematical Systems* (Vol. 690). https://doi.org/10.1007/978-3-030-39891-0_6

Rodríguez-Rosa, M., Gallego-Álvarez, I., Vicente-Galindo, M. P., & Galindo-Villardón, M. P. (2017). Are Social, Economic and Environmental Well-Being Equally Important in all Countries Around the World? A Study by Income Levels. *Social Indicators Research*, 131(2). https://doi.org/10.1007/s11205-016-1257-x

Sabbaghi, H., & Tabatabaei, S. H. (2023). Regimentation of Geochemical Indicator Elements Employing Convolutional Deep Learning Algorithm. *Frontiers in Environmental Science*, 11. https://doi.org/10.3389/fenvs.2023.1076302

Sari, M., Berawi, M. A., Larasati, S. P., Susilowati, S. I., Susantono, B., & Woodhead, R. (2023). Developing Machine Learning Model to Predict HVAC System of Healthy Building: A Case Study in Indonesia. *International Journal of Technology*, 14(7). https://doi.org/10.14716/ijtech.v14i7.6682

Sari, M., Berawi, M. A., Zagloel, T. Y., & Triadji, R. W. (2022). Machine Learning Model for Green Building Design Prediction. *IAES International Journal of Artificial Intelligence (IJ-AI)*, 11(4), 1525–1534. https://doi.org/10.11591/IJAI.V11.I4.PP1525-1534

Sarker, I. H., Kayes, A. S. M., & Watters, P. (2019). Effectiveness Analysis of Machine Learning Classification Models for Predicting Personalized Context-Aware Smartphone Usage. *Journal of Big Data*, 6(1), 57. https://doi.org/10.1186/s40537-019-0219-y

Sdoukopoulos, E., Boile, M., Tromaras, A., & Anastasiadis, N. (2019). Energy Efficiency in European Ports: State-of-Practice and Insights on the Way Forward. *Sustainability (Switzerland)*, 11(18). https://doi.org/10.3390/su11184952

Sobieralski, J. B. (2021). Transportation Infrastructure and Employment: Are All Investments Created Equal? *Research in Transportation Economics*, 88. https://doi.org/10.1016/j.retrec.2020.100927

Testas, A. (2023). Naive Bayes Classification with Pandas, Scikit-Learn, and PySpark. In *Distributed Machine Learning with PySpark*. https://doi.org/10.1007/978-1-4842-9751-3_11

Thacker, S., Adshead, D., Fay, M., Hallegatte, S., Harvey, M., Meller, H., O'Regan, N., Rozenberg, J., Watkins, G., & Hall, J. W. (2019). Infrastructure for Sustainable Development. *Nature Sustainability*, 2(4), 324–331. https://doi.org/10.1038/s41893-019-0256-8

Thomas, T., Vijayaraghavan, A. P., & Emmanuel, S. (2020). Applications of Decision Trees. *Machine Learning Approaches in Cyber Security Analytics*, 157–184. https://doi.org/10.1007/978-981-15-1706-8_9

Vijayakumar, A., Mahmood, M. N., Gurmu, A., Kamardeen, I., & Alam, S. (2022). Social Sustainability Indicators for Road Infrastructure Projects: A Systematic Literature Review. *IOP Conference Series: Earth and Environmental Science*, 1101(2). https://doi.org/10.1088/1755-1315/1101/2/022039

Vourdoubas, J. (2024). Use of Solar Photovoltaics for the Achievement of the National Goals for Energy and Climate in Greece. *European Journal of Applied Science, Engineering and Technology*, 2(5), 4–15. https://doi.org/10.59324/EJASET.2024.2(5).01

Wei, T., Zhou, J., & Zhang, H. (2019). Rebound Effect of Energy Intensity Reduction on Energy Consumption. *Resources, Conservation and Recycling*, 144. https://doi.org/10.1016/j.resconrec.2019.01.012

15

From Classical Models to Intelligent Systems: AI and Machine Learning in Transportation Planning

Soroush Rashidi

15.1 Introduction

The contemporary urban environment is defined by rapid urbanisation, growing travel demands, and persistent challenges such as traffic congestion, carbon emissions, safety risks, and environmental degradation (Abduljabbar et al., 2019). For many years, urban planners and transportation engineers have relied on classical models – grounded in statistical analysis and simulation – to analyse, forecast, and manage the flow of people and goods (Meyer & Miller, 2001). While these traditional approaches have formed the backbone of transportation planning, they increasingly struggle to address the complexity, scale, and dynamic nature of modern transport systems (Bastarianto et al., 2023). In particular, their limitations become evident when faced with the need to integrate heterogeneous data sources, respond to real-time conditions, and provide adaptive solutions for evolving urban landscapes (Xu et al., 2024b). As cities continue to expand and mobility patterns shift, the demand for more advanced and sustainable planning tools is more urgent than ever (Nikitas et al., 2020). Against this backdrop, Artificial Intelligence (AI) and Machine Learning (ML) have emerged as transformative technologies, offering innovative methods to tackle longstanding transportation challenges and drive the evolution of 'smart cities' (Nikitas et al., 2020). By leveraging computational techniques inspired by human cognition, AI and ML enable a new generation of solutions that surpass the constraints of classical models. These technologies enhance predictive capabilities, support the development of autonomous systems, and open up possibilities for more responsive, efficient, and equitable urban mobility.

This chapter contributes by synthesising the evolution from classical, sequential transport modelling to AI and machine learning-enabled

DOI: 10.1201/9781003480167-18

intelligent systems; systematically comparing the strengths, limitations, and applications of both paradigms; consolidating the main techniques now central to practice – such as neural networks, evolutionary optimisation, fuzzy logic, agent-based models, deep learning, and generative AI – and highlighting their roles in transport. It also demonstrates a practical LLM–SUMO pipeline for translating natural-language policy into microscopic simulation, and outlines the ethical, explainability, and governance challenges, as well as research priorities – including digital twins, hybrid models, transfer and meta-learning, and the integration of AI with agent-based modelling – for achieving sustainable and equitable urban mobility.

15.2 Literature Review/Background

For many decades, classical models have formed the foundation of transportation planning, designed to understand, predict, and manage the movement of people and goods within both urban and regional contexts. These approaches are grounded in established statistical and simulation techniques and have traditionally relied on manual data collection alongside static models built upon simplified assumptions.

15.2.1 Review of Classical Models in Transportation Planning

Classical models have long provided the foundation for transportation planning, serving as the principal tools to understand, forecast, and manage the movement of people and goods across urban and regional systems (Meyer & Miller, 2001). These approaches are typically underpinned by established statistical analyses and simulation techniques (Da et al., 2025; Meyer & Miller, 2001), frequently involving manual data collection and static assumptions about traveller behaviour and system operations (Sadek, 2007). Among these traditional approaches, the trip-based model – commonly known as the four-step travel demand model – remains one of the most widely recognised and utilised frameworks. It processes aggregate travel choices through a sequential methodology involving trip generation, trip distribution, mode choice (modal split), and route assignment; each stage is typically modelled independently, with the output from one stage serving as input for the next (Bastarianto et al., 2023). Beyond urban travel demand, classical railway scheduling and planning algorithms have included exact methods (e.g., integer programming, linear programming, mixed integer linear programming), ad hoc heuristics, simulation models, expert systems, and constraint propagation techniques – valuable for small to moderate-scale applications but often unsuited to large, complex, or dynamic networks (Zhang & Zhang, 2023). Traditional transportation planning and traffic management have likewise been expert-driven and labour-intensive, with limited sensors and data collection, one-way and static information dissemination (signage, printed maps, timetables, radio), and little capacity for real-time adaptation or feedback (Meyer & Miller, 2001; Zemmouchi-Ghomari, 2025).

Despite their long-standing utility, classical models exhibit significant limitations that have become more pronounced as systems and behaviours have grown more intricate. Their aggregate focus makes it difficult to capture the diversity of individual decision-making and derived demand, while the rigid, sequential structure restricts simultaneous simulation of all modelling stages at a disaggregate level, reducing realism and adaptability (Bastarianto et al., 2023). Initial assumptions embedded within these models limit flexibility in the face of evolving urban challenges, and traditional techniques struggle to represent interdependencies and feedback, particularly when empirical data is incomplete or ambiguous (Sadek, 2007; Abduljabbar et al., 2019). Handling qualitative data and uncertainty is another challenge: classical analytical methods prioritise quantitative certainty and definitive logic, which is often insufficient for problems involving human judgement, qualitative evidence, and inherent vagueness; probability theory becomes problematic when observations are imprecise or propositions ill-defined (Sadek, 2007; Kikuchi, 2007). Resource intensity and static processes further hinder scalability, while limited, fixed-logic traffic management constrains responsiveness to real-time or complex network conditions; computational limits similarly confine classical scheduling/planning algorithms to small-scale instances (Zhang & Zhang, 2023; Zemmouchi-Ghomari, 2025). Data bias and generalisability compound these issues: models calibrated for specific contexts – may not transfer well, and incomplete or biased training data can yield implausible outputs and unreliable predictions (Guo & Liu, 2024). These limitations are summarised in Figure 15.1.

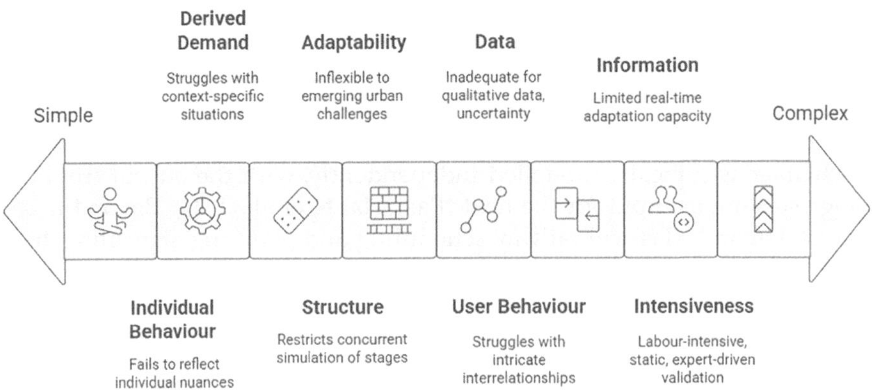

FIGURE 15.1
Classical models' limitations in capturing travel demand complexity.

To address some of these constraints, activity-based models (ACBMs) emerged as an evolution of the trip-based paradigm, aiming to reflect individual-level travel choices by considering sequences of activities, time-space constraints, and personal characteristics. They assume individuals seek to maximise activity utility by selecting the optimal set of activities and corresponding trips (Bowman & Ben-Akiva, 2000). While this offers greater behavioural realism, it introduces fresh challenges: computational complexity, demanding data requirements for detailed synthetic populations, integration issues between demand generation and traffic assignment, incomplete activity chains, limited rescheduling or departure-time adjustments, and difficulties in modelling multimodal interactions (Bastarianto et al., 2023; Rasouli & Timmermans, 2014; Ionescu et al., 2024). These burdens can be substantial – simulating nationwide demand-responsive systems or large metropolitan regions may require days or even weeks on high-performance computing clusters (Sanford Bernhardt, 2007; Waraich et al., 2015).

In sum, the traditional four-step framework and related classical methods provided a practical scaffold for decades, but their aggregate orientation, rigid sequencing, static data flows, and limited treatment of uncertainty now constrain performance in complex, data-rich, and dynamic contexts (Bastarianto et al., 2023; Nikitas et al., 2020; Xu et al., 2024b; Zemmouchi-Ghomari, 2025). ACBMs push towards richer behavioural representation yet inherit and introduce their own computational and integration hurdles (Bastarianto et al., 2023; Bowman & Ben-Akiva, 2000).

15.2.2 Transition to AI and ML Approaches

The dynamic, large-scale, and increasingly complex nature of contemporary transportation systems – combined with diverse data sources and the need for real-time responsiveness – has pushed traditional methodologies beyond their practical limits. This reality has driven a paradigm shift towards the adoption of AI and ML approaches (Xu et al., 2024b). AI and ML offer transformative computational tools capable of modelling relationships and uncertainties beyond the scope of classical techniques (Abduljabbar et al., 2019; Haenlein & Kaplan, 2019). In the transportation domain, these methods provide the means to address pressing challenges, including increasing demand, emissions, safety, and environmental impacts. Unlike traditional models that often eliminate uncertainty through simplifying assumptions, AI approaches allow for the direct modelling of uncertainty, incorporating both quantitative and qualitative data, and supporting more robust analysis of complex systems (Sadek, 2007).

15.2.3 Key Milestones and Developments in AI and ML for Transportation

The evolution of AI in transportation reflects a profound transformation, progressing from manual, expert-driven models to data-driven and

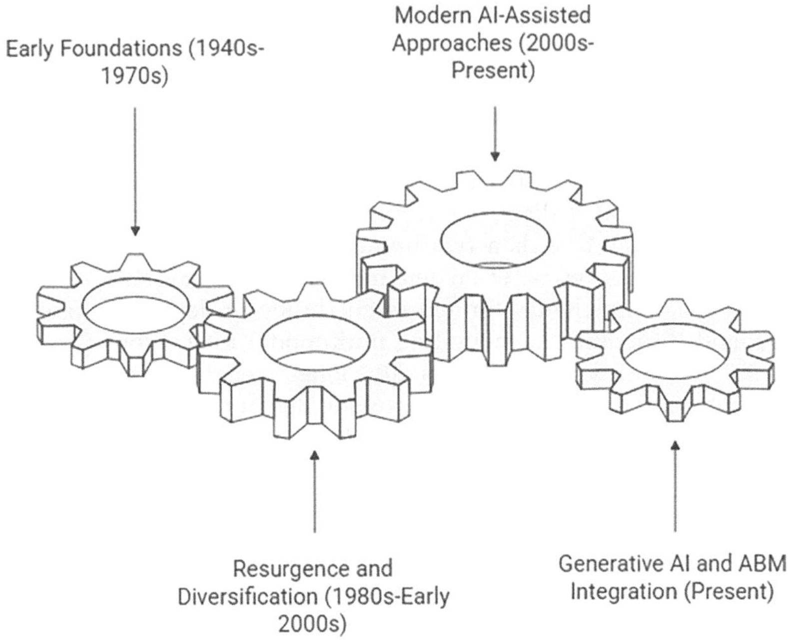

FIGURE 15.2
Evolution of AI in transportation.

generative approaches and can be understood across three major phases (see Figure 15.2).

- **Early Foundations (1940s–1970s)**

  The origins of AI trace back to 1956, when John McCarthy coined the term. Early efforts focused on knowledge-based systems (KBS), or expert systems, which utilised rule-based reasoning ('if X, then Y') to support decision-making under uncertainty. Initial work on neural networks (NNs) also began, though progress was limited by technical challenges during this period (Abduljabbar et al., 2019; Sadek, 2007; Haenlein & Kaplan, 2019).

- **Resurgence and Diversification (1980s–Early 2000s)**

  Renewed interest in neural networks followed the introduction of the backpropagation algorithm, enabling the modelling of complex systems with limited understanding of internal relationships (Negnevitsky, 2005). The field also saw the rise of genetic algorithms (GAs) and fuzzy systems (FS) (Sadek, 2007), which addressed optimisation and uncertainty in transportation tasks. Cellular automata models and the introduction of agent-based modelling

(ABM) enabled the simulation of complex, emergent behaviours within transport systems, particularly for pedestrian movement and intelligent traffic control (Bastarianto et al., 2023).

- **Modern AI-Assisted and Generative Approaches (2000s–Present)**

  The 2000s saw the integration of intelligent transport systems (ITS), combining communication, sensing, and control technologies to deliver data-driven, proactive, and user-centric management of transport networks (Zemmouchi-Ghomari, 2025; Nikitas et al., 2020). Deep learning has emerged as a crucial tool for pattern recognition in transportation data, particularly for applications such as long-term traffic prediction (Wu et al., 2018) and autonomous vehicles (Abduljabbar et al., 2019). More recently, large language models (LLMs) and multimodal models (MLLMs) have expanded the capabilities of AI in transportation, enabling the interpretation of diverse data types, the generation of scenario analyses, and the automation of policy evaluation and stakeholder engagement (Xu et al., 2024b). Generative AI, including GANs and diffusion models, has further advanced capabilities in synthetic scenario creation, demand forecasting, and traffic simulation, supporting greater scalability, automation, and innovation in planning processes (Da et al., 2025).

The integration of AI with Agent-Based Modelling (ABM) represents a significant area of progress, with AI supporting the generation of synthetic populations, the calibration of agent behaviours, and the evaluation of model performance. Open-source frameworks such as MATSim, SimMobility, and AnyLogic now facilitate the integration and management of complex, multimodal transport systems (Bastarianto et al., 2023).

15.3 Overview of AI and Machine Learning Concepts

AI encompasses a broad field of computer science dedicated to mimicking aspects of human intelligence, enabling machines to interpret external data, learn from experience, and adapt flexibly to accomplish specific tasks or objectives. AI approaches are commonly categorised into symbolic AI, which underpins knowledge-based systems (KBS), and computational intelligence, encompassing neural networks (NNs), fuzzy systems (FS), and evolutionary computing (Sadek, 2007; Abduljabbar et al., 2019; Nikitas et al., 2020; Negnevitsky, 2005).

ML represents a key subfield within AI, focused on developing algorithms that allow computers to learn from data without explicit programming for each task. By processing large and varied datasets, ML systems are able

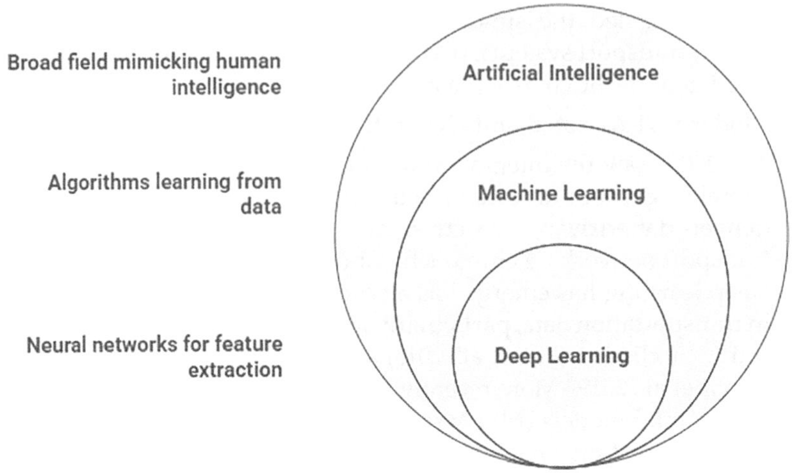

FIGURE 15.3
Hierarchy of AI technologies.

to extract salient features and identify patterns (Abduljabbar et al., 2019; Zemmouchi-Ghomari, 2025; Da et al., 2025), thereby supporting advanced analytical and decision-making processes in transportation planning and management.

Deep Learning (DL), situated within ML, involves the use of deep neural networks – comprising multiple hidden layers – to model highly complex, non-linear relationships in data (Schmidhuber, 2015). Deep learning techniques are increasingly vital in the analysis of complex and high-dimensional datasets (Lv et al., 2015), and aim to deliver more connected, responsive, and adaptive solutions. The hierarchical relationship between these is illustrated in Figure 15.3.

15.4 Modernising Transport Modelling: A Classical–AI Synthesis

A variety of AI and machine learning models have become central to transportation planning and management, each bringing distinct capabilities to address complex mobility challenges.

Artificial Neural Networks (ANNs) are computational systems inspired by the human brain, composed of interconnected 'neurons' organised in layers (Sadek, 2007; Abduljabbar et al., 2019). These networks, including feed-forward neural networks, convolutional neural networks (CNNs) for image analysis, and recurrent neural networks (RNNs) for processing sequences, are widely used in road planning, traffic incident detection, public transport optimisation, and short-term traffic forecasting (Abduljabbar et al., 2019). Their strength lies in handling large, noisy datasets and modelling nonlinear relationships (Sadek, 2007), enabling effective prediction and analysis across diverse transport applications.

Evolutionary computing offers a family of optimisation algorithms based on natural processes (Abduljabbar et al., 2019). Genetic algorithms (GAs) iteratively improve solutions by mimicking natural selection, making them well-suited to problems such as network design, railway timetabling (Zhang & Zhang, 2023), and route optimisation. Other evolutionary techniques include simulated annealing, and swarm intelligence (Teodorović, 2008), such as ant colony optimisation and bee colony optimisation, which model the collective behaviour of social insects to solve complex routing and scheduling challenges in bus operations and road networks.

Fuzzy logic models address the inherent ambiguity and uncertainty found in transportation systems by allowing for gradual transitions and partial set memberships, rather than rigid classifications (Kikuchi, 2007). This flexibility is invaluable in scenarios where qualitative data, human judgement, and vagueness are prevalent (Kikuchi, 2007; Sadek, 2007). Fuzzy logic has found success in dynamic traffic optimisation, prediction tasks, and in contexts requiring adaptability and reasoning under uncertainty (Wang et al., 2016).

Knowledge-based systems (KBS), or expert systems, encapsulate human expertise in the form of rules or cases (Sadek, 2007), providing valuable guidance in domains lacking robust analytical models or where multiple stakeholders present conflicting objectives (Spring, 2007). These systems have supported railway operations and dispatching, especially in disrupted scenarios (Schaefer & Pferdmenges, 1994; Yin et al., 2014), while more advanced forms, such as case-based reasoning, solve new problems by adapting solutions from prior experiences (Spring, 2007).

Agent-based models simulate transportation systems as collections of interacting autonomous agents, capturing emergent behaviours in traffic and pedestrian flows, travel demand, and land-use patterns (Bonabeau, 2002; Crooks & Heppenstall, 2012). The integration of AI enables the enhancement of agent behaviours using data-driven and learning-based techniques, supporting the modelling of complex, adaptive transport systems (Sadek et al., 2003).

Reinforcement learning (RL) and deep reinforcement learning (DRL) further advance transportation modelling by enabling agents to learn optimal strategies through trial and error (Haydari & Yılmaz, 2022; Liu, 2018). RL techniques underpin adaptive traffic signal control and autonomous vehicle navigation (Haydari & Yılmaz, 2022), while DRL extends these capabilities to large-scale operational challenges, such as automatic train operations and timetable rescheduling (Liu, 2018; Yin et al., 2014).

Computer vision leverages AI to process and analyse visual data, supporting advanced driver assistance systems, vehicle and pedestrian detection, licence plate recognition, and traffic law enforcement (Ibrahim et al., 2020; Englund et al., 2021). By allowing machines to interpret images and videos, computer vision significantly enhances safety and operational efficiency across transportation networks (Englund et al., 2021).

Natural language processing (NLP) empowers computers to comprehend and generate human language, facilitating improved communication between users and intelligent transport systems (Mehri, 2022; Kang et al., 2020). NLP applications range from voice-controlled navigation to the analysis of social media streams for real-time traffic incident detection and public sentiment analysis (Tsai et al., 2022).

Generative AI represents a cutting-edge class of models capable of producing novel content, such as text, images, and problem-solving strategies (He et al., 2025; Da et al., 2025). Large language models (LLMs) are now used for policy analysis, stakeholder engagement, and transport data interpretation (Wang et al., 2024), while multimodal large language models (MLLMs) extend this capacity to process visual and spatial data alongside text (Xu et al., 2024b; Le et al., 2024). These generative techniques are poised to revolutionise demand forecasting, infrastructure design, policy evaluation, and scenario generation, bringing greater creativity, automation, and scalability to transportation planning (Chatterjee & Byun, 2023; Huynh et al., 2020).

Taken together, these AI and machine learning models are transforming the transportation sector by providing advanced tools for prediction, optimisation, and adaptive decision-making, ultimately supporting the development of more efficient, safe, and sustainable mobility systems (Abduljabbar et al., 2019; Nikitas et al., 2020).

AI and ML represent a profound advancement over classical methods in the field of transportation planning and management. As discussed in the previous section, classical approaches – reliant on statistical analysis, static models, and labour-intensive data collection – have served as the foundation of the discipline (Sadek, 2007; Da et al., 2025). Their limitations become apparent when addressing the increasing complexity, dynamism, and scale of contemporary transport systems (Abduljabbar et al., 2019). In contrast, AI and ML techniques offer adaptive, data-driven solutions that are better suited for the multifaceted challenges of modern urban mobility (Zhang & Zhang, 2023; Da et al., 2025), though they also introduce a new set of practical and ethical considerations (Nikitas et al., 2020; Zemmouchi-Ghomari, 2025).

AI and ML methodologies excel in contexts where traditional computational techniques falter (Abduljabbar et al., 2019; Nikitas et al., 2020). These approaches can ingest and interpret vast quantities of heterogeneous data, including both quantitative and qualitative sources (Kikuchi, 2007; Negnevitsky, 2005), thus providing a more nuanced understanding of system and user behaviours (Da et al., 2025; Abduljabbar et al., 2019). Expert systems and fuzzy logic models, for example, are particularly effective in dealing with ambiguity, uncertainty, and the vagueness of human judgement – domains in which classical models often struggle (Sadek, 2007; Spring, 2007).

Neural networks, with their universal function approximation capabilities, are robust in modelling non-linear relationships and managing large, noisy datasets (Ishak & Trifirò, 2007; Sadek, 2007). They are especially useful for tasks such as empirical modelling, prediction, and pattern recognition where the internal mechanisms of the system are only partially understood (Abduljabbar et al., 2019; Negnevitsky, 2005). Similarly, genetic algorithms (GA) and other evolutionary computing methods are adept at tackling complex optimisation problems that are intractable using traditional mathematical programming (Katoch et al., 2021; Xu et al., 2009), while generative AI systems enable the autonomous generation of solutions and rapid scenario simulation in response to real-time data (Da et al., 2025).

The adaptability of AI-assisted methods extends to real-time decision-making and dynamic control, enabling more efficient management of congestion, traffic rerouting, and incident response (Abduljabbar et al., 2019; Da et al., 2025; Sadek et al., 2003). These models also underpin significant advances in predictive accuracy, enabling the detection and forecasting of traffic volume, incidents, and travel demand, which, in turn, support more reliable and efficient use of transport infrastructure (Nikitas et al., 2020; Zhang & Zhang, 2023; Zemmouchi-Ghomari, 2025).

Despite these advantages, classical computational techniques continue to offer value, particularly in contexts where a clear understanding of the internal problem structure is paramount (Zhang & Zhang, 2023). Methods such as mathematical programming provide interpretable solutions, supporting transparency and insight into the relationships between variables and outcomes (Chowdhury & Sadek, 2012). However, these approaches are inherently limited by their scalability, reliance on simplified assumptions, and inability to handle high-dimensional, dynamic, or ambiguous systems (Da et al., 2025; Sadek, 2007). In many instances, hybrid approaches that integrate AI/ML with classical models have proven most effective, leveraging the strengths of each and mitigating individual shortcomings (Abduljabbar et al., 2019; Talbi, 2021; Guo & Liu, 2024).

15.5 Building Ethical, Explainable AI for Transport Systems

The deployment of AI/ML systems in transportation introduces several new challenges (Abduljabbar et al., 2019; Nikitas et al., 2020; Zemmouchi-Ghomari, 2025). Foremost among these is the need for large, high-quality, and diverse datasets, which are essential for model accuracy and robustness (Da et al., 2025; Zemmouchi-Ghomari, 2025; Xu et al., 2024c). Data scarcity, inconsistency, and labour-intensive preprocessing remain significant barriers, particularly for emerging generative AI applications (Da et al., 2025).

Additionally, the computational demands of training and deploying large models, such as deep learning architectures and agent-based simulations, can be prohibitive (Liu, 2018; Waraich et al., 2015), necessitating advanced hardware and distributed computing frameworks (Saprykin et al., 2019). AI-driven transportation systems also raise critical privacy and security concerns, as they often rely on sensitive personal data and are vulnerable to malicious attacks, adversarial manipulation, and data breaches (Lv et al., 2020).

Public acceptance and trust are further complicated by the 'black box' nature of many AI models, which often lack transparency and explainability (Nikitas et al., 2020). This opacity can also contribute to algorithmic bias (Haenlein & Kaplan, 2019; Abduljabbar et al., 2019), with the risk of perpetuating inequities present in training data (Nikitas et al., 2020).

Interpretability is therefore a crucial area of ongoing research (Da et al., 2025), with the emerging field of explainable AI (XAI) dedicated to developing systems that provide clear, understandable rationales for their decisions (Xu et al., 2019; Gaur & Sahoo, 2022). Ensuring transparency, trustworthiness, and fairness is essential for the successful adoption of AI in critical applications such as intelligent transportation systems (Nikitas et al., 2020; Zemmouchi-Ghomari, 2025).

Ethical considerations extend to issues of accountability, responsibility for errors, job displacement (such as with the rise of autonomous vehicles), and the need to maintain human oversight (Ogundare, 2024; Abduljabbar et al., 2019). The integration of human expertise – whether as 'human-in-the-loop' or 'human-on-the-loop' – remains indispensable for defining objectives, validating results, and ensuring alignment with societal values (Fagnant & Kockelman, 2015).

15.6 SWOT Analysis of AI/ML and Classical Methods

The balance of these strengths and limitations is effectively summarised in the SWOT analysis presented in Figure 15.4. This figure illustrates the adaptive capacity of AI/ML to handle complex data and revolutionise the future of transport, contrasted with their dependence on large, high-quality datasets and the ethical and practical risks – such as bias and safety concerns – that must be managed.

The figure highlights the adaptive data solutions and potential for innovation offered by AI/ML, set against the backdrop of data dependency and the ongoing ethical and practical risks associated with their deployment.

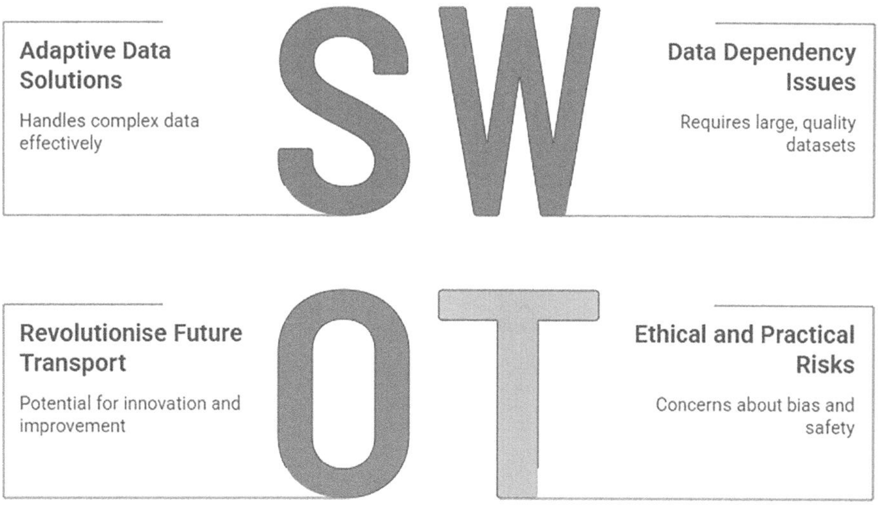

FIGURE 15.4
SWOT analysis: AI/ML in transportation versus classical methods.

As the analysis shows, while AI/ML excels in managing complexity and enabling innovation, addressing challenges around data dependency, ethical risks, and practical implementation remains essential for the successful and responsible integration of these technologies in transportation systems.

15.7 Example: LLM-Integrated Framework for Flexible Traffic Intervention Analysis

A state-of-the-art framework was developed to illustrate the integration of open-source Large Language Models (LLMs) with established transport simulation tools. The objective was to demonstrate how recent advances in artificial intelligence can facilitate the translation of high-level, natural language policy interventions into detailed, microscopic transport simulations.

The framework leverages Llama 3 (an open-source LLM) in conjunction with SUMO (Simulation of Urban Mobility), a widely adopted, open-source microscopic traffic simulation package (Da et al., 2024). A user-friendly graphical user interface (GUI) (see Figure 15.5) was developed, which serves as the control centre, enabling users to select geographic areas (e.g., 'Auckland Huapai Triangle') and describe traffic interventions in plain English, such as 'reduce the speed limit to 40 km/h on all roads with more than one

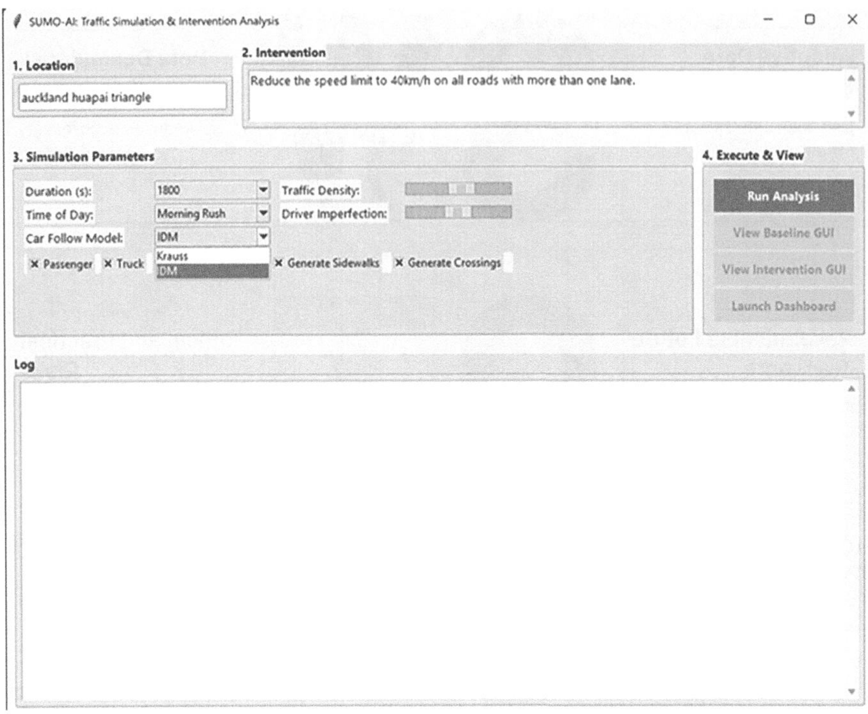

FIGURE 15.5
SUMO-AI traffic simulation GUI: scenario and intervention configuration window.

lane'. The LLM processes this input and automatically generates executable Python code that programmatically modifies the SUMO network files.

Upon user input, the framework retrieves real-world road network data from OpenStreetMap, converts it into SUMO-compatible files, and visualises the baseline network within the SUMO GUI. The interface provides granular control over simulation settings, including time profiles, traffic demand, and driver behaviour models (e.g., selection between 'Krauss' and 'IDM' car-following models). The generated code is applied to implement the specified intervention. A robust fallback mechanism ensures reliability: if the LLM's generated code fails (for instance, due to syntax errors or unexpected input), the system triggers an unmistakable default intervention – such as colouring all roads yellow and uniformly lowering speed limits – so users are immediately aware of the fallback state.

Both baseline and intervention scenarios are simulated in parallel. Key performance indicators (KPIs) – such as average speed, waiting time, and travel time – are extracted and automatically displayed on a web-based dashboard for easy comparison. Initial experiments showed that impacts may be minimal in uncongested conditions but become more pronounced in

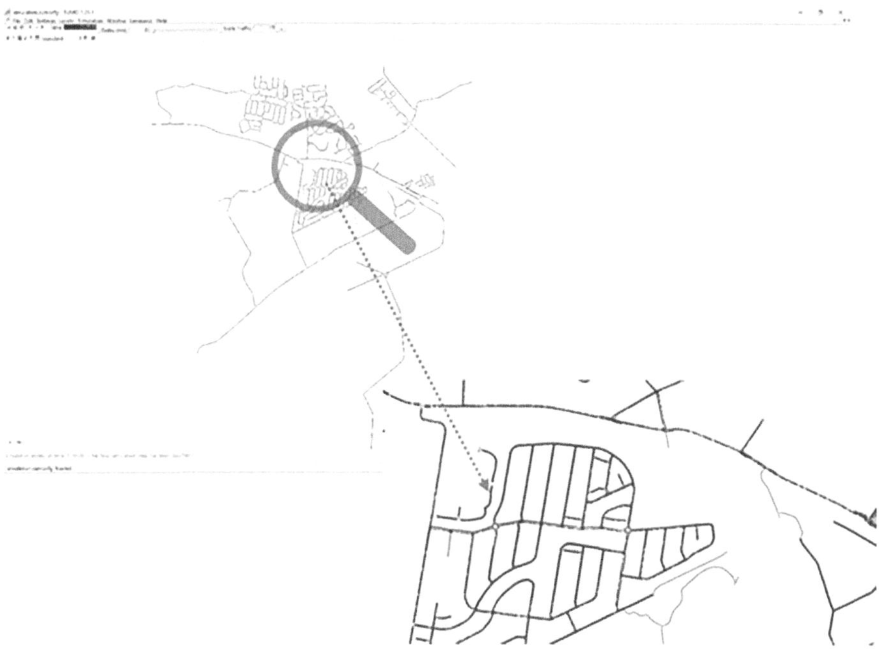

FIGURE 15.6
Visualisation of LLM-automated SUMO network extraction for Huapai Triangle, Auckland, New Zealand.

higher-density, complex scenarios. As shown in Figure 15.6, the integration of the LLM-driven framework with the SUMO traffic simulation environment enables fully automated network extraction and visualisation. By entering a natural language prompt specifying the location ('Auckland Huapai Triangle') within the graphical user interface, the system seamlessly connects to OpenStreetMap and retrieves the correct road network for the specified area, with no further manual input required.

The extracted map accurately reflects the Huapai Triangle's real-world road geometry in Auckland, New Zealand, confirming the reliability of the automated workflow. In addition, the simulation display illustrates vehicle objects as yellow markers, indicating the successful execution of a SUMO-based microscopic traffic simulation. This process demonstrates the capability of the framework to translate high-level user instructions into tangible, ready-to-analyse transport simulation scenarios using only natural language and a user-friendly interface.

This approach demonstrates the feasibility of integrating LLMs into end-to-end transport modelling workflows. The framework can be extended to interact with live data feeds (such as loop detector APIs) for real-time model calibration and validation. This paves the way for genuinely intelligent, adaptive traffic analysis and management systems driven by natural language input.

15.8 Future Directions and Research Priorities

Looking ahead, several emerging trends and research priorities are poised to shape the future of AI/ML in transportation (Nikitas et al., 2020; Abduljabbar et al., 2019; Zemmouchi-Ghomari, 2025). Deep learning continues to drive advances in handling complex, high-dimensional datasets and delivering accurate, real-time insights (Schmidhuber, 2015; Liu, 2018).

Generative AI, encompassing large language models and multimodal large language models, is rapidly evolving (Da et al., 2025; He et al., 2025), with the potential to revolutionise demand forecasting, infrastructure design, policy evaluation, and scenario generation through creative and adaptive outputs (Xu et al., 2024b). The integration of AI with agent-based modelling (ABM) is particularly promising for simulating complex urban phenomena (Guo & Liu, 2024; Zhang & Zhang, 2023).

Explainable AI (XAI) is gaining prominence as a means to enhance transparency and trust in automated systems (Xu et al., 2019; Gaur & Sahoo, 2022). Similarly, the rise of digital twins, enabled by AI, offers opportunities for the real-time simulation and management of transport networks (Bao et al., 2021; Wang et al., 2022; Xu et al., 2024a). Finally, transfer learning and meta-learning approaches may reduce the data requirements for new applications by leveraging existing knowledge (Pan & Yang, 2010; Weiss et al., 2016).

Hybrid models that combine generative AI with traditional transportation models will be essential to ensure realism, interpretability, and domain-specific relevance (Da et al., 2025; Zhang & Zhang, 2023). The synergy between AI and ABM offers opportunities for dynamic, data-driven agent behaviour (Guo & Liu, 2024; Turgut & Bozdağ, 2023), while generative AI stands to transform not only predictive tasks but also public engagement and knowledge dissemination, potentially offering multilingual access to transportation expertise (Yu & McKinley, 2024; He et al., 2025).

However, significant research gaps persist (Abduljabbar et al., 2019; Nikitas et al., 2020). There is a pressing need for unified, systematic frameworks to guide the integration of AI/ML – particularly generative AI – into transportation workflows (Guo & Liu, 2024; Da et al., 2025). Domain-specific adaptations are necessary to address data bias (Nikitas et al., 2020), computational efficiency (Waraich et al., 2015; Kaddoura & Schlenther, 2021), and the unique challenges of transportation systems (Da et al., 2025).

Finally, novel evaluation criteria are required to assess the real-world impact, fairness, and interpretability of AI-driven solutions, moving beyond traditional performance metrics (Nikitas et al., 2020; Da et al., 2025).

Other key areas requiring attention include the calibration and validation of large-scale agent-based models (Waraich et al., 2015), the mitigation of hallucinations in generative models (He et al., 2025), improvements in long-term traffic state prediction, and the capacity to forecast under unexpected events or adverse conditions (Vlahogianni et al., 2014). Further research is also needed to address equity concerns (Ogundare, 2024), as most case studies remain concentrated in developed economies (Abduljabbar et al., 2019), and to explore the integration of LLMs in large-scale ABM environments (Guo & Liu, 2024).

Finally, as AI systems become increasingly embedded in critical infrastructure, research on AI safety and value alignment, as well as the consideration of social networks within agent-based frameworks, will be vital for ensuring that future intelligent transportation systems are not only efficient and effective but also ethical, inclusive, and resilient.

References

Abduljabbar, R., Dia, H., Liyanage, S. & Asadi Bagloee, S. (2019) 'Applications of artificial intelligence in transport: An overview', *Sustainability*, 11(1), p. 189.

Bao, L., Wang, Q. & Jiang, Y. (2021) 'Review of Digital Twin for Intelligent Transportation System', in *Proceedings of the 2021 International Conference on Information Control, Electrical Engineering and Rail Transit (ICEERT)*. IEEE (Piscataway, NJ), pp. 309–315.

Bastarianto, A., Dewi, V. K., Candrakirana, R., Diswandi, D., Mahmudi, M., Prayitno, S. & Yaqin, A. (2023) 'European Transport Research Review', *European Transport Research Review*, 15, p. 19. Available at: https://doi.org/10.1186/s12544-023-00590-5

Bonabeau, E. (2002) 'Agent-Based Modeling: Methods and Techniques for Simulating Human Systems', *Proceedings of the National Academy of Sciences*, 99, pp. 7280–7287.

Bowman, J. L. & Ben-Akiva, M. E. (2000) 'Activity-Based Disaggregate Travel Demand Model System with Activity Schedules', *Transportation Research Part A: Policy and Practice*, 35, pp. 1–28.

Chatterjee, S. & Byun, Y.-C. (2023) 'Generating Time-Series Data Using Generative Adversarial Networks for Mobility Demand Prediction', *Computers, Materials & Continua*, 74(3), pp. 5507–5525. Available at: https://doi.org/10.32604/cmc.2023.032843

Chowdhury, M. & Sadek, A. W. (2012) 'Advantages and Limitations of Artificial Intelligence', in *Artificial Intelligence Applications of Critical Transportation Issues, Chapter: Why Artificial Intelligence*? The National Academies Press, pp. 6–8.

Crooks, A. T. & Heppenstall, A. J. (2012) 'Introduction to Agent-Based Modelling', in *Agent-Based Models of Geographical Systems*. Dordrecht, Netherlands: Springer, pp. 85–105.

Da, L., Chen, T., Li, Z., Bachiraju, S., Yao, H., Li, L., Dong, Y., Hu, X., Tu, Z., Wang, D., Zhao, Y., Zhou, X., Pendyala, R., Stabler, B., Yang, Y., Zhou, X. & Wei, H. (2025, March) *Generative AI in Transportation Planning: A Survey*. Preprint. Available at: https://doi.org/10.48550/arXiv.2503.07158

Da, L., Chen, T., Li, Z., Bachiraju, S., Zhou, X. & Wei, H. (2024) *ChatSUMO: Large Language Model for Automating Traffic Simulation Scenarios*. Preprint.

Englund, C., Aksoy, E. E., Alonso-Fernandez, F., Cooney, M. D., Pashami, S. & Åstrand, B. (2021) 'AI Perspectives in Smart Cities and Communities to Enable Road Vehicle Automation and Smart Traffic Control', *Smart Cities*, 4(2), pp. 783–802.

Fagnant, D. J. & Kockelman, K. (2015) 'Preparing a Nation for Autonomous Vehicles: Opportunities, Barriers and Policy Recommendations', *Transportation Research Part A: Policy and Practice*, 77, pp. 167–181.

Gaur, L. & Sahoo, B. M. (2022) *Explainable Artificial Intelligence for Intelligent Transportation Systems: Ethics and Applications*. Cham: Springer Nature.

Guo, Z. & Liu, X. (2024) 'How Artificial Intelligence Cooperating with Agent-Based Modeling for Urban Studies: A Systematic Review', *Transactions in GIS*, 28(3), pp. 654–674. Available at: https://doi.org/10.1111/tgis.13152

Haenlein, M. & Kaplan, A. (2019) 'A Brief History of Artificial Intelligence: On the Past, Present, and Future of Artificial Intelligence', *California Management Review*, 61(4), pp. 5–14. Available at: https://doi.org/10.1177/0008125619864925

Haydari, A. & Yılmaz, Y. (2022) 'Deep Reinforcement Learning for Intelligent Transportation Systems: A Survey', *IEEE Transactions on Intelligent Transportation Systems*, 23(1), pp. 11–32. Available at: https://doi.org/10.1109/TITS.2020.3008612

He, R., Cao, J. & Tan, T. (2025) 'Generative Artificial Intelligence: A Historical Perspective', *National Science Review*, 12(5), p. nwaf050. Available at: https://doi.org/10.1093/nsr/nwaf050

Huynh, N. V., Du, H., Hoang, D. T. & Niyato, D. (2020) 'Spatiotemporal Scenario Generation of Traffic Flow based on LSTM-GAN', *IEEE Access*, 8, pp. 186191–186198.

Ibrahim, M. R., Haworth, J. & Cheng, T. (2020) 'Understanding Cities with Machine Eyes: A Review of Deep Computer Vision in Urban Analytics', *Cities*, 96, p. 102481. Available at: https://doi.org/10.1016/j.cities.2019.102481

Ionescu, Ş., Delcea, C., Chiriţă, N. & Nica, I. (2024) 'Exploring the Use of Artificial Intelligence in Agent-Based Modeling Applications: A Bibliometric Study', *Algorithms*, 17(1), p. 21. Available at: https://doi.org/10.3390/a17010021

Ishak, S. & Trifirò, F. (2007) 'Neural Networks', in *Transportation Research Circular E-C113: Artificial Intelligence in Transportation*. Washington, DC: Transportation Research Board.

Kaddoura, I. & Schlenther, C. (2021) 'Scenarios of Automated Mobility in Vienna: A Multi-Agent Simulation Approach', *Cities*, 107. Article number: 103205.

Kang, Y., Cai, Z., Tan, C.W., Huang, Q. & Liu, H. (2020) 'Natural Language Processing (NLP) in Management Research: A Literature Review', *Journal of Management Analytics*, 7(2), pp. 139–172.

Katoch, S., Chauhan, S. S. & Kumar, V. (2021) 'A Review on Genetic Algorithm: Past, Present, and Future', *Multimedia Tools and Applications*, 80, pp. 8091–8126. Available at: https://doi.org/10.1007/s11042-020-10139-6

Kikuchi, S. (2007) 'Fuzzy Sets Theory Approach to Transportation Problems', in *Transportation Research Circular E-C113: Artificial Intelligence in Transportation*. Washington, DC: Transportation Research Board.

Le, D., Nguyen, A., Tran, Q., Nguyen, T. & Pham, H. (2024) *Multimodal LLM for Intelligent Transportation Systems*. Preprint.

Liu, X. (2018) *Deep Reinforcement Learning for Intelligent Transportation Systems*. Preprint.

Lv, Y., Duan, Y., Kang, W., Li, Z. & Wang, F.-Y. (2015) 'Traffic Flow Prediction with Big Data: A Deep Learning Approach', *IEEE Transactions on Intelligent Transportation Systems*, 16(2), pp. 865–873.

Lv, Z., Qiao, L. & Singh, A. K. (2020) 'Advanced Trustworthy Computing for Medical Cyber-Physical Systems', *IEEE/ACM Transactions on Computational Biology and Bioinformatics*, 18(6), pp. 2224–2236.

Mehri, B. (2022) 'Textual Data and Natural Language Processing for Next Generation Intelligent Transportation Systems: Perspectives, Techniques, and Challenges', Doctoral dissertation, Ecole Polytechnique, Montreal (Canada).

Meyer, M. D. & Miller, E. J. (2001) *Urban Transportation Planning: A Decision-Oriented Approach*. 2nd edn. Boston: McGraw-Hill.

Negnevitsky, M. (2005) *Artificial Intelligence: A Guide to Intelligent Systems*. 2nd edn. Harlow, England: Addison-Wesley.

Nikitas, A., Michalakopoulou, K., Tchouamou Njoya, E. & Karampatzakis, D. (2020) 'Artificial Intelligence, Transport and the Smart City: Definitions and Dimensions of a New Mobility Era', *Sustainability*, 12(7), p. 2789. Available at: https://doi.org/10.3390/su12072789

Ogundare, E. (2024) 'Understanding the Mediating Role of Artificial Intelligence in Urban Transportation Planning for Smart City Development and Its Implications for the United States', *International Journal of Innovative Science and Research Technology*, 9(12). Available at: https://doi.org/10.5281/zenodo.14613884

Pan, S. J. & Yang, Q. (2010) 'A Survey on Transfer Learning', *IEEE Transactions on Knowledge and Data Engineering*, 22(10), pp. 1345–1359.

Rasouli, S. & Timmermans, H. (2014) 'Activity-Based Models of Travel Demand: Promises, Progress and Prospects', *International Journal of Urban Sciences*, 18(1), pp. 31–60. Available at: https://doi.org/10.1080/12265934.2013.835118

Sadek, A. W. (2007) 'Artificial Intelligence in Transportation', *Transportation Research Circular*, E-C113, pp. 72–79.

Sadek, A. W., Spring, G. & Smith, B. L. (2003) 'Toward More Effective Transportation Applications of Computational Intelligence Paradigms', *Transportation Research Record*, 1836(1), pp. 57–63.

Sanford Bernhardt, K. (2007) 'Agent-Based Modeling in Transportation', in *Transportation Research Circular E-C113: Artificial Intelligence in Transportation*. Washington, DC: Transportation Research Board, pp. 84–98.

Saprykin, A., Chokani, N. & Abhari, R. S. (2019) 'GEMSim: A GPU-Accelerated Multi-Modal Mobility Simulator for Large-Scale Scenarios', *Simulation Modelling Practice and Theory*, 94, pp. 199–214. Available at: https://doi.org/10.1016/j.simpat.2019.03.002

Schaefer, H. & Pferdmenges, S. (1994) 'An Expert System for Real-time Train Dispatching', in *Proceedings of COMPRAIL* '94. Madrid: Computational Mechanics Publication, pp. 27–34.

Schmidhuber, J. (2015) 'Deep Learning in Neural Networks: An Overview', *Neural Networks*, 61, pp. 85–117.

Spring, G. (2007) 'Knowledge-Based Systems in Transportation', in *Transportation Research Circular E-C113: Artificial Intelligence in Transportation*. Washington, DC: Transportation Research Board.

Talbi, E. G. (2021) 'Machine Learning into Metaheuristics: A Survey and Taxonomy', *ACM Computing Surveys*, 54(6), pp. 1–32.

Teodorović, D. (2008) 'Swarm Intelligence Systems for Transportation Engineering: Principles and Applications', *Transportation Research Part C: Emerging Technologies*, 16(6), pp. 651–667.

Tsai, M. J., Cui, Z., Yang, H., Kopca, C., Tien, S. & Wang, Y. (2022). *Traffic-Twitter Transformer: A Nature Language Processing-joined Framework for Network-wide Traffic Forecasting*. arXiv. https://doi.org/10.48550/arXiv.2206.11078

Turgut, Y. & Bozdağ, C. E. (2023) 'A Framework Proposal for Machine-Learning-Driven Agent-Based Models through a Case Study Analysis', *Simulation Modelling Practice and Theory*, 123, p. 102707.

Vlahogianni, E. I., Karlaftis, M. G. & Golias, J. C. (2014) 'Short-Term Traffic Forecasting: Where We are and Where We're Going', *Transportation Research Part C: Emerging Technologies*, 43, pp. 3–19.

Wang, B., Wang, Y., Shi, X., Li, Y., Zhang, L., Xu, H. & Li, Z. (2024) *Traffic Performance GPT (TP-GPT): Real-Time Data-Informed Intelligent Chatbot for Transportation Surveillance and Management*. Preprint.

Wang, Z., He, Q., Khattak, A. J., Kandil, A. & Yuan, F. (2022) 'Mobility Digital Twin: Concept, Architecture, Case Study, and Future Challenges', *IEEE Internet of Things Journal*, 9(18), pp. 17452–17467. Available at: https://doi.org/10.1109/JIOT.2022.3180892

Wang, Y., Wu, B. & Du, W. (2016) 'Fuzzy Logic Dynamic Traffic Optimization', *Journal of Traffic and Logistics Engineering*, 4(2), pp. 146–151.

Waraich, R. A., Charypar, D., Balmer, M. & Axhausen, K. W. (2015) 'Performance Improvements for Large-Scale Traffic Simulation in MATSim', in *Computational Approaches for Urban Environments*. Cham: Springer, pp. 211–233.

Weiss, K., Khoshgoftaar, T. M. & Wang, D. (2016) 'A Survey of Transfer Learning', *Journal of Big Data*, 3(1), p. 9. Available at: https://doi.org/10.1186/s40537-016-0043-6

Wu, Y., Tan, H., Qin, L., Ran, B. & Jiang, Z. (2018) 'A Hybrid Deep Learning-Based Traffic Flow Prediction Method and Its Understanding', *Transportation Research Part C: Emerging Technologies*, 90, pp. 166–180.

Xu, H., Yuan, J., Zhou, A., Wang, Y., Chen, Y. & Zhu, J. (2024a) 'Leveraging Generative AI for Urban Digital Twins: A Scoping Review on the Autonomous Generation of Urban Data, Scenarios, Designs, and 3D City Models for Smart City Advancement', *Urban Informatics*, 3(1), p. 29.

Xu, H., Yuan, J., Zhou, A., Zhao, B., Ding, G., Chen, Y. & Zhu, J. (2024b) *GenAI-Powered Multi-Agent Paradigm for Smart Urban Mobility: Opportunities and Challenges for Integrating Large Language Models (LLMs) and Retrieval-Augmented Generation (RAG) with Intelligent Transportation Systems*. Preprint.

Xu, W., Wain, J. & Qie, Y. (2019) 'Explainable AI: A New Era of Intelligent Transportation Systems', *Proceedings of the 2019 International Conference on Intelligent Transportation Systems (ITSC)*.

Xu, T., Wei, H. & Wang, Z.-D. (2009) 'Study on Continuous Network Design Problem Using Simulated Annealing and Genetic Algorithm', *Expert Systems with Applications*, 36(2), pp. 2735–2741. Available at: https://doi.org/10.1016/j.eswa.2008.01.071

Xu, X., Zheng, Z., Hu, Z., Feng, C., Ran, B. & Peng, H. (2024c) 'A Unified Dataset for the City-Scale Traffic Assignment Model in 20 U.S. Cities', *Scientific Data*, 11(1), p. 325.

Yin, J., Chen, D. & Li, L. (2014) 'Intelligent Train Operation Algorithms for Subway by Expert System and Reinforcement Learning', *IEEE Transactions on Intelligent Transportation Systems*, 15(6), pp. 2561–2571.

Yu, J. & McKinley, G. (2024) 'Synthetic Participatory Planning of Shared Automated Electric Mobility Systems', *Sustainability*, 16(13), p. 5618.

Zemmouchi-Ghomari, L. (2025) 'Artificial Intelligence in Intelligent Transportation Systems', *Journal of Intelligent Manufacturing and Special Equipment*, 6(1), pp. 26–42. Available at: https://doi.org/10.1108/JIMSE-11-2024-0035

Zhang, J. & Zhang, J. (2023) 'Artificial Intelligence Applied on Traffic Planning and Management for Rail Transport: A Review and Perspective', *Discrete Dynamics in Nature and Society*, 2023, Article ID 1832501. Available at: https://doi.org/10.1155/2023/1832501

Index

Note: **Bold** and *Italic* page numbers refer to **tables** and *figures*.

For Product Safety Concerns and Information please contact our
EU representative GPSR@taylorandfrancis.com Taylor & Francis
Verlag GmbH, Kaufingerstraße 24, 80331 München, Germany